Dismantling Glory

Dismantling Glory

TWENTIETH-CENTURY SOLDIER POETRY

Lorrie Goldensohn

Columbia University Press / New York

Columbia University Press
Publishers Since 1893
New York   Chichester, West Sussex

Library of Congress Cataloging-in-Publication Data
Goldensohn, Lorrie.
    Dismantling glory : twentieth-century soldier poetry / Lorrie Goldensohn.
        p.   cm.
    Includes bibliographical references (p.) and index.
    ISBN 0–231–11938–0 (acid-free paper)
        1. Soldier's writings, English—History and criticism.   2. English poetry—20th century—
History and criticism.   3. Vietnamese Conflict, 1961–1975—Literature and the conflict.
4. American poetry—20th century—History and criticism.   5. Soldier's writings, American—
History and criticism.   6. World War, 1914–1918—Literature and the war.   7. World War,
1939–1945—Literature and the war.   8. War poetry, American—History and criticism.
9. War poetry, English—History and criticism.   I. Title: Twentieth-century soldier poetry.
II. Title: 20th century soldier poetry.   III. Title.

    PR120.S64G65 2003
    821'.9109358—dc21

                                                                                        2003051500

For Barry, as always;
for Matthew and Rachel, who were scouts and runners;
and for all the Vassar students, in class after class,
    who read this poetry with me.

Contents

Illustrations

Preface: A Preliminary

NOT an introduction, nor a road map to the commentaries on war poetry that occupy the rest of the book, these pages describe a little of how and why this book came to be written by someone who is neither a military specialist nor served and suffered in war. For me, as for most Americans, wars or battles happen elsewhere. Spottily remembered, my life in World War II shrinks to sitting on a curbstone with other nine-year-olds, wondering what the news of the death of Franklin Delano Roosevelt meant. The curbstone, fending off the street and its 1940s traffic, was very real; death and the American president were not.

This is a slender memory to draw on. But in a book that focuses so heavily on other people's experience of war, I seem to myself quaintly bound to notice how the vantage and timing of my own insertion into history may have shaped my analysis. The size of war, of what I, the writer, and now you, my hoped-for reader, begin to search for, in the huge and dual act of reconstruction that we perform together in a book, is so immense and unwieldy. A thousand jumpy perspectives are in play. For scholarly work, there seems little reason to attach personal detail, even briefly. But when the subject becomes fear, rage, destruction, suffering, and blood sacrifice—or extremes of experience on a scale unfamiliar and incomprehensible to most noncombatants—we are curious about who asks us to look at these things, and with what authority: if we *are* familiar with war, then so much more do we ask for its right representation.

The book I have written is the effort of a reader. No doubt part of my fascination with war stems from its active contrast to the almost actionless life of reading. But the pressure to write about war proceeds as well from several sources, not the least of which flows from ten years and more of teaching war literature in college classrooms at Vassar.

Before that, I spent a good part of the 1960s teaching in alternative schools and colleges. Living first in California and then Vermont, my husband and I went to antiwar lectures and demonstrations, wrote letters, and joined the pacifist campaigns, beginning in 1962 in America and stretching out from that time for more than a decade. In Montpelier, Vermont, I went with a group of Quakers every Wednesday to stand in front of the capitol dome for an hour, where we silently registered our protest to the Vietnam war. Once, a woman came to our line of people and, addressing us in ringing tones, said: "I am ashamed of you. My father and my uncle died in our country's wars, and you are dishonoring their memory."

I didn't have the presence of mind to answer her with the obvious counterarguments, about lulling and fatal misuses of commemoration, in which a great, blind space can swallow up the single human body lost in social policy. Nor can I trace a straight line between the private and public wars of my parents' lives and those of my own; World War I shoved my German Jewish mother across one ocean and my Filipino father across another, each to meet unhappily in an interwar America. Nor can I, made of their collision of culture and character, even now, without a confusing prolixity of detail, try to explain away the barriers that lay between the lady who challenged the Quakers and their friends in Montpelier, to her satisfaction and theirs. But surely part of what has pulled me into the work of this book is the need to find how and where grief can be twisted by public and private lies, letting anger and revenge convulse into broader violence.

While it is a stale commonplace to talk about wanting to erase war, there is no other motivation worth acknowledging. This study of twentieth-century war poetry is largely bound to the poetry of those who experienced war as soldiers. In it, I aim to track the nature of antiwar feeling in soldier poetry, to explore the reluctant, but defensive reaffirmation of violence and bloodletting that so often resurfaces in these poems, even during moments of the most apparent revulsion to war. Following on the heels of this contradiction are other equally central, equally urgent issues: how an awareness of female and civilian experiences of war began to flood the twentieth-century soldier; and how the radical difference between rear echelon and front line enters into poetry.

Nearly all of the poetry or prose of the poets that I choose to dwell on represents, in my mind, a largeness of literary being, an intensely varied formal excellence that accounts for the vibrancy of both work and genre for any attentive reader. In a recent class on war poetry at Vassar, however, I was struck by a comment in a student's journal, in which the writer remarked with some bewilderment on how unendurably moving she found what she was reading; alone with these poems, she would cry over them, only to find that in talking about them in class, all tears dissipated. I hope I never forget this student or, in the earnest desire to be true to the complexity of war, betray her respect for the bitter harvest that this poetry represents.

Again and again, I have been buffeted by the need to break the isolation around anyone's private, internal, and revolted outcry against war and have crashed against the solemn placidity, the general suffocating acceptance, of the public ritual celebrating it. Such a tension between feelings occurred in a visit to the Imperial War Museum in London in January 1998.

It was a good exhibit for children, all those *vehicles* crowding in the center, a kind of war parking lot: a century's worth of artillery and military transport used on the ground, in the air, and over mud and sand. There were cannons. A very highly varnished little boat stretched across a bare fifteen feet of flooring—the smallest boat to take part in the rescue at Dunkirk. Then Monty's tank. Other tanks used at El Alamein. I was surprised at how huge they were in person, looming over me on the polished wood. There were small airplanes. Howitzers.

Quite a few groups of schoolchildren streamed past on this Wednesday afternoon. They seemed to know their way around, heading single-mindedly for particular exhibits in small knots. Boys patted the tanks they passed. Girls in navy blue school uniforms and white blouses applied lipstick in the loo. When I went across to the museum shop there was a small display section on "Forties Fashion." Large poster displays, rosy-cheeked women supporting the war effort, soldier laddies, and so on. Glass shelves held little miniaturized tanks, planes, and jeeps. That year, they printed battle scenes on jigsaw puzzles.

I followed two elderly men as they trailed through the glass tunnels of an exhibit marked "1918: Year of Decision." As we passed a painted dummy dressed in German battle gear, I was wondering about the strange giant matchsticks extruding from burlap sacks slung around his neck and sides. "Stickbombs!" one of the codgers barked to the other, pausing briefly. The whole area offered amazingly interactive, three-dimensional displays. I squatted to have a better look at the vintage of the barbed wire at the foot of the dummy. On one wall an eight-inch television monitor showed grainy black and white footage of gassed and blinded soldiers with white folds of cloth over their eyes; each of the men, in single file, stumbled along by laying his hand on the shoulder of the soldier in front of him. A photograph of the same famous moment, blown-up to three feet high extended across an adjacent wall. Among the blocks of text, there was nothing that could not easily be read in a few minutes—nothing to slow down any visitors if the place were crowded. A niche in another wall held slatted wooden packing cases and, under glass, field glasses, operators' manuals for wireless sets, wireless sets, and a disassembled flame thrower. Using an attached telephone, you could call up two pilots and an infantryman and get a recorded selection of their remembrances.

I stood there with the phone in my hand, listening to their quiet, patient, affable voices describing strafing and mowing people down, then being strafed and mowed down themselves. On another wall hung a huge photo of German prisoners of war massed in hundreds, their blackened, tired faces, staring eyes, all crammed tight on the wall. One picture showed British recruits being trained for duty overseas, a couple of them with their shirts off, their over-long leather belts cinching the full trousers that bunched around their skinny waists, their bare, narrow, concave chests and sticklike arms clearly that of undernourished sixteen and seventeen-year-olds. By then, the generals were so hungry for men they were taking anything nominally male they could get.

At this demonstration of waste and indifference to men who were virtually children, a kind of bile rose in my throat, an involuntary water blurred my sight—foiled movements of bodily revulsion with nowhere to go. Whatever one writes, one should be faithful to the historic breadth of this experience of frustration and powerlessness, but also be pulled to face the stubborn resurgence within most of us of an instinctive, almost involuntary, assent to this incommensurable and horrifying wrong that any truthful writing on war sooner or later must expose. Since the outset of writing about war, people have marked its pitiableness, but for every text with a pitiful victim and a pitiless enforcer, another story exists of courage and indomitability. In pursuit of any of these qualities, I find again and again that infinitely seductive word, *courage*, which means *of the heart*; if only that rising of the heart to do greatness never meant the extinction of others, if only it always meant a canny and forceful self-preservation in the face of undeniable threat—always to disarm, rather than to annihilate. It is our painful task to keep imaginative faith with the species by ceasing to long for that kind of destroying courage—which only harms and never truly defends—even in the rubble surrounding us when we are stricken.

Acknowledgments

WITHOUT the prior example of other historians and literary scholars like John Keegan, Michael Howard, Paul Fussell, and Samuel Hynes, this book on war poetry would never have been written. In addition to my large debts to them, both visible and invisible, I have been helped by discerning and demanding readers like Steven Gould Axelrod, Alida Gersie, David Huddle, Paul Nelson, Raymond Oliver, and Jane Shore.

I also owe a great deal to a 1997 faculty seminar at Vassar on the history of war, sponsored by the Gladys Krieble Delmas Foundation and memorably led by Distinguished Visiting Professor John Keegan. This seminar, with its stimulating contributions from a group of colleagues in a variety of academic disciplines from classics to economics, began my writing on war. Faculty grants from Vassar for research and travel kept the spark alive.

Stephen Crook and Philip Milito at the Berg Collection in the New York Public Library have been efficient and expediting among the treasures of their archive. Other immensely useful manuscript collections at the British Library in London and at the Harry Ransom Research Center in Austin have formed my thinking beyond any possibility of fairly acknowledging. Nor would this project have taken any shape without the steady stream of intelligent and inquisitive Vassar students, from Ivor Hansen to C. J. Anderson to Mark Salter, Stinson Carter, and Lindsay Danis. Other undergraduates who riffled pages, toted books, and xeroxed inordinately to help this project at early and late stages were Betsy Reichert at Vassar and Kelly Sullivan and Justin Rogers-Cooper at Skidmore. Library staff at both Vassar and Skidmore were indispensable.

My great thanks to Jennifer Crewe at Columbia for seeing this project through from start to finish, to Juree Sondker for helpful backup, and to Michael Haskell for his patient and meticulous editing of the final draft.

The Dignities of Danger

WHY should the short, tight little lyric be the form that modern poets choose for the outsized subject of war? At the birth of English, a good, big epic was the natural home for the war poem, where the Beowulf poet spread out battles and dangers over 3,000 lines of Anglo-Saxon. Centuries later, even the Americans felt compelled to make their first attempt at a national literature in this genre with Joel Barlow's interminable opus, *The Columbiad*. Somehow, full statements about manhood and national definition find war their proper subject and the epic the proper vehicle for starting up a national history.

Nevertheless, after *Beowulf*, the brotherhood of English war poets turned from epic to the myth and protonovel writing of Malory's *Morte D'Arthur*. By the Renaissance, in another switch of genre, war poetry found a vital and commodious second home in drama in Shakespeare, in a parade of historical dramas featuring armed hostility from the Romans on through the Wars of the Roses. War, and its epic scale was the subject, even if the Chorus of *Henry V* urges us past the "unworthy scaffold" of the Globe Theater, asking that we make "imaginary puissance" fit the vasty fields of France within the Globe's wooden "O" (*Henry V* 1.1.8–34). Unenhanced by Kenneth Branagh's cinema techniques, for nearly four hundred years *Henry V* managed to reduce the actual battle of Agincourt to alarms and a tucket or two, plus off-field exchanges, and a couple of scenes between rogue soldiers who are dodging battle.

Yet in the face of the broad, or sometimes provocatively scanty, pleasures of enactment, the long, narrative war poem served standing needs. At ceremonial length throughout the Enlightenment and on into the Romantic Revolution, Dryden, Byron, and others carried forward the cultural consensus about the bulky fearsomeness of war. Even so late as 1937, David Jones shaped a long, albeit prickly, narrative poem on World War I, *In Parenthesis*. In quite traditional thinking, if not in orthodox form, Jones celebrates the continuities of war spirit for the English fighting man.

Yet for twentieth-century American and English war poets, novels—and films with suitably loud, slushy scores—have largely preempted the imaginative energy that might have gone into epic or drama. But given a channeling push by the growing egalitarianism of industrial democracies, the tight scope of the lyric has narrowed epic, unruly war into first-person-singular depth of feeling. This generic shift has been enough to give any critic a handsome density from which to cull the war poems of lasting significance. The fractured attention and restless, ground-covering speeds that mark our lives leave many of us poorly adapted to the silent, sit-still contemplation of accumulating columns of print without pictures; film, photograph, and television coverage very efficiently and seductively minister to our durable need for epic thrill. Any seven days of the week will find, real or simulated, war's nerve-quickening action and ear-injuring sound, in full-spectrum color, somewhere up on a public screen at least a half a block long. Yet because the incandescent and immaterial word still assembles and multiplies meaning beyond even the clearest visual image, writers and readers continue to be drawn to the short flare of the war poem.

Our reasons for preferring a concentrated brevity in war poems are also rooted in the war poem's long-standing relation to elegy and ceremonial mourning. The war poem, even in its modern expression as lyric rather than epic, comes to share some of the elegy's developmental fate, turning its lyric purpose away from any simple celebration of the heroic and deadly. More particularly, the war lyric shares in the cultural aftermath of the change in rituals, identified by Jahan Ramazani, that took death out of our houses and brought it to hospitals and funeral "homes" in the late nineteenth and early twentieth centuries, thereby creating the expressive need for the antisentimental, the antielegiac, and, ultimately, the antiheroic and antiwar.

In parallel resistance to a standardized and institutional response to the gravest events of our emotional lives, the lyric elegy—the usual prop of the war poet—has over the course of the last century metamorphosed into antielegy. In a peculiar transformation of the customs and ceremonies of dying, we have left off washing our corpses at home and turned them over instead to the professional ministrations of the undertaker, while we relinquished our traditional obsequies to the funeral parlor and the commercial greeting card. In a backlash of reappropriation, however, twentieth-century elegy in general and war poetry in particular have come to retrieve the intimate details, needing to give full voice back to the private, irreducibly individual narrative of death, wounding, grief, and loss.

For this, no more fit instrument than the intense focus of the lyric can be found. The same drive towards antielegy and the same aversion to an industrialized death, growing from the same need to assert the unquenchably personal, the radically unstandardizable, boosts the development of the poem opposed to war. Within the modern war lyric sits the best register of changing attitudes toward the wasteful heroic, as these poems move against the savaging of body and mind that war calls forth from its community of citizens, both male and female. More and more, the short lyric, a form as old as the human impulse to shape the species' singing or crying into coherence, makes a fertile, flexible cultural object within which to trace both the fearful, atavistic impulses that propel war forward and the countersurge that attempts to contain or deflect the civic violence that it represents.

Yet while antiwar poetry may represent a largely twentieth-century perspective, the split between celebrating and abhorring war is not an entirely new division of mind. Homer turns the ugly, cowardly Thersites, who alternately taunts and whines, into the one, only, and quite unsympathetic commoner that he bothers to insert in the *Iliad*. His description does everything it can to make you feel contempt and dislike for Thersites. But Lawrence Tritle, a Vietnam veteran whose reading of classics is inflected by his own experience of ground combat, reads Homer's Thersites from another angle. For Tritle, the given details of Thersites' speech reveal the truths of "a war-weary soldier who has at last realized that his sacrifice means nothing and only serves to enrich his lord, Agamemnon" (Tritle, 12). That war-weary and reluctant soldier appears in the Greek lyric, in the poems of Archilochos.

In the *Iliad*, Homer undercuts Thersites' outburst by having Odysseus ridicule him and beat him up, to general approval in the Greek camp (2.250–324). Close to the birth of the epic tradition, however, Archilochos (whose possibly self-chosen name meant "first sergeant," or the leader of a company of hoplites) introduces a more subversive view of military hierarchy and military necessity. Archilochos's lyrics, born from a point of view much closer to Thersites than to Odysseus, spew out pungent and suspiciously anarchic accounts of military life, which, featuring a sturdy and antiheroic self-defense, would have drawn praise from many a corporal or second lieutenant of later wars.

As Guy Davenport translates the poem that most draws Tritle's attention:

Some Saian mountaineer
Struts today with my shield.
I threw it down by a bush and ran
When the fighting got hot.
Life somehow seemed more precious.
It was a beautiful shield.
I know where I can buy another
Exactly like it, just as round.
                    (Archilochos, 79)

For Tritle, Archilochos prefers "discretion over valor" (Tritle, 41). Bernard Knox tells us the context in which Archilochos's preference has come to stand for the Greek antiheroic; in fifth-century Sparta, a member of a hoplite phalanx never threw away or abandoned his shield: he came home either with it or on it (Knox, 203). In Davenport's poem 191, he gives us another look at Archilochos's soldiering:

Kindly pass the cup down the deck
And keep it coming from the barrel,
Good red wine, and don't stir up the dregs,
And don't think why we shouldn't be,
More than any other, drunk on guard duty.

Guy Davenport calls his translation of Archilochos one that was "as much from the barracks of the XVIII Airborne Corps and of the 756th Heavy Artillery" (xviii) as from archaic Greek. Urged by this fraternity, Davenport nonetheless finds a grimmer, doughtier Archilochos than the drunk on guard duty who is careless of his shield; Archilochos says the following lines, with taut and urgent modernity:

From hill to hill in retreat
We walked backward under their javelins
Until we reached the rampart of stones
She, Zeus' daughter, led us toward.
We attacked later, chanting hymns
Of Mytilenian Apollo, while they,

Keeping their courage with harp and song,
Fell back to their hill, withered by arrows.
We crossed a harvest of our dead.

Minus the Olympians and the implements of attack, this poem's bleak admissions could belong to the twentieth century. The classical tradition did allow the occasional rebel to the heroic mode, but it is largely the modern war poem that fleshes him out and explores the dignities and rights inherent in the insubordinations of a character like Archilochos.

While writing a book on war poetry, studded with frequent reference to poets' memoirs and letters, I found myself rocked back and forth between the undeniable appeal of the heroic—the irrepressible glamour of its self-forgetfulness in the face of great danger to achieve a public good—and revulsion at what traffic in the heroic has always brought about. How often in appalled retrospect we have had to recognize that public good has meant a vengeful dominance, merely the mean and brutal exchange of lives for lives, of blood for blood. Yet antiwar thinking advances in the twentieth century: as traditions of war and masculinity break down under the redefinition of industrial warfare, an ideologically ungainly but persistent pacifism keeps returning.

Dismantling Glory

Continuity in the war lyric competes with change, and antipathy to war clashes with love of war in a long and tidal argument. But decade by decade, century by century, it becomes harder to justify heart-sinking results that continue to bring us dubious freedoms, qualified victory, and immersion in suffering; or that make us part of populations become vengeful or complicit or indifferent about the regressive savagery inflicted on others. Nine million people have been killed in lesser conflicts since World War II.[1] As the number of genocidal massacres since 1945 continues to rise, the need to view war as pathology, as an illness from which all need to be healed, puts itself more insistently beside the fatalism that accepts the inevitability of war or wallows too comfortably in its tragic dignities, which are unarguably many.

The war poetry that forms the meat of this book spans World Wars I and II and the American-Vietnamese conflict. Each of these wars produced a distinctive poetry, with different shades of antiwar thinking. My aim is not to conduct a survey, but to focus on poets who wrote memorable poetry and who advanced the scope and thinking of the war lyric. Chapter 2 concerns Wilfred

Owen on World War I. Owen writes a poetry of victimhood, which was where his passionate questioning of the ethic of stoic endurance led him. Chapter 3 suggests how W. H. Auden's poetry of the 1930s influenced the wartime poetry of the 1940s. Chapters 4 and 5 investigate the World War II poems of Keith Douglas and Randall Jarrell. Both Douglas and Jarrell rejected Owen's largely sinned-against rather than sinning soldiers, describing a much more complicated picture of internal involvement in military violence. The very different character of Douglas's and Jarrell's military service brought them to poems both alike and different in ambition and preoccupation. Like Owen, these poets were intensely literary; all three found ways to fit their poems uniquely within traditional devices, but they also taught themselves how to use war as subject so that they stretched both the formal and subjective reach of the war lyric.

Unpredictably, Keith Douglas, the poet with combat experience, wrote much less about combat than Randall Jarrell, who had none. The poems of Douglas's war years anchor more in anticipation and aftermath, slipping the immediate conflicts into metaphysical confrontations with death, time, and will. Jarrell, a flight instructor who never left American air bases, in contrast to both Owen and Douglas, went beyond autobiographical witness. Using fictional detail, his war poems directly project combat, aiming at an understanding of war as a general phenomenon. Douglas saved this aim for his prose. In Jarrell's handling, Owen's tenderly lamented youth became modernity's drained and depersonalized child-victim. In ways typical for World War II poets, both Jarrell and Douglas concerned themselves with a wider angle on the relation between civilians and soldiers, and in the global theater of World War II they began the process of hinting at the geopolitics in which the soldier finds himself. Either because they were more stoic or less personally involved, World War II poets were in the habit of observing others' status as pawns of war rather than their own. But, like the young men of World War I, for the American soldier-poets of the 1960s and 1970s, warfare was more enveloping and painful.

Chapter 6 concludes with late-twentieth-century poems, which contain the self-doubt that did not penetrate so deeply the poems of the world wars, as well as the ardent and angry questioning of authority that suffused only the earlier poems of World War I. This final discussion of war poetry takes up a group of Vietnam War soldier-poets, using various technical, but largely non-traditional literary means. This consideration of a group of innovative poets ends, like a snake with its tail in its mouth, by returning to Homer's *Iliad*, and the impact of classical heroic poetry on two soldier-poets of the American-Vietnamese conflict.

Looking at the increasingly eroded lines drawn between combatants and noncombatants during hostilities, I contrast Doug Anderson's sequence re-working the Iliad in *Raids on Homer* with R. L. Barth's *Forced Marching to The Styx*. The doubled perspective of Anderson and Barth's poems encompasses both literary and mythic history and shows how very unevenly, and often in what masquerade, change moves through a genre.

My attention is about evenly split between English and American war po-etry. Another important binary, between civilian and soldier experience—sometimes starkly evident, sometimes unrecognizable in its blurring continu-ities—begs for notice in the jarring complexities of the witness position. While I found myself mostly drawn to the contribution of the soldier-poet, in the case of World War II, it became impossible to write about either Keith Douglas or Randall Jarrell without considering W. H. Auden, a predecessor whose style of politics was so influential on both English and American poets of the forties. Yet the contribution of any forties war poet cannot be fairly evaluated without some acknowledgment of how, within the span of global wars, even the soldier-poet's immersion in direct experience of war varied as terrifically as the experience of the civilian.

During World War I, for English and American alike, there was an enor-mous gap between combatant and home front. During World War II, every survivor became aware of the varied deployment of risk over changing fronts; English noncombatant women and children could be bombed and killed, while in the United States, war factory employees collected bonus checks for over-time, in more danger from their machines than from their enemies. A rear-echelon soldier in an occupied country could sleep more peacefully than a civilian whose homeland was the target of an invasion. Safety depended on where you were and who you were and not on whether you were in, or out, of uniform. The American-Vietnamese War brought even more permutations and combinations of these alignments of soldier or civilian, hostile or friendly.

Generally, the antiwar inclinations of the soldier seem to me peculiarly in-teresting, and I find them compelling beyond those of the civilian involved in various degrees of conflict. While many soldiers serving as backup to armies behind the front lines never find themselves directly facing risk over the course of a war, many civilians do. Yet the articulated resistance of the soldier to war has overtones that the protest of the civilian, who is bound by a less immedi-ate commitment to war and to reciprocal exchanges of threat and injury, does not. When the soldier protests—a being meant to give as well as to receive war's outrages—his protest is always a knot in the working out of war itself, an internal contravention of the use of force. At best, soldiers represent the courageous, heroic mode of defense; at worst, as both perpetrator and victim of violence, the citizen as soldier stands in most fitly for all of us needing to resolve the ethics of militarism.

It is also true that while many notable and determined pacifists have suffered jail and physical and mental torment for their beliefs, so far in the twentieth century, none of them, neither men nor women, with the exception of the American Robert Lowell, are visible as distinguished poets as well. W. H. Auden, the most brilliantly focused exponent of a general citizen's guilt for the crises of war in the twentieth century, and whose impact I could not ignore in this study, dropped war poems shortly after arriving in America, leaving us thereafter with soldier poetry as the most fertile ground for the exposure of both war and antiwar thinking. But the model of political and pacifist engagement that Auden initiated cast a long shadow.

Far with the Brave We Have Ridden

The shorter poem, whose paper intensity can be blanketed by spread palms, its duration pinched between thumb and forefinger, makes plain a real transition in representing war. From poet to poet, the best of them record the steadily evolving tension between the older heroism and contemporary antimilitarist values. Cleared of the novelist's need for backstory, a poem can cut to the pivotal balances between life and death, courage and cowardice, or winning and losing, as the subject covered goes from glory of killing, to glory of being killed, to fear of being killed, and finally, in a move looking to dismantle glory altogether, to shame in killing. And yet the line of development is never wholly linear, never wholly pacifist. What remains fascinating and tormenting is the loop back to earlier positions, the persistent eruption in modern poems of old styles of sensation and focus, assenting not only to war's necessity, but to its terrible grandeurs.

The oldest tradition accepts war as a test of courage and sees that test as the apotheosis of masculinity. Few men find themselves immune to the rasp of that tradition. Any man writing war poetry is interrogated, directly or indirectly, as to whether he has passed or failed or evaded the test; for a long while, any woman writing of war has tended to see herself as looking over the fence of gender in relation to a show going on in a distant yard. Because of their apparent detachment from war's causation and its active duties, with the unique exception of poems like Elizabeth Bishop's "Roosters," English and American women have written the odd poem generally excoriating war, even as the writers assumed a conventional posture of lament, but they have not written a war poetry advancing either form or substance in the genre. Critics like Susan Friedman make a strong case for the importance of H. D.'s *Trilogy*, written during the Blitz in London, yet to me H. D.'s approach in that poem philosophizes and generalizes away any solid connection to a specific historical reality, winding up with a remote and fleshless ecstasy of religion that bypasses the rage, violence, and misery of actual people at war.

The value of being either a passive, suffering conquest or an active, enthusiastic conqueror crumples given what the century cannot help but know of indiscriminate, mechanized slaughter. In the face of that experience, clinging to models of Homeric or chivalric dueling as justification for war seems criminal lunacy. No culture, no language, for either gender, seems quite able to let go of war as a prompt for self-transcending sacrifice, but at least a gain in the ethics of war turns approval away from heroic attack and towards heroic defense even if the test of courage through violence lingers to shape reality.

In the fourteenth century, as a soldier and hero exulting in the exercise of his craft, the troubadour Bertran de Borns could sing:

> My heart is filled with gladness when I see
> Strong castles besieged, stockades broken and overwhelmed,
> Many vassals struck down,
> Horses of the dead and wounded roving at random.
>
> . . . .
> I tell you I have no such joy as when I hear the shout
> "On! On!" from both sides and the neighing of riderless steeds,
> And groans of "Help me! Help me!"
> And when I see both great and small
> Fall in the ditches and on the grass
> And see the dead transfixed by spear shafts!
>
> (Tuchman, 16)

And so on through many more lines of joyful bloodbath, earning Bertrans a place in Dante's *Inferno*, where with upright trunk and severed neck he walks in the Ninth Chasm, his hand swinging the lantern of his head by the hair (Dante, 300–301).

Since the passing of chivalry and the horse-borne fighter, a thirst for personal glory appears a vain and shallow reason for murdering or being murdered. But in the modern vamping of the theme of being challenged by death, combatants manage to idealize war by setting aside the part about killing in favor of the part that risks being killed; in this way, war shines most convincingly as the will to risk life for others. Pleasure in wartime killing retreats to a mythic underside, the dense, fantastic undergrowth where cinematic renegades from Rambo to those saving Private Ryan can still dress up carnage as the unavoidable by-product of loyal rescue missions, where the good fellas go in to get the good fellas out.

Charles Carrington takes a passage from Boswell's *Life of Johnson* as the epigraph for his World War I memoir, *Soldier From The Wars Returning*, and nothing I have read puts the adaptable, tenacious appeal of militarism more cleanly:

JOHNSON: "Every man thinks meanly of himself for not having been a soldier, or not having been at sea.

Were Socrates and Charles the Twelfth of Sweden both present in any company and Socrates were to say, 'Follow me and hear a lecture on philosophy'; and Charles, laying his hand on his sword, were to say, 'Follow me and dethrone the Czar'; a man would be ashamed to follow Socrates. The impression is universal; yet it is strange. But the profession of soldiers and sailors has the dignity of danger. Mankind reverences those who have got over fear, which is so general a weakness.'

SIR WILLIAM SCOTT: "But is not courage mechanical, and to be acquired?"

JOHNSON: "Why yes, Sir, in a collective sense. Soldiers consider themselves only as parts of a great machine." (Carrington, 10)

In Johnson's talk, "dignity" may be found in defense of the goals of that larger, collective self, of which the army forms a necessary part, manufacturing courage for soldiers within its "great machine." While it is "strange" that a man should reject the call of intellect to pursue the deposition of tyrants, it is nonetheless a universal urgency to wish to have such freedom of action, beyond fear, rushing into danger with one's fellows at one's side. This validation of blood spill, strengthened by the glow that continues to radiate from sacrifice for the public good, holds us atavistically.

More atavistic still is the all-too-swift conversion of stranger into enemy, a change that elicits a primal need to retaliate and ascribe damage to communal malignancy. In this scheme, faceless or obscurely motivated opponents slide into the reductionist conception of war in which only friends and foes are felt to exist. And yet few nations wish to look like the schoolyard bully who initiates offense, so a second oversimplification occurs, in which, after transforming complicated socialities into friends and foes, a nation further reduces motive into dubious claims of original innocence. Every modern country, even as it begins the rituals of war, explains itself to itself as a fearless and righteous people countering, but never truly initiating or precipitating, violence or elemental evil. If poets like Keith Douglas in poems like "How to Kill" offer new insights into this basic equation, they do so by reading the male test of war not as a surmounting of the fear of being killed, but as a grim surmounting of the doubts and fears involved in killing itself, in a mode subverting righteousness.

This is quite an advance from Tennyson, whose position as a bystander led him to ask of a cavalry charge in the Crimea, which even at the time it fatally took place was acknowledged as a "hideous blunder,"

When can their glory fade?
O the wild charge they made!
    All the world wondered.
Honor the charge they made!
Honor the Light Brigade,
    Noble six hundred!
        ("The Charge of the Light Brigade," 1854; Tennyson, 207)

Tennyson carries out manly identity by hailing and encouraging the extension of empire by its professional builders. When lettered poets stood on one side of war and unlettered soldiers on the other, poetry on military glory became a kind of benevolence that the distantly involved could bestow in tones mixing an Olympian pity tinged with irony and admiring gratitude. Tennyson, Kipling, and many others provided this formula in plenty. Here's a good measure of it from A. E. Housman, as he assumes appropriate voice and costume in "Lancer" (1922):

And over the seas we were bidden
    A country to take and to keep;
And far with the brave I have ridden,
    And now with the brave I shall sleep.

For round me the men will be lying
    That learned me the way to behave,
And showed me my business of dying:
    Oh who would not sleep with the brave?
       (Housman, 103)

Housman administers more of the same in even more famously elevated tones in "Epitaph on an Army of Mercenaries" (1922):

These, in the day when heaven was falling,
    The hour when earth's foundations fled,
Followed their mercenary calling
    And took their wages and are dead.

Their shoulders held the sky suspended;
    They stood, and earth's foundations stay;
What God abandoned, these defended,
    And saved the sum of things for pay.
      (Housman, 144)

Which, by 1935, in "Another Epitaph on an Army of Mercenaries," drew this retort from Hugh MacDiarmid:

It is a God-damned lie to say that these
Saved, or knew, anything worth any man's pride.
They were professional murderers and they took
Their blood money and impious risks and died.
In spite of all their kind some elements of worth
With difficulty persist here and there on earth.
     (MacDiarmid, 100)

That Hugh MacDiarmid was a soldier returned from the Great War and that Housman was a civilian bystander has some relevance; only veterans have come to have the right to scorn the glory trader. It is quite clear, though, that some perspectives changed conclusively during the mass conscriptions of two world wars, when more people than the village ne'er-do-well or a lord's younger son took care of the business of dying. MacDiarmid's reply to Housman emphasizes the widening rift between poets on war, between those who watch and those who fight.

An ailing Thomas Hardy bicycled fifty miles and back to be at Southampton in 1899 to cheer the departure of British troops for the Boer War. Summoning up the grim, historical weight of such moments and amplifying the tragedy of their recurrence by noting how the repetition of place hammers home the repeated, but also expanding, arc of action, he says in "Embarcation,"

> Here, where Vespasian's legions struck the sands,
> And Cerdic with his Saxons entered in,
> And Henry's army leapt afloat to win
> Convincing triumphs over neighbor lands,
>
> Vaster battalions press for further strands,
> To argue in the selfsame bloody mode
> Which this late age of thought, and pact, and code,
> Still fails to mend.
>> (Hardy, 1:116)

With bitter helplessness, Hardy sees that it's the British thing to go to war for empire. Even if, at the poem's end,

> Wives, sisters, parents, wave white hands and smile,
> As if they knew not that they weep the while.

"Drummer Hodge" lets Hardy's sadness at the death of the English drummer boy spill over into the pathos of final and absolute estrangement from the home turf, but in "The Man He Killed" (1902), he frankly allows for the vulnerable interchangeability of soldier parts, whether they wear one uniform or another:

> "Yes; quaint and curious war is!
> You shoot a fellow down
>> You'd treat if met where any bar is,
> Or help to half-a-crown."
>> (Hardy, 1:122)

Yet in this poetry, the gulf between onlooker and man of war stays disheartengly firm. Even as industrial war from one end of the century to the other increased the flooding of war over combatant and noncombatant alike, those who write about war intensify awareness of the different feelings that each position entails. Those who suffer war directly, in uniform or not, as their number and access to publication swells, begin to speak in louder and louder admonition and reproach to those on the sidelines in perceptible safety.

World War I, with a severe censorship of battlefield events in place, also intensified changes in the conventional codes of mourning when the logistics of twentieth-century warfare prohibited the return of corpses after huge engagements and notoriously extended lines of command. A crisis of mourning arose when literate, grieving soldiers were immersed in a carnage that was allowed to have only a distant connection with home-front life and continuity. Soldiers were killed; bodies vanished in the mud, later memorialized at mass cenotaphs. A gap persisted between war and home. The combat soldier's memory was filled with degraded and mutilated flesh. For those at the rear and the home front, loss was the abstraction of a growing casualty list, difficult to square with frenzied patriotism or initial hopes of lightning success—a loss to be balanced against protracted shortages and a battlefield stalemate finally obvious even at home. But when the unbearable discrepancies of knowledge between home front and front lines finally burst through in the soldier's memoirs of the late 1920s, like Blunden's *Undertones of War* (1928) and Robert Graves's *Good-Bye to All That* (1929; reprint, 1998), interest sharpened in the anguish of what direct battlefield witness reported. From the 1920s on, after the publication of Siegfried Sassoon's *War Poems* and the first edition of Wilfred Owen's poems in 1920, war poetry by soldier-poets began to receive what developed into a wide hearing.

There had been troubled soldier-poets in English before, of course. While Richard Lovelace was an early advocate of a stiff upper lip for the home front, counseling Lucasta to understand the paradox of the love that made him abandon her for honor, George Gascoigne's picture of war was less summary and less kind. In "The Fruites of Warre," he plainly writes:

> I set aside to tell the restless toyle,
> The mangled corps, the lamed limbes at last,
> The shortned yeares by fret of fevers foyle,
> The smoothest skinne with skabbes and skarres disgrast,

The broken sleepes, the dreadfull dreames, the woe,
Which wonne with warre and cannot from him goe.

(Gascoigne, 149–50)

War trauma clearly existed before the Great War, and the shame of fighting and killing was named long before the Vietnam War by Gascoigne as he described the hunt for honor during the campaigns of Elizabeth I:

"And fie," (sayeth he), "for goods or filthie gain,
I gape for glory, all the rest is vayne."

Vayne is the rest, and that most vayne of all,
A smouldring smoke which flieth with every winde,
A tickell treasure, like a trendlyng ball,
A passing pleasure mocking but the minde,
A fickle fee as fansie well can finde.
A sommers fruite whiche long can never last,
But ripeneth soone, and rottes againe as fast.
. . . .
Searche all thy bookes, and thou shalt finde therein,
That honour is more harde to holde than winne.

(149)

Nothing written by the poets of trench warfare exceeded these admissions. What has become in the late twentieth century an almost ritual popular reference to "the horrors of war" has never been entirely new, but it is as if the soldier-poets of World War I created an almost codifiable awareness of those horrors. Yet even so, a broad popularity for the grimmer poems of World War I did not arrive until well after the 1930s.

During World War I, the bewildering stoppage of information would only make the trench soldier's indignation keener, as in many cases he put into his writing his sense of betrayal by politicians at home and chateau generals, as well as by citizen ignorance. As Allyson Booth describes the situation:

The extremely restricted space within which trench warfare was fought simultaneously ensured that Great War soldiers would live with the corpses of their friends and that British civilians would not see dead soldiers. . . . British policy dictated that the civilian bereaved would never have anything to bury.

Soldiers inhabited a world of corpses; British civilians experienced the death of their soldiers as corpselessness. In England, then, World War I created two markedly different categories of experience, a discrepancy that complicated the gap that always separates language from experience. (Booth, 21)

These "markedly different categories of experience" helped to push into being the literature by which we have lastingly come to know industrial war.

In *A War Imagined*, Samuel Hynes explains the impact of a severe and often arbitrary censorship, which in effect curtailed both description and criticism of the conduct of the war. But out of human need for mourning and closure, the ordeal of the war then flared up in the peculiar niche of the World War I poet. His pain, suffered millionfold by literate men in uniform, was unforgettably conveyed and assumed as the burden and type of heroism by the next generation of soldiers. By that next generation, however, the medium of reportage went from the verbally symbolic to the visual, and war poetry in World War II yielded to the popular transmission of newsreel and photographic journalism. We might use the red paper poppy as a telling illustration of the difference between World Wars I and II: the World War I veteran drew his symbolic strength from a line of poetry ("In Flanders field, the poppies grow . . . "); an equivalent symbol from World War II probably derives from a photo archive, maybe the shot of the flag raising at Iwo Jima or an image of a mushroom cloud. Both symbols are visual, but the earlier one originates from a print medium. While the writers of World War II were as literate as the poets of World War I, their witness reached a comparatively altered home audience, already receiving broad war coverage through popular journalism.

Speaking of changes in the cultural function of war poetry, Gregory Woods remarked about the poems of the Vietnam War:

Siegfried Sassoon used his poetic abilities to present the jingoistic British public with a true and appropriately melodramatic picture of the horrors of the Western Front. Why should anyone even begin to perform such a task, by sending home poems from Vietnam, when that war's iniquities had become already the commonplace fare of televised news bulletins? In fact, the poet of the Vietnam war generally sought to come to terms with the grey pictures which flickered endlessly in a corner of his bedroom. Given the public, exhibitionistic nature of the fighting, we need not expect the memorial function of the poetry of that war to operate quite as did that of the First and Second World Wars. When a nation flies its dead home as efficiently as the United States did from Vietnam, retrospective paper head-stones are not needed to commemorate lost corpses; and when a man dies on film, one need not publicise his death in written stanzas months later. (Woods, 70)

Yet both elegiac and antielegiac poems were written. Vietnam veterans shoul-dered the burdens peculiar to their war and requiring their expressive confir-mation, even as did the soldier-poets of World War II. World War I poetry stood in a historically unique position of attention: but mindful of their belat-edness, soldiers of subsequent wars absorbed and revived at least in part what their predecessors offered as motivation in word and action.

The World War I soldier-poet wrested irony and pity away from the class of disengaged elders like Housman or Kipling or Hardy and deployed his own. The World War II soldier-poet had not only to cede the freshness of first-person battlefield epiphany to the older generation, but also to deal with new segregations in readership, new realignments of generation, genre, and gen-der. As the range of effective weaponry kept enlarging the distance between soldiers, World War II also introduced a new form of dehumanization, in which death managed at such distances becomes a matter of precision me-chanics. For World War II, R. N. Currey observed, "This is a civilization in which a man, too squeamish to empty a slop pail or skin a rabbit, can press a button that exposes the entrails of cities" (Currey, 43); in such a civilization, pity—or pathos—is definitively redistributed, moving each successive gener-ation of poets to grope for pivotal meanings in both the rending and preserv-ing of flesh at war.

What moves with new force in Keith Douglas's 1943 poem "How to Kill," is not only its refusal to use the easy pathos of victimhood for its soldier-speaker, but its emphasis on the cage of otherness which combat itself impos-es from within. In Douglas's memoir, *Alamein to Zem Zem*, issued after his death in 1944, he affirms the necessity of battle to his self-conception, saying, "I never lost the certainty that the experience of battle was something I must have." (15) A year after Alamein, he concentrated on battle as conferring a kind of election, a boost into a zoned apartness of being: "to read about it can-not convey the impression of having walked through the looking-glass which touches a man entering a battle." (16)

Besides the reverence men accord being moved beyond fear of death, how-ever death may come, war may have a stubborn and resilient purchase as topic because of its otherness. War exists as an inflected zone in which participants know they live in a space set aside by its terms, and which they approach to struggle with the alienation of death, striking into the borderlands of mortality, right there, to move and do in the dark and frightful place that dream and transcendent vision also occupy. It may be that the Faustian demiurge not only to defy death, but to know it directly or by proxy is one of the more durable parts of our acceptance of war, our attachment to its abattoirs.

The Burdens of Heroic Masculinity

Age, temperament, education, class, and nationality—all the odd quirks of individual talent and experience—shape the poetry that ends up being understood as representative of its time. As I read the remarkable writers I've picked for a closer look, the juggler's trick will be to keep a steady and supple sense of the individuality of each. In order to resist both the typifying that blurs and reduces complicated people in the speeding mesh of their lives, and to avoid the formalist myopia of pretending that poems are written by pens and typewriters alone, my readings are laced, wherever possible and relevant, with letters and memoir. Because they are commonly thought to initiate the antiwar posture that dominates twentieth-century war poetry, Wilfred Owen's poems of the trench warfare of World War I, which frequently gild the memory of fellow soldiers as hapless sacrificial victims, make the best place to begin. Owen's own death in battle in 1918 folded him back inside his own pictures of the Fated Boy: his poems generally bifurcate into visions of golden lads nobly lost or horrific visions which try to make real to the reader the rawness and ugliness of the human slaughter in which the body is broken to carrion. These poems, both horrified and tenderly elegiac, are told by a junior officer. Owen followed Siegfried Sassoon's lead in looking at the higher leadership with hostility and suspicion, but midlevel or junior officers, like himself, and their men, conspicuously overrepresented in casualty lists in both world wars, were part of the sacralized brotherhood of battle.

Celebrating the fraternity of battlefield is hardly new. Shakespeare planted the idea of the "band of brothers" beyond removal from our memories in 1599. Henry V proclaimed a brotherhood for any soldier that fought "be he ne'er so base" (*Henry V* 4.3.62); Wilfred Owen and other World War I poets, however, seriously broadened that "base," or lowered our eyes to look at it longer and closer. The focus is moved from the top of the military pyramid closer to its bottom: not the affirmation of fraternity, but the egalitarian embrace of the foot soldier marks Owen's poems as particularly twentieth century.

FIGURE 1. Michael Sheen as Henry V, Royal Shakespeare Company production, directed by Ron Daniels. 1997. Malcolm Davies, The Shakespeare Centre Library.

Wilfred Owen's inclusiveness did not take in the soldiers on the other side, however. Only "Strange Meeting" throws up a mirror image of the dead enemy, holding up to the living soldier his reproachful counterpart:

> "I am the enemy you killed, my friend.
> I knew you in this dark: for so you frowned
> Yesterday through me as you jabbed and killed.
> I parried; but my hands were loath and cold.
> Let us sleep now. . . ."
>   (*Complete Poems*, 1:149)

But only one or two poems deal with killing rather than being killed; while the poems were taken as pacifist in spirit, especially in postwar readings, Owen explicitly relinquished "pacifist" as the name of his own beliefs. Later poems, like Keith Douglas's "How to Kill," are more direct about what soldiers do as well as have done to them. Douglas's "Dead Men," and "Vergissmeinnicht" play on actual or ghost or violent dream encounters with dead soldiers, or they have speakers who burrow empathically inside the enemy psyche, as in Siegfried Sassoon's "The rank stench of those bodies haunts me still."[2] In poems of soldierly meeting from World War I and II combat veterans, however, there's none of the comfortably ironic, ruefully gentle equality posed by the civilian Hardy in "The Man He Killed" (Hardy, 1:344); this tone is not readopted until Yusef Komunyakaa looks at his Vietnamese equivalent late in the century. But all the newer poems show their men as mutually and indelibly fouled by the ugliness, or what Owen referred to as the "cess of war."

In "Dulce et Decorum Est" Owen associates his ghost with the guilt of abandonment. This revenant seems the harbinger of a number of the poems of World War II, which will, in equal pain but in more explicit and more intensified self-reproach, represent the soldier as one who maims and kills, as well as one who is killed, is maimed. The officer-poets of World War I may have more freely dissociated themselves from the agency of bloodshed, accustomed to thinking, in John Keegan's words, that the military code had evolved to one in which "soldiers on the whole are given medals for killing and officers for doing other things" (Keegan, *Face*, 315). In later wars, however, written up by other ranks, this job ticket became less relevant, increasingly less exculpatory. When race influenced how one disposed of the enemy, as in Vietnam, strange conjunctions of belated respect and past fear and contempt for the enemy become visible, as in Yusef Komunyakaa's "Tunnels" (*Dien Cai Dao*, 5) or Bruce Weigl's "Surrounding Blues on the Way Down" (in Ehrhart, *Carrying*, 258).

But the deep and defiant trench between combatant and noncombatant that Wilfred Owen and Siegfried Sassoon dug to ward off the sentimental falsification of war witness by civilians and the antagonism towards the home front and sense of betrayal that these poets expressed seem hotly special to all of the poet-veterans of World War I. What came undone for them, to the greatest surprise of everyone, was the agreement that those doing their duty were not to talk of it or to bring the war home. The Englishmen of World War I, broadly conscripted and tightly woven into the social fabric, were not the soldiers that Wellington's officers had brutally flogged into shape during the Peninsular Wars, whom Wellington called "the scum of the earth" because "none but the worst description of men enter the regular service" (Hibbert, 139). Neither were they the old-style professionals of the late-nineteenth- or early-twentieth-century peacetime armies, whose fossilized styles of leadership so offended Robert Graves, prompting the title of his World War I memoir, *Good-Bye to All That*. For these soldier-poets, industrial war destroyed shallow codes of sportsmanship and undermined the loyal son, the Christian stoic, and the jingoistic patriot.

The institutional props of their identities, playing-field slogans, church platitudes, newspaper clichés—all that they had of moral armor— failed to serve. For Rebecca West, as quoted by Samuel Hynes, the crisis of World War I represented the following:

> the precipitation of a class bred from its beginnings to eschew profundity, into an experience which only the profoundest thinking could render tolerable, with no words to express their agony but the insipid vocabulary of their education, no gods to guide them save the unhelpful gods of Puritan athleticism. (Hynes, *War Imagined*, 443)

Yet the problems that West identified were not limited to the middle and upper classes. The war poets of World War II could not point to a puerile cultural optimism as the source of their discontent with war, and they did not wholly share the heightened sense of generational, specifically patriarchal, division that marked the protest of the World War I generation. They could, however, appropriate from their predecessors some sense of inexpungeable difference from the worlds of civilian value, as well as the familiar bitterness at the foreshortening of their lives.

But the warfare of 1939–45, with even vaster suffering on both home front and battlefront, bore other distinguishing marks than just the conflict of generations. A crucial shift gradually occurred in World War II. Lyric poets like Keith Douglas and Randall Jarrell could and did advance their perspectives by beginning to articulate responsibility for, in Owen's words from "Spring Offensive" (*Complete Poems*, 1:183), the "superhuman inhumanities . . . [and] immemorial shames" of war as well as its epic grandeur. The earlier poets defined their relationship to war in terms of battlefield realities, incurious about much else but the features of that landscape; but the poet of World War II, placed in a wider geography, wrote his poems within a bigger, and more restive cultural and political arena. Influenced by W. H. Auden and his renditions of the politics of crisis building in the 1930s, the tilt of World War II poets seemed inevitably farther left but also, in an odd twist, more hopeless and more passive about either political evolution or revolution.

Swatting away at Egyptian and Tunisian flies, writing on the run in "hospitals, Con Depots, Base depots etc—" Keith Douglas complained to Tambimuttu, his editor, that if his circumstances changed, he would send him "bags of literature, in all forms & on all subjects" (Douglas Papers, Add 53773): that is, if he could commandeer a house, with his own room, and a vehicle at his disposal.

Wilfred Owen shared Douglas's anxiety about billeting and might gladly have traded sand flies for trench lice, but Owen never pressed for wheels as part of his poetic identikit. While Douglas believed that "almost all that a modern poet on active service is inspired to write would be tautological," that is, merely an illustrated rerun of the earlier hell of World War I, he added that "the mobility of modern warfare does not give the same opportunities for writing as the long routine of trench warfare" (*Prose Miscellany*, 120).

Where Wilfred Owen wistfully hoped to see more of England and France through his postings, soldiers like Keith Douglas spanned continents in abrupt and discontinuous rhythms. If we compare Owen with the English and American poets of World War II, like Keith Douglas, Alun Lewis, and Henry Reed or Randall Jarrell, Karl Shapiro, and Louis Simpson, we quickly encounter not only the difference between compulsory induction and mobile air and tank warfare, but also the difference that occurs when one generation of poets glances back, in extreme self-consciousness, invidiously to measure its own perceptions and accomplishments against that of another.

World War II poets were doubly weighted by the condition of belatedness and diminished in the glow of their soldierly individuality by stunning increases in men and materiel. Paul Fussell points out that a conscript in World War I was lumped as one of four million men; his counterpoint in World War II stood, or hid, as one of sixteen million: "But if in the Second World War you're one of sixteen million, you're really nothing" (*Wartime*, 70). A poet like Wilfred Owen, bursting out from behind the screen of censorship, could count on the new, raw impact of the horror of the Western Front to bring home, quite literally, what he was saying about modern battle. But by World War II, the home front, surveying bomb damage after air raids, knew very well what war entailed. T. S. Eliot, inspecting damage as a firewarden, or Philip Larkin, jumping on his bicycle to see if his family had survived the bombing of Coventry, were privy to fear and horror: that war was nasty, wasteful of life and youth, and, furthermore, often badly led became a less novel observation.

Like Wilfred Owen and Isaac Rosenberg in World War I, in World War II equally talented poets like Keith Douglas, Alun Lewis, and Sidney Keyes all died on active duty; Randall Jarrell's war experience was in uniform, although he never made it overseas. While this time, unlike in 1914–18, English and American war poets shared almost the same dragging weight of years at war, interwar national politics and the spread-out geography of World War II, as well as their very different and varied educations in poetic tradition, separate

English and American accomplishments. Any discussion trying to encompass both needs to filter judgment with some clear sense of how personal and temperamental singularities might impinge on cultural circumstance.

The poetry that spilled from the politics of the Vietnam War describes soldier-civilian interaction, with shame, guilt, and futility as the overwhelming climate of wartime behavior. In these late-century poems, responsibility for atrocity and indiscriminate slaughter moves critically from being largely the function of bad leadership toward something that is inherently part of war at all levels of soldiering. All the war poetry of this century, however, took a heightened awareness of politics as part of its poetical equipment, pervaded by what Samuel Hynes describes as the legacy of the thirties generation, "the sense of crisis, the menace of the future, the need for action;" (*The Auden Generation*, 82) but for the post-Auden sensibility, both action and inaction are threaded with moral unease. Nor is the soldier to be separated from what his civilian counterpart must feel.

As antiwar themes in poetry deepened, so did the egalitarian strain, questioning and dissolving the more crudely top-down perspective of officers versus other ranks. Vietnam War poets also saw a more intense and varied articulation of the relations between soldier and civilian, as well as between the older generation and younger generation of home front and battlefront. But in their war, even the divisions between men and women at war became part of the story, as well as the isolating underside of combat, undermining battlefront fraternity; this is a new development in war poetry. For post-Eliot and post-Auden poets like Randall Jarrell, Karl Shapiro, and Roy Fuller, the leftist politics of the thirties are the point of departure. In the late–Atomic Age poems, the technology of war itself becomes the urgency propelling war resistance. New wounds accompany new wars, and the lurching asynchronicity of new weapons and new systems of medical recovery only provokes further revulsion at war making itself.

Not until later in the twentieth century does exactly what it is that women or older people or children do to augment the masculine effort in war or to share men's subjections and hazards begin to register on the poet as part of the totality of industrialized war, and hence something appropriate for the literary record. The war poets of World Wars I and II were steeped in the English pastoral tradition; in *A War Imagined*, Samuel Hynes shows how the continuities of this tradition were broken and filtered through the betrayals of the Great War, how the breakage led to a characteristic antipastoral poetry that worked in by contrast and ironic implication how war ruinously transformed ordinary life. World War I poetry, however, went only so far in tracking the ripped threads.

Hynes quotes statistics showing how losses in World War I made lasting impact on women and family:

> In the 1921 census there were 19,803,022 females in England and Wales, and only 18,082,220 males—a difference of a million and three-quarters women. This situation was not indeed a new phenomenon: there had been more women than men in England for nearly a hundred years—a million more in the last pre-war census. But in 1921 that number had nearly doubled, by a figure that was almost exactly the number of the English war dead. If you look at the numbers for persons of child-bearing age, the point is even more striking: there were more than nine and a half million women between the ages of fifteen and forty-four in 1921, and less than eight and a half million men. More than a million women—one in nine of the child-bearing group—would not marry or bear children. For them, the war would be a continuing reality in their lives until they died. (Hynes, *War Imagined*, 379)

The making of widows and childless women registers only at a slant for Wilfred Owen, Siegfried Sassoon, Isaac Rosenberg, Edmund Blunden, or Robert Graves. Whether the World War I poet was gay, killed on the battlefield, or later replete with progeny, the poetry of war's aftereffects was largely silent on questions involving women or families. Wilfred Owen's widely anthologized "Anthem for Doomed Youth" has an odd shot of women mourning, static apparitions at dusk behind "a drawing-down of blinds" (*Complete Poems*, 1:99). But elsewhere, he merely scolds women for their inability to care, or care properly, for the dead or wounded male. Given the lesser frequency of homosexuality among the prominent soldier-poets of later wars, one might ask what emphasis should be placed on a wider spread of homoerotic themes and authorship in World War I. In World War II, there was certainly a shift away from the anguished mourning for boys, the boys goldenly handsome as Rupert Brooke, that characterized the World War I elegy. And the angry burden of accusation against the useless mothers and sweethearts—who failed to understand the trials that soldiers had undergone, or who frivolously backed the greedy war profiteers—lightened, as so many more of these mothers and sweethearts joined the wartime labor force or were hurt and maimed by aerial bombardment. In World War II poems, while women hardly figure in wartime roles, whether because of a generally lessened tension about sexual expressivity of any sort or because women themselves were more directly plunged into war, the former gender animus dissipates. More World War II poems remember shore leave or furloughs, express hunger for women, and suggest the pains of arrested or interrupted domesticity. Poetry from the Vietnam War expands these subjects yet further.

The question that reformulates in the war poetry of 1939–45 not only nibbles at the edges of heroic masculinity, but also asks to know what that preoccupation excludes. War is about battles, one colleague said to me, and battles take place between soldiers. Therefore, he said, with truly impeccable logic, war has little to do with women. If there are victims in war, as Wilfred Owen paints it, they are soldiers, and the origin and source of their victimhood flows from men behind desks far behind battle lines and from the false women who exhort the soldiers to follow where the men behind desks point them. When Wilfred Owen dedicates his most famous antiwar poem to Jessie Pope, indignantly rejecting the war fever of her patriotism, we might also remember how earlier Julia Ward Howe's "Battle Hymn of the Republic" similarly swept Americans into trampling and sampling the grapes of wrath in civil war. Those who prefer to think of women as leaders of pacifist causes must ignore the women who belie that stereotype. But whether women are thought to be naturally or unnaturally bellicose, fear and rejection of women—the desire to shut them out, to displace them from the pure maleness of war—uneasily ride the war poetry so tenaciously haunting its male readers.

The Boundaries of War

Edmund Blunden's prose opened to occasional glimpses of the people among whom soldiers in World War I billeted or drove from their homes. Blunden, whose poems were alive to the feel of country roads at the front, the sounds of rivers and trees, and the ghostly presence of farms, animals, and barns, took no pains to fill in the farmer, the farmwife, the farm children, or the townspeople whose nonmilitary world intersected with him or any other soldier. Indeed, the reverse: like Henri Barbusse, in whose *Under Fire* the surrounding peasantry of the Western Front often represented truculence, stinginess, and suspicion, Blunden reported hostile contact as typical, writing home to say:

> I regret to say that the French villagers show a nasty spirit in many cases,
> to the Tommies—they dismantle wells and pumps to prevent them getting

water, they swindle outrageously in their everyday deals, and they are constantly probing them for information. (Webb, 61)

He added optimistically, though with what prescience is debatable, that "another war will see some remarkable differences, for the men are not encouraged by these things from the people they are defending."

Later yet, Blunden doubtlessly became more deeply aware that "defense" for the French and Belgian alike along this wasteland meant an aftermath, in which, as Denis Winter points out, "a war zone of 250 miles in length and thirty miles in breadth had consumed 1,659 townships and over half a million houses" (Winter, 263). Neither do Blunden's remarks reflect on the historical enmity between French and English, nor the legacy of peasants and villagers being caught between the hammer and the anvil in even older wars: the soils of the low country contain relics of other conflicts, which are currently being dug up along with the still-lethal war debris of the twentieth century.

Whatever the intercourse between these populations caught in their common dilemma may have been—antagonistic, amorous, avaricious, or merely civil—the soldier poets of 1914–18 saved their memory for other subjects. The broad stock-in-trade of the World War I memoirists or novelists, veterans of combat like Robert Graves or Ernst Junger or Erich Maria Remarque, proved of little interest to the poet. Wilfred Owen borrowed the image of troop movement as caterpillar-like from "The Vision" in Henri Barbusse's *Under Fire*, to describe No Man's Land for his poem, "The Show": "Across its beard, that horror of harsh wire, / There moved thin caterpillars, slowly uncoiled" (*Complete Poems*, 1:155). But he left Barbusse's tender grotesque of civilian and soldier interface strictly alone or shunted the like observation to the more random spontaneity of his letters home.

Although World War II saw the stimulating effects of a less insular soldier-writer, habituated to both travel and desire for travel, war poets still spent many stanzas more on antipastoral description of the battlefield through which combat moved or stagnated, and only gradually enlarged the view of the people on whom the soldiers depended for bodily comfort of one sort or another. In a Renaissance painting by Giovanni Bellini, hung in the National Gallery in London, Saint Sebastian is martyred by a group of helmeted and cuirassed soldiers, while behind a nearby grove of chestnut trees an indifferent farmer steadily plows his field. Most of the war poems of World War I see what happens adjacent to the battlefield, or in the city or village whose perimeter is increasingly penetrable by modern total war, much less clearly than Bellini.

The terrain occupied by civilian populations has been late in coming into the literary view of English and American twentieth-century war poetry, no doubt reflecting the geopolitical circumstances of each conflict. All of Walt Whitman's Civil War poems present the full imbroglio of people on fraternal battlefields wherein all speak the same language, but his own experience as a journalist and wound dresser also left him poised at the nerve center of operations both hostile and recuperative, on the battlefield and at the skirmish line and in the aftermath of hospitals. Later, when English and American soldiers went away to war, they did so at a time when national borders continued to figure prominently, and the soldiers' receptivity to other nationals fluctuated with the content of their own prior exposure, or rather lack of it, to different languages, classes, and cultures.

In *Good-Bye to All That*, Robert Graves recounts a prototypical experience of the trench soldier going home. Listening to civilians trade bombardment scares, Graves offers his own memory of hapless involvement: as soon as his hearers understand that he is speaking of French casualties, they turn away in complete indifference: "'Oh,' they said. 'but that happened in France!' and the look of interest faded from their faces as though I had taken them in with a stupid catch" (142). If the front line was only partly tuned to civilians, the front line was not always the object of civilian interest either; nor was the gap between English and French sympathies closed by wartime alliance. English civilians, relatively protected, were not about to waste condolence on their opposite number across the Channel.

Two generations of soldier-poets wrestled with this split, each in its own way. Robert Graves said in his essay "The Poets of World War II" that "on the whole the soldier has lived a far safer life than the munition maker whom in World War I he despised as a 'shirker'; he cannot even feel that his rendezvous with death is more certain than that of his Aunt Fanny, the firewatcher" (Graves, *The Common Asphodel*, 310). Although casualty figures on specific sectors of World War II must modify Graves's rhetoric about the comparative safety of soldiers in relation to civilians, overall figures of World War II show how, depending on what part of the war one was in, neither soldier nor civilian escaped hazard. George Vassiltchikov, annotating Marie Vassiltchikov's *Berlin Diaries, 1940–1945*, says that Allied bombing from 1942–44 reduced every major city in Germany and Austria to ashes, plus quite a few in the rest of occupied Europe. The cost in civilian lives for this was some 600,000, compared to a similar British loss of civilians at 62,000, or roughly a tenth of the German and Austrian dead (77).

Fiction and memoir, perhaps because they were bound to younger and looser literary genres, scanned noncombatant experiences of war long before the lyric did. As late as 1965, however, an anthology of World War II poetry included a particularly feculent example of English colonial racism.[3] Norman Cameron's blinkered and casual manipulation of stereotype in "Black Takes White" reveals the complacency about how we peg others, which would not survive the more closely noticed but still harrowing divisions of race and class riding soldier and civilian contact in Vietnam, for instance. But in World War II, a sophisticated or sensitive probing into the nuances of the collision of cultures in wartime mostly stayed the preserve of novelists and short-story writers. Crossing to the United States, where the periods of immersion in war were so much briefer, we discover increasing consciousness of the festering vulnerability between the subject who practices war and the object on whom war is practiced, expanding throughout the period of the Vietnam War. This awareness emerged strongly during World War II, in Randall Jarrell, but fitfully elsewhere. It was the Vietnam War era, however, that produced the American poems notably and graphically spelling out the system of dominance and terror to which the exertion of masculinity in wartime so often descends, worked on by factors of class, caste, and racial politics. In the Vietnam War, the educated, young, American, middle-class male who would have been the soldier counterpart to Wilfred Owen and Keith Douglas was largely shielded by class privilege from the fire zones of Vietnam. While the generation of American men who were of draft age during the 1960s and 1970s remains alive to comment, the bitterness of the gulf between those who served in the military and those who resisted or evaded war still sparks fiercely, and both sides often remain actively unforgiving in the personal histories still being written.

This division of ideology and experience registers more faintly in the main vein of English war poetry, as if *all* the poets were too well-bred and basically middle class to speak with any resentment of class assignment in war. And radically pacifist politics seem too sparsely or unmemorably written to matter in the poetry of that era that has lasted. English antiwar poetry since World War I belongs about evenly, with no great seismic rupture visible, to combatants and noncombatants, with poems not conspicuously divided into officers at home and other ranks in the field. In World War I, the higher-ranking officers generally faced less combat, and poets like Wilfred Owen and Siegfried Sassoon reserved their harshest reproof for the civilians clearly in support of the war and the generals behind the lines. But in 1958, Robert Graves, lecturing on World War I in "What Was the War Like, Sir?" could say:

In World War I, a great gulf of heroism and incommunicable horror separated the trench soldier from the civilian. In World War II, no such gulf existed: conscription had placed everyone on equal footing. Little virtue could be attached to the wearing of uniform especially in the long pause between Dunkirk and the invasion of France, when civilians worked harder than most soldiers, faced more responsibilities and worries, ate worse, slept worse, and in heavily blitzed towns or sea-ports, suffered hideous casualties. (238)

In the later American poems, governed by the free-verse forms of postmodern idiom, Wilfred Owen's soldier-victim translates vividly to a soldier-victim who has victimized others. The grunt in the 'Nam does not become a murdered boy worthy of the crown of martyrdom, but a murderous, hapless nineteen-year-old conscript with gun, grenade, and phallus pointed in many directions. If either soldier shares anything with the other, it is a mutinous contempt for the rear echelons responsible for his wartime placement. Even as total war effaced the usual distinctions between frontline and rear-line action, the division between the attitudes and perspectives at home and at the front still handily reasserts itself because danger and risk mark the standpoint in modern war of only some men and only some women.

The heavy impact of photographic imagery and war newsreel footage gave new shapes to the verbal rhythms and forms of war experience. The aftermath of war also emerges more insistently as a subject in the Vietnam War literature; there is a higher proportion of poems written about the lingering impact of war by tormented survivors of combat. These are still war poems, but their long-term witness to the psychic damage of war and their use of wartime memory clearly distinguish these poems from the more familiar burdens of those written at white heat in the midst of the World War I battlefield. When I pick up the collections by Vietnam veterans Bruce Weigl, Yusef Komunyakaa, and Robert Balaban, the last a conscientious objector assigned to Vietnamese hospitals, large questions frame themselves around audience and tradition and bespeak new anxieties about the fit of race and culture within war.

The ways in which civilians, particularly women, enter these poems, represents a striking change. For Siegfried Sassoon or Wilfred Owen, fathers are impotent or vindictive, women crucially misunderstand, mothers are occasionally called on in the final extremity. No doubt drawing on a burgeoning of naturalistic war fiction, in the Vietnam poems the homefront figures take on greater shading. For these heterosexual soldiers, their representation of wartime sex also undergoes less self-censorship than in the work of earlier poets; the flooding memory of the women encountered overseas is a constant and graphic source of shame, anguish, and mutilated desire.

Rape and sexual abuse, which had earlier been subjects only for the propagandists, enter post–Vietnam War poems as literary events. Poem after poem underscores the relevance of Susan Brownmiller's grim observations about the place of rape in war: Rape is not merely an act of sexual release brought on by a general loosening of homefront morality—in which a regressive violence enters sexual relations—or a displacement of repressed anger at the exemption of women from war making or an expression of contempt for what is perceived as the generic weakness of women, although all of these motivations may figure. Above all, rape is an act of warfare in which the penis becomes the weapon controlling virility:

> Rape by a conquering soldier destroys all remaining illusions of power and property for men of the defeated side. The body of a raped woman becomes a ceremonial battlefield, a parade ground for the victor's trooping of the colors. The act that is played out upon her is a message passed between men—vivid proof of victory for one and loss and defeat for the other. (Brownmiller, 31)

Prostitution constitutes another aspect of the same thinking: "the two acts—raping an unwilling woman and buying the body and services of a more or less cooperating woman—go hand in hand with a soldier's concept of his rights and pleasures" (Brownmiller, 28 n).

In examining all of these poems, from all three of these wars, one cannot help inquiring into the constant relation between the assertion of masculine dominance and the fixing and blunting of memory of women's wartime acts or sufferings as negligible, irrelevant, or hostile. The fence between high and low art, or art and propaganda, does not quite account for the habitual disappearance of women from the poetry of war. The war posters of each world war featured women in broad stereotype, yet these crude images translated uneasily or not at all to literary artifacts trying to better or correct these simplicities. In the twentieth century, as women became a larger and larger part of the labor force that supported war, these old social myths of dominant male protectors and passive feminine protected are visibly subject to ongoing revision—with enormous consequences for the erotics of desire that undergirds war making.

"Half in love with the horrors which we cried out against"

Whatever may have been the actual desire to end war of the various soldier-poets of the Great War, one of their paradoxical effects was to render their war experience as something fatally attractive to younger men. In his memoir, *Friends Apart*, Philip Toynbee describes his conflicted feelings:

> Siegfried Sassoon and Wilfred Owen, Remarque and Barbusse had not convinced us that war is dull and dispiriting: still less could they have persuaded us that our own war might disillusion us. In fact, it seems to me now that our picture of war was as falsely romantic, in its different way, as anything which had stirred the minds of Edwardian boys, brought up on Henty and the heroics of minor imperial campaigns. The desolate No-Man's-Land pictures of Paul Nash, Bernard Partridge cartoons of the kaiser; songs from *Cavalcade* and the compassionate poems of Wilfred Owen had made a powerful, complex and stimulating impression on us, so that we felt less pity than envy of a generation which had experienced so much. Even in our antiwar campaigns of the early thirties we were half in love with the horrors which we cried out against, and as a boy, I can remember murmuring the name "Passchendaele" in an ecstasy of excitement and regret. . . . Disillusionment was half-expected from the beginning: it had become an element of romantic experience. (Toynbee, 91–92)

Readily and inventively, boys accommodate themselves to the new negatives to be incorporated in their ardent assimilations of war mystique. In 1938, Christopher Isherwood comments:

> Like most of my generation, I was obsessed with the idea of "War." "War," in this purely neurotic sense, meant The Test. The test of your courage, of your maturity, of your sexual prowess. "Are you really a man?" (*Lions and Shadows*, 74–75)

The fascination with the torments of 1914–1918 lasted well beyond the impress of the Second World War. Ted Hughes, aged fifteen when World War II ended, nonetheless carries the traces of that seduction into several poems in his first collection. Two among several early poems from 1957, "Griefs for Dead Soldiers" and "Six Young Men" both demonstrate the occupation of

Hughes's imagination by this earlier English history and his consequent sense of historical weightlessness. Staring at a snapshot of men who became his hallowed war dead, the poet says,

> Such contradictory permanent horrors here
> Smile from the single exposure and shoulder out
> One's own body from its instant and heat.
>> (Hughes, *Hawk*, 55)

Hughes's father fought at Gallipoli in World War I. As Erica Wagner reports, he was one of only seventeen from his entire regiment to survive: "a diary in his breast pocket had stopped a bullet" (Wagner, 59). For Ted Hughes, World War I reached out to mark not only what he felt about his father, and his father's generation, but even to blast his sense of the landscape of his childhood:

> Everything in West Yorkshire is slightly unpleasant. Nothing ever quite escapes into happiness. The people are not detached enough from the stone, as if they were only half-born from the earth, and the graves are too near the surface. A disaster seems to hang around in the air there for a long time. I can never escape the impression that the whole region is in mourning for the first world war. (Wagner, quoting Hughes, 59–60)

Still caught by that mourning in *Wolfwatching* in 1989, Hughes grapples vicariously with the war experience of the men of his own family as well as earlier poets like Wilfred Owen and Charles Causley. "For the Duration" tries to put together the scraps of what he knows about his father's war experience: uncles talked; his father did not. From him, only a frightening and numbing silence:

> Your day-silence as the coma
> Out of which your night-dreams rose shouting.
> I could hear you from my bedroom—
> The whole hopelessness still going on,
> No man's land still crying and burning
> Inside our house, and you climbing again
> Out of the trench, and wading back into the glare
>
> As if you might still not manage to reach us
> And carry us to safety.
>> (Hughes, *Wolfwatching*, 27)

World War I remains a bulky, displacing presence even in post–World War II English poetry. Typically enough for his generation, Hughes's "contradictory permanent horrors" permeate the watching or listening boy not with a glad sense of horrors escaped, but with an uneasy sense of challenges ducked by his fortunate date of birth in 1930. Decades later, he attributes his pervasive sense of childhood insecurity not to the war that he himself was experiencing from age nine to fifteen, but from the psychic contagion of his father's earlier ordeal.

Even in the dialogue of wars shared between generations of English soldiers, the Great War poets continued their overshadowing mark. Vernon Scannell, who fought in World War II with the Gordon Highlanders, writes in "The Great War":

Whenever the November sky
quivers with a bugle's hoarse, sweet cry,
The reason darkens; in its evening gleam
Crosses and flares, tormented wire, grey earth
Splattered with crimson flowers,
And I remember,
Not the war I fought in
But the one called Great
Which ended in a sepia November
Four years before my birth.
    (*Collected Poems*, 69)

His own war was merely a continuation of the nightmare that the first called into being and memory.

Philip Larkin, a critical two years younger than Keith Douglas, and eight years older than Ted Hughes, almost entirely and quite conspicuously evaded representing the years that he was a student and civilian throughout World War II. The personal history made known in the "Recollections," published by Larkin in 1982, supplemented by Andrew Motion's 1993 biography *A Writer's Life*, and spelled out in detail through the publication of Larkin's correspondence in 1992, invites speculation about the later and more high-minded thoughts set out in his essay "The War Poet." Larkin's family was unhurt by the bombing raids on Coventry, but at the time, Larkin was spending enormous energy in scheming for ways to avoid being called up. While as an adolescent he worshipped at the shrine of a leftist Auden, Larkin's father, Sydney, was a fervent admirer of Hitler who bore untouched during the war his prewar convictions that German National Socialism was bound to—and indeed ought to—prevail over the decadent inefficiencies of England's democracy. Larkin's published handful of World War II poems, the poems of a boy, were surely influenced by ambivalent reactions to his father's unrepentantly reactionary politics and to his own terrified squeamishness about military service, flamboyantly evident in his letters from the 1940s.

"After Dinner Remarks,"written sometime before June 1940, catches the teenage Larkin in High Audenesque, reflecting on an unloving, incompetent, and powerless self, who frames his identity and fate while "Exploding shrapnel" bursts the men of his time. But describing himself deliberately in a comfortable indolence, Larkin says: "Choose what you can: I do remain as neuter" (*Collected Poems*, 241). "Conscript," written with a close friend in mind in October and November 1941, is a little sharper in its refusal to endorse masculine duty; Larkin's sense of the wrong and futile waste of a militarized manhood is no less keen than Wilfred Owen's. He writes of the hapless conscript:

> The assent he gave
> Was founded on desire for self-effacement
> In order not to lose his birthright; brave,
> For nothing would be easier than his replacement,
>
> Which would not give him time to follow further
> The details of his own defeat and murder.
> (*Collected Poems*, 262)

Yet in "Stone Church Damaged by a Bomb," where the dead lie "shapeless in the shapeless earth" (*Collected Poems*, 269), Larkin's tone retreats to the same haze of nostalgia and passive fatalism marking his best-known war poem, "MCMXIV." As notable a presence in twentieth-century poetry in English as either Ted Hughes or Randall Jarrell, Philip Larkin's zigzag treatment of the legitimacy of war poetry shows the impossibility of divorcing biography from the formation of one's opinions on war. "MCMXIV," an elegy written in 1960, powerfully but comfortably returns to the more personally remote and therefore more manageable earlier history of war. Larkin takes up the familiar themes of lost innocence and irrevocable change:

Never such innocence,
Never before or since,
As changed itself to past
Without a word—the men
Leaving the gardens tidy,
The thousands of marriages
Lasting a little while longer:
Never such innocence again.

(*Collected Poems*, 127–28)

What besides a tidy Edwardian domesticity went missing from that innocence, becoming either ignobly truant or expendable in the next war, is still nothing upon which an adult Larkin cares to invest more than a menaced, understated, but still rather gilded regret. The raw recruits in "MCMXIV" are so dead and gone that even the date of their exit from the present cannot make it to the modernity of Arabic numeration. But like Hughes and Scannell, Larkin, too, acknowledges the primary weight and vividness of the prior generation, his own English manhood a twilight run off of theirs.

Even across the ocean in the United States, James Tate in "The Lost Pilot" of 1967, understood being haunted by his war dead in the same remote and glazing terms. If the explicit historical pointing of the English poem is replaced in the American poem by deific mythicizing, the effect on vitality and potency appears the same:

All I know
is this: when I see you,
as I have seen you at least

once every year of my life,
spin across the wilds of the sky
like a tiny, African god,

I feel dead. I feel as if I were
the residue of a stranger's life,
that I should pursue you.

(Tate, 27)

Similarly, David St. John's "Six/Nine/Forty-Four," written decades later, clings numbly to a dead pilot-father:

> these sons
> putting their faces to pillows as cold
> as a father's leather chest.
> These sons picking through the silences
> of abandoned Quonset huts, where they were born.
> These fathers: suddenly air. Blown from cockpits
> into the shrugs of sons, the shrugs of my friends
> & poets; all of us walking out of these pages,
> & the wars, & these fathers.
> (*Study for the World's Body*, 11)

In David St. John's poem, unlike in James Tate's, the image of a dead poet attaches itself to the flyer father; under the "Six/Nine/Forty-Four" title, which commemorates the day of his death, Keith Douglas appears, on his way from North Africa to D day:

> To a ragged
> France, the slow clack of blood, & a soft
> black window in his gut. No poem, & drawings
> in his pocket. A loosed bête noire. The third day
> of Normandy. Keith Douglas.

With a kind of causative energy, all the fathers of poetry become war heroes, however reluctant, because "Poetry / deserves legacies" (*Study*, 9).

For both David St. John and James Tate, the war that dogs memory skips from World War I to World War II. American losses in World War II, if not equalling the burden of the English in 1918, still registered the weight of overpowering numbers. For the Americans, the most significant and crushing global conflict lasted from 1941 to 1945; for the English, the most sobering memory of world conflagration rested in 1914 to 1918.

The Troubled Stream

It is never easy to make out whether people within a given historical moment or geography are closer to or farther from the angels in their opinions about the use of violence, or whether they are more or less ingenious or self-deceiving in their arguments of blood. Our capacities for renewing moral justification for violence, along with our critiques of such justifications, merely expand and proliferate. Still, it seems worth probing the idea that there now exists a greater predisposition to behave, at least in theory, as if the violent answer of war were the wrong one. Daily, however, the sequence of responses after violent affront still visibly and mechanically descends from "we grieve" to " we retaliate and punish," or responses to violence tend toward the awesome satisfaction of heaping murder on murder, in the place where *lex talionis* still functions as the ground zero for our moral characters. In 2001, photo and film exhibits from crashed planes, crushed buildings, and pulverized bodies furnished us, over and over again, with reasons for evading war to be subverted, recharged, and redirected into reasons for continuing it. Part of this recharging and redirecting certainly concerns the motivation of the war hero and the shifting of the constraints governing his, and now almost certainly her, behavior.

The notion of war as the birthing ground of heroic myth refuses to die, in literature or anywhere else. Regardless of the wide and fertile spread of forms attempting to present fairly even the most noxious of its truths, war is at war with its own literary annihilation. In the memory of those who have not suffered them, accounts of atrocity fade and give way to the old, exciting myths of an empowering valor. There is something about speaking of war that tends to favor the impulse to burnish the recitation; what does not burnish, we have an inborn reluctance to touch. Swift's Gulliver, when carried away by enthusiasm for the ingenious and potent destructiveness of his fellow Yahoos, is cut off in his description of their war making by his beloved Houyhnhnm master, who says:

> Whoever understood the Nature of Yahoos might easily believe it possible for so vile an Animal, to be capable of every Action I had named, if their Strength and Cunning equalled their Malice. But as my Discourse had increased his Abhorrence of the whole Species, so he found it gave him a Disturbance in his Mind, to which he was wholly a Stranger before. . . . That, although he hated the Yahoos of this Country, yet he no more blamed them for their odious Qualities, than he did a Gnnayh (a bird of prey) for its Cruelty, or a sharp Stone for cutting his Hoof. But, when a Creature pretending to Reason, could be capable of such Enormities, he dreaded lest the Corruption of that Faculty might be worse than Brutality

itself. He seemed therefore confident, that instead of Reason, we were only possessed of some Quality fitted to increase our natural Vices; as the Reflection from a troubled Stream returns the Image of an ill-shapen Body, not only *larger*, but more *distorted*. (Swift, 234–35)

Again and again, our narratives return to the troubling stream, again and again attempting to clear it. And yet each return seems to embed more firmly the original disturbance and to fix within it the distorted body.

It begins to seem important not only to stress the role of the witness in war, but to understand the wounding forces that act on the witness, making him complicit and limiting and compromising witness itself within what we have come to term traumatic experience. In a natural desire to shut down the expression of obscene cruelty, we refuse it passage into our imaginations, thinking like the Houyhnhm that what we do not imagine need not exist. And yet what we shut our eyes upon exists and repeats for others, and they, too, become our responsibility.

Within the compressed space of lyric poetry, I want to track the possible inflections of style, rhetoric, tone, and point of view that literary language allows and try to analyze the waves of conflicting attitudes for which poems serve as such puzzling or stubbornly ambivalent testimony. Language, in these focused instances, roughly within the territory of a century, seems to form a trace, a peer forward, a lean, an inclination, toward a sensibility that war represents an aberrant pathology, yet "hegemonic masculinity" seems the most certain guarantor of war's longevity. Just as we have shifted the term for a group of men carrying weapons against other men from "warrior band," which is what we have called war-making preliterate peoples, to "armies," our modern term descending from the Romans, and then again mutated an "army" into a "peacekeeping force," so I believe that the language of poetry reflects similar changes in nomenclature signalling deep changes in how we think force may be legitimately applied.

Reading about the effects and aftereffects of armies in the twentieth century, I find it hard to avoid daily confirmation that both corrupt politics and collective psychosis hinge on an outmoded code of virility. Yet is it not one of the bleaker contemporary ironies that technological advance has made possible and inevitable a large incursion of women into the armed forces of all countries? As industrial and postindustrial war has fixed the terms of engagement, and hugely extended the theater of war to include both combatant and noncombatant populations, obliterating or blunting the usual distinctions between these classes of citizens, so war is fast becoming an equal opportunity employer.

Just as feminists, both men and women, have concluded that the one true enemy of peace is an ancient and driven style of masculinity, the masculinity of war as warrior *virtu* is undergoing profound redefinition. Human war making itself devolves once again to another plane of possibilities regarding the shapes of murderous extinction. Just as the Mameluke or the steppe warrior or the code of Bushido have become obsolete in modern war, so the next throw of the technological dice game may eliminate gender as the defining element in militarism, leaving both men and women to press the buttons of extirpation, forcing new templates, new sources of aggression, on pacifists and generals alike.

Revulsion against war has always existed in English poetry: alongside the usual celebrations, there follow the usual regrets. Yet even our translations from classic texts reveal the odd fluctuations of our notice, the old obeisance, the forced accommodation. Our dilemma is not only the manufacture of new insights into the new ways we make war, but the old problem of how badly the rationale for socializing violence fits our glimmering and fitful sense of how civilized human beings really ought to meet conflict. More urgently for this book, even the war poems that show what we might or must not do when war blocks the civilized impulse often blot out or distort context, collapsing into useless generality.

In a collection of antiwar poems that he gathered in the United States in 1969, entitled *Poems of War Resistance*, Scott Bates excerpts Alexander Pope translating from the *Iliad* this speech of Nestor's to his Greek allies:

"Curs'd is the man, and void of law and right,
Unworthy property, unworthy light,
Unfit for public rule, or private care,
That wretch, that monster, that delights in war:
Whose lust is murder, and whose horrid joy
To tear his country, and his kind destroy! . . ."
    (Bates, 169)

The last three lines, embroidering Homer, isolate for us the rogue who loves war, laying the emphasis on that love. By now, we know we ought not to like war. Since the happy bloodlust of warriors like Bertrans de Born has gone with them to their berths in hell, much has become a given. We have learned, if not to be ashamed, at least to be uneasy in our tolerance of the familiar bombast that accompanies our bleak acquiescence to inflicting casualties as the best answer to inflicted casualties, of our following a bullet with a bullet given back.

The most current definition of civilized retort seems to rest on a highly subjective calibration: will the give-back equal the given, or will it be topped with collateral damage? How much collateral damage has to accumulate before both sides acknowledge that the damage inflicted equals atrocity and that the moral advantage has just been canceled as the erstwhile victim turns to victimizer? In the seesaw between the perception of these two states, between infliction and affliction, war sustains itself. In millennia of survival as a species, we seem only to have "progressed" by developing retaliation to such a murderous finality that we have learned to check the retaliatory impulse, but we have no secure intraspecies system for figuring out how or when. From Pope, and really from before Pope, the bewildering quality of war, for those who see no alternative to it, is war's moderation. A pacifist war poetry careens back and forth between an absolute of abjuring violence—usually only briefly entertained—to merely abjuring its unchecked practice.

What Pope makes Homer do in the passage quoted and pressed by Bates into his anthology, is to add a little hand-wringing at murderous lust, at "horrid joy." In the passage extracted from Book IX of Alexander Pope's *Iliad*, the force of the free-standing lines becomes a clear condemnation of delight in war. But both Homer and Pope follow immediately with Nestor's war counsel: the key to violence is *not* not doing it, but doing it right—and doing it successfully, according to tribal rule. In the barbered poem of Scott Bates's creative misprision, Pope thunders briefly, and honors a 1960s pacifist revulsion. If however, we pick up a contemporary translation by Robert Fagles, we find a story of the fluctuations of feeling and principle enclosed in the objection, and then a long, slow, staged assent to violence that Homer and Pope record in the book's unfolding. The Fagles version reads:

> Lost to the clan,
> lost to the hearth, lost to the old ways, that one,
> who lusts for all the horrors of war with his own people.
>   (9.73–75)

The thrust here is on misrule and tribal anarchy, not on bloodlust itself. Pope, through Bates's excision, gives a round dismissal of the violence of war instead of an aside over the shoulder, added in the course of the Greeks' figuring out a viably aggressive strategy, to bring Achilles back on board. Fagles's more stripped reading of Nestor's speech highlights not a condemnation of war but a cautious affirmation of good leadership in its prosecution. In the formula of the thrice-repeated "Lost . . . lost . . . lost," closer to Homer's actual syntax, Nestor counsels that the tribal leader who wrongly wars with his "people"—the other Greeks—is the horror; which supports even Pope's earlier affirmation of Homer's meaning:

> Concord, among Governors, is the preservation of States, and Discord the ruin of them.

War is not so bad; you just have to make war with strong leaders, in union, at the appropriate time. What practitioner of *realpolitik* would ever disagree? And with this reading of the old poem, a passive fatalism with respect to the ancient argument of blood resumes its sway, intact: Scott Bates advances pacifism only by selectively remembering tradition.

There has to be a better way for Pope's Nestor or for Wilfred Owen or for anybody to dissent from the old reasons that sent people to arm and to take part in more of that tearing, that lustful murder, that destroying of kind. If I concern myself with the war poems of the twentieth century, it is because I believe that in spite of massive continuities in feeling and approach to war making, many of these poems nonetheless can be seen as moving with conviction both direct and indirect towards peace witness. Their mode of war resistance, shaped by new methods of representation from the photograph to television, has been helped into being by stylistic developments like the complex growth of realism and naturalism, as well as egalitarian and liberationist ideology. It would be a chronic and immoral pessimism that would deny newness its room to change for the better as well as the worse.

One of the most intractable problems in reading and even writing antiwar texts, however, is that representing the horror of war is not the same thing as committing oneself or others to ceasing its practice. Horror is an amazingly elastic sensation. And what Owen earnestly indicts as the "scorching cautery of battle" becomes the next poet's test of manhood; one soldier's savage accusation becomes the next war's recruiting romance. How to prevent that dulling and blunting of the original indignation is still so palpably more than Owen's or Pope's or Homer's problem.

2

Wilfred Owen's "Long-famous glories, immemorial shames"

Introduction: The Fellowship of Death

Awe before the magnitude of war, at the sheer scale of the thing, never quite dies away; loud echoes of this can still be heard in descriptions of the massing of bodies and weapons mobilizing for war, even as technology chooses metal alloy and plastic increasingly over flesh in its assembly for hostilities. But the idea of war's grandeurs also attaches gravely and persistently to war lamentation, as a union in death is figured as the exaltation of a noble company, indeed, a Sacred Band. From King David's time, when David mourns the death of Jonathan in battle, we are pierced by the sorrow of a surviving warrior, keening that the love of men passes the love of women:

> How are the mighty fallen in the midst of the battle! O Jonathan, thou
>   wast slain in thine high places.
> I am distressed for thee, my brother Jonathan: very pleasant hast thou been
>   unto me: thy love to me was wonderful, passing the love of women.
> How are the mighty fallen, and the weapons of war perished!
>   (2 Sam. 1:25–27)

These verses from 2 Samuel, passed to us from the liquid eloquence of the King James Bible, echo the earlier eroticized dying of the Sacred Band, the shock troops of the Theban forces that gained their unity of purpose from the intimate bonding of soldiers paired as lovers. The pathos of the sight of these lovers as they lay dead on the plain at Chaeronea, each married to death and war in the person of the other, is carried forward, with only a slight lessening of erotic emphasis, into the "band of brothers" that fought and died at Agincourt with Henry V.

If we turn to Shakespeare's *Henry V* and read Exeter's lines on the fate of York and Suffolk, we get an idea of the luminous glaze that a death in battle applies to corpses and of the glory of the fellowship that can come to displace all other bonds. Exeter announces York's death to Henry at the close of the battle of Agincourt:

> and by his bloody side
> Yoke-fellow to his honour-owing wounds,
> The noble Earl of Suffolk also lies.
> Suffolk first died, and York, all haggled over,
> Comes to him where in gore he lay insteeped,
> And takes him by the beard, kisses the gashes
> That bloodily did yawn upon his face.
> He cries aloud "Tarry, my cousin Suffolk.
> My soul shall thine keep company to heaven.
> Tarry, sweet soul, for mine, then fly abreast,
> As in this glorious and well-foughten field
> We kept together in our chivalry."
> Upon these words I came, and cheered him up.
> He smiled me in the face, raught me his hand,
> And with a feeble grip says "Dear my lord,
> Commend my service to my sovereign."
> So did he turn, and over Suffolk's neck
> He threw his wounded arm, and kissed his lips,
> And so, espoused to death, with blood he sealed
> A testament of noble-ending love.
> The pretty and sweet manner of it forced
> Those waters from me which I would have stopped,
> But I had not so much of man in me,
> And all my mother came into mine eyes
> And gave me up to tears.
>
> (4.6.8–32)

In the Cambridge *Henry V*, Andrew Gurr notes that the wordplay flickering through York and Suffolk's espousal in death turns on the blood that usually seals a testament of marriage as the breach of virginity (176 n). One might say additionally that the blood testament acknowledges a traditional suppression or suspension of the knight's sexuality, or will to heterosexual marriage, for the sublimated satisfactions of service to a feudal master and feudal brother on the field of war. The virgin blood is redistributed in a marriage consummated between fellow warriors, who "kept together" in chivalry; in this passage, a mortal blow provides the body's final ecstatic and submissive seizure.

Death in war replaces the little deaths of erotic pleasure; moreover, "the pretty and sweet manner of it" forces the tears from the battle survivor's eyes that by right and custom are the tears of the mourning mother, here one more casualty of war's usurpation of intimate relations. It is not only a bride who re-treats, to have her place taken by another, but also the loving mother. As all "my mother" swells into Exeter's eyes, we witness the all-sufficient family of warrior men weeping the first and keenest tears in recognition of their dead.

The poets of World War I, most particularly Wilfred Owen in poems like "The Parable of the Old Man and the Young" or Siegfried Sassoon in "Glory of Women," probed the intricacies of these psychic economies. For Owen, glory abandons service to a kingly master and firmly renounces the patriarch and what Henry V called the "*royal* fellowship of death" (4.8.101; italics mine), handing over whatever bloody or stained praise is left to the brotherly band of dying soldiers, as the top-down patriarchal is put behind and the leveling fra-ternal is brought forward. If we read toward religious myth, the New Testa-ment son with his brotherly love displaces the jealous and vengeful Old Tes-tament father-judge. In a broadly allied psychological twist, the united brotherhood of sons displaces daughters, sisters, wives, and mothers as people whom one should die to defend. Brothers and sons become the primary objects of affectionate need and the most visible participants in the working out of war's gains and losses, as war's family constricts to the loving and hating of men alone, with here and there a substitutive fathering going on between so-licitous field officers and their charges: not too solicitous, or the devotion of all to the hazard of death suffers. In their flow of development through Wilfred Owen's varying experiences of battle, his war poems show the fluctuating struggle between commitment to the ongoing life of the community and to that of the band of brothers pushed to dying for it.

From the *Iliad* to the World War I elegy, in the approved routing for hos-tile and aggressive emotion, poets affirm that masculinity arrives through shedding blood but allow the feminine experience of bloodshed a ritually ex-pressive outlet only within the rigors of childbed. The menstrual blood flow that signals a woman's cycle of fertility is usually inaccessible to civil speech. But if women are not a society's designated warriors and defenders, then female aggression will lack the sanction permitted to men in war, and its onset will always provoke a special terror of the lawless and unlimited. Our deepest apprehension then springs from this stifled maternal rage, leading us to anticipate the terrible mother's angry abandonment, which denies us the life support that the long infancy of our species requires.

Culturally, we may repress that fear of maternal fury or abandonment and its concomitant acknowledgment of the power of female anger, but by doing so, we then strengthen the ongoing essentialist substitutions that make masculinity and war making one and the same. Not only does war become what men do with each other in place of loving women in the dark, parodic intimacies of the battlefield—as Agincourt's yokefellows are seen dying to do—but war also becomes what men make instead of babies.

Nancy Huston shows in "The Matrix of War: Mothers and Heroes," how deeply imbedded in linguistic practice these thoughts are:

> In Greece, the rapprochement between combat and confinement is not only ritual but lexical as well: the two events are informed by one and the same vocabulary. According to Nicole Loraux, *luchos* signifies, on the one hand, "the place for lying down," and on the other hand, "the name of the ambush, and later of the armed troops themselves"; *ponos* is "one of the words that designates the pains of labor" and also "the name of a long and toilsome effort, such as that of the Achaean warriors in the *Iliad*, engaged in the interminable labor of war." (Huston, 131)

In many literary traditions, childbed travail equals the labor of the battlefield, and our English word *labor* contains the same shadings. Huston suggests that in segregating women from either battlefield or war council, men compensate themselves for being biologically cut off from childbirth and thus only indirectly linked to paternity. A man's power for dealing death then becomes not simply equivalent to, but of greater consequence than, the female power of giving life.

In this tight, rigid schematic, a man daring to become the sacrificial lamb in war corresponds to a woman undergoing the trial of maternity, as both warrior-hero and mother act with ideal selflessness, in defiance of the body but through the body's ability to suffer, they offer to sustain their community. Men defend women, and women breed for men a constant supply of would-be defenders and defended for the maintenance of the communal equation. While all the overt choice for this channeling of human energies apparently rests with men, and indeed protects and insures their sexual advantage, the resilient comfort of the code's attraction for both men and women cannot be overstated.

And for what an amazing length of time this narrative of human purpose has survived and lent itself to various ideologies, often quite awkwardly: for the brief cultural moment of World War I, Paul Fussell in "The Fate of Chivalry, and the Assault Upon Mother" in *Thank God for the Atom Bomb and Other Essays*, describes a reigning belief which marries the chevalier to the bourgeois family, seating him at the family board in deference to maternal power. Fussell writes of this sentimental archaism that is based in nostalgia and in denial of modernity: "The Victorian celebration of the chivalric is an attempt by the traditional imagination to posit that the modern world, with its political compromises and gross materialism, its scientism and urban squalor and proletarianization, does not exist" (Fussell, *Thank God*, 222). Left over from a nineteenth-century social organization and its English weave of domesticities, this Victorian rendition of a medieval chivalric code installs a mother backstage at the theater of war whose primary task is to feed dutiful sons into the maw of the cannon.

While feminism and pacifism converged with the onslaught of what social historians like Betty and Theodore Roszak call "compulsive masculinity" (Roszak, 90–92, 102), suffragette women were sharply divided in their attitudes toward militarism. The popular cult of the mother as the primary domestic bond for the soldier, however, was behind assertions like the following, taken from General Seeley and cited by Denis Winter: "It is strange and touching that, when men die of dangerous wounds, in almost every case 'mother' is the last word that crosses their lips." Winter concludes that this final utterance is "almost one of the litmus tests of veracity," and he gives us the impact of such a test in this battlefield report by a soldier named Griffith:

> After a thunderous crash in our ears, a young boy began to cry for his mother in a thin, boyish voice. "Mam, Mam. . . ." He had not been hit but was frightened and crying quietly. Suddenly he started screaming again, screaming for his mother with a wail that seemed older than the world. The men began to mutter uneasily. We shook him and cursed him and even threatened to kill him if he did not stop. The shaking brought him back.
> (Winter, 118)

Such reports are common in war literature; even in 1981, Lynda Van Devanter collects nurse Bobbie Trotter's observation, "every man who has died, / had the same last word on his lips—"'Mother'" (Van Devanter, *Visions*, 40). But as other feelings about the gap between field and home surface, with more complex anxieties and with greater doubt about the centrality of the homefront mother's capacity to assuage, the battlefront soldier's capacity to protect other people's mothers decreased, even as his need to invoke his own in extremity seems not to have wavered. The bond between mother and son may have been vestigially strong for the post-Victorian soldier of World War I, about to cast off the patriarch's dominion in the new family order assembling at the start of the twentieth century, but by World War II, one could find the mothers among the women and children who lay at the bottom of the frantic heaps clawing for the last moment of air in the gas chambers of Auschwitz. Within the rule of the machine, perhaps the final lesson of the industrialized warfare initiated in the twentieth century is its perfect disregard of any family alignment.

In the male company of war, men continue to imitate familial bonds, playing all the parts normally reserved for both sexes. While the twentieth-century nation-state may have muted the patriotism expressed as love toward a father- or even motherland, the erotics of war continue to show a libidinal battlefield energy deflected from heterosexuality and redirected towards a split of emotions that supports murderous ferocity towards one set of fellows and an expense of protective tenderness towards another. Women, concluded Siegfried Sassoon contemptuously:

You love us when we're heroes, home on leave,
Or wounded in a mentionable place.
You worship decorations; you believe
That chivalry redeems the war's disgrace.
You make us shells. You listen with delight,
By tales of dirt and danger fondly thrilled.
You crown our distant ardours while we fight,
And mourn our laurelled memories when we're killed.
   (*Collected Poems*, 79)

At that point in "Glory of Women," Sassoon switches from the mother's fond enthrallment to the still living, narrating son and takes up the reality of a death in trench warfare, something beyond a mother's belief or comprehension:

You can't believe that British troops "retire"
When hell's last horror breaks them, and they run,
Trampling the terrible corpses—blind with blood.

Ultimately, the mother's dream is also blind and false:

O German mother dreaming by the fire,
While you are knitting socks to send your son
His face is trodden deeper in the mud.

Sassoon's poem appears to limit his critique of mothers at the end to German women supporting militarism, as the poem travels through British lines to end in a German death, but the applicability of the lines to all the co-opted women of either side is unmistakable. A mother's notion of "Glory" ends in a final, ironic subversion of that show, in which all soldiers of either side are overrun by a quite ignoble and inglorious reality.

By lowering an accusation against mothers rather than the fathers who acquiesced to this horror by instigating war, Sassoon makes room for a critique of sentimental codes: it is where we set the limit of love that determines our eventual corrupt resort to hostilities. Finally, those who trash us by assenting to our sacrifice in their defense are more guilty; as the complicit guardians of civil life as the soldier knows it, mothers, indeed all of those knitting women, earn the soldier's horrified revulsion by their blind acceptance of their sons' deaths. In the communal prosecution of war, no one, especially not the mother, is morally above or free of its bloody conclusions.

In his war poems, Owen's handling of soldiers' love and bonding concentrates on his perception of their largely passive victimhood in the Great War, while it only indirectly tracks his sense of war's deflected sexualities and loyalties. In letters and poems, his reproaches of the civilian front's practice of a collection of sins ranging from ignorance, indifference, and blind glory hunger and greed for profit, tends to fall equally on mothers, wives, lovers, and home-front officialdom. It is the suffering of the practiced-upon soldier, however, that truly becomes his subject.

Because his poems cover the widest range of topics, closing in on pacifism, heroic masculinity, battlefield fraternity, and the like, and represent the most sustained poetic achievement of World War I, my discussion of that war's poetry for the most part rests on Wilfred Owen. For the injustices of trench warfare, Siegfried Sassoon got there first and hardest. But his poems, often

FIGURE 2. Wilfred Owen in 1916. National Portrait Gallery.

memorable, thump along with blunter rhythms, narrower moods and tones, and a less versatile diction, even as they remain a necessary part of the historical as well as the literary record. For different masteries, and other views, Isaac Rosenberg, Edmund Blunden, and Robert Graves are indelibly part of the canon of war poetry. And yet, for a cluster of reasons substantive as well as aesthetic, their part of the spectrum is less compelling for someone looking at the general trajectory of World War I.

Wilfred Owen's war poems do not say everything about war and its world; what they do say about soldiers, however, bursts with a real freshness over this century. They repress any full contemplation of the murderous rage of the soldier, sexual or otherwise, while amplifying all that lives of his tender, eviscerating helplessness. Damnably indifferent, and damnably distant, feminine tenderness exists on the far side of the war, in the homeland where war profiteers, wives, and mothers blur in a common ignorance. Of all the soldier-poets, his concentration on his fellows is most arresting and provocative and also exists in the purest arc of definition. That this concentration did not survive his final battlefield very likely adds intensity to Owen on soldier love and death. Unlike Edmund Blunden, Robert Graves, and Siegfried Sassoon, Wilfred Owen never moved into the community of postwar memoirists, nor was he able to extend the perspective of age to what he had undergone.

Freshly aware of his own drive towards same-sex love and newly liberated by his discovery of a welcoming underground homosexual community, yet still deeply attached to his mother and younger siblings both male and female, Wilfred Owen in his war poetry sustains Henry V's binding "fellowship of death." Yet Owen wipes his poems, if not his letters, free of any lingering domination by what Paul Fussell identifies as the late-nineteenth-century cult of the mother and of praise or support for that grade of affection by which women were to be kept ready at the mythic hearthfire, rocking the future soldier, while men marched away. Owen's poems, in the intricacy with which they prod gender positions, are also led over various roads unpredictably to the exposure of old and new terms of brotherhood in relation to old and new terms of soldier victimization.

"One must see and feel"

While there is nothing in Wilfred Owen that quite resembles the Greek view of the dead homosexual couples twined at the Battle of Chaeronea, or even York and Suffolk at Agincourt, certainly the question of what kind of reverence is due, and from whom, hangs over the bodies of his young soldiers. "Greater Love" vigorously rejects the female lovers at home as unworthy. The speaker of the poem turns his back on them to celebrate his own "greater love" of the English war dead. The "red lips" that open the poem cannot compare with "the stained stones kissed by the English dead." And so on: a woman's "slender attitude" or soft voice or lukewarm heart are, item by item, matched to the dearly bought sacrifices of soldier-companions and found to be no match at all. The love of women pales beside that offered by the "eyes blinded in my stead!" And the whole fractured assemblage of womanhood is progressively swept from the field. The real bonds remain fast in the place of their making and supersede any claim made by the ostensible but undeserving objects of soldiers' risk:

> Heart, you were never hot
> Nor large, nor full like hearts made great with shot;
> And though your hand be pale,
> Paler are all which trail
> Your cross through flame and hail:
> Weep, you may weep, for you may touch them not.
>> (Owen, *Complete Poems*, 1:166)

A similar insistence on irreconcilable wartime zones of feeling occurs in "Dulce et Decorum Est," which, C. Day Lewis notes in his edition of Owen's poems, was in draft form alternately dedicated to Jessie Pope or "To a certain Poetess." The poem may well be answering and dismissing James Rhoades's earlier patriotic effusion, "Dulce et Decorum Est":

> We, nursed in high traditions,
> And trained to nobler thought,
> Deem death to be less bitter
> Than life too dearly bought. . . .
>> (Cited in Fussell, *Thank God*, 235)

But the poem is also a clear reply to Jessie Pope's "The Call," published in 1915, in which the poet beats out her brash interrogation to the tune of these repetitions: "Who's for the trench— / Are you, my laddie? // Who'll follow French— / Will you, my laddie?" And ends with an implied denunciation of anyone resisting recruitment, or wanting to "wait a bit," with these blandishments:

Who'll earn the Empire's thanks—
    Will you, my laddie?
Who'll swell the victor's ranks—
    Will you, my laddie?
When that procession comes,
Banners and rolling drums—
Who'll stand and bite his thumbs—
    Will you, my laddie?

To this versification, Owen made his reproof. Against her call, he juxtaposes a postcombat nightmare of wretches suffering in the trench, forced to abandon one of their number to gas. The poem swells to overwhelm any impertinent manipulation of the idea of heroic death to be taught to school children by homefront patriots:

Gas! Gas! Quick, boys!—An ecstasy of fumbling,
Fitting the clumsy helmets just in time;
But someone still was yelling out and stumbling,
And flound'ring like a man in fire or lime . . .
Dim, through the misty panes and thick green light,
As under a green sea, I saw him drowning.

In all my dreams, before my helpless sight,
He plunges at me, guttering, choking, drowning.

If in some smothering dreams you too could pace
Behind the wagon that we flung him in,
And watch the white eyes writhing in his face,
If you could hear, at every jolt, the blood
Come gargling from the froth-corrupted lungs,
Obscene as cancer, bitter as the cud
Of vile, incurable sores on innocent tongues,—
My friend, you would not tell with such high zest
To children ardent for some desperate glory,
The old Lie: Dulce et decorum est
Pro patria mori.

The chief features of the Lie are its claims of sweetness and decorum; this death by gassing is as bitter, ugly, and indecorous as Owen can make it. Sending the poem to his mother, Owen translates and embellishes the Horatian tag with incredulous underlining and exclamation points: "*It is sweet and meet to die for one's country. Sweet! and decorous!*" (*Collected Letters*, 552)

But the other error Owen often seems anxious to correct in his battlefield poems is the belief that soldiers die for those at home; often as not, they die for each other and for the combat fraternity. A later poem, "The Next War," rejects patriotic nationalism:

> Oh, Death was never enemy of ours!
>   We laughed at him, we leagued with him, old chum.
> No soldier's paid to kick against His powers.
>   We laughed,—knowing that better men would come,
> And greater wars: when every fighter brags
> He fights on Death, for lives; not men, for flags.
>
>   (*Complete Poems*, 1:165)

Death is the enemy, not the other man, and the fighting is certainly not for the flags of nations. *Why* one does this fighting at all stays in a muddle: nothing clarifies how it is that one can fight death in wars without fighting men. But Owen liked this poem, and its emphasis on the selflessness of the soldier, well enough to send it to his younger brother, echoing the phrasing of the Anglican catechism, to say: "I want Colin to read, mark, learn etc. it" (*Collected Letters*, 550).

"Dulce et Decorum Est" is one of the first poems to give witness against war trauma: it is a combat nightmare that pulls the speaker stark upright months later, and it is the piercing recall of a moment when the brotherhood of war leaves behind one of its members to a death made hideous to reader and complicit speaker alike. This deeply honest poem builds on an experience of uncontrollable dreaming now widely recognized as a symptom of combat trauma; part of war's truly unbearable reality is its freakish demolition of just such ambitions of heroic protectiveness. In this poem Owen does not only reserve his accusation for others, but makes a rare record of his own helpless entrapment by war guilt.

Owen's sense of the split between home- and battlefront knowledge went on, intensifying in the new expressive freedom he was teaching himself from exposure to the fierce candors and direct style of Siegfried Sassoon's poems. He met man and poems at Craiglockhart War Hospital, where he and Sassoon had been sent for treatment for shell shock. Back from his first profound immersion in combat, both the respite of the hospital itself and the exposure to

Sassoon's supportive attention brought about decisive changes in Owen's poetry. After intensive engagement at the Somme, and in yet another episode in France during April 1917, Owen's poetic language settled into a kind of dichotomy of before-the-war and after-, in which his sense of the fissure between his own preaction and postaction selves widened to articulate and explore the troubling chasm between men away and women at home, and between the generations, one sidelined but commanding and the other fatally and obediently engaged.

The poems Owen wrote during and after the Craiglockhart period use these appositions as the framework for his war, and women constitute one of the two pegs on which he hangs difference and definition. In "The Send Off," soldiers are mobilized, "secretly, like wrongs hushed-up" (*Complete Poems*, 1:172); later, presumably, they feel mockery for the women who send them off so ingenuously with flowers. "Disabled" shows not only women's infuriating incomprehension, but their disloyal treachery as well, as the wounded youngster who joined the army to please "the giddy jilts" now sits propped alone in the dark:

Tonight he noticed how the women's eyes
Passed from him to the strong men that were whole.
How cold and late it is! Why don't they come
And put him into bed? Why don't they come?
    (*Complete Poems*, 1:175)

Only Owen, the officer-poet who sends his voice breathing through this teenage paraplegic and sublates the maternal to his own person, is there to speak these questions for him, if not to answer them.

The very first of Owen's war poems, one he never completed, aestheticizes death in the best decadent tradition. In the fragment "Has your soul sipped," Owen witnesses a "strange sweetness," which he rhetorically and progressively declares the sweetest of all: "that smile, / Faint as a wan, worn myth, / Faint and exceeding small, / On a boy's murdered mouth" (*Complete Poems*, 1:90). There is a fair amount of adolescent boy love in the less well known poems of these months, but a reading of the work in the dating given by Jon Stallworthy makes clear the switch of subject that Owen undergoes, maturing quickly through the shocks of combat. Owen surrenders the arbitrary application of pathos to the passive corpses of lovely boys, as a generalized amorous posturing yields to a wider field of actual relations between men and boys, leaders and followers, in games of horrific consequence. The sexual tension of the surface is also diffused and displaced, as erotic attraction between men becomes only one aspect of texts capable of being read as dominantly conventional representations of male bonding in the larger heterosexual male community of war.

At the cusp of declaring his own sexual preference for men, there is a moving tenderness, marked by both desire and the restraint of desire, flowing from Owen's poems, so many of which were based on his experience of being in charge of younger men, first as tutor and companion in civil life then as an officer in the army. As Douglas Kerr points out, there is yet another model for Owen's role of caretaker, originating in his early family life where, as the firstborn of a mother frequently disabled by illness, he was often left in charge of his three younger siblings; identifying completely with his mother, he referred to them as "the children." But he took well to soldiering, even if in the opening years of the war he reported to his mother on being the green recruit who spent time practicing salutes on trees (*Collected Letters*, 387).

Philip Larkin notes that one of the strong plot threads in Owen's war narrative is the steady progression from the self-absorption of seeing his men as blank ciphers outside his interest to seeing them as objects of intensely focused, compassionate care. By 10 January 1917, he writes:

> I have to take a close interest in feet, and this very day I knelt down with a candle and watched each man perform his anointment with Whale Oil; praising the clean feet, but not reviling the unclean.

This was not an idle task; amputations and casualties stem from maimed and frostbitten feet in any infantry campaign, and by the autumn of 1918 Owen was complaining that his own trench feet barely allowed him to walk (*Collected Letters*, 645). He took his responsibilities for oversight seriously, but with good humor, writing home copious details about his command.

In pleased embarrassment he wrote to Susan Owen (627): "Drummer George of Dunsden *wept* when I said goodbye. (I had seen him 3 times!) This you must not tell *anybody*" (627) A month before he died, he wrote to Sassoon, "I don't take the cigarette out of my mouth when I write Deceased over their letters" (664). But once while censoring letters for his company, he came upon a reference to himself, which he passes on to his mother with great pride: "'Do you know that little officer called Owen who was at Scarborough; he is commanding my Company, and he is a *toff* I can tell you. No na-poo. Compree?' Interpreted:

'a fine fellow, no nonsense about him!'" (666) And again he reports, with a relish for the notice that included its misspellings, "from another Letter to Scarboro '—Mr. Owen is my Coy. Commander, and his such a desent chap'" (666).

On women, apparently, he was, if not harder, then less appreciative. On 30 July 1918, he wrote:

> I am glad to Have Done with the W.A.A.C's. It is almost impossible to control them. They either weep or take flight when reprimanded. 2 of Priestley's deserted today. One of 'mine' 'cries' several times every day.
>
> Their work it is true is terribly hard: but I was responsible for the men's food, and had to 'slave' them. Tell Mary [his sister] I overheard one W.A.A.C say after me "I'd like to smack 'is brown face forrim." (*Collected Letters*, 565)

The breasts of Britannia on a prize-winning design for a bronze memorial plaque "for the Fallen" flummoxed him; he found them "somehow not the breasts of a chaste woman, excuse me" (611). He boasted to his mother about his indifference to ladies of the night, although a fairly late poem about a district in London apparently known for both female and male prostitutes, "Who is the god of Canongate," tells another story of attraction:

> *What shall I pay for you, lily-lad?*
>   Not all the gold King Solomon had.
>
> *How can I buy you, London Flower?*
>   Buy me for ever, but not for an hour.
>
> *When shall I pay you, Violet Eyes?*
>   With laughter first, and after with sighs.
>
> *But you will fade, my delicate bud?*
>   No, there is too much sap in my blood.
>
> *Will you not shrink in my shut room?*
>   No, there I'll break into fullest bloom.
>   (*Complete Poems*, 1:132)

But the picture of Owen's general indictment of women alters when you look over his shoulder and read his mail home. Owen's war correspondence was no doubt subject to all the usual constraints; nevertheless, through these letters, three-quarters of which went to his mother, he was able to represent to some degree what wrenched and changed him. His letters to Susan Owen, and to his brothers and sister, are sharp and particular, all of his senses on pour to the paper—the look of his billets, the weather, the sounds rattling the wall beside him, the crump of the artillery—the vibration of which shakes fine particles from the roof down onto the paper which he is just now blowing off—he was excited about all that was happening to him and pleased to tend to that excitement. By temperament neither a rebel nor an ironist, this is his initial response to artillery fire: "As I was making my damp bed, I heard the guns for the first time. It was a sound not without a certain sublimity" (*Collected Letters*, 477).

For the whole of his war, he was eager to tell the family at home as much as he could get down and to receive the lifeline of their letters in return. He forwards endless imperious requests to his mother—this gets the tone of many: "I believe there lies in my Drawers a medium-thickness vest. Could you send it *at once* here?" And: "Shall be glad of socks as soon as you can send them. Would you include my enamel *mug*, left on my dressing table" (459), and so on. One of the last letters home says severely: "*I don't* want old, shrunk, darned socks. No use at all" (667). With all the self-importance and confidence of a well-loved child, he reminds his youngest brother (twice) to disinfect his hands when coming out of the stables, advises his parents as to the safest branch of the military for Colin (553), and scolds his sister Mary about not taking an interest in things (625). He buys gifts for all and writes anxiously wherever possible to inquire about reunion.

From the Advanced Horse Transport Depot on Sunday, 4 February 1917, he wrote his mother in the aftermath of one prolonged assault:

> I forgot hunger in the hunger for Life. The intensity of your Love reached me and kept me living. I thought of you and Mary without a break all the time.

Again, in similarly fervent vein a few months later (502):

> Without your letters I should give in. *What to* [Owen's underlining] I know not, but I 'sorter' feel I should 'give up the unequal contest!'—without a definite object for carrying on. And that object is not my Motherland, which is a good land, nor my Mother tongue, which is a dear language, but for my Mother, of whom I am not worthy to be called
> *The Son* [Owen's underlining] x x x

Under fire, England is the Motherland; a year before, stiffly dutiful before his baptism of fire, he wrote, "On the whole, I am fortunate to be where I am, and happy sometimes, as when I think it is a life pleasing to you & Father and the Fatherland" (*Collected Letters*, 387).

About the experience that eventually furloughed him to Craiglockhart War Hospital for treatment of "neurasthenia," he wrote fairly openly to his sister Mary, then a nurse (508):

> You know it was not the Bosche that worked me up, nor the explosives, but it was living so long by poor old Cock Robin (as we used to call 2/Lt. Gaukroger), who lay not only near by, but in various places around and about, if you understand. I hope you don't!

His mother receives a more covert description: "My brother officer of B Coy, 2/Lt Gaukroger, lay opposite in a similar hole. But he was covered with earth, and no relief will ever relieve him, nor will his Rest be a 9 days-rest" (505). For Susan Owen, he flings a little cover of dirt over the lingering parts of 2/Lt Gaukroger that had so tormented him and adopts euphemism, manners that in poetry Siegfried Sassoon's example and his own growing experience help him to shed.

Paul Fussell shows with precision how Owen's poems "about individual victims ground themselves . . . in physical attributes"; his mind unfolds, "feeling always towards male particulars." Owen's literary imagination is not, however, only open to the subtly erotic and sensuous in masculine bodies, but is also schooling itself to a more exact observation as he learns to part the veils of sentimental respectability. Fussell says of Owen:

> To speak of "sufferings" is not enough; one must see and feel the bloody head cradled dead on one's own shoulder. In early October, 1918, he writes his mother to explain why he had to come to France again: "I came out in order to help these boys—directly by leading them as well as an officer can; indirectly, by watching their sufferings that I may speak of them as well as a pleader can." And then, sensing that "their sufferings" is too abstract to do the job, he indicates what he's really talking about: "Of whose blood lies yet crimson on my shoulder where his head was—and where so lately yours was—I must not now write." But he does write about it to a less shockable audience, Sassoon: "The boy, by my side, shot through the head, lay on top of me, soaking my shoulder for half an hour." *His head.*

My shoulder. An improvement over *watching their sufferings*. (Fussell, *The Great War*, 296)

In Fussell's analysis, Owen identifies his true subject and moves steadily towards a style revised "to replace the pretty of 1913 with the nasty of 1917."

Yet it seems to me that Owen's growing mastery of particularity is more like Keats's "stationing": on 31 October, in the last letter he was to write, intent on complete placement within the sensory, he quickly compresses a scene to details of touch, sound, smell, and sight:

Splashing my hand, an old soldier with a walrus mustache peels & drops potatoes into the pot. By him, Keyes, my cook, chops wood; another feeds the smoke with the damp wood.

"It is a great life," the passage concludes.

Douglas Kerr argues persuasively that the army was as much a schoolmaster for Owen's language and style as war itself. "After his enlistment the bodily consciousness of Owen's poems becomes more substantial." Then, "the represented body evolves, developing muscles, teeth, back and thighs, and a tanned skin" (289). A poem of this earlier period of the war, "Training," however, does not lose the sense of a body in mental and spiritual training for sacrifice, while it keeps all of Owen's prewar interest in sensuous, homoerotic detail. Dipping into the books that Owen carried with him, Kerr shows that the army's preference for bald, impersonal description was probably a useful stylistic correction, as well as eventually a ripe source for parody; oddly, modernism and the *Field Service Pocket Book* alike cultivated in Owen a new, spare, concrete, and "masculine" style. Kerr says: "The masculine disciplines of war extended the register of his writing. He never lost the lyrical and private tones which, I would suggest, have their earliest origins in communing with his mother. The repertoire was now increased by the mixing-in of the voice of the good soldier" (295).

Yet learning to put away euphemism and, more gradually, vague, generalizing diction and overheated Georgianism was one side of development; having his soul abruptly tempered in a bath of death, mutilation, and dismemberment was another. Still, neither a changing style nor traumatic immersion in war ever quite erased Owen's essentially romantic temperament or made a pacifist of him. Both wartime events, and the change of social and intellectual worlds brought about by recognition stemming from the publication of Owen's poems, would inevitably have loosened or frayed even the bond to his mother. But what was sturdiest in his commitment to the war lay in the tie to his men and in his consciousness of the indissoluble zone of difference between his soldiering and the life of the civilian.

Whatever guilt or uncertainty he may have felt about homoerotic desire could easily be sublimated by an emphasis on the quasi-religious nature of soldier sacrifice; whatever he or others owed, they paid out in blood for civilians. But some part of Owen fused death, sexuality, and the exclusive company of men as a unified field commanding his unadulterated loyalty, and this fusion inexorably pushed him to choose frontline life over rear-echelon safety. In May, before his final assignment, C. K. Scott Moncrieff was trying to get him a safer posting teaching a Cadet Battalion; Owen did not reject these efforts on his behalf, although they came to nothing. Sheer common sense and a basic appetite for survival seems to have urged gratitude for everything that removed him from immediate danger. But much of the pull for staying, besides fraternal loyalty to other men still under fire, might have been the need to exercise publicly an approved brand of masculinity in the undeniably male theater of war.

Owen welcomed membership in the elect brotherhood of the fired upon, if not always the firing. This election was at least as much an indelible mark on the brow as the laurel, and for someone of Owen's ambition for high singularity, it was doubly welcome. Exposure to danger also has its highs, its own erotic flare. For Paul Fussell, "there are numerous testimonies associating masturbation and exhibitionism with the fears and excitements of infantry fighting." He illustrates the point over several paragraphs, ending with these lines from Robert Graves: "we . . . thrust out / Boastful tongue, clenched fist and valiant yard" (*The Great War*, 271–72).

Remembering moods of alternating terror and exultation, Wilfred Owen wrote to his younger brother on 14 May 1917 from a Casualty Clearing Station. The letter opens: "Here is some Loot, from a Pocket I rifled on the Field. I was thinking of you when I was unbuckling the Bugle from the equipment, and being in a particularly noble frame of mind, meant to present it to you some day." In turmoil, he capitalizes all the critical nouns, then finds he can't bear to part with the "Bugle." In a compressed intensity of descriptive detail he continues:

The sensations of going over the top are about as exhilarating as those dreams of falling over a precipice, when you see the rocks at the bottom surging up to you. I woke up without being squashed. Some didn't. There was an extraordinary exultation in the act of slowly walking forward, showing ourselves openly.

First it was not exhilarating; then when he woke up without being "squashed," it was. There is an important crossover here, as in a dreamlike, time-expanding intensity Owen appears to himself to traverse the boundary from life to death and exultantly back again, with a potency having sexual overtones. Writing the battle narrative was a stimulus: he erupts for pages more. The letter closes; after telling Colin he may show the letter to Harold, his other brother, but must return it, like the precious souvenir of the bugle, back to Wilfred himself, he then ends, "You must *not* show these sheets at home" (*Collected Letters*, 408). Who is left not to show it to, but his little sister and his parents' generation?

Owen's respect for his own experiences was keen, and he treats their recall carefully. But it would be a mistake to scant the complexities of his feelings about war and try to cram them into either the prowar or the antiwar camp. If he has become famous for poems brooding over the injustice of waste and loss of youth in war, those poems nonetheless run parallel to other poems and letters that also show a never-extinguished sense of the high mission of war, of its honorable continuities. A lot of war and poetry was packed into a few very short years, and he was not given a lifetime to sort it all out.

Like Siegfried Sassoon, Isaac Rosenberg, Ivor Gurney, and Edmund Blunden, a major theme for Wilfred Owen was the unrelenting brutality of trench warfare. He had no use for what he called "washy pacifists," but in the same breath disdains "whiskied prussianists" (*Collected Letters*, 551). In 1916 Owen was frank about his fears of the designated foe but made unequivocal the neutrality of his feelings towards Germans as a nation: "I am terrified of Fritz, the hideous, whom I do not hate" (*Collected Letters*, 408). A little over a year later, having wriggled to a trench abandoned by the Germans, he remarks with studied neutrality on having fed himself on the remains of their meal and notes of that same Fritz: "It was curious and troubling to pick up his letters where he had left off writing in the middle of a word!" (*Collected Letters*, 454).

By the end, his letters indicate an awareness of civilian casualties; on 29 October 1918, he begins: "The civilians here are a wretched, dirty crawling community, afraid of *us*, some of them, and no wonder after the shelling we gave them 3 weeks ago." But the letter ends:

The people in England and France who thwarted a peaceable retirement of the enemy from these areas are therefore now sacrificing aged French peasants and charming French children to our guns. Shells made by women in Birmingham are at this moment burying little children alive not very far from here.

For the first time, Owen directly pities a civilian population, but he assigns no real blame for their misery except to the people who thwart treaties. The most direct causal connection for atrocity is to those shells made by women, which bury little children alive. When "we" shell, it's on the "wretched, dirty crawling," and so on.

Owen still has a somber interest in placing himself and others in a line that, if it does not promote glory, does allow for a military tradition with mantlings of tragic dignity and full of a subdued religiosity only partly muffled by the occasional fun he took in parodying the biblical cadence and phrasing that had soaked his boyhood. He was not immune to nationalist legend. In Bordeaux, in 1915 before he enlists, an impressed Owen had toured the battlefield of Castillon, noting to his mother that there, "in 1453 Talbot Earl of Shrewsbury suffered the defeat which lost Guienne and Bordeaux to the English forever" (*Collected Letters*, 367). He has doubts about his future as a soldier, though:

> I am already quaking at the idea of Parade; and yawning with the boredom of it. *Now if I could make it a real, live adventure, a real, old adventure, by flinging myself into Italy . . . ?*

Army drill is one thing, combat another, and the image of flinging himself about in a properly adventurous war certainly has its imaginative appeal. "Yesterday we rode not far from the field of Crecy!" (485) he writes to his cousin, Leslie Gunston. He says of a poem of his own that he is enclosing for Leslie, "I crossed the long backs of the downs after leaving you. It is written *as from* the trenches. I could almost see the dead lying about in the hollows of the downs." The dead are familiar in this landscape, and the living army is still close to them. He plumes himself on looking like past English soldiers: "You must know I am transformed now, wearing a steel helmet, buff jerkin of leather, rubber waders up to the hips, & gauntlets. But for the rifle, we are exactly like Cromwellian troopers"(485).

As late as December 1917, he sees himself in the mournful, fatalistic tradition of the chivalric knight. Discussing "Hospital Barge" in his edition of Owen's *Complete Poems and Fragments*, Jon Stallworthy notes that Owen had

picked up a copy of Tennyson's *The Holy Grail and Other Poems*, and underlined these lines from "The Passing of Arthur" (Tennyson, 439):

> Then saw they how there hove a dusky barge,
> Dark as a funeral scarf from stem to stern,
> Beneath them; and descending they were ware
> That all the decks were dense with stately forms,
> Black-stoled, black-hooded like a dream—by these
> Three Queens with crowns of gold: and from them rose
> A cry that shiver'd to the tingling stars,
> And, as it were one voice, an agony
> Of lamentation, like a wind that shrills
> All night in a waste land, where no one comes,
> Or hath come, since the making of the world.

Apocalyptic mystery and ritual caught at him, so that his own death, and all
the dead that he had kept company with, could be seen to fit into a familiar
wasteland imagery, in its own category of ordered, heroic necessity.

Owen's December 1917 sonnet, "Hospital Barge," builds from a remembered sail on a steam tug down the Somme Canal from Gailly, where he had
been an "inmate" at the 13th Casualty Clearing Station, before proceeding to
Craiglockhart. Of the trip, he writes his mother (*Collected Letters*, 509): "The
scenery was such as I never saw or dreamed of since I read the *Faerie Queene*.
Just as in the Winter when I woke up lying on the burning cold snow I fancied
I must have died & been pitch-forked into the Wrong Place, so, yesterday, it
was not more difficult to imagine that my dusky barge was wending up to
Avalon, and the peace of Arthur, and where Lancelot heals him of his griev-
ous wound." In his letter, he's on the barge; in the sonnet, on the bank:

> Budging the sluggard ripples of the Somme,
> A barge round old Cerisy slowly slewed.
> Softly her engines down the current screwed,
> And chuckled softly with contented hum,
> Till fairy tinklings struck their croonings dumb.
> The waters rumpling at the stern subdued;
> The lock-gate took her bulging amplitude;
> Gently from out the gurgling lock she swum.

One reading by that calm bank shaded eyes
To watch her lessening westward quietly.
Then, as she neared the bend, her funnel screamed.
And that long lamentation made him wise
How unto Avalon, in agony,
Kings passed in the dark barge which Merlin dreamed.

> (*Complete Poems*, 1:127)

What works so well is the poem's bold plunge into a diction that holds all the crass, jarring sounds of modern machinery but suspends those sounds within the slow, stately pace of a funeral dirge. In all that contented engine hum— even the unforgivable "fairy tinklings" that unrumple the waters—in the release of the barge through the gurgling canal, it is as if there were one clear line from Malory to Tennyson to Owen, one compelling and enveloping dream of war.

"The pity of War"

Wilfred Owen's combat duty split roughly into two halves. The first half plunged him into the battle of the Somme with the 2nd Manchesters as the year turned to 1917. While on duty with his battalion in April, he entered a farmhouse and fell fifteen feet through a hole in the floor to the cellar, receiving a knock on the head on the way down. This slight concussion was jarred again after renewed exposure on the line:

> For twelve days I did not wash my face, nor take off my boots, nor sleep a deep sleep. For twelve days we lay in holes, where at any moment a shell might put us out. I think the worst incident was one wet night when we lay up against a railway embankment. A big shell, lit on the top of the bank, just 2 yards from my head. Before I awoke, I was blown in the air right away from the bank! (*Collected Letters*, 505)

When this explosion terminated, Owen was in another hole covered with corrugated iron, where he was pinned down by shelling for several days with the body of Gaukroger, "in various places around and about." After this, he had periods of high fever, and by 2 May was taken out of the line with "neurasthenia," pronounced "unfit" for General Service, and sent to Craiglockhart War Hospital in Edinburgh. After rest, more duty in the rear, and a series of examinations, Owen was declared "fit" by 4 June 1918, when he joined the 5th Manchesters, and by late September he was in action again in France.

A certain symmetry marks this career: a first part ends with wounds, fever, and shell-shock, and a declaration of being unfit for service; after a long hiatus governed by treatment at Craiglockhart, meeting Siegfried Sassoon, and having the first real flush of literary success, a second part ends with a declaration of fitness, being awarded a Military Cross for gallantry in action, and then death on the Sambre Oise Canal a week before Armistice Day. The first intense exposure to combat ends in retreat and shattered nerves. Owen regroups at Craiglockhart and recovers, reborn as both soldier and artist, learning how to handle his recurrent nightmares and to develop a writing style adequate to new experience. He then returns to combat with a new resolve, a new sophistication about the politics of war, and a desire to wipe out earlier questions about "nerves." Following his second immersion in the line, on 4–5 October 1918, he reports with almost palpable relief to both Sassoon and his mother, "My nerves are in perfect order." He describes the encounter, which won him a Military Cross, in the same letter to his mother, heading it with the phrase "Strictly private," and says: "It passed the limits of my Abhorrence. I lost all my earthly faculties, and fought like an angel."

The earlier unfitness rankled Owen. After reading Stallworthy's careful reconstruction of Owen's last engagement, John Bayley concludes that the episode was "an epic fight frequent enough even in that war, but common to every kind of ancient and pointless heroism of battle." Owen's commanding officer— whom Owen referred to as "the most arrant utterly soldierly soldier I ever came across" (cited in Bayley, 1274)—becomes Achilles, and Bayley writes:

> A handful of volunteers, of whom Owen was one, surrounded this Achilles, already ten times wounded, as he struggled—in defiance even of the minimum military common sense practiced at the time—to get his company across the Sambre-Oise Canal in the face of point-blank machine-gun fire. Almost all were killed, including the Major, and later in the day an unopposed crossing was made further down.

Something like a crowded half year after Wilfred Owen wrote "Hospital Barge" from his memory of 1917 at the Casualty Clearing Station, in July 1918, on his way back to the front again, he finished "The Parable of The Old Man and The Young." This poem allegorizes the military and civilian leaders of World War I as a vindictive Old Testament patriarch, and Owen's myth takes quite another turn from the Arthurian "Hospital Barge." In the later poem, soldier death is neither stoically nor beautifully received:

> Then Abram bound the youth with belts and straps,
> And builded parapets and trenches there,
> And stretched forth the knife to slay his son.
> When lo! an angel called him out of heaven,
> Saying lay not thy hand upon the lad,
> Neither do anything to him. Behold,
> A ram, caught in a thicket by its horns;
> Offer the ram of pride instead of him.
> But the old man would not so, but slew his son,
> And half the seed of Europe, one by one.
>
>   (*Complete Poems*, 1:174)

Reality does not offer the traditional symbolic sacrifice, where Abram replaces Isaac with "the ram of pride"; in Owen's revised text, an Old Testament Jehovah is met by an insubordinate Abraham, who defies God and his emissary, who denies obedience to an ultimately merciful authority to whom he should bend and does not. A divine dispensation does not cover this military world; the only relevant myth seems to be Saturn devouring his sons. Around the time that Owen was writing the elegiac "Hospital Barge" and more than half a year before the bitter outcry of "The Parable of the Old Man and the Young," at twenty-four, Owen looked in summary at the arc of his life in poetry, and on New Year's Eve 1917 wrote to his mother, Susan Owen, with quiet joy: "I am started. The tugs have left me; I feel the great swelling of the open sea taking my galleon." But immediately thereafter he wrote,

> last year I lay awake in a windy tent in the middle of a vast, dreadful encampment. It seemed neither France nor England, but a kind of paddock where the beasts are kept a few days before the shambles. I heard the revelling of the Scotch troops, who are now dead, and who knew they would be dead. I thought of this present night, and whether I should indeed—whether we should indeed—whether you would indeed—but I thought neither long nor deeply, for I am a master of elision.
>
> But chiefly I thought of the very strange look on all the faces in that camp; an incomprehensible look, which a man will never see in England,

though wars should be in England; nor can it be seen in any battle. But only in Etaples.

It was not despair, or terror, it was more terrible than terror, for it was a blindfold look, and without expression, like a dead rabbit's.

It will never be painted, and no actor will ever seize it. And to describe it, I think I must go back and be with them. (*Collected Letters*, 520–21)

Nothing in his life seems more compelling than this act of witness to a dumb and brutal slaughter.

In this letter, and in other poems of these months, there is a terrible isolation, a cosmic disordering in which life and mercy are refused and where death falls as a huge, immitigable punishment visited on the innocent. As Modris Eksteins describes the 1914–18 schism between home front and battlefield, in imposing broad censorship in the name of maintaining morale, the home leadership undercut both soldier and civilian trust in their conduct of the war, and in the reading of actuality for each:

Defeats were presented as victories, stalemate as tactical maneuvering. Truth became falsehood, falsehood truth. As euphemism became the official order of the day, language was turned upside down and inside out. Atrocity stories were invented, and real atrocities buried. (Ecksteins, 233)

The enormity of industrialized death and injury inflicted broke the survivor's ability to speak of it and left him unable in any case to put together the savage disjunctions of war experience and any life that might exist in time and space beside it.

In two paragraphs of his memoir, *Undertones of War*, Edmund Blunden presents one of those instances in which the incommensurable occurs:

The tunnellers who were so busy under the German line were men of stubborn determination, yet, by force of the unaccustomed, they hurried nervously along the trenches above ground to spend their long hours listening or mining. At one shaft they pumped air down with Brobdingnagian bellows. The squeaking noise may have given them away, or it may have been mere bad luck, when one morning a minenwerfer smashed this entrance and the men working there. One was carried out past me, collapsing like a sack of potatoes, spouting blood at twenty places. Cambrin was beginning to terrify. Not far away from that shafthead, a young and cheerful lance-corporal of ours was making some tea as I passed one warm afternoon. Wishing him a good tea, I went along three firebays; one shell dropped without warning behind me; I saw its smoke faint out, and I thought all was as lucky as it should be. Soon a cry from that place recalled me; the shell had burst all wrong. Its butting impression was black and stinking in the parados where three minutes ago the lance-corporal's mess tin was bubbling over a little flame. For him, how could the gobbets of blackening flesh, the earth-wall sotted with blood, with flesh, the eye under the duck-board, the pulpy bone be the only answer? At this moment, while we looked with dreadful fixity at so isolated a horror, the lance-corporal's brother came round the traverse.

He was sent to company headquarters in a kind of catalepsy. The bay had to be put right, and red-faced Sergeant Simmons, having helped himself and me to a share of rum, biting hard on his pipe, shovelled into the sandbag I held, not without self-protecting profanity, and an air of "it's a lie; we're a lie." (Blunden, *Undertones*, 63–64)

The description ticks along quietly in a scene of industrial labor with men and machines above and below ground, even with the nervousness of the tunnellers, almost in the normal delving of peacetime. The "wrong" events are put with minimum fuss, maximal efficiency: it's a harmless, unlucky squeak that starts a bad business, which escalates in intensity like a mine accident, not like a war. The first visible casualty collapses in a metaphor of homely familiarity, "like a sack of potatoes"; only then without warning those potatoes are incongruously stained with blood spouts—in a further grinding of particularity—in twenty places. After this, the tool of understatement is joined by that of juxtaposition, as the lucky escape from the shell for the speaker turns out symmetrically to be the unlucky hit for the lance-corporal, incongruously and with such monstrous irony "wished a good tea"; and then the cheerful lance-corporal pairs with the exploded lance-corporal; and so on, in a cascading series of calamities and indignities that never once give way to any facile control by the mode of heroic attack or heroic resistance. Thing triggers thing: squeak to minenwerfer to scaffolding to flesh-as-potatoes, finally all going into a sandbag, which the speaker holds in receptive hand and memory. Blunden's is a cooler and a crueler, a less obviously mediated report of war than Owen's: when the familial relation is invoked, a brother can only stumble upon a brother's horribly concluded life, and in the end, it's the "bay" that has to be put

FIGURE 3. Lt. Edmund Blunden, ca. 1916. Imperial War Museum.

right, while sergeant and speaker can only say, wordlessly, "it's a lie; we're a lie." The gaps between the thought and the shattered pieces of action, too, are enormous; what fills them? The "lie" of soldiering? Of heroic war? Of familial caring?

Managing those gaps by direct, material presentation becomes the mode of twentieth-century war writing, born out of the collision between industrial war and the literate conscript who remains faithful to the project of telling a truth. No explanation or recognizable or bearable law that dictates a just and comprehensible ordering could be put to these events of death, dismembering, and mutilation. With even grimmer and more condensed effect, Blunden uses the same technique of juxtaposition for an even more inward accusation of the casual brutality of soldiering in "Concert Party in Busseboom," published only in 1928. An actual concert opens the nightmare ballad, and then Blunden sets his pair going:

> And standing on the sandy way,
> With the cracked church peering past,
> We heard another matinee
> We heard the maniac blast
>
> Of barrage south by Saint Eloi,
> And the red lights flaming there
> Called madness: Come, my bonny boy,
> And dance to the latest air.
>
> To this new concert, white we stood;
> Cold certainty held our breath;
> While men in the tunnels below Larch Wood
> Were kicking men to death.
>   (*Selected Poems*, 77)

A paralysis exists between the beholder and the act beheld which is the antithesis of heroism, pointing to the passivity of the new heroic mode. The almost limp predictability of the monosyllabic rhymes—"past / blast," "there / air," "breath / death"—is in fierce contrast to the shock of the subject. In *A War Imagined*, Samuel Hynes says of this aspect of World War I:

> Once the soldier was seen as a victim, the idea of a hero became unimaginable: there would be no more heroic actions in the art of this war. And if entire armies could be imagined composed of such victims—if indeed every army was an army of martyrs—then Victory too must fade from the story, and war become only a long catastrophe, with neither significant action nor direction, a violence that was neither fought nor won, but only endured. (215)

What shadows the ending of Blunden's "Concert Party at Busseboom," however, is not only the inert, fixed helplessness of the listeners, but the internalized and unresolved guilt at participation in these pitiless rites, even if only remotely. In subsequent wars these tones become a stronger part of acceding to the growth of the war story as the antiheroic, moving passivity towards the more active positions of pacifism: if not a pacifism towards all wars, then at least a pacifism towards the one ravaging the soldier-poet and his fellows. But Samuel Hynes quotes Blunden's wry, postwar comment on how these strong feelings tended to evolve: "Now the danger is, perhaps, that the horror and crime of war are being transformed into a glib axiom" (*Auden Generation*, 39).

Yet the evolution from passive, horrified onlooker to a still revolted, but uneasily complicit, speaker becomes visible in Wilfred Owen, the war poet most widely acclaimed as pacifist in intention and effect. "War poetry," according to Simon Featherstone, "as now generally presented and interpreted in the anthologies, is the poetry of 1914–18. Its purpose is seen to be telling the truth about war, and its prevailing attitudes as pacifist" (Featherstone, 7). Owen's book of war poems was posthumously published with a memoir by Edmund Blunden and introduction and notes by C. Day Lewis. Taken as an exemplary war poet by other poets, Lewis in this collection notes of Owen that he was the poet who "made poems which radically changed our attitude towards war" (Owen, *Collected Poems*, 12). On a separate sheet of paper, which, to W. B. Yeats's extreme indignation, was preserved in the manuscript collections of the British Museum, Owen, with many revisions still visible, had described his book in terms that quickly became famous; this sketch for a preface is reproduced in all currrent collections of Owens's poetry:

> This book is not about heroes. English poetry is not yet fit to speak of them.
> Nor is it about deeds, or lands, nor anything about glory, honour, might, majesty, dominion or power, except War.
> Above all I am not concerned with Poetry.
> My subject is War, and the pity of War.
> The poetry is in the pity.
> Yet these elegies are to this generation in no sense consolatory. They may be to the next. All a poet can do is warn.

Pity is the issue here, and it becomes a problem of both style and substance for Owen. An unsympathetic reader like C. H. Sisson can say, "It is an embarrassing statement" and, "it comes near to being absolute rubbish." Sisson regrets Owen's "progressivist" politics, thinking that English poetry has no need to wait for Wilfred's good reports on its progress. Most importantly, he takes exception to Owen's saying "the poetry is in the pity—" which Sisson unfairly takes to mean "that if you look after the pity the poetry will take care of itself" (Sisson, 82–83). Sisson charges Owen's aesthetic with handling poetic device too lightly and accuses Own of going crabwise into poetry by way of ideas, or feelings about ideas; Owen's poetry runs counter to Mallarmé's saying that all one ever has are the words: poetry is made of words, not ideas or feelings. But if one takes Keats's judgment as the model, as Owen so often did, an X by "the voice of true feeling" will always mark the worthy lyric. In defying Keats, to Owen's partial advantage, John Bayley writes:

> [Owen's] poetry not only has "a palpable design upon us"; but the bad taste to buttonhole us with its sufferings and to allege (a further irritation) that we haven't the remotest idea how terrible they are. Heroes have never presumed before to behave, or to write, like that. And—as a last straw—it is magnificent. No wonder a lot of people prefer to praise without looking. (1273)

Owen was not gifted with Blunden's taste for understatement, and because by temperament he was more attracted to the florid and full-mouthed style usually blamed on Keats, critics have always been divided about the literary worth of Owen's poetry. Along with the dense, springy thickness of the phrasing Owen preferred, readers are often repulsed by his penchant for archaisms and inverted syntax. This anachronisitc style, syntax, and diction, plus the habit of indignation and, in the late pieces, Owens's fondness for the accusatory mode, made up traits at least in part responsible for Yeats's excluding him from *The Oxford Book of Modern Verse* and for his blasting away at Owen privately in letters to Dorothy Wellesley.

Yeats's introduction to this anthology, however, with its public formulation of Yeats's rejection of Owen, contains some very strange elements. Pity in war ought not to be held as a fit subject at all in Yeats's code; speaking of unnamed officer-poets, and seeming to have both Siegfried Sassoon and Wilfred Owen in mind, he says:

> they were not without joy—for all skill is joyful—but felt bound, in the words of the best known, to plead the suffering of their men. In poems that had for a time considerable fame, written in the first person, they made that suffering their own. I have rejected these poems for the same reason that

made Arnold withdraw his *Empedocles on Aetna* from circulation; passive suffering is not a theme for poetry. In all the great tragedies, tragedy is a joy to the man who dies; in Greece the tragic chorus danced. (xxxiv)

Yeats seems to say that there is an inadmissible edge of didactic and partisan pleading in this war poetry; he goes on to remark that it is not tragic, or worth poeticizing, when "some blunderer has driven his car on to the wrong side of the road—that is all." Winding up with a curious analogy, and an even curiouser anecdote, he says:

> If war is necessary, or necessary in our time and place, it is best to forget its suffering as we do the discomfort of fever, remembering our comfort at midnight when our temperature fell, or as we forget the worst moments of more painful disease. Florence Farr returning third class from Ireland found herself among Connaught Rangers just returned from the Boer War who described an incident over and over, and always with loud laughter: an unpopular sergeant struck by a shell turned round and round like a dancer wound in his own entrails. That too may be a right way of seeing war, if war is necessary; the way of the Cockney slums, of Patrick Street, of the *Kilmainham Minut*, or *Johnny I hardly knew ye*, of the medieval *Dance of Death*. (xxxv)

War is not made by men; it's made by Forces! There is surely something grotesque here about Yeats's fanatic acceptance of war's necessity, with all its attendant cruelty. In his ancient, glittering eyes, any bitching about getting killed for no discernible cause seems to miss the point: dying heroically and uncomplainingly is all the point, since war exists perpetually. Dying is a soldier's job. He seems to insert as well a bad-faith effort at "balance," making a nod to the lower-class view by noting the constant antagonism that exists between leader and led in all war, and coming around to an unexpected approval of war's cruelty once again by applauding the vicious humor of those who are led when their antagonism is played out against the leader. He rounds off his observation on the willfulness of pleading the suffering of your men by pleading the hearty masculine hilarity of Florence Farr's Connaught Rangers instead.

He was even less temperate in a letter to Dorothy Wellesley, saying about Owen:

> My Anthology continues to sell & the critics get more & more angry. When I excluded Wilfred Owen, whom I consider unworthy of the poets'

corner of a country newspaper, I did not know I was excluding a revered sandwich-board Man of the revolution & that some body has put his worst & most famous poem in a glass-case in the British Museum—however if I had known it I would have excluded him just the same. He is all blood, dirt & sucked sugar stick (look at the selection in Faber's Anthology—he calls poets 'bards,' a girl a 'maid' & talks about 'Titanic wars'). There is every excuse for him but none for those who like him. (Yeats, *Letters*, 124–26)

There's an exasperation in the punishment that Yeats metes out—it is not merely Owen's naive lack of the kind of modernization that Yeats received at Pound's hands, but sheer outrage that attention should be paid to a revolutionary politics at all, which Yeats here plasters on the very generalized dissidence of poor Owen like that sandwich-board.

Is Owen's blood unclean because Yeats finds it sentimentally eulogized or because Owen is refusing to swallow what Yeats thinks he should? Yet the "dirt" of war that Owen reports is probably the modernist specificity of whose lack Yeats makes a point in fastening with distaste on Owen's diction and the details of his very bloody and dirty war.

As Bayley makes the linkage, Yeats's "sneers" are parallel to that "flicker of distaste" that Robert Graves expressed in a letter written to Owen in December 1917: "For God's sake cheer up and write more optimistically—the war's not ended yet but a poet should have a spirit above wars"(quoted in Seymour-Smith, 65). Maintaining the stiffest of upper lips, Graves lets through only the thinnest, sharpest wedge of irony. Owen makes both Yeats and Graves queasy: Yeats partly on grounds of style, but also by what he perceives as Owen's evasion of *amor fati*, or the tragic acceptance of fate, and Graves by the new manners of Owen's war. Both regret the disintegrative sugar of the pity that Owen pours into the military gas tank. For Yeats and Graves, Owen's critique of war disrupts a social and literary order, perverting the tradition that rightly assigns war a place as epiphenomena to the greater dramas of human will.

A gloss on what Robert Graves meant by "above wars" can perhaps be seen in William Butler Yeats's poem "An Irish Airman Foresees his Death" (1918). "Those that I fight I do not hate, / Those that I guard I do not love"; of the poor he serves, the airman declares:

No likely end could bring them loss
Or leave them happier than before.
Nor law, nor duty bade me fight,

Nor public men, nor cheering crowds,
A lonely impulse of delight
Drove to this tumult in the clouds;
I balanced all, brought all to mind,
The years to come seemed waste of breath,
A waste of breath the years behind
In balance with this life, this death.

(*Poems*, 135)

Yeats's airman is death's man, renouncing all for inhuman passionlessness. It fits Yeats's code that this icon of war is an aristocratic spokesman for the one aspect of World War I that derived from the anachronism of the duel, in which pilots fought each other from airborne palfreys like medieval knights.

Owen's witness for the passive victimhood of his soldiers appears to be what most annoyed Yeats, though not because it denies agency, heroic or otherwise, to the soldier, because for Yeats soldiers seem by their profession above choice, pure instrumentality. More seriously for Yeats, Owen's formulation of war witness implies that experience cannot be permeated by imagination. The idea of authentic witness relies on something Yeats called "that cult of sincerity, that refusal to multiply personality which is characteristic of our time" (xxxvi). In Yeats's argument against what has become particularism, each poet then stands islanded, "a man so many years old, fixed to some one place" (xxxvi); resident, too, within a literature of covenanted housing.

Part of what repels Yeats may be exactly what recommends Owen ever more strongly to new readers. If we consider the traumatic content of his experience of war, it fits within other parameters in which events are sharply and radically in excess of what a noncombatant can know. Through the volatility and openness of literary witness, we are reconciled with the estrangements of that radical experience. Quoting Elie Wiesel, Shoshana Felman says:

> It has been suggested that testimony is the literary—or discursive—mode par excellence of our times, and that our era can precisely be defined as the age of testimony. "If the Greeks invented tragedy, the Romans the epistle, and the Renaissance the sonnet," writes Elie Wiesel, "our generation invented a new literature, that of testimony." (Felman, 17).

Current interest in Wilfred Owen's poetry may be evoked by the directness with which he raises questions about the nature of literary witness.

The victims in Owen's reading of war are fairly exclusively Other Ranks. The dominant irony in a poem like "Spring Offensive," may be that there *is* no offensive: it's "the whole sky" that burns with fury against the soldiers, "earth" that "set sudden cups / In thousands for their blood; and the green slope / Chasmed and deepened sheer to infinite space" (1:192). In the apocalyptic landscape of one of the last poems Owen wrote, there's nobody in it but the sacrificed. In Owen's mechanized world, to be pure instrument as an infantryman is to be degraded and vulnerable. In their helplessness, Owen's soldiers do not kill, but get killed.

Owen's true originality is to have swept up all the new ways of looking at war and soldiering—the comprehension of the soldier as a dehumanized fighting particle of a mass machine, who endures the industrial ugliness of sound, sight, and smell and the impersonal, overwhelming weapons tearing into the human body—and to have reinstated the old appreciations, in a presentation of the new and frightful amalgam as tragic glory. Heroism now lives in the preemptive maternality of Owen's brooding care for the dead, the mutilated, and the mutilated dead of war. As these soldiers enter their purgatory of suffering, it is their animal sacrifice that enhances our indifferent, underrealized and uncaring life: crossing the line separating our life from their transfiguring death is the only grace available to us, or to Owen.

Those poems that speak mainly in what Patrick Swinden calls Owen's "ventriloquial style" are the ones that settle most narrowly for pathos; in part, poems like "The Dead-Beat" or "The Letter" extend the range of vividness and round out the portraiture, much as Shakespeare's yokels bulk out the lower end of the scale of emotional complexity while the true heroes go on about their business on the heights. Besides his fix on tragic youth, Owen takes a good look at all the different ways to die; he lets his poems visit hospitals, listen to soldiers' nightmares, and play the whole keyboard of wartime injury, mental and physical.

But the poems that through elevated language and image convey the battlefield scene are those that confer something else, essentially a religious language without a religious conviction, and one that by force of beauty transforms anguish, pain, and suffering into a nobility of heroic endurance in which the apprehension of this nobility is all that exists. The reduction of men in the circumstances of war becomes the paradoxical means of their rising to be born again in something finally very close to Yeats's "terrible beauty."

The successful execution of Owen's pararhyme, or consonantal rhyme and half rhyme, convey the terror and somber satisfaction of this negative position. As Swinden puts it,

para-rhyme is often most effective in Owen's poetry when the aural dislo-
cations produced by its syntactic form and semantic reference are matched
by a degree of rhythmic irregularity in the whole of the two lines in which
it appears. (Swinden, 324)

For Swinden, good examples occur in several poems, including "the uneven
and uncertainly rhyming stanzas of 'Insensibility.'" If we look at "Insensibility," the faltering line length and the slight concussion at the ends of lines
where the pararhymes and the half rhymes meet, or only half meet, is like the
chink of metal meeting metal and glancing away. In every particular, syntactic, metrical, and rhymed, the off-balance nature of the whole intensifies the
sense of a pattern, but a pattern being blunted or twisted by pain and doubt.
Form and expressive function are so skillfully blended that an effect is created,
whereby a fluid, shapeless reality seems, in Ezra Pound's words, "just coming
over into speech" (*Gaudier-Brzeska*, 82).

"Insensibility" (*Complete Poems*, 1:145), a poem that Jon Stallworthy tells
us was likely written in by Owen 1917 in ironic response to Wordsworth's
"The Happy Warrior"), begins:

> Happy are men who yet before they are killed
> Can let their veins run cold.

We might pause here to note that the happy men with cold veins represent an
abhorrent insensibility of numbed feeling to Owen; yet that insensibility or
coolness seems to be exactly what Yeats treasures as a virtue both manly and
aristocratic in "An Irish Airman Foresees His Death." Owen's poem continues:

> Whom no compassion fleers
> Or makes their feet
> Sore on the alleys cobbled with their brothers.
> The front line withers.
> But they are troops who fade, not flowers,
> For poets' tearful fooling:
> Men, gaps for filling:
> Losses, who might have fought
> Longer; but no one bothers.

"Longer" staggers over onto the next line with a real hopelessness. There's almost a jarring silliness in that "fooling / filling" pairing, which conveys the

amoral and surreal absurdity of the acceptance of such losses, and then the end-sounds of "brothers / withers / bothers," as well as "fleers / flowers," make a linkage of further sour and desolate sounds in the mouth. Stanzas 2 and 3 continue:

> Dullness best solves
> The tease and doubt of shelling,
> And chance's strange arithmetic
> Comes simpler than the reckoning of their shilling.
> They keep no check on armies' decimation.
>
> Happy are these who lose imagination:
> They have enough to carry with ammunition.
> Their spirit drags no pack.
> Their old wounds, save with cold, can not more ache.
> Having seen all things red,
> Their eyes are rid
> Of the hurt of the colour of blood for ever.
> And terror's first constriction over,
> Their hearts remain small-drawn.
> Their senses in some scorching cautery of battle
> Now long since ironed,
> Can laugh among the dying, unconcerned.

Here, the drag and skip of true rhyme across the stanzas—"imagination / dec-imation"—and the pararhyme, "imagination / ammunition," only enhance the dulling and flattening impact of both. The single unrhymed line, "Their senses in some scorching cautery of battle," flares as the one patch where metaphor burns through, but only with some unhappy truth.

Stanzas 4 and 5 continue the pattern of overlapping sounds and the jerky, repetitive, and wearying abruptness wherein sound mimics qualities of motion and emotion:

> Happy the lad whose mind was never trained:
> His days are worth forgetting more than not.
> He sings along the march
> Which we march taciturn, because of dusk,

The long, forlorn, relentless trend
From larger day to huger night.

We wise, who with a thought besmirch
Blood over all our soul,
How should we see our task
But through his blunt and lashless eyes?
Alive, he is not vital overmuch;
Dying, not mortal overmuch;
Nor sad, nor proud,
Nor curious at all.
He cannot tell
Old men's placidity from his.

"March / much / besmirch" echo the "scorching" of earlier, and the poem reaches conclusion in the sixth stanza:

But cursed are dullards whom no cannon stuns,
That they should be as stones.
Wretched are they, and mean
With paucity that never was simplicity.
By choice they made themselves immune
To pity and whatever moans in man
Before the last sea and the hapless stars;
Whatever mourns when many leave these shores;
Whatever shares
The eternal reciprocity of tears.

Even the variation in monosyllabic and polysyllabic rhyme endings—pairings like "stuns / stones" versus "paucity / simplicity"—adds to the complexity of rhythms. It's a bumpy, leaden poem that rises blimplike, loaded with Romantic echoes, to something truly astonishing, in which nothing more is affirmed than the never-ending existence of pain. God does not save these men, or keep their souls in heaven. All that we can and must assert in their honor is the stir of our own reciprocal feeling.

But of course our feeling does not count unless we can offer it as one of them. And to be truly one of them one must die, or attempt to die, as they do.

In a much-cited letter to Osbert Sitwell on 4 July 1918, while Owen helped train troops and prepared himself to return with them to the front, he unburdens himself of the sense of sacrifice which these young men meant to him:

> For 14 hours yesterday I was at work—teaching Christ to lift his cross by numbers, and how to adjust his crown; and not to imagine he thirst till after the last halt. I attended his Supper to see that there were not complaints; and inspected his feet that they should be worthy of the nails. I see to it that he is dumb, and stands at attention before his accusers. With a piece of silver I buy him every day, and with maps I make him familiar with the topography of Golgotha.

Douglas Kerr shows how the parodic, biblical phrasing has its source not only in the New Testament, but in the specimen report of the duties of the Subaltern of the Day, as quoted by Kerr from Captain Hood's *Duties for All Ranks*. Kerr takes this from the subaltern's standardized specimen form: "I inspected rations yesterday, and saw them weighed and issued. They were of . . . . quality. I visited the breakfasts and found them . . . . The men were . . . . properly dressed." And so on. Kerr comments further:

> The pro forma accountability of bureaucratic utterances like this could be brought face to face with the language of quite a different code, with a different idea of what responsibility might mean. It is one of Owen's most studied discursive confrontations. (294)

Owen used Biblical language, popular culture, and the whole of English poetry as his treasure horde of pieces to be turned, faceted, and backlit by his own subverting intention, in ways that scholars are still scrambling to follow.

But however often he used Christ as his model of high soldierly sacrifice, his ambivalent rejection of Christian humility seems essential to defining his own war code:

> [O]ne of Christ's essential commands was: Passivity at any price! Suffer dishonour and disgrace, but never resort to arms. Be bullied, be outraged, be killed; but do not kill. It may be a chimerical and an ignominious principle, but there it is.

Acting on chimerical and ignominious principles proved unacceptable to Owen, as the letter swerves from accusing men of the pulpit for deceit to this eventually self-justifying self-reproach: "And am I not myself a conscientious objector with a very seared conscience?" (*Collected Letters*, 461)

And here we may arrive at one of the worst of Owen's condemnations of war; through letters like these, testing the limits of conventional religious and ethical principle, and through poems like "Insensibility," we are brought to see that war *does not* necessarily provide us with life-transfiguring knowledge. In his metaphors, war knowledge brings about the "searing" of consciences like his own by the "scorching cautery of battle." About the engagement which won him the Military Cross, he writes to Siegfried Sasson: "I cannot say I suffered anything; having let my brain grow dull: that is to say my nerves are in perfect order." And later, "perfect order" means: "My senses are charred" (*Collected Letters*, 581) War's worst murder is the destruction—dulling, blunting—of our capacity to care.

This is plainly visible even in the labored, archaized diction of "Sonnet On Seeing a Piece of Our Heavy Artillery Brought into Action":

> Be not withdrawn, dark arm, thy spoilure done,
> Safe to the bosom of our prosperity.
> But when thy spell be cast complete and whole,
> May God curse thee, and cut thee from our soul!
>> (*Complete Poems*, 1:151)

War has to be actively renounced; the mentality of the garrison-state is dangerous. "Dulce et Decorum Est" scolds facile civilian assumptions about war, but it also registers the deaths of fellow soldiers, for whose deaths Owen himself is not yet wholly absolved. It is important to read the admonishing German soldier of "Strange Meeting" as more than an abstract allegorical figure or mere double of Owen himself; for the first time, Owen shows his own unresolved conscience about killing the enemy.

In this visionary poem, triggered, as Denis Welland has shown, by a passage from Shelley's "The Revolt Of Islam" (Welland, 99), Owen stands his two soldiers in Hell. "I went hunting wild / After the wildest beauty in the world," says the enemy soldier, but now death nullifies everything:

> I mean the truth untold,
> The pity of war, the pity war distilled.
> Now men will go content with what we spoiled,

Or, discontent, boil bloody, and be spilled.
They will be swift with swiftness of the tigress.
None will break ranks, though nations trek from progress.

Finally, there's no absolution from this figure, even though he wants to wash away "the cess of war." The poem ends,

"I am the enemy you killed, my friend.
I knew you in this dark: for so you frowned
Yesterday through me as you jabbed and killed.
I parried; but my hands were loath and cold.
Let us sleep now. . . ."
(*Complete Poems*, 1:148)

Above ground nobody breaks ranks, and below ground there is an unusable wisdom and nothing but rest. Twenty years later everybody was at it again, doing that trek from progress.

On 4 February 1917, Owen sets down the battleground in these terms:

[E]xtra for me there is the universal pervasion of *Ugliness*. Hideous landscapes, vile noises, foul language and nothing but foul, even from one's own mouth (for all are devil ridden), everything unnatural, broken, blasted; the distortion of the dead, whose unburiable bodies sit outside the dugouts all day, all night, the most execrable sights on earth. In poetry we call them the most glorious. But to sit with them all day, all night . . . and a week later to come back and find them still sitting there, in motionless groups, THAT is what saps the "soldierly spirit.

Above all, Owen's language was struggling to keep faith with the unburiable, and with the sense of a self-fouling impotence that also accompanied that struggle, a sense to which later soldier-poets undeniably responded. In this passage, the unburiable, execrable corpse beats out glory. But Owen and others keep laboring to find that glory: even in the most material witness, something unaccountable leaks through, and at the match point of Owen's authentic witness and Yeats's imaginative reconception, war poets keep trying to force its ignition.

3

W. H. Auden: "The great struggle of our time"

IT is not the custom to talk about American and British poems of World War II as if they belonged to the same language. Typically, English critics attempting to judge or sort out World War II poems push their fellow members of the Commonwealth into one drawer and then set aside a separate bin for the Americans, if they bring them on at all. American critics, perhaps mindful of the greater prominence of their national poetry in the early decades of modernism, or alive to the deluge of talent occurring in the United States after 1945, write fewer histories of the 1940s; when they do anthologize war poems, they tend to divide less by decade than by larger temporal units, for example, "Midcentury Poetry." Or, like the American poet Stanley Kunitz, they dismiss the category of World War II poetry altogether, inclining to Kunitz's view that with the exception of Randall Jarrell, successful World War II poetry does not exist. Yet whatever English or American critics allege about its character, the poetry of World War II, with its irony and formal good manners, looks and sounds similar in both countries.

The Anglo-American cross-fertilization, although more pervasive at the millennial marker, nonetheless reached into the 1940s as well. Both Keith Douglas and Randall Jarrell are palpably indebted to W. H. Auden, and Auden, even before emigrating, had to shake both his style and his substance free of the American T. S. Eliot and the Anglo-Irish Yeats. But in order to explain the Americans' war, Vernon Scannell in *Not Without Glory* (like Ian Hamilton in his *The Poetry of War, 1939–45*), bags them in a separate chapter which Scannell calls "American Poets of the Second World War." Randall Jarrell, Richard Eberhart, and Karl Shapiro make the cut, and Scannell lumps them in with the quality because he finds them behaving like members of a familiar, traditional school, which would have traced its origins back to the English metaphysical poets of the seventeenth century and would have vigorously rejected any paternity claims from Walt Whitman, eschewing free forms, expansive verbal gesticulations and the exclusive use of the idioms and rhythms of demotic speech in favour of wit, lucidity, grace and traditional prosody. (Scannell, 228)

Writing in 1976, his back braced for defense against the hordes of American free-versers then rushing to overwhelm British poetry with their sodden demotic, Scannell only occasionally intersperses remarks accounting for the historic differences that compelled much of the nationally separatist vetting of war poets. What finally persuades Scannell to fold Americans into the poets fit to be recognized is their adherence to English tradition.

From the 1940s and beyond, however, besides the question of national exclusivity and fidelity to the right traditions, English readers worried whether the poems of World War II were advancing or even maintaining the standards set by the previous generation: no new Wilfred Owens or Siegfried Sassoons seemed to be turning up. In May 1943, the bulk of his war poems, from one major campaign, and his battle wounds behind him, Keith Douglas took up the question of the absence of significant World War II poetry in a short piece called "Poets in This War," declaring: "In the fourth year of this war we have not a single poet who seems likely to be an impressive commentator upon it." Baffled as to why this should be, Douglas looks back to his immediate predecessors and writes:

During the period 'entre deux guerres' we were listening alternately to an emphasis of the horrible nature of modern war and to the vague remedies of social and political reformers. The nation's public character remained, in spite of all, as absurdly ignorant and reactionary as ever.

Those who wrote of war looked back to the last even when they spoke of the next. (Douglas, *Prose Miscellany*, 118)

Even while British mortality in World War II would climb to 350,000 deaths, including civilians, that suffering could not erase the lingering impact of the soldier deaths in World War I, which stood at 700,000—double the combined number of soldier and civilian fatalities in World War II. But Douglas, as he senses the weight of this comparison, also goes on to link the slightness of his generation's war poems to the style of World War II, which "began and continued in such a disconcerting way." Complaining of "long inaction on all fronts," he remarks that "Dunkirk was over almost before most people had rubbed the sleep out of their eyes," and then asks:

> Why did all this happen? Why are there no poets like Owen and Sassoon who lived with the fighting troops and wrote of their experiences while enduring them? (*Prose Miscellany*, 119)

Douglas is confident that whatever comes, war poetry will be written after the event by soldiers; yet as he continues to frame his questions and mount his explanations, the blank of the missing soldier-poet remains:

> There are such poets, but they do not write. They do not write because there is nothing new, from a soldier's point of view, about this war except its mobile character. There are two reasons: hell cannot be let loose twice: it was let loose in the Great War and it is the same old hell now. The hardships, pain and boredom; the behaviour of the living and the appearance of the dead, were so accurately described by the poets of the Great War that everyday on the battlefields of the western desert—and no doubt on the Russian battlefields as well—their poems are illustrated. Almost all that a modern poet on active service is inspired to write, would be tautological. (*Prose Miscellany*, 119)

For Douglas, inside the global conflagration later adopted by both English and Americans as "The Good War," the burden and the silence of its poets was created by belatedness and ideological muddle. One ear fed by "the horrible nature of modern war" and the other fed by "vague remedies of social and political reformers" (*Prose Miscellany*, 118), the lessons to be extracted canceled each other out; the mood and the mode were left to plod on, in grim hope and glum cognizance of somebody's, if not one's own, imminent and inevitable sacrifice. This is not a state in which new perceptions flash and fuse with new forms to contain them.

England's Auden

Any estimate of how good the poetry of World War II may be will surely rest, however, not only on the other war poetry with which it is compared, but on its viable relation to what was written immediately before it in

English by the still numbingly outsized figures of W. B. Yeats, T. S. Eliot, Ezra Pound, and Wallace Stevens. And as if these presences were not sufficiently intimidating, poets of the 1940s wrote in the over-hang of W. H. Auden's political poetry of the 1930s. Auden himself, by 1940, had stopped all ardent voyaging to troubled frontiers; his best war lines, those prepping for the onrushing conflict with fascism, were largely expended prior to his leaving England for the United States at the outset of global war. Having lost him as either war correspondent or embattled home-front citizen, the English found no commanding replacement to frame in poetry the hostilities that swept them through 1945.

By the end of the 1930s, W. H. Auden found himself unable to choose either a bully patriotism or a confirmed pacifism, and he backed away from war to the shores of the New World. In the summer of 1939, he wrote in *The Prolific and the Devourer*:

> If one reviews the political activity of the world's intellectuals during the past eight years, if one counts up all the letters to the papers which they have signed, all the platforms on which they have spoken, all the congresses which they have attended, one is compelled to admit that their combined effort, apart from the money they have helped to raise for humanitarian purposes (and one must not belittle the value of that) has been nil. (20)

And with finality, reiterating his phrase from "In Memory of W. B. Yeats"— "poetry makes nothing happen"—Auden says now in broader terms: "Art makes nothing happen" (26).

W. H. Auden's "Spain 1937," written for an express political cause, medical relief to loyalists in the Spanish civil war, in the throes of its composition and decomposition offers some insight into Auden's growing perplexities in response to the use of violence and into his subsequent renunciation of any poetry rallying or not rallying for war. Using "yesterday," "today," and "tomorrow" as the three legs of a tripod on which to seat his arguments, Auden's poem first declares "Yesterday all the past." In hammering chains of anaphora, all the past yesterdays are made to yield to this repeating conclusion: "but today the struggle." And in the dimensions of that struggle, Auden's poet "whispers" a request for vision; his investigator peers "through his instruments / At the inhuman provinces" and inquires sputteringly for the lives of

his friends. In a fierce round-up of the weak and complicit bound to these duties, Auden then submits his ironized cry invoking the struggle:

> And the nations combine each cry, invoking the life
> That shapes the individual belly and orders
> The private nocturnal terror:
> "Did you not found the city state of the sponge,
>
> "Raise the vast military empires of the shark
> And the tiger, establish this robin's plucky canton?
> Intervene. O descend as a dove or
> A furious papa or a mild engineer, but descend."

And of course the response to this equivocal injunction is a further equivocation:

> And the life, if it answers at all, replies from the heart
> And the eyes and the lungs, from the shops and squares of the city:
> "O no, I am not the mover;
> Not today; not to you. To you, I'm the
>
> "Yes-man, the bar companion, the easily duped;
> I am whatever you do. I am your vow to be
> Good, your humorous story.
> I am your business voice. I am your marriage.
>
> "What's your proposal? To build the just city? I will.
> I agree. Or is it the suicide pact, the romantic
> Death? Very well, I accept, for
> I am your choice, your decision. Yes, I am Spain"

And from that poisoned docility, the entity Spain, if not the entity Auden, becomes "precise and alive" in its struggle towards the just city of Tomorrow:

> The beautiful roar of the chorus under the dome;
> Tomorrow the exchanging of tips on the breeding of terriers,
> The eager election of chairmen
> By the sudden forest of hands. But today the struggle.

And finally in that struggle:

> Today the deliberate increase in the chances of death,
> The conscious acceptance of guilt in the necessary murder;
> Today the expending of powers
> On the flat ephemeral pamphlet and the boring meeting.
>   (*Spain*, 7–12)

George Orwell exploded against "The conscious acceptance of guilt in the necessary murder," although he initially misquoted the line, dropping the word "conscious"; for him, the phrase, rightly or wrongly quoted, negatively represented all of Auden's ambivalent commitment to a gritty activism. Of course Orwell's assessment of the grim politics of antifascist resistance was no less steeped in irony and repugnance than Auden's; his judgment of Auden, however, depended not only on a sharp-fanged and virtually open personal attack on Auden's homosexuality, but on a serious misreading of his poem as well.

Orwell's first line of attack was on Auden's masculinity. In the *Adelphi* (December 1938) he wrote:

> Our civilisation produces in increasing numbers two types, the gangster and the pansy. They never meet, but each is necessary to the other. Somebody in eastern Europe "liquidates" a Trotskyist; somebody in Bloomsbury writes a justification of it. And it is, of course, precisely because of the utter softness and security of life in England that the yearning for bloodshed—bloodshed in the far distance—is so common among our intelligentsia. Mr. Auden can write about "the acceptance of guilt for the necessary murder" perhaps because he has never committed a murder, perhaps never had one of his friends murdered, perhaps never seen a murdered corpse. The presence of this utterly irresponsible intelligentsia, who "took up" Roman Catholicism ten years ago, "take up" communism today and will take up the English variant of fascism a few years hence, is a special feature of the English situation. ("Political Reflections," 244)

And yet as James Fenton points out, there is an important difference in the killing that Orwell and Auden each behold: Orwell understands Auden to be speaking of political assassination; Auden, though, is really looking at the acceptance of death in war. While inveighing against Auden's squeamishness in beholding dead bodies, Orwell quite unfairly portrays the killing Auden names as a kind of coy, lustful peekaboo at the dreaded. He ignores the possibility that Auden's equivocal consciousness is an acceptance of the unpopular assertion that killing in war itself is murder.

Killing in war is just killing; Orwell, who toted guns for the loyalist cause, is perhaps mistaking the nerve Auden has touched in him for another sensitivity, that towards the value of a stoic witnessing of combat: Auden has surprised in Orwell the quick of his own uneasy acceptance of wartime killing. Orwell now masks this uneasiness by brushing aside Auden's judgment of war as lack of experience. An unarticulated argument remains in Orwell's fulminations: only those initiated in actual combat may know or speak of its mysteries; only he who has faced combat is capable of measuring its realities. James Campbell's phrase, "combat gnosticism," describes "a construction that gives us war experience as a kind of gnosis, a secret knowledge which only an initiated elite knows." Campbell indicates how this knowledge tacitly excludes women: "It is not the label of 'soldier' that is privileged so much as the label of 'warrior.'" And he concludes:

combat is a liminal experience that sets the veteran irrevocably apart from those who have not crossed the ritual threshold of war. It can, indeed has, been seen as the ultimate rite of passage: a definitive coming to manhood for the industrial age, in which boys become men by confronting mechanical horror and discovering their essential masculinity, perhaps even their essential humanity, in a realm from which feminine presence is banished. (Campbell, 204)

The crux of these references in Orwell seems to me to come together not only in Orwell's acceptance of the primitive and essentialist doctrine that war is the test of manliness, but in the further assumption that Auden's resistance to war comes from a derogated and passive unmanliness. As Campbell sees "combat gnosticism," not only does it fall into the further error of validating a narrow aesthetic of realism, but it creates "an ethical criterion of a humanism of passivity" (203). The nature of Orwell's reactions to Auden on war short-circuits his ability to examine whether true manliness consists of exposure to battle, and, finally, stops him from even asking the truly sticky questions that Auden puts to himself about whether killing may be battle's justifiable outcome.

Long after the war, in a 1963 letter to Monroe K. Spears about this poem, Auden wrote to set the record straight:

I was *not* excusing totalitarian crimes but only trying to say what, surely, every decent person thinks if he finds himself unable to adopt the absolute pacifist position. (1) To kill another human being is always murder and should never be called anything else. (2) In a war, the members of two rival groups try to murder their opponents. (3) *If* there is such a thing as a just war, then murder can be necessary for the sake of justice. (Quoted in Davenport-Hines, 167)

In James Fenton's summary "the fact remains that Auden was emphasizing, rather than overlooking, the nastiness of war, rather than condoning political liquidations" (Fenton, 222).

Not only was Auden emphasizing the "nastiness" of war, but he saw no reason to allow himself any comfort through his own peculiar brand of pacifism, which seems to have amounted to a personal distaste for violence, in his eyes and Orwell's much akin to what they both characterized as "squeamishness." He tried to summarize his positions in *The Prolific and the Devourer*, a manuscript eventually abandoned and only retrieved in posthumous publication. In the tortured question and answer session that ends this book, with an unnamed interlocutor that allows Auden to interrogate Auden, he writes:

Certainly my position forbids me to act as a combatant in any war. But if by pacifism you mean simply the refusal to bear arms, I have very little use for it. Nothing costs one less to do, for no one wants to do it. . . . To think that it is enough to refuse to be a soldier and that one can behave as one chooses as a private citizen, is to be quite willing to cause a war but only unwilling to suffer the consequences. (87)

And reluctantly, to his interlocutor: "You know that I loathe violence and shall make a very bad revolutionary, but I recognise that this is a weakness and I don't try to justify it" (91).

In these years, Auden holds that "poetry is not a substitute for life." And thereby renounces the Romantic or Shelleyan premise that "Poets are the unacknowledged legislators of the world." In fact, his essay "Writing," openly mocks Shelley: "'The unacknowledged legislators of the world' describes the secret police, not the poets" (*Dyer's Hand*, 27). And with this, the ascendancy of Blake's visionary "shaping Imagination" also goes down the drain. What happens on the page remains in the world of the page, and the flesh holding the pen or tapping a keyboard needs additionally to act—but how? Elsewhere in the text, back one way and on again over another, there is an agonized awareness of the eventual, incremental efficacy of private act, but in their haphazard massing, like the irregular fault lines of a log jam, such acts define and check the progress of history. Word or act, though, it's all just another stick: yet when the romantic premise, with its faith in the primacy of the word, is undercut, the idea of poetry as anything but one more incidental witness leaves a major poet with very little support for his art. It is a position of extreme humility, offering little but frustrating irrelevance.

For W. H. Auden, as well as for Randall Jarrell, the word "murder" was not inappropriate for the moral default position that they both clearly felt war to be; yet both of the poets who reached for this word were noncombatants. As a soldier, Jarrell remained stateside; as a journalist, Auden had been briefly under fire in trains passing through disputed territory in the Sino-Japanese War. Yet Orwell's description of Auden's blood innocence does not quite hold up. In Auden's and Isherwood's jointly produced *Journey to a War*, even for two writers playing at being war correspondents and camping on the role, war impinged: armed planes flew over their heads; bombs dropped; guns fired. In a coolness of recording akin to Orwell's own, a paragraph from *Journey to a War* reads:

> Meanwhile there was time for a stroll around the village. It was a glorious, cool spring morning. On a waste plot of land beyond the houses a dog was gnawing what was, only too obviously, a human arm. A spy, they told us, had been buried there after execution a day or two ago; the dog had dug the corpse half out of the earth. It was rather a pretty dog with a fine, bushy tail. I remember how we had patted it when it came begging for scraps of our supper the evening before. (Auden and Isherwood, 112)

Auden *had* witnessed what he felt to be murder, and he maintained a "monumental calm" under fire unnerving to Isherwood. While Isherwood lay wakeful on a train through a Chinese countryside experiencing threats of imminent bombardment, Auden in the opposite bed "slept deeply, with the long, calm snores of the truly strong" (75). In response to possible Japanese shelling, Auden's coping tactic was simple denial, probably backed by a sense of his own personal irrelevance at the axis of violent experience. While Isherwood opened their windows to prevent being assaulted by breaking glass, Auden withdrew emotionally and physically. When they finally emerged safely from the train, Isherwood reports: "'You see,' said Auden. "I told you so. . . . I knew they wouldn't. . . . Nothing of the sort ever happens to *me*'" (128).

As spectators in Hankow, Isherwood and Auden had lain on the lawn of the British consulate to get a good glimpse of the night sky, in which Japanese fighters were closing in for a raid. After the all-clear sounded, they hired a taxi, and scrambled up a bank to tour the results of the bombing on a derelict arsenal, in which five civilian victims had apparently been killed. Auden's handwritten notes record:

> In a shed nearby, lay some of the victims, mostly old men and women—one still breathing spasmodically, waiting for the coffins to arrive. Blood and guts oozed out from under the sack coverings, like the stuffing of an old sofa. They looked very small, very poor, and very dead. (Auden manuscripts, British Library, Add 61838)

Auden's tone is not merely dispassionate; it is heartless. His own need for distance from these frightening injuries forbids him to see anything human under the sack coverings. At a later point in their travels, however, the text comments on Auden and Isherwood's appearance in an active war zone:

> We waited. At last the commander himself appeared. Although very polite he couldn't conceal his dismay at our presence. We were tiresomely notorious foreigners, who might add to his responsibilities by getting killed. Our proper place was on a platform in London—not here, amongst exhausted and overworked officers and officials. We might have to leave, he warned us, in the middle of the night. The evacuation of the civilian population had started already. Touched, and rather ashamed of myself, I thought of those men and women who had wasted their last precious hours of safety, waiting to welcome us with their banner in the rain. (Auden and Isherwood, 222)

From the convention of the pronouns in the published text, it is Isherwood who feels this shame, but both writers collaborated in assembling these reflections on the bumble of their witness.

For other poets whose exposure to fire would build to something more prolonged and intense, the word "murder" will be more hesitantly applied, especially for those accepting as part of their consciousness that a proper masculinity requires an assent to killing in war. For these generations, the assent to killing seems unbreakably soldered to manhood. In Auden's case, it is hard to dissociate his feelings about homosexuality from the tangle of his feelings about pacifism and the application of military force. To the extent that he himself could not quite accept his queer status as a part of normal or admirable sexual behavior, perhaps sleeping with women and being a soldier, like skill at games, were all life acts that he renounced in basic ambivalence about his own kind of maleness. In answer to the row that Orwell had raised about "Spain 1937," Auden altered the offending line to read: "The conscious acceptance of guilt in the fact of murder;" this change removes all the original and complicitous sting of the line. The guilt in the alteration is now pretty randomly spread.

Waspishly, and quite unfairly, in 1941 the *New Statesman* commented on Auden's remove to the United States by claiming that Henry James and W. H. Auden had one thing in common: "they both changed nationality for the same reason—the neutrality of the United States" (quoted in Davenport-Hines, 207). George Orwell in "Inside the Whale," never impugns Auden's courage so directly, but describes Auden's change of residence as a change of heart in which letting go of pacifism moved into the taking on of Christianity. For Orwell, Auden's real error appears not only to be political, politics, but rather, a wrongheaded attitude about religion. Orwell's redefinition in the later essay of what bothered him in Auden's poetry actually left very little substantive disagreement with Auden's newer positions of disengagement; Orwell merely reserved the right to dismiss poetry on account of its inferior ability to speak truth compared with the novel. But as Auden did, Orwell lauded that art which hangs on to subjectivity over didactic purpose. Sucked inside the whale, Jonah, in Orwell's eyes, has the duty merely to feel and describe, and to do what he can to stay away from pronouncement. After all, the hero of "Inside the Whale" is an apolitical Henry Miller. Orwell thinks it's fine to stay away from politics:

> If I had been a soldier fighting in the Great War, I would sooner have got hold of "Prufrock" than *The First Hundred Thousand* or Horatio Bottomley's *Letters to the Boys in the Trenches*. I should have felt, like Mr. Forster, that by simply standing aloof and keeping touch with pre-war emotions, Eliot was carrying on the human heritage. What a relief it would have been at such a time, to read about the hesitations of a middle-aged highbrow with a bald spot! So different from bayonet drill! After the bombs and the food queues and the recruiting posters, a human voice! What a relief! ("Inside the Whale," 110)

It is not Auden's bystanding with which Orwell picks his quarrel, but his generation's particular flirtation with communism. In explaining why the young writers of the 1930s flocked to communism, Orwell says:

FIGURE 4. W. H. Auden and Christopher Isherwood at the Bryanston School, 1937. Berg Collection, New York Public Library.

It was simply something to believe in. Here was a church, an army, an orthodoxy, a discipline. Here was a Fatherland and—at any rate since 1935 or thereabouts—a Fuehrer. All the loyalties and superstitions that the intellect had seemingly banished could come rushing back under the thinnest of disguises. Patriotism, religion, empire, military glory—all in one word, Russia. Father, king, leader, hero, saviour—all, in one word, Stalin. God—Stalin. The devil—Hitler. Heaven—Moscow. Hell—Berlin. All the gaps were filled up. So, after all, the "Communism" of the English intellectual is something explicable enough. It is the patriotism of the deracinated. ("Inside the Whale," 110)

Even Orwell comes back to the necessity of English roots.

But Auden and especially Isherwood, in his memoirs of the time, touch on the attractions that a disguised lean toward fascism held for them within the leftist orthodoxies that both began to abandon on emigrating to America. Of this early Auden, collaborating with him on *The Ascent of F6*, Christopher Isherwood wrote:

As a child, he enjoyed a high Anglican upbringing, coupled with a sound musical education. The Anglicanism has evaporated, leaving only the height: he is still much preoccupied with ritual, in all its forms. When we collaborate, I have to keep a sharp eye on him—or down flop the characters on their knees (see F6 passim): another constant danger is that of choral interruptions by angel-voices. (Isherwood, "Some Notes," 74)

Signing off on World War II from the distance of uninvaded America, Auden left unsolved the dilemma of how to bring socialist and antifascist practice into poetry, the writing of which remained another and stiller kind of act. His retreat into what looked like safety robbed him, in his own and others' eyes, of the ability to write with any urgency about war's enmeshing violence, and he left that task to those who bombed and shot or those who were bombed and shot at.

Again and again, poets and critics return to Auden's wartime emigration to America as a factor in the evaluation of his art, measuring what left his poetry when Auden extricated himself from what he then regarded as the parochialism of the English and from that steeping in the political which Louis MacNeice declared a necessary consequence of swinging back "to the Greek preference for information over statement" (21). But as poets in the 1930s opted for information, or for what would in later decades in America roll trendily into view as "relevance," they were clearly trying to check what they perceived as the detachments and isolations of pure formalism. This left the vatic high ground to previous generations, and more than anything else, as poets trundled downhill towards an ethical engagement with public issues, they were exposed to their own ineffectualities of class and kind. It was a positioning in my memory brutally parodied by Ernest Hemingway in "The Earnest Liberal's Lament":

I know monks masturbate at night,
That pet cats screw,
That some girls bite
And yet
What can I do
To set things right?
(Hemingway, *Collected Poems*, 12)

What followed led to self-laceration. Words wrung from a sense of unease about what remained alive and well in Auden's poetry appear in the passage that Davenport-Hines quotes from Lincoln Kirstein, from Kirstein's response to Auden's Chinese sonnets:

> He can be hateful. He is the relentless adversary of the kind of weak conscience-money conspiratorial optimism which now identifies so many of us within the fringes of protest and action—where we have our precious moral safety just under the angle of our real defenders.

Auden's real courage, one might say, lies in his refusing the easy moral consolations afforded a poet who applies himself to simply recording personal truth. For Kirstein, Auden accepts a terribly high measure of personal futility, even though "The reason Auden is writing the greatest poetry of our speech is because his one subject is personal responsibility. He assumes for himself, as a man, the entire load, the whole blame" (quoted in Davenport-Hines, 176).

Surely, one of Auden's most attractive qualities lies in his avoidance of pathos. In 1942, he advised James Stern to "beware of the poignant note, which, because we are all such masters of self-pity, is the easiest of all to strike" (Auden, Letters to the Sterns).

In taking leave of his birth country, however, Auden exiled himself from any active engagement with "the entire load, the whole blame." In "September 1, 1939," what does it mean, to "sit in one of the dives / on Fifty-Second Street" and say as a response to the outbreak of a shooting war in Europe,

> There is no such thing as the State
> And no one exists alone;
> Hunger allows no choice
> To the citizen or the police;
> We must love one another or die.
>
> Defenceless under the night
> Our world in stupor lies;
> Yet, dotted everywhere,
> Ironic points of light
> Flash out wherever the Just
> Exchange their messages:
> May I, composed like them
> Of Eros and of dust,

Beleaguered by the same
Negation and despair,
Show an affirming flame.

(*English Auden*, 245–47)

What relation is this flame to "the crowned knot of fire" where "the fire and the rose are one"? In T. S. Eliot's "Little Gidding," published in 1942, we can see how both poets trod pavements in a dead patrol with their own literary ghosts, but it was the American who declared: "Here, the intersection of the timeless moment / Is England and nowhere. Never and always" (Eliot, 139). At what height in relation to the daily and local does war poetry as a genre disappear? It was Auden's appointed but uncertain task to find that lyric altitude and try to sustain it. War from that height, however, is not war, and it evades the perfectly usable medium of lyric war poetry to become instead a generalized, more remote poetry of meditation.

Auden, in "Making, Knowing, and Judging," sorts out the tensions between what I am regarding here as the loftier, higher ranking poetry of meditation, versus the lower breed of the war poem. He describes the dynamics of these tensions as existing between two enduring poetic affinities, the *romantic* and the *classical*. These terms, he decides are stand-ins for "the Aristocratic and the Democratic, which have always existed and to one of which every writer belongs, though he may switch his party allegiance, or, on some specific issue, refuse to obey his Party Whip." The oppositions he spells out are interesting:

The Aristocratic Principle as regards subject matter:
No subject matter shall be treated by poets which poetry cannot digest. It defends poetry against didacticism and journalism.

The Democratic Principle as regards subject matter:
No subject matter shall be excluded by poets which poetry is capable of digesting. It defends poetry against limited or stale conceptions of what is "poetic."

The Aristocratic Principle as regards treatment:
No irrelevant aspects of a given subject shall be expressed in a poem which treats it. It defends poetry against barbaric vagueness.

The Democratic Principle as regards treatment:

No relevant aspect of a given subject shall remain unexpressed in a poem which treats it. It defends poetry against decadent triviality. (Auden, *Dyer's Hand*, 21)

This program fits all too handily what we incline to mark as American or English, over the years, or even modern versus traditional. And war poetry as others came to practice it falls within the "Democratic Principle" in its defense of fresh against stale, in its embrace of the apparently journalistic and didactic, and in its acceptance of what looks to be barbarically vague in its defiance of the decadently trivial.

But whatever the acuity of his various diagnoses, Auden's own situation and his responses to it remained a great, stiffening scab over broken tissue, emblematic of the blocked or euphemistically abstract speech that Keith Douglas rejected as the defining product of his contemporaries. Whether one left like Auden or stayed in England like MacNeice or Day Lewis made little difference. Committed to a war that seemed inevitable, but resisting facile optimism, World War II brought poets like Stephen Spender, H. D., and Edith Sitwell a varied species of retreats to religious symbol and endorsements of passive suffering on the cross of the air raid. Younger poets like Keith Douglas or Alun Lewis or Roy Fuller, taking their chances on living and dying, underwrote the traditional testing of manhood by plunging into soldiering. They looked to enlarge their poetry through more conscious witness, even if that witness were only to replicate the features of what the World War I poet had already so horrifically spelled out to them, in the novel largesse of a stubborn lyricism they felt no certain hope to match.

Some thirteen years before Auden died, Philip Larkin dissed him in "What's Become of Wystan?" Larkin sums up Auden's peculiar subject as "the gathering dread of the next war that was half-projected guilt about the last" (Larkin, *Required Writing*, 124); "this dominant and ubiquitous unease" lies at the center of Auden's verse. We come upon a familiar and peculiarly English plangency when we note again that for Larkin and for Scannell, in their uppish mode, good poetry only emerges from tradition and roots. When Auden leaves England, according to Larkin:

At one stroke he lost his key subject and emotion—Europe and the fear of war—and abandoned his audience together with their common dialect and concerns. (*Required Writing*, 125)

In Larkin's assessment, transferred to America, Auden's English "dialect" would disconnect from any immediate audience, leaving Auden to perform Auden in a void. He concludes:

> My guess is that the peculiar insecurity of pre-war England sharpened his talent in a way that nothing else has, or that once "the next war" really arrived everything since has seemed to him an anticlimax. (*Required Writing*, 128)

The argument about Auden's apprehensions projects Larkin's own style of connecting fear and poetry. Larkin's more trenchant observation, however, surely lies in his assumptions about the tie between a poet and his national audience, about healthy and damaging distances, and about the elasticity and adaptability of language, an oddly and unpredictably pliable clay.

Auden himself tied together nationalism and insularity, seeing both as restraints on the imagination, and, for him, being in America meant jettisoning the load of his insular roots. In January 1940, Auden wrote to Mrs. E. R. Dodds (Bucknell and Jenkins, 111) that he found America "a terrifying place," but that in it he could usefully try "to live deliberately without roots." Two months later, he wrote to Mrs. Dodds again, and, framing an argument that in the letter took a question-and-answer format, he asked himself, "Do you care what happens to England?" And he answered:

> Qua England, not in the least. To me England is bits of the country like the Pennine Moors and my English friends. If they were all safely out of the country, I should feel about the English as I feel about the Spanish or the Chinese or the Germans. It matters what happens to them as it matters what happens to all members of the human race, but my concern is as a fellow human being not as a fellow countryman. (Bucknell and Jenkins, 113)

This soaring degree of detachment, or the desire for it, surely had negative consequences for Auden's poetry, perhaps by effectively removing the barb of self-interest that stings one into passion over the politics of one's age.

Whether one agrees with Larkin's dismissal of W. H. Auden's poetry after his departure for the New World, it is clear that Auden did turn his back on any further engagement in poetry with invasion or occupation. Missing a core of ideology and belief in the local subject that would hold his interest, Auden in his war poems did not advance the form, even in his most sustained engagement with the political. Thus in ways inscrutably historical,

FIGURE 5. W. H. Auden and James Stern in occupied Germany, 1945. Auden served as a civilian research chief in the Morale Division of the U.S. Strategic Bombing Survey from April to August 1945. Berg Collection, New York Public Library.

circumstantial, and biographical, World War II poetry in England, a poetry so firmly stamped by Auden in the prewar decade, dropped into a kind of aesthetic limbo.

Where the War Poets Were

For a poet like Roy Fuller, soldiers lacked the capacity for prophetic insight, being merely followers, and war poetry was an inferior and circumscribed genre. His "Follower's Song" derides the heroic in war:

Oh to be mad with marching and May,
To be bold, to be brutish,
To dream in the night and by day
To delight in duties.

And oh for the pointing finger to cube
To a gun and the feeling
Inside to come out of the tube
And kill with its healing;

The earth to be gone with its grave and the sky
With its season: forever
To shake in God's voice and to lie
Next his iron and leather.
     (Fuller, 30)

An ironic god, a Mars of "iron and leather," rules the soldier's world, a god to be evaded. Even if one exercised choice by dodging the military hierarchy of officers and men, of followers and leaders, one would still be trapped within a morally diminished and brutal place, where "healing" is merely death. For Roy Fuller, soldiers who follow the virtue of obedience to duties are bound in other ways, so that war poetry as a genre must emanate from some inferior place broadly lacking even imaginative choice; this is quite clear in "War Poet." After a plaintive call-up of poets' fates, where sad fatality as a subject divorced from war receives adequate treatment at Donne and Shakespeare's hands, what the war poet of the title does with death in war is inevitably lesser:

Donne, alive in his shroud,
Shakespeare, in the coil of a cloud,
Saw death very well as he
Came crab-wise, dark and massy.
I envy not only their talents
And fertile lack of balance
But the appearance of choice
In their sad and fatal voice.

        (Fuller, 38)

Most of us who grew up to memorize this poem, reprinted in scores of anthologies, especially loved the part about "fertile lack of balance"—but we tended to forget the poem's title, "War Poet," and the larger message of its speaker's identity as one of a limited breed.

In the spreading anxiety over fascism and imperial domination that, with the help of the Auden set, had saturated and politicized poetry from the 1930s on, anyone could fairly ask if the antiwar fervency of the Great War had become a quaint or misdirected model for the next generation. Where did the high modernist revolutions of T. S. Eliot fit the tone and diction of the war poem? Were they manageable for a subgenre of the lyric linked to public modes of affirmation, and by tradition only intermittently attached to the practice of realism over the demands of glory? In 1941, Julian Symons tried to retrieve war poetry from the exclusive grip of the soldier-poet. In the introduction to his *Anthology of War Poetry*, he announced that looking for "war poets" was a game for the "silly season": "War poetry is not a specialized department of poetry; it is . . . quite simply the poetry, comic or tragic, cynical or heroic, joyful, embittered or disillusioned, of people affected by the reality of war" (Symons, vii).

Yet no one could quite leave it at that. The question of where one stood in a war continues to affect one's reading of the act of witness. If, in Keith Douglas's words, the "England can take it" school of poetry lacked heft or resonance, the only voice left for him and many others appeared to belong to the combat soldier, even if little remained for the soldier-poets of World War II to do but reiterate, or amplify, the witness given in 1914–18.

Another way to gauge the real strength and authority of World War II poetry is to look at its tentative approach to another register of war's participants. Dylan Thomas's "Refusal to Mourn the Death, by Fire, of a Child in London" and Randall Jarrell's "The Truth" and "Protocols" introduced children as prominent victims of war in ways that have not left our consciousness since. Written for and by everybody affected, World War II poetry contends with traditional expectations of war poetry—that it be written by men in general and soldiers in particular. Both the resurgence of articulate citizen sufferers and an enlargement of the idea of who suffers in war definitively altered ideas of what either reader or writer should expect, even as the cultural need to cast resistance to war in myths of dynamic masculinity still lends most weight to the narratives of soldiers who prosecute war.

But the shifting character of military involvement complicates this expansion of the subjects of war. When the historian and memoirist Charles Carrington, a soldier in both World War I and II, named the psychological barriers between combatant and noncombatant in World War I, he described how that condition came into view, noting dryly: "Nothing is stranger in the history of the First World War than the sudden outburst of soldiers' autobiographies which reached its climax in 1929 and 1930. Until then a dumb protest, now a phase of exhibitionism." But in World War II, "there was no distinction between combatant and non-combatant":

> Within ten minutes of the Declaration of War the air-raid sirens were telling the people of London that they were in the fighting line. No one supposed that it was the duty of every able-bodied man to fight in France while the women and the weaklings kept the home fires burning. For the first half of the war the main strength of the Army was at home in the comparative comfort of training camps and enjoying periodical week-end leave. Often the soldier going home from his safe country quarters found his wife, booted and helmeted, dealing with air-raid incidents under fire. (Carrington, 14)

These changing conditions of war making only intensified the degrees of difference between the situations faced by the poets of World War I and II.

When the civilian poets of the 1940s donned uniforms, many had been shoehorned into their conflict by way of the leftist political allegiances of the 1930s. With the full memory of what Wilfred Owen, Siegfried Sassoon, Isaac Rosenberg, and Robert Graves had said about the last war, Roy Fuller, Alun Lewis, and the like could see that the pattern of ruptured innocence followed by dawning horror could not be theirs. Unlike the soldier-poets of the previous war, reaction and belatedness were their portion.

The character of the World War I victim in its most memorable poetry had been the Fated Boy, the young man cut down in his prime like Owen or

Rosenberg or even Rupert Brooke, Julian Grenfell, or Alan Seeger. But as Carrington indicates, the World War II poet-conscript, unlike most of his World War I counterparts, spent fewer hours on actual battlefields, was usually a little older and already married, and after the war generally went on to write about other things, slipping from any claim to the mantle of the war poet. Besides, there had already been the pattern of a grand mobilization followed by a great slaughter in 1914–18. The poet of 1939–45 had been led past the trench warfare of his fathers and uncles, past the rearmed Ruhr District, past service in the Spanish civil war, past the Sino-Japanese War, the dismemberment of Czechoslovakia, Anschluss in Austria, and by degrees of violence on into the War to Preserve Democracy. The poets in uniform who survived beyond their war would write of aftermath and postnuclearity, as they struggled to understand the relentless continuity of military violence, cutting across and belying as it did any formal dates certifying outbreak and cessation of hostilities.

Roy Fuller's "During a Bombardment by V-Weapons" sounds as if it deals with the world at war; instead, it writes hopelessly about an interim period in which war will slide easily into the littleness of the ongoing domestic war. Fuller's poem matches the intensity of observation in T. S. Eliot's magnifications of domestic decay in "East Coker":

> Houses live and die: there is a time for building
> And a time for living and for generation
> And a time for the wind to break the loosened pane
> And to shake the wainscot where the field mouse trots
> And to shake the tattered arras woven with a silent motto.
>   (Eliot, 123)

But Fuller cannot fold everything into a majestic echoing of the poet of Ecclesiastes, where decay fits within the comfortably revolving cycles of a Christian history. His poem narrows its eyes to read:

> The little noises of the house:
> Drippings between the slates and ceiling;
> From the electric fire's cooling,
> Tickings; the dry feet of a mouse:
>
> These at the ending of a war
> Have power to alarm me more

Than the ridiculous detonations
Outside the gently coughing curtains.

And, love, I see your pallor bears
A far more pointed threat than steel.
Now all the permanent and real
Furies are settling in upstairs.

> (Fuller, 99)

All the hostilities that poetry can focus on blur from external into internal threat.

When the American Howard Nemerov wrote "Redeployment" in 1947, he wrote a poem well within stylistic earshot of Fuller and the English war poets, and in conformity with much later poetry that will slide into consciousness of the transition not from war to peace, but from hot to cold war. "Redeployment," with its ambiguously sinister title, begins:

They say the war is over. But water still
Comes bloody from the taps, and my pet cat
in his disorder vomits worms which crawl
Swiftly away. Maybe they leave the house.
These worms are white, and flecked with the cat's blood.

The poem ends:

The end of the war. I took it quietly
Enough. I tried to wash the dirt out of
My hair and from under my fingernails,
I dressed in clean white clothes and went to bed.
I heard the dust falling between the walls.

> (Nemerov, 16)

This end-of-the-war poem with its spill of uninterruptable civil menace nonetheless meets the flat, flayed sensibility of W. H. Auden's sonnet sequence *In Time of War*—which constituted his most open contribution to the book he wrote with Isherwood, *Journey to a War*—in which the time of war is really all time, within *l'univers concentrationnaire*.

Auden's sonnet sequence was completed in 1938 but written before British engagement in World War II, when Auden, tracking war elsewhere on the planet, had returned from China. In it, war bears the prosaic features of an urban bureaucracy, even as it melds with peasant simplicities of food:

> Here war is simple like a monument:
> A telephone is speaking like a man;
> Flags on a map assert that troops were sent;
> A boy brings milk in bowls.
>
> (Auden and Isherwood, *Journey*, 274)

In 1938, back home from touring elusive foreign wars nevertheless coming closer and closer, Auden put a cooler, more abrupt spin on the unknown soldier treated at such passionate, reverent length after 1914–18. He adds to this poem his signature feature of inclusive detail, the tone that mixes war with peacetime bureaucracy:

> He will not be introduced

> When this campaign is tidied into books:
> No vital knowledge perished in his skull;
> His jokes were stale; like wartime, he was dull;
> His name is lost forever like his looks.
>
> (*Journey*, 276)

Even before the global devastation of 1939–45 was underway, the wide scan of Auden's landscape took it in, and presciently placed in a precisely calibrated emotional miniature all the tiny figures of war woe. Sonnet XIX supplied the sweeping resignation and the chilly, authoritative understatement, to which younger English and American poets, like Fuller and Douglas, Jarrell and Nemerov, and, later, Auden himself, would try to restore an enlarging warmth and texture.

I quote the sonnet in its entirety:

> But in the evening the oppression lifted;
> The peaks came into focus; it had rained;
> Across the lawns and cultured flowers drifted
> The conversation of the highly trained.

> The gardeners watched them pass and priced their shoes;
> A chauffeur waited, reading in the drive,

For them to finish their exchange of views;
It seemed a picture of the private life.

Far off, no matter what good they intended,
The armies waited for a verbal error
With all the instruments for causing pain:
And on the issue of their charm depended
A land laid waste, with all its young men slain,
The women weeping, and the towns in terror.
    (*Journey*, 277)

Auden left room for *le trahison des clercs*, betrayals by "the conversation of the highly trained." He left room, even if he could not entirely fill it, for a growing comprehension of an internalized war guilt within a universal and boundless bureaucracy, whose edges blended both civil and military.

In "The Unknown Citizen" Auden celebrated in Orwellian style the passivity and automatism of the citizen-soldier as *l'homme moyen sensuel*. Under the marble monument erected by the state, this Unknown Citizen lies:

Except for the War till the day he retired
He worked in a factory and never got fired.

The poem concludes:

When there was peace, he was for peace; when there was war, he went.

George Orwell, or the Charlie Chaplin of *Modern Times*, recognized this man. But the later poems welling up out of these anxieties wanted to move their picture beyond simplistic declarations in favor of the soldier-victim to question more ruthlessly what the complicity of both soldiers and civilians aided and what each understood within their predicaments.

Yet even if the scenario of donkey generals leading hapless innocents to war had been replaced by one in which goose-stepping dictators and their jackbooted followers imposed conquest on compliant or passive or helpless populations, what place was there for any sort of ideology in a poem with formal and lyrical good manners? The hoist and soar, the unquenchable intensity of diction of even the most greatly despairing of Owen's poems were impossible for the 1940s generation of civilians in uniform. The high, tender pity for men, the ardent love of men for men that marked the World War I lyric was deflected even before World War II officially opened by Auden's and others' astringencies. Haplessly, even, the later poets were committed to the narrowing fortunes of Auden's Democratic Principle. Even as we might regret the disappearance of those feelings, however, the new astringency could be understood as a defense against the turgid and declamatory rhetoric, or the stale of the Aristocratic Principle, to which the poets of the period, sunk in the inevitability of a resumption of old hostilities, were otherwise led.

Innocence, or the ecstasy that can accompany it and intensify the music of the lyric of sacrifice, was not tenable. A demoralizing guilt existed for all reflective inhabitants of the "low, dishonest decade" preceding the ultimate conflagrations. In "Where are the War Poets?" C. Day Lewis trumpeted against a "They," against the oligarchic forces who were now belaboring the appalled and grudging intelligentsia to strike up a new "immortal verse" for war:

> They who in panic or mere greed
> Enslaved religion, markers, laws,
> Borrow our language now and bid
> Us to speak up in freedom's cause.
>
> It is the logic of our times,
> No subject for immortal verse,
> That we who lived by honest dreams
> Defend the bad against the worse.
>   (C. Day Lewis, 228)

There cannot be a war poetry in a language subject to such homegrown abuses of meaning, and the "we" of this disheartened poem, still living by their "honest dreams," can only "Defend the bad against the worse." In the disgruntled climate that hung over England and drifted on in waves of co-optation, lingering in the 1930s and on into the 1940s, both war protest and war support had soured, their energies contravened.

A terrifying individual helplessness and a numbing deluge of ideological fatigue seeped out of the 1940s. Trying to talk up the best of the World War II generation, Ronald Blythe (or his publisher), on the back cover of his 1966 anthology, *Components of the Scene*, ran this advertising copy:

> They refused to preach—as the writers of the thirties had done; they refused to become propagandists—as the writers of 1914 had been; and

they never became—as the writers of 1918 became—disenchanted and despairing.

The gentleman protests too much. That "never became" in fact signals the ongoing distress of a pervasive disenchantment and despair. Given the helplessness of being saddled with what was merely a defense of the bad against an inundating worse, lyric poetry had to mount a victory for the imaginative life over the stale crush of wartime reality. A disconsolate and hardly heroic Roy Fuller could write of "What Is Terrible":

> The year, the month, the day, the minute, at war
> Is terrible and my participation
> And that of all the world is terrible.
> My living now must bear the laceration
> Of the herd and always will. What's done
>
> To me is done to many. I can see
> No ghosts, but only the fearful actual
> Lives of my comrades.
>> (Fuller, 80)

In "The Soldier," a tormented Alun Lewis would "Feel the dark cancer in my vitals / Of impotent impatience grope its way," and then conclude:

> But leisurely my fellow soldiers stroll among the trees.
> The cheapest dance-song utters all they feel.
>> (Alun Lewis, 70)

Having found the serviceable limit to the 1914–18 model of the war poem, with its exalted lyric anger, no compelling form, rooted in the modernist disjunctions of the post–World War I era or ripened in the politics of the 1930s, brought containment or definition to those enduring the global, industrialized world war of 1939–45. Echoing Keith Douglas's sense of belatedness and helpless persevering, C. Day Lewis wrote sourly in "Will it be so again?":

> Will it be so again—
> The jungle code and the hypocritic gesture?
> A poppy wreath for the slain

And a cut-throat world for the living? that stale imposture
Played on us once again?
      (C. Day Lewis, 234)

The overall weariness and deadened energy of this position show themselves in the rather mechanical rhyme, the undistinguished diction of Lewis' poem.

For many not suffering bombardment or the goad of combat, war settled into a depressing nullification, a grinding down into the crude generalizing emotion despised by Virginia Woolf in her journals and wartime writing. The dullness also seems to have induced a formal timidity, a revulsion and pulling away from experimentation to acknowledge the impotence of purely aesthetic concern. Fighting the squeeze of cultural solidarity and the descent into the conformities of "war effort," the best bet for the majority of English poets in the 1940s was to be faithful to familiar linguistic moves, to stick to the central clearinghouse of word and gesture understood to be the tradition through which a beleaguered but civilized "we" must always pass. This approach tightened into other restraints. As an English critic-reviewer in *The Spectator* in 1942 saw the business of connecting to reality,

> all good poets are essentially and inevitably of their age—but directly only if they are the most conscious aspirants for a cheap and immediate notoriety. (Quoted in Davidson, 156–57)

War poetry, thought this noncombatant, needs to deal with the present, but should not vulgarly reek of it. Before his term of active duty began, Sidney Keyes, a talented youngster killed on the second day of his first battle in 1941, had prepared a portrait of the "War Poet":

I am the man who looked for peace and found
My own eyes barbed.
I am the man who groped for words and found
An arrow in my hand.
I am the builder whose firm walls surround
A slipping land.
When I grow sick or mad
Mock me not nor chain me:
When I reach for the wind
Cast me not down:

Though my face is a burnt book
And a wasted town.

> (Keyes, 82)

Characteristically for the period and much of its less successful poetry, this Oxford twenty year old, who died of gunfire in Africa, pictured himself as an obsolescent bowman, fingering the arrow unaccountably substituted for the words he would rather have. But why an arrow? This war poet averts his face from the actual details of industrial warfare, and no second chance will be given him for revision in light of experience.

Keyes's poem stands in interesting contrast to one of the most widely published of World War II poems, Henry Reed's "Naming of Parts," a poem Reed published in 1946 that, in its precise and layered naming, gives us one of those credible moments of boredom and incapacity in which the voice of the drill instructor and the parallel thoughts of the conscript are perfectly balanced in their comic and dangerous incompatibility. It begins "Today we have naming of parts." And from there, among the neighboring gardens with flowering japonica, we move to the uses of sling and piling swivel, "which in your case you have not got." Also present are the tree branches holding "their silent, eloquent gestures, / Which in our case we have not got." The poem jumps to:

This is the safety catch, which is always released
With an easy flick of the thumb. And please do not let me
See anyone using his finger. You can do it quite easy
If you have any strength in your thumb. The blossoms
Are fragile and motionless, never letting anyone see
Any of them using their finger.

And this you can see is the bolt. The purpose of this
Is to open the breech, as you see. We can slide it
Rapidly backwards and forwards; we call this
Easing the spring. And rapidly backwards and forwards
The early bees are assaulting and fumbling the flowers:
They call it easing the spring.

> (In Hamilton, 36)

And so on. Like a perfectly framed and focused snapshot, the poem freezes its war, and sets the contours of the imperfect transformation of man into soldier in motion within the irrepressible pastoral sexuality that the drill instructor can only deflect, or jar, but cannot quell. It also fits that Henry Reed stayed only a few months in the army before switching for the duration of the war to a desk in the Foreign Office. The poem is representative of the World War II soldier poem, written from both frontline and rear echelon stations. Because in World War II there was not what the historian John Ellis ("Reflections on the 'Sharp End' of War," 15) calls "a unitary iconography," and because in comparison to World War I, so much more of the war was fought by soldiers who stayed rearward, Reed's poem as a war poem has as much truth as any earlier, doughtier effort.

Perhaps it is not so curious that resolutely archaic attitudes persisted in a postimperial England, hanging on grimly in the collapse of its cultural and economic ascendencies after 1945. Increasingly, in the latter half of the twentieth century, an asymmetrical development occurred in the practice of poetry in English. As England diminished as both a political and cultural power, her lyric poets' sense of possibility shrank, their fists clenching on traditionalism, just as American poets were demobilized into a rising nation-state.

In the decades after World War II especially, American poems began to flower enterprisingly in what Vernon Scannell dismissed as "free forms, verbal gesticulation and the exclusive use of the idioms and rhythms of demotic speech" (Scannell, 228). After 1945, poets increasingly came to argue for these instruments as a true expansion of literary possibility; personal data, rooted in immediacy and liberated for poetic use, took off in a wider idiom and with newer rhythms, rhythms simultaneously looser but gaining in complexity as poets learned novel ways of miming and exploiting prose. While American war poets of World War II stayed in the same, largely static position as their English counterparts, poets of the Vietnam War found new moods, new urgencies, new literary devices to use; the English, however, came to at least a temporary halt in the name of their tradition, their rhymed and metred representations of reality, or, in Larkin's words, their "common dialect and concerns" (*Required Writing*, 125).

Philip Larkin, in his 1963 evaluation of Wilfred Owen, decided that Owen was to be valued beyond war poetry precisely because he transcended the weakness of the poet strapped to his inciting occasion. Larkin, too, reviewing C. Day Lewis's edition of Owen's poems, works over the definitions available for a "war" poet:

A "war" poet is not one who chooses to commemorate or celebrate a war but one who reacts against having a war thrust upon him: he is chained, that is, to a historical event, and an abnormal one at that. However well he does it, however much we agree that the war happened and ought to be written about, there is still a tendency for us to withhold our highest praise on the grounds that a poet's choice of subject should suit an action, not a reaction. "The Wreck of The Deutschland," we feel, would have been markedly inferior if Hopkins had been a survivor from the passenger list. Again the first-rank poet should ignore the squalid accident of war: his vision should be powerful enough to disregard it. Admittedly, war might come too close for his vision to be maintained. But it is still essentially irrelevant. (Larkin, *Required Writing*, 159)

"We feel": for a magisterially plural Larkin, the higher truth is the envisioned, imaginative truth cut loose from the solitary, experiencing body bound in the pit of its idiosyncratic flesh. Down there with the lower truths, soldier-poets must wrestle to keep their eyes from wandering away from vision toward a trivializing personal history with which they dare not mingle too freely, for fear of encountering the dreaded "bathos," or "the cheap notoriety," of which a pop heroism could be compounded.

But Philip Larkin's stiffening against the reactive becomes an inability to acknowledge both the human design and the human imposition of that "squalid" suffering imposed by war. The inadequacy of making war the analogue of disasters of weather like "The Wreck of the Deutschland" also conveniently sidesteps past thinking about cause and effect or, critically, about service in war. When war is whittled down to a mere disaster to be suffered, poets move themselves squarely into the passive reactivity that Larkin then seizes as the main reason for excluding it as subject, and the passivity he derides becomes a self-inflicted wound of the imagination, shared in some measure by most of the poets of World War II.

Larkin, born in 1922, only two years younger than Keith Douglas—and still smarting from Sidney Keyes's exclusion of his poems from the 1941 *Eight Oxford Poets* that featured Douglas, Keyes, and others of his contemporaries— skirts his own wartime experience. Bombing raids in Coventry, the bad eyesight that rendered him "unfit for service," and the fascist sympathies of his father, which may have affected the thrust of his genuine enthusiasm for Auden, are features of the Larkin biography. Although an Olympian consideration of the war poet that rejects the personal is wholly congruent with much formalist thinking of the 1940s, when Larkin tacitly frees himself from any possible link to war as legitimate subject, he raises the questionable circumstances of his own relation to it, and we begin to peer at the judgments barely submerged beneath the steam of his own experience.

His reactions in the 1940s were youthfully muddled. In July of 1942, he shows his horror at friends' account of their stints in the military: up close, the British look to be mutinous bunglers, and the Germans untouchable heroes, and Larkin decides that "England cannot win this war: there's absolutely no spirit in this country. I feel everything is in a mess . . . And I agree we don't deserve to win." He writes:

> If there is any new life in the world today, it is in Germany. True, it's a vicious and blood-brutal kind of affair—the new shoots are rather like bayonets. It won't suit me. (*Selected Letters*, 36)

Andrew Motion, Larkin's biographer, extracts these comments from an unpublished diary entry from 1940, before call-up was an imminent threat: "Nobody could have been expected to understand that without being a conscientious objector I did not want to join the army on moral grounds. . . . I was fundamentally—like the rest of my friends—uninterested in the war" (Motion, 70; ellipsis in original). "Uninterested"! In November 1941, these feelings had coalesced a little more recognizably as fear of death. He wrote to a contemporary, "I have a strong presentiment I shall get killed in this war . . . not that I am resigned to it, far from it" (Motion, 70) Frantic to get out of military service, in December of the same year he wrote to J. B. Sutton, one of his prime sources on army life:

> Perhaps you think I'm being a bit selfish but I just don't want to go into the Army. I want to pretend it isn't there: that there's no war on. When I do get into it, it will be a hell of a struggle of readjustment. I dare say I shall get over it in about 5 months.
>
> I wonder if Suicide is *very* easy? (Patient dragged away howling by airmen—in the Orator sense.) (*Selected Letters*, 29)

But these worries were obviated by his failure to pass his medical exam.

By January 1943, writing again to Sutton, he had reverted to calm pastoral in the face of war, producing a Lawrentian prose very like what any writerly citizen, noncombatant or combatant on leave, an aged or a juvenile, might have rendered as impersonal judgment on war's effects:

Do you know the kind of morning—cold, with a pale, diffused light over everything, with frost on the grass and hedges, and ice in the puddles and cartruts? . . . The sky was half ice-blue, and half misty and dove-coloured. Occasionally an aeroplane swam across. And the land was so richly brown and green, with occasional flocks of grey and golden sheep; and red brick farms rising up. Then here and there was a big country house, white, set in a dip or on a hillside against the sun, with a lodge and iron gates. The sun flashed blindingly from frozen puddles and there wasn't a breath of wind. I saw some yellowhammers—silly little buggers—and some little shaggy ponies. Everything seems filled with the glory of God, except that I got caught up in an enormous convoy for the last 6 miles or so. An unending drawling caterpillar of diarrhoea-coloured lorries. (*Selected Letters*, 54)

The world is redeemed with a dash of Hopkinsian splendor, even through the momentary inconvenience of wartime transport. The passage, laid on with such careful strokes, minus a word or two for decency censorship, would fit a BBC wartime broadcast about Deep England, the resilient pastoral that came to take over industrial England as the exaggerated image of its alternate peacetime self. The range of the emotions that Larkin went through about being conscripted anticipate the later panic and distress of American college boys during the Vietnam War. Larkin glorifies and simplifies the enemy even as they did and savages the army with similar contempt; yet the language and structure of their pacifism were temperamentally and practicably unavailable to him. And so the wartime feeling of Larkin's poems went into a closet, reemerging as an affirmation of sentimental nostalgia but clothed in an aesthetic disdain for the literarily obvious.

In the apparent detachment of "The War Poet," Larkin's prose does allow for the traditional war elegy, but he fudges the gap between what he publicly venerated and what he was lucky enough to privately dodge. In this straitened space of regard, acts of commemoration or celebration may indeed elevate one to be free of reductive experience, lofted to the higher ground of that feeling and universalized "We." Yet a moment of bad faith obtrudes for him in the interval when a poet crosses from commemorating or memorializing to reacting. What securely identifies the nobility or squalor of the issue or detail to be "transcended"? Why would Philip Larkin, who took on the shrivelling and dirtying of virtue in his adult treatment of sexual riot and repression, and who fully explored imaginative impotence and congenital emotional failings in his own work, proscribe any similar debts of experience for the genre of war poetry?

In 1975, when a more detailed exposition of Owen's homosexuality came by way of the publication of Jon Stallworthy's biography, a ruffled Larkin in his essay "The Real Wilfred" demoted Owen from "the only twentieth-century poet who can be read after Hardy without a sense of bathos" (from "The War Poet," *Required Writing*, 163) to someone whose tie to his subject was tainted by an impure, "private involvement, something that seemed part of his isolation, his frustrated ambitions in poetry, his sexual hang-ups" (239). There could be too near, too loving a grasp of the soldier bodies engaged in war; in all senses, the war poet must keep from embracing his subject too tightly. Or even, in Larkin's case, too loosely.

At some point the tug away from a loathsome bondage to solipsistic experience started to weaken imaginative embodiment, and English poets other than Larkin shied away a little precipitously from artless realism. But in trimming too assiduously the inevitable ties to material being that any genuine attempt at mimesis demands, the war poet cannot sustain a fidelity to the live act. What comes instead may be an offensively and sentimentally faked recollection that obscures the real death and horror of modern war. Here are the earnest histrionics that open C. Day Lewis's heroic opera, "The Nabara" (1938):

> Freedom is more than a word, more than the base coinage
> Of statesmen, the tyrant's dishonoured cheque, or the dreamer's mad
> inflated currency. She is mortal, we know, and made
> In the image of simple men who have no taste for carnage
> But sooner kill and are killed than see that image betrayed.
> Mortal she is, yet rising always refreshed from her ashes:
> She is bound to earth, yet she flies as high as a passage bird
> To home wherever man's heart with seasonal warmth is stirred:
> Innocent is her touch as the dawn's, but still it unleashes
> The ravisher shades of envy. Freedom is more than a word.
>   (C. Day Lewis, 191)

This fustian makes freedom very little more than words, and the blood that decorates this stagy affirmation of suicidal attack by "simple" partisans is quite of a piece with any of the earlier brainless and enthusiastic citizen kitsch of World War I. After World War I, for Philip Larkin himself in "MCMXIV," there was "Never such innocence again"; never an innocence within which the heroic could be clad with decorum. Although poets like him may have thought to preserve poetry from the bald programming of the emotions that sentimentality and bathos undeniably represent, postwar historical momentum could not clear the poetry of the 1930s, or eventually the 1940s, from the clutter of circumstance, or from the necessity of engagement with acts of direct witness binding the war poem to a painful immediacy.

Both English and American poets of World War II made little or ambiguous or often clumsy rhetoric of the 1930s realization that all of us are complicit in the reign of militarism. In the 1940s, with war upon them, poets found it difficult to resist their particular war's numbing and brutalizing presence with new aesthetic practice, new habits of diction, novel sounds and rhythms. Auden seemed to provide one model; but in the twentieth century's second onset of global hostilities, nothing replaced the convictions that persuaded, filled, and lifted the otherwise traditional forms of World War I poetry with their ring of newly opened truth. World War II poetry remained in some tentative interstitial space, for most practitioners cramped or short-circuited in both England and America by the diffused variety of the formal strategies bent to its scattered meanings.

World War I poetry was saturated by trench warfare; World War II poetry gaped even wider. Even though Hew Strachan (Strachan, 370) reminds us that by 1929 less than 1,500 copies of the 1920 edition of Wilfred Owen's poems had sold, in contrast to over 300,000 total sales for Rupert Brooke's collected poems, the shape of World War I, or the larger sense of it, heart and soul has come to belong to the poets of the trenches. World War II, however, was gutted and sold to Hollywood culture. But in the anticipatory phase, and even during and after the war, a large residue of this literature—in English the best of it mostly written by soldiers with very mixed feelings about the glory of either soldiers or battle—still manages its pierce and dazzle in the salvaged ruck of its dispersal.

4

Keith Douglas: Inside the Whale

IF war could no longer be said to be the thing painted in glory by Dryden or Tennyson, who had never been there, then what was it? Even more, *why* was it? W. H. Auden's biographer, Richard Davenport-Hines notes that

> Victorian Christians like Auden's clergymen grandfathers had regarded pugnacity and violence as expressions of original sin, and therefore as inescapable parts of human nature. This outlook, it seemed to many people who lived through the First World War, had led to an easy acceptance of ferocity in public policy. Most progressive people after the war insistently denied what their Christian grandfathers thought self-evident. (Davenport-Hines, 152)

Davenport-Hines singles out the occasion that epitomized this "easy acceptance of ferocity," for Auden, lighting up as it did the embeddedness of a casual and pervasive human brutality the very idea of whose necessity revolted him.

In 1937, Auden and MacNeice's *Letters from Iceland* described a whale as "something alive, enormous, and gentle, with the functional beauties of modern machinery." A seventy-ton whale lay on the slip-way "like a large and very dignified duchess being got ready for the ball by beetles." Seeing it torn apart with steam winches and cranes clarified the further steps of a death-dance:

> The sun was out; in the bay, surrounded by buoys and gulls, were the semi-submerged bodies of five dead whales: and down the slip-way ran a constant stream of blood, staining the water a deep red for a distance of fifty yards. Someone whistled a tune. A bell suddenly clanged and everyone stuck their spades in the carcass and went off for lunch. The body remained

alone in the sun, the flesh still steaming a little. It gave one an extraordinary vision of the cold controlled ferocity of the human species. (Auden and MacNeice, 149–50)

Auden shows us a creature of enormous gentleness on a vast field of bloodflow, over which the Lilliputian swarms make their dissection while the beast steams in its own fading body heat. Abandoned at lunchtime, that flensing spade stuck in the whale's carcass is made to stand for the unthinking, confident cruelty, without recess, of the little species which presides so decisively over it. From this image it is a short trek to Stephen Crane's battlefield surgeon hacking the limbs of the wounded in a similarly unrelenting calendar of efficiencies.

While the bleak vision of the whales may have superficially aligned Auden with the faith of his grandfathers, Auden and others sharing a progressive streak saw their duty as the revocation of easy acceptance of violence, even if protest left them swamped in feelings of futility and largely mute or inarticulate in the face of every country's descent into the maelstrom. It fell to every poet after Auden to struggle for the terms that would allow them recognition of universal malevolence while still leaving enough hope to stiffen the spine for living.

"Simplify me when I'm dead"

Keith Douglas was twenty-four when he was killed by mortar fire on 9 June 1944, four days after he had first driven his tank onto the beach at Normandy. He amply fills the requirement created by World War I for soldier poetry followed by tragic early death. But perhaps an equally vital reason for his nomination by readers like Desmond Graham as the strongest of the English poets of World War II stems from the transitional ambiguity—sometimes argued as the almost archaism—of his refusal to deny war's potent attractions, its fitness as epic subject. Like many other schoolboys of his generation, he spent a childhood doodling cartoons—fairly good ones—of World War I soldiers, and then as a young man he was pitched into war. With a cool intelligence bent toward trying out the necessity of war, and aided by his own peculiar fatalism, Douglas probed verbally at the nature of death and killing in battle. Going after exact witness, World War II provided Douglas the occasion to immerse himself in his own experiment in war consciousness.

In 1937, precocious, seventeen years old, and writing autobiographical fiction and speaking of himself in the third person, Douglas begins, "As a child

FIGURE 6. Keith Douglas in North Africa, 1942. The Brotherton Collection, University of Leeds.

he was a militarist" (*Prose Miscellany*, 13). Yet the whole of his brief adult life—its terms split exactly between two years of college and two years of military service, a life moving in a seamless gradient from schoolmasters to commanding officers—begins to fray or undo that militarist propensity. Few in final number, but quite prolific given the time available for their completion, Douglas's poems from those years, poems about a tour of service eagerly undertaken, offer a crucible of development within which Douglas works toward a stoical disregard of any conventional heroic ideal.

We pay the attention that we do to Keith Douglas's small, intense oeuvre of war poems at least partly because more and more twentieth-century writing about war nears resistlessly what James Campbell calls "combat gnosticism," or the belief that requires personal experience of battle as a precondition for understanding and writing of war. In combat gnosticism, it is always an improvement to replace A. E. Housman's voice behind the lancer with the voice of the lancer himself, to replace the miming voice of Kipling as journalist with that of the Tommy himself, or with the Tommy's officer: the voice of authority must always issue directly, and not from the rear of the battle scene in a fairly remote retrospect. Although the flavor of retrospect is inevitable because writing instrument and instrument of lethal force may not as yet be held simultaneously, Douglas's poems sustain their singular balance of interests partly because the dead young man who is their author came back to us hot on the heels of battle to report on killing and dying and, having observed a variety of corpses during his service, on being dead.

In the artwork by Keith Douglas housed at the British Library, the sketches of soldiers charging and bayoneting that he made as a schoolboy at Christ's Hospital indicate a not uncommon absorption of English boys born in the interval between world wars, but they also reveal a crisp mastery of perspective in complex forms. Douglas was the son of a World War I soldier who, having failed in business and deserted Douglas's mother for the family maid, disappeared from his life when Douglas was about six years old. Quite fond of his rough but affectionate father, Douglas learned early to read the character of the soldier for the layered composition it surely must be.

In the dry, dispassionate tones of an early fiction, Douglas describes "Keir's" turn towards the masculine and militarist:

> His father did not spend very much time with him, but would speak to him of war and boxing and shew the boy his great muscles, for here at least he could shew them off to unbounded admiration. He teased his son, and pinched and tormented him sometimes, but Keir liked his father better than his mother, who fondled him a deal too much and cried sometimes. (*Prose Miscellany*, 13)

There is a stolid acceptance of male cruelty and male vanity here, as well as a keen eye for the comparative weakness and vulnerability of women and children in the family hierarchy. Other paragraphs efficiently include other prime data:

When he was four, his mother had been very ill. He never sensed anything wrong when she came back from hospital, and when his father, a hearty playmate whom he secretly feared and wholeheartedly admired, disappeared and Olwen too, he wept as much as his mother. (16)

In another autobiographical fragment, where "Peter" substitutes for "Keir" as the name of choice, the following paragraph indicates how Peter's mother's severe illness entailed his being packed off to the first of the preparatory schools that shaped him. With the insight gained at seventeen, Douglas takes the measure of moneylessness paired with male desertion: "It was soon apparent that lack of a father meant lack of money, and after a curtailed prep-school career, Peter entered Christ's Hospital" (Douglas Papers, British Library, Add 56359). Douglas's attachment to the only parent left to him, a mutual attachment, remained strong and stubborn, but he recognized very early that only under the male aegis is real power obtained. Equally early, however, are the manifest signs of a sturdy self-reliance. In 1931 when he was eleven and away at school, he appealed briefly to his mother in an odd mix of studied cool and suppressed panic, his tone both plaintive and self-possessed (British Library, Add 56355): "shall I be able to come home this term or any Sunday or not? I hope I shall Don't you?" At roughly the same age, and in another instance of carefully unchildlike precision he asks her, "In what way are you not feeling well?"

His mother had begun a complicated series of removals in order to support herself that left both of them experiencing a disorienting homelessness. Marie Douglas was rarely able to offer her son a stable or secure household outside of the schools where she managed to place him. It is this early instability that Ted Hughes links to the temperament that "reveals the curiously despairing nature of Douglas' search for emotional anchorage, his loneliness, the frailty of his equilibrium, and his fatalism." His "passionate, fatalistic outlook" becomes

the gimbal control of Douglas' balancing act, where the nonchalance is also, as on a puppet's face, anguish, the bravura a harrowing posture of doll's hands, the gallantry a cool acceptance of the worst possible fate. (Hughes, in Douglas, *Complete Poems*, xx)

What tilts the balance is "a vision of his own early death, his own death already foresuffered." Although Hughes also concludes: "It is impossible to say which exercises most sway: the premonition of this death in action, or the sealed hopelessness of his 'long pain.'"

A version of Douglas's sense of being marked for tragedy erupts in 1940, where it is part of a letter written in the wake of what eventually became several failures to acquire family and home through marriage: "I shall never get over the idea of the world in general as a powerful force working for my hurt: nor would I wish to, for this conception of things saves me many disappointments" (quoted in Graham, 7). Yet his fatalism is only part of the balancing act of Douglas's outlook. The vitality of this poet, coursing with insight and active observation, should not be shrunk down to fit a passive, masochistic acceptance of death. Even in this letter Douglas is describing a dialectic of forces which he energetically resists. He was always quick enough to ward off blows of adversity by new attempts at breaking through his difficulties, even when the very bounce of his resilience only thickened the scar tissue that burdened him with doubt and skepticism.

William Scammell has a clear grasp of the relation of Douglas's schooling to his militarism. He sees militarism as one more instance for Douglas of the welcome triumph of formal discipline over unruly existence, which he had witnessed

at close quarters all his life: boys become blue-coated scholars, young men became uproarious or pompous undergrads, older men became officers and gentlemen. In all these cases, a uniform was ready and waiting, literal and social, and the majority were happy to slip it on and act out their allotted role. (Scammell, 29)

Looking at Douglas's life as a cadet in 1940, Scammell writes:

He functioned well in closed, hierarchical societies both because he had to, or go under, and because they provided him with a sort of family, and the family's twin possibilities of conformity and revolt. (10)

Yet it would be a mistake to read Douglas's accommodation within these hierarchies as complete, or even consistent, or to misread the growing depth and extent of his critiques of them. Through all the phases of his life in barracks as a cadet in England, then as an officer on active duty in Palestine, Egypt, and North Africa, and then back in England again, Keith Douglas's poems maintain a curious and skeptical neutrality as to all aspects of military life. This expresses itself in shrewd delineation of the barriers between man and officer, friend and foe, and civilian and soldier. Having enlisted as soon as war was declared, Douglas took war as his worthy subject: an exploration of basic questions that allowed him a full measure of war's rules of existence, its compass points, and the rules of its termination. Figuring out how to define life, its edges and endings, made the death on offer both fascinating and metaphysically compelling to a temperament primed for risk and headlong adventure, as well as one steeped in his own early experience of loss and isolation. But in the main, the treatment of war in Douglas's poems does not differ distinguishably from other poets of the era who lacked the extent or fact of his combat experience. The eye that surveys a war-blasted Enfidaville, the one that so astutely and persuasively assesses the predatory sexual moves of men and women in a wartime Cairo cafe, or even the one that looks into the desert in the wake of engagement in "Cairo Jag" and "Vergissmeinnicht" could as readily belong to a journalist as a frontline soldier.

In "Cairo Jag" he remarks on the world reached by a day's traveling; the frame of reference, that of the tourist, seems oddly precise for someone who could blend the world of tourism and war, even on active duty. The implied tourism suggests for us the element of show and display now attaching openly to every war, an element heightened by everyone's access to cameras of all sorts. In the literature of World War II, the ubiquity of this need to record, to witness, and the consequent self-consciousness it brings to modern warfare only deepens the complexity of the act of witnessing war; again we are shown how the line between combatant and noncombatant, between object and subject, fades. Here is the last stanza of "Cairo Jag":

> But by a day's travelling you reach a new world
> the vegetation is of iron
> dead tanks, gun barrels split like celery
> the metal brambles have no flowers or berries
> and there are all sorts of manure, you can imagine
> the dead themselves, their boots, clothes and possessions
> clinging to the ground, a man with no head
> has a packet of chocolate and a souvenir of Tripoli.
>
> (Douglas, *Complete Poems*, 102)

The grotesque, headless corpse survives with the detritus of global civilization; like the soldier-traveler who "snaps" this moment for us, the dead soldier-traveler also scurried about for the war loot, the objects and experiences, that equally preoccupy the man who now looks at him with such seeming imperturbability. Either as war correspondent, as medic, or as soldier, chances are fair that the observer may soon share his posture on the ground in the new, iron world enveloping the living and the dead in the queasy richness of its manure. In this war, the unique specificity of the soldier's perspective may broaden to include other trades, but the taste of fatality is still the attraction.

That "Cairo Jag" was written in hospital in 1943 while Douglas was recovering from wounds received in the North African desert campaign does not alter its applicability to much nonmilitary experience of war. The number of Keith Douglas's poems that contemplate bodies in the aftermath of engagement far outweigh the number dedicated to ongoing battlefield episodes. While he is largely known as a war poet because he came to his abbreviated maturity during wartime service, Douglas saw himself as a poet before he saw himself as a soldier. His poems treat war as one more nugget, albeit a large one, within the circle of acts and objects greedily scavenged for poetry by a young man greatly gifted, burdened, and hungry for love and recognition. War becomes his laboratory for the trial and assay of death, death as subject subsumed within the greater lyric tradition in which he saw himself a player.

In the aggregate, Keith Douglas's poems assemble the picture of someone whose own struggle to see his life as viable and resurgent coincided with the exploding conflict in which his generation, given to war, found itself caught and striving—not just for life itself, but for an ethical, emotional, and intellectual survival. Acknowledging death as the major by-product of war, and fitting this by-product within the traditional, and equally congenial, subject of the metaphysics of human death, Douglas set himself to examine all the consequences of extinction in war with a certain remoteness and philosophical abstraction. From start to finish, in tone and technique, the poems fit within not only the subgenre of war poetry, but the broader Romantic crisis of mutability. More intimately, Douglas's work tugs at us to follow not just the exercise of memory, but his calculus of the future, and the teasing out not only of death, but the spray of its aftertaste.

Once dead, how does it look, how do I look, and what happens then to the pulsating vibrance of everything I think, the poems ask with nervy sobriety. In "Dead Men," surveying the dead in the desert after his experience in the North African campaign sometime in 1943, Douglas writes:

All that is good of them, the dog consumes.
You would not know, now the mind's flame is gone,
more than the dog knows: you would forget
but that you see your own mind burning yet

and till you stifle in the ground will go on
burning the economical coal of your dreams.

Then leave the dead in the earth, an organism
not capable of resurrection, like mines,
less durable than the metal of a gun,
a casual meal for a dog, nothing but the bone
so soon.

        (*Complete Poems*, 100)

There is here some submerged refusal to believe that death is really death. Something in the phrasing or timing of the lines stubbornly continues to gasp for breath underground—even as the speaker exhorts himself to leave the dead to their nonresurrection and to bring up, as a raised but untouched subject, the likelihood of his own soon stifling underground, one more extinguished furnace in the lot, the whole thing a dog meal, as we look at what the poet's world has set out for his and the dog's consumption.

From the beginning of his army poems, what accompanied Douglas's apprehension of early death, along with his need to feel what his own afterlife would be like, was a galvanizing probe into all experiences of love from that position of desperate resignation and eager hope which seems uniquely Douglas's mode. While still in army training at twenty, he wrote a poem, called "The Prisoner," for a former girlfriend, which ends:

but alas, Cheng, I cannot tell why,
today I touched a mask stretched on the stone-

hard face of death. There was the urge
to escape the bright flesh and emerge
of the ambitious cruel bone.

        (*Complete Poems*, 67)

Death is in us always thrusting to come out, even in defiance of the experience of union that love offers.

Dead bodies and soldiers, dead or otherwise, lurked in Douglas' poems long before he came upon them during and after actual combat. It is not kind to go into too much detail about the work of these very early years, but at fifteen Douglas declaimed: "I saw men curse, weep, cough, sprawl in their entrails" (*Complete Poems*, 6). By twenty, in passing, he is commemorating a Great War battlefield in "A God Is Buried," and—since the date of the poem is 1940—noting "another madness begun this year" (*Complete Poems*, 42). "Russians," also from 1940, remembers an incident in the Russian campaign against Finland, in which "a Russian regiment was reported to have been discovered frozen to death, the soldiers still holding their rifles ready to fire" (*Complete Poems*, 145 n) This poem affects a grim nonchalance in closing:

Think of them as waxworks, or think they're struck

with a dumb immobile spell
to wake in a hundred years with the merry force
of spring upon them in the harmless world. Well,
at least don't think what happens when it thaws.
(*Complete Poems*, 37)

With so many corpses dug and undug in these paper soils, it's clear that Keith Douglas had little security about what will be left of him, or made by others of his life. In 1941, still in training he wrote "Simplify Me When I'm Dead," and, in an ironic bid to deflect the inevitable, he begins and ends the poem with the same hopeless hope, "Remember me when I am dead / And simplify me when I'm dead." The poem continues:

Time's wrong-way telescope will show
a minute man ten years hence
and by distance simplified.

Through that lens see if I seem
substance or nothing: of the world
deserving mention or charitable oblivion

not by momentary spleen
or love into decision hurled
leisurely arrive at an opinion.

Remember me when I am dead
and simplify me when I'm dead.
(*Complete Poems*, 74)

The thudding repetition, like a dull drumbeat, shoves us into the complex after-shocks of simplicity. Other poems interest themselves not only in the fused perspective of the living and dead, but balance the eternal soldier's dyad of friend and enemy in the one being. With tolerance and compassion for his opposite number, Keith Douglas from the beginning of his soldier poetry acknowledged the twinship of the soldier seeing himself in the mirror of the other army: in war, your enemy, like you, is merely doing his job. Desmond Graham's biography repeats a friend's recollection of Douglas at a university film showing, where

> they witnessed the usual newsreel in which an aerial dogfight was concluded with the German plane spinning to the ground in flames. The audience cheered. Even in the semi-darkness of the cinema Beaty could see that Douglas was trembling with rage. He climbed on to his seat, shouting at the audience, 'You shits! You shits! You shits!' until he was forcibly removed by the doorman. (Graham, 100)

He was not a pacifist, and at that stage in his life before actual recruitment, he believed in the preservation of a military class whose honor existed beyond national boundaries. While his perception remained that the war was being fought against fascism, an ideological opposition that he wholly supported, characteristically he could not and would not translate this into the usual partisan oversimplifications.

Keith Douglas's "How to Kill" is the successor of Siegfried Sassoon's "How To Die" (1917). Sassoon, with what shades of crossbred irony or sentimentality may be hard to tell, marks in "How to Die" the sober decency with which his hero ends:

> But they've been taught the way to do it
> Like Christian soldiers; not with haste
> And shuddering groans; but passing through it
> With due regard for decent taste.
>   (Sassoon, *The War Poems*, 72)

Surely other poems, including "Counter-Attack" and its corpses, are a better guide to Sassoon's thoughts on the decency of dying at trench warfare:

> The place was rotten with dead; green clumsy legs
> High-booted, sprawled and grovelled along the saps

And trunks, face downward in the sucking mud,
Wallowed like trodden sand-bags loosely filled;
And naked sodden buttocks, mats of hair,
Bulged, clotted heads slept in the plastering slime.

(*War Poems*, 105)

Every verb in this stomach-turning description is picked to convey a maximum degradation of the body and to follow with exactitude what decay and rottenness are thrust on the attacking soldier's eye as he moves either to evade or contribute to the human and inhuman debris around him. Everything in these lines counters the traditional elegy of the heroic; the legs of the dead do not race with a noble determination, but sprawl and grovel. Decomposing faces wallow, inexorably sucked down into the mud. Death and its undoing of the body become gross parodies that reverse birth and becoming. Even in this world of nauseated, suffocating immersion in rot and decay, ignominious exposure is equally present in the matted hair and naked, obscene buttocks.

An older decorum of war poetry might have forced such scenes off page in deference to the mythic honor accruing to a death in war. When Housman or Tennyson omit such particulars, they appear to be instinctively editing to remove all possibility of an ugly dying; there will be no rot and slime, only hints of the smells that might edge their version of patriotic sacrifice. But in Sassoon's combat realism, ugliness undermines the authority that commands slaughter because the elision of unpleasant detail would bow to the susceptibilities of unblooded civilians, who, otherwise informed, might not affirm the wartime actions done in their name. Inevitably the faithful reporting of the style of such losses reflects on those who order them, and responsibility cannot be wholly displaced onto the backs of enemy forces. In showing an effect, one is halfway to implying a cause, and any honest account of war necessarily embroils itself in the complex motivations behind blood violence.

Dismissing realism in war always runs the risk of trivializing if not falsifying the event, and by shallowing and gutting substance, to eviscerate any subsequent literature. To say, with Philip Larkin, that an aesthetic sharply recording the particulars of war fails because it forces attention on the particular over the universal, the local over the transcendent, is to hamstring the artist, to make him behave as if the transcendent could always be readily found, and not fumbled after in blind or bewildered retrospect by way of the local.

Inevitably, a spotlight on the death of soldiers forces uncomfortable questions about necessity and benefit, and about the volatile relationship of attentive reader and committed writer. Nor can we avoid awareness that the war elegy—directly and indirectly—has its traditional political function directed to a complex hearing, in which listeners are solicited to pity the results, with approval or disapproval linked to what and who may have commanded the outcome. To gild the death of any one person as a form of boosting safety for all people ties aesthetics to a morality that affirms violent social action. Whatever our announced aesthetic, we cannot evade the locking of realist principles to moral practice. When we read or write violence it is never a wholly formal matter; we are inevitably implicated in both the setting forth and the reception of the details.

In "How to Kill," Douglas makes his contempt for tasteful or gratifying death quite plain: yet unlike much of World War I poetry, his figures and explanations circle to enclose those targeting as well as targeted. A soldier sighting a gun speaks into his cross hairs a soliloquy at the point of another man's death:

Now in my dial of glass appears
the soldier who is going to die.
He smiles, and moves about in ways
his mother knows, habits of his.
The wires touch his face: I cry
NOW. Death, like a familiar, hears

and look, has made a man of dust
of a man of flesh. This sorcery
I do. Being damned, I am amused
to see the centre of love diffused
and the waves of love travel into vacancy.
How easy it is to make a ghost.

The weightless mosquito touches
her tiny shadow on the stone,
and with how like, how infinite
a lightness, a man and shadow meet.
They fuse. A shadow is a man
when the mosquito death approaches.

(Douglas, *Complete Poems*, 119)

"This sorcery / I do" is said very quietly in Douglas's stripped diction. But there is more than a shade of swagger in Douglas's "damned" and "amused" response to this easy shatter of flesh and bone. The mood of foreknowing acceptance in this piece is decades away not only from Sassoon, but from Isaac Rosenberg's "swift iron burning bee," whose insect temperature Douglas's mosquito seems to lower, perhaps because in this second of the twentieth-century world wars, death in general is not less painful but at least less surprising. Rosenberg wrote:

> None saw their spirits' shadow shake the grass,
> Or stood aside for the half-used life to pass
> Out of those doomed nostrils and the doomed mouth,
> When the swift iron burning bee
> Drained the wild honey of their youth.
>   (Rosenberg, 81)

The savage title of Isaac Rosenberg's poem, "Dead Man's Dump," written before he was killed in action in 1918, is closer to the blunt sensibility of "How to Kill" than to Sassoon's "How to Die"; yet even here, Rosenberg's caressive, pitying tone, and the evocative pastoral-elegiac, find no match in Douglas, whose coverage of death always mutes pathos.

Although Douglas cried out in "Desert Flowers," "Rosenberg I only repeat what you were saying—" his bullet-flowers are a decisively different version of the natural world of both missile and blossom, matter and spirit. While the speakers of Keith Douglas's poems may walk a world in which the dead are eerily and unnervingly present alongside the living—embedded in the stars, inscrutable in bird, sand, or swordfish—they are above all audible in the literary echo chamber of the poet's head, in the spirit-world of writing. In Douglas's "How to Kill" and elsewhere, death resembles Milan Kundera's "unbearable lightness of being," where, like the landing of a mosquito, death becomes a barely detectable move from one neighborhood to the other, from that of the living to that of the dead, one footfall with a shadow's weight and a shadow's consequence. That professional bloodsucker, the mosquito, is no bee, either; his job in hell is to extract a more viscous nectar. Altogether, Douglas seems less convinced than Rosenberg that his life was ever a matter of wild honey. Along with his greater foreknowledge, the later poet's world had bred a lesser hopefulness.

Douglas also had an ear tuned to a wider spectrum of black humor for the soldier's predicament than the World War I soldier-poet. In "The Last

Laugh," Wilfred Owen hears bullets chirp, machine-guns chuckle, and the Big Gun guffaw when a man cries, "Oh! Jesus Christ! I'm hit," and dies. "My Love!" moans another:

> And the Bayonets' long teeth grinned;
> Rabbles of shells hooted and groaned;
> And the gas hissed.
> (*Complete Poems*, 1:168)

In a less cosmic, more acid commentary on the manners and amours of his fellow comrades, and with an irony more self-consciously tuned to sexual as well as social complexity, Douglas's poem, "Gallantry," observes the last moments of three heroes:

> Into the ears of the doomed boy, the fool
> whose perfectly mannered flesh fell
> in opening the door for a shell
> as he had learnt to do at school.
>
> Conrad luckily survived the winter:
> he wrote a letter to welcome
> the auspicious spring: only his silken
> intentions severed with a single splinter.
>
> Was George fond of little boys?
> We always suspected it,
> but who will say: since George was hit
> we never mention our surmise.
>
> It was a brave thing the colonel said,
> but the whole sky turned too hot
> and the three heroes never heard what
> it was, gone deaf with steel and lead.
>
> But the bullets cried with laughter,
> the shells were overcome with mirth,
> plunging their heads in steel and earth—
> (the air commented in a whisper.)
> (*Complete Poems*, 104)

Douglas's view of the menace narrows the reference beyond Owen's cosmic accusation: artillery will obliterate any brave thing that the colonel says because war making itself takes precedence over the power of the hero; neither Douglas's victims or the death they die are robed in dignity. Douglas's acceptance of bonds between men is less trusting, less erotically and nostalgically tinged, although the view of the viciousness of indifference within which soldiers finish looks the same in both poets: what alters crucially is the degree of self-deception about the nature and possibility of gallantry in a machine-tooled war.

In "Aristocrats," alternatively titled "Sportsmen," there is no brief presented either, for the heroic mold. Douglas writes:

> The noble horse with courage in his eye,
> clean in the bone, looks up at a shellburst:
> away fly the images of the shires
> but he puts the pipe back in his mouth.
>
> Peter was unfortunately killed by an 88;
> it took his leg away, he died in the ambulance.
> I saw him crawling on the sand, he said
> it's most unfair, they've shot my foot off.
>
> How can I live among this gentle
> obsolescent breed of heroes, and not weep?
> Unicorns, almost,
> for they are fading into two legends
> in which their stupidity and chivalry
> are celebrated. Each, fool and hero, will be an immortal.
>
> (*Complete Poems*, 117)

These dying soldiers are recognizably kin to Sassoon's or Rosenberg's unceremoniously dumped dead men. But in their bifurcation into "fool" and "hero" they are sharply antithetical to Owen's soldiers of "Spring Offensive,"

> who running on that last high place
> Leapt to swift unseen bullets or went up
> On the hot blast and fury of hell's upsurge,
> Or plunged and fell away past this world's verge,
> Some say God caught them even before they fell.
>
> (Owen, *Complete Poems*, 1:92)

The easy sentimentality of the last line lay beyond Douglas's reach. As Edmund Blunden, Keith Douglas's mentor at Oxford put it a little dryly, "Owen had no immediate conception that war was "disenchantment, obscenity, and torture" (Owen, *Collected Poems*, 153). And much of the time, this remark feels truthful; Douglas, the inheritor of all their poems and metaphors, had no such luxury of ignorance. Even as one disabused by battlefield terror, however, Owen's unforced visionary eloquence could still exalt his fated victims in a glory of hellfire.

But in a sly stab at both the superiority of Swift's noble Houyhnyms and the glamorous centaur's tradition of lancer or cavalryman, well into his war Douglas will have the maimed immortal seen only through the fused stupidity and archaism of a subhuman animal loyalty. Before shellburst and disintegrating explosive, injury remains more horrifying than ennobling, more haphazard than heroically chosen. The very sporting code that sent the Great War recruits out into battle kicking footballs in front of them is definitively shredded by Douglas's irony, an irony shading into pitying contempt:

> These plains were their cricket pitch
> and in the mountains the tremendous drop fences
> brought down some of the runners. Here then
> under the stones and earth they dispose themselves,
> I think with their famous unconcern.
> It is not gunfire I hear, but a hunting horn.
>
> (*Complete Poems*, 117)

If there is more than a faint, collusive nostalgia for this archaic ideal of the defeated Roland, Douglas makes clear that simple rather than complex elegy always hides selective, narrowing deafness and retrograde stupidity.

Douglas, who fancied himself as an equestrian, had his pride in his unorthodox horsemanship bruised early in his military career and had managed to dissociate himself from any easy equations of war as sport, or as heraldic manifestation. In one rejection of conventional masculine symbolism, colleagues remember Douglas's moment of irritation at the constant flow of cricket-inspired metaphor in intertank communications, when in order to pass on information he was heard to interrupt peremptorily by asking for a break from the coverage at Lord's. The horsey, sporting diehards of his regiment had effectively shown him his true distance from the anachronisms of chivalry.

Desmond Graham describes the regimental background of the Sherwood Rangers, and the anomalous character of Douglas's service within it, as the regiment itself switched from horses to tanks, becoming a mechanized cavalry, for which Douglas had been specifically trained (although he was conspicuously neither a wonderful horseman nor mechanic). In an old regiment ruled by a deeply stratified caste, horses figured prominently. A major took along to war three of his own valuable hunters: when somewhere in France one of these future chargers fell sick, a railway waiting room was requisitioned for the horse's convalescent needs, and a corporal was left behind to administer brandy. As the horse recovered, he eventually caught up with his two-footed and four-footed fellows by means of a carriage ordered by the Duke of Gloucester. The first cavalry charge brought the regiment, swords drawn, down a street in Jaffa, where they rescued police from a riot; this was not a wartime charge against fascists, but the ordinary imperial duty of the British in what was then Palestine. As Graham puts it,

> Douglas neither hunted, fished, nor shot; he knew no one in Nottinghamshire and nothing of the regiment; the qualities for which his school [Christ's Hospital] was famous—intellectual excellence, classlessness, and its place in the mercantile history of London meant little to these country gentlemen. (Graham, 136)

When he wrote about these soldiers amongst whom he served, his alienation from them makes both attraction and repulsion evident. The tight bonds born of the battlefield that grow between fellow soldiers gave small sign of thickening for Douglas; his struggle for individuation remains the texture of his war.

In assessing Douglas as a soldier, one of his peers commented that "he always seemed to me somewhat wasted in the Army. Regimental life with its discipline, its thoughtless automatic routine, its conventions . . . must have been terribly difficult to accept" (quoted in Graham, 204). Again, in summary of these traits, Graham reports:

> Instead of moving strictly according to the plans of the colonel and the squadron leader, Douglas had a tendency to regard his job as a roving commission. If he saw something which interested him, he would take his Crusader across for a closer look. If a battle was on, instead of remaining hull-down while the heavy tanks fought it out, Douglas would join in. If

nothing was happening, he would get down from his tank and wander around, while his gunner and driver replied to urgent radio commands that they did not know where he was. Jack Holman recalls that Douglas enjoyed jumping from his tank to throw hand grenades, a practice which always earned him an order to leave 'the cowboys and Indian stuff' to the infantry. (Graham, 204)

This independent streak left Douglas with little sense of the Army as anything but a way station in his life: if he survived or not, the Army would not be the site of his surrender to the intimate relations that would press and haunt his future world, as Siegfried Sassoon had been pressed and haunted. Nor could the exclusive company of men hold out the same attractions for him that it did for Wilfred Owen. Not in his work, or indeed that of other World War II poets, is there anything like the bald and hopeless shock of grief in Ivor Gurney's "To His Love," which, after Housman-like delicacies of fond and loving memory, concludes:

> Cover him, cover him soon!
> And with thick-set
> Masses of memoried flowers—
> Hide that red wet
> Thing I must somehow forget.
>   (Gurney, 76)

But neither is Gurney's rage of betrayal by death related to the stoic and satisfied musing on the beauty of death in battle that Shakespeare put in the mouth of Exeter, as he notes "The pretty and sweet manner" of Suffolk and York's dying on the field of Agincourt. In both twentieth-century poets, the growing openness of expression to either the numbness or the rawness of grief seems more than the difference in stages of decay undergone by corpses subject to swordplay and arrows against the ravage set in train by shellburst, machine gun, and mortar fire. Whether we turn to Gurney's rage or Douglas's irony-deflected horror, the newer reactions expose some further collective sense of the belittled body as just another mechanism vulnerable to industrial demolition, a demolition set going not by a paternalistic warrior god but by a devil-ridden human inventiveness.

The poems of World War II seem to require delivery or release from myths of heroic comradeship. In this war as in all others, moving testimonials exist of the power of battlefield friendship; in photograph and film, young men in extremity cradle and console other shocked and hurt young men, assuming maternal and fraternal powers of consolation for each other. But the warrior bonds of World War II are often effaced by a greater need to put on record the fearful loneliness of the mass recruit in the drill of his army existence, whose only real double is that of his opposite number on the other side, visible to him through the crazed mirror of battle.

There are nearly twenty pages in draft that show how Keith Douglas's poem "Sniper" struggled to become the four completed stanzas of "How to Kill." Dropping the focus of the speaker as victim by the time he worked out the fourth stanza of the first draft, he realized that he wanted the arc of a ball dropped in the speaker's childhood to equal the arc of the mosquito's flight meeting its shadow on stone as well as the arc of the sniper's bullet. Douglas got the ending of the poem first. He begins: "As a weightless mosquito who approaches her own shadow on the stone"; this weightless extinction initiates the poem's fatality, in which death becomes the extreme simplicity of a meeting between mosquito and the mosquito's shadow, just as the crosshairs of a sighting mechanism touch a target. As the metaphor gathers, in a parallel weightlessness time blurs between boyhood meeting manhood, and the parabola of a child's ball echoes the round of the sniper's glass, in a curved space in which the beginning of one is made to resemble the ending of another. The final version began:

Under the parabola of a ball,
a child turning into a man,
I looked into the air too long.
The ball fell in my hand, it sang
in the closed fist: *Open Open*
Behold a gift designed to kill.
        (Douglas papers, British Library, Add 53773)

It takes the rest of the finished poem to get back to the mosquito's flight that triggered the whole.

Initially, it is an "I" who glides "in my own silence as in a glass sphere" toward erasure in "the minute when shadow and self are one." Four lines scrawled on the reverse side of the MS of "Snakeskin and Stone" show the genesis of "How to Kill" and locate the death as the speaker's own (italics mine; alternate pronoun Douglas's):

I like a snakeskin or a stone
a bald head or a public speech,
I hate. *I move towards my end*
as a mosquito moves toward [his] her shadow.
(British Library, Add 53773)

In the many transformations of the poem, before the beginning flipped to become the end and Douglas definitively decided to tell it from the sniper's point of view, exactly which mother's son was to remain caught in the parabola of death's gift—the ball—and how many people were in the poem blurred. Well into a fifth patient working out of the poem's structure, Douglas tried to reintroduce "a new stranger" into the poem, who would "erase me." Yet this stranger was scratched out in a fishhatch of crossed and trailing phrases, which netted Douglas a final insight, which he kept: "It is easy to be a ghost."

And from there, the poem holds to its two-man membership, toiling towards its concluding examination of the eerily murderous calm that marks a death by gunfire in the twentieth-century evolution of the warrior's duel. Both rifleman and target are closed in the glass sights of the lethal and impersonal instrument. Douglas's revisions and reworkings of "How to Kill" complicate the burden of where guilt will fall, eventually lifting crucial weight away from the moment of death and onto the circle of the aim, and so proleptically into the earlier process of targeting itself. Hanging over the poem is the vestigial sense that the damned self who kills will complete the circuit with his own death. In the lightness of the mosquito's landing a life ends, and the diffusion of love that this sorcery creates draws down its own infernal consequence. It is *not* easy to be a ghost. That adjective "easy," wavered a half-dozen times in drafts into "sad": it is sad, it is sad, it is sad making a ghost, the typewriter reiterated, before, like a runner clearing the crest in a final bound, Douglas landed the phrase with "It is easy to make a ghost." The "sorcery" or potent magic of rendering life into death went through similar convolutions before departing from simple guilt and arriving at "amused" damnation. This murderous poise might not have been achieved if the rigorous hold on the figures of the poem had been loosened. Its central fusions— the convergence of mosquito and shadow flight on the stone, the ball dropping into the child's fist, the child grown into sudden manhood as the man himself travels in soundless waves from man to sudden dust—keep agency within the mental play of the one beholder of all these processes. Brilliantly, in complex, subtle movements, "How to Kill" ties together sadness, lightness, inevitability, and death:

> The weightless mosquito touches
> her tiny shadow on the stone,
> and with how like, how infinite
> a lightness, man and shadow meet.
> They fuse. A shadow is a man
> when the mosquito death approaches.
>
> (*Complete Poems*, 119)

In "How to Kill," soldiers represent a fatal redundancy, a nullification in which, whoever dies, each means to eliminate his double and therefore himself. Douglas's fix on this situation oddly echoes traits said to belong to the North African campaign which was his introduction to battle. In Hamish Henderson's forward to a book of his own poetry set on these battlefields, he begins with the remark of a captured German officer, who says: "Africa changes everything. In reality we are allies, and the desert is our common enemy" (Henderson, 59). This "allying" reshuffles the war, so that friend and foe stay to one side, and the terrain and its victims exert their own tremendous force on the other side:

> The troops confronting each other in Libya were relatively small in numbers. In the early stages of the desert war they were to a large extent forced to live off each other. Motor transport, equipment of all kinds and even armored fighting vehicles changed hands frequently. The result was a curious 'doppelgaenger' effect.

Henderson concludes:

> After the African campaign had ended, the memory of this odd effect of mirage and looking-glass illusion persisted, and gradually became for me a symbol of our human civil war, in which the roles seem constantly to change and the objectives to shift and vary. It suggested too a complete reversal of the alignments and alliances which we had come to accept as inevitable. The conflict seemed rather to be between 'the dead, the innocent'—that eternally wronged proletariat of levelling death in which all the

fallen are comrades—and ourselves, the living, who cannot hope to expi-
ate our survival but by 'spanning history's apollyon chasm.' (59)

Keith Douglas rarely misses the sense that observer and observed are inter-
changeable. While earlier war poets may have played up the essential brotherhood of friend and foe, much as Hamish Henderson does in the quoted passages, Douglas's leveling eye puts him in brotherhood with the dead.

Besides "How to Kill," Douglas's "Vergissmeinnicht" amplifies this sense of
the spectator-soldier helplessly viewing a dead self through the mirror of battle,
and, like Douglas's other memorable poems of war death, "Vergissmeinnicht" is
a static poem of aftermath. Initially, however, when it was called "A Dead Gunner," "Vergissmeinnicht" was a much more straightforward battlefield report.
Douglas began the draft of "A Dead Gunner" with a certain amount of exposition involving flashback (the brackets represent later insertions by hand):

Three weeks since pierced by flung metal
the sound steel broke beside my belly
[drew us back shattered]: the turret in a flurry
of blood and Bilby quite still, dribbling spittle,

and we advanced and knocked out that gun
and the crew got away somehow
to skulk in the mountains until now
the campaign over. [But] they left one,

they left you, perhaps the boy
to whom Steffi had written Vergissmeinnicht
on this photograph in the ditch. Perhaps the hand
that gave Evans and Bilby their last gift

For we see you with a sort of content
Abased, seeming to have paid
mocked by your own durable equipment
the metal beneath your decaying hand undecayed.

    (Douglas papers, British Library, Add 53773)

At this point the material switches into the conclusions of the final draft of
"Vergissmeinnicht," merely awaiting Douglas's smoothing hand to pull the

whole straight. But Douglas stripped all the drama of onslaught and active engagement away; he erases Evans and Bilby, attaches Steffi's photo in the ditch to the dead gunner without perhapses, and with the cancellation of Evans and Bilby amps up the love interest while scrapping the details of the possible revenge play between the fighters. The poem concentrates instead on the fact of human decay in the face of metal and weapon indomitability.

In the final version of "Vergissmeinnicht," the apposition of dead man and lover or beloved that is a subtheme in "Dead Men" and "How to Kill" comes to the fore, with all the essential props the same as in the other poems: a dead man, an observer, and a spill of the dead man's belongings, including that inscribed photograph of Steffi, the girlfriend, who enjoins us, "Vergissmeinnicht," or in Bavarian dialect, "Forget-me-not." In the near misses of battle, this is still the soldier who came on to attack the speaker "like the entry of a demon," but the emphasis is on his lying now in stillness as a harmless corpse:

> Three weeks gone and the combatants gone
> returning over the nightmare ground
> we found the place again, and found
> the soldier sprawling in the sun.
>
> The frowning barrel of his gun
> overshadowing. As we came on
> that day, he hit my tank with one
> like the entry of a demon.

In a flash of satisfaction at surviving his antagonist, the speaker can say,

> Look. Here in the gunpit spoil
> the dishonoured picture of his girl
> who has put: *Steffi. Vergissmeinnicht*
> in a copybook gothic script.

But the poem can only close, "almost content" with the victory of metal over man, killer over lover, death over life:

> We see him almost with content,
> abased, and seeming to have paid
> and mocked at by his own equipment
> that's hard and good when he's decayed.

But she would weep to see today
how on his skin the swart flies move;
the dust upon the paper eye
and the burst stomach like a cave.

For here the lover and killer are mingled
who had one body and one heart.
And death who had the soldier singled
has done the lover mortal hurt.

Not only does the erectile capacity of the weapon and not the man dominate, but also the static result over the dynamic of action.

A glance at C. Day Lewis's poem, "Reconciliation" (1943) makes clear the indelible originality of Douglas's "Vergissmeinnicht." If we could forget the way in which a combatant like Wilfred Owen occasionally sugared heroic death—as in a poem like "Asleep"—we might unfairly stigmatize Lewis's poem as the kind of opera only to be written by a noncombatant. "Vergissmeinnicht," however, whatever its relation to authentic experience, shows how genuinely sharp, clear-eyed, and unsentimental Douglas is about a gunner's death in the desert. There are striking differences in tone, point of view, and diction in Lewis's "Reconciliation":

All day beside the shattered tank he'd lain
Like a limp creature hacked out of its shell,
Now shrivelling on the desert's grid,
Now floating above a sharp-set ridge of pain.

There came a roar, like water, in his ear.
The mortal dust was laid. He seemed to be lying
In a cool coffin of stone walls,
While memory slid towards a plunging weir.

The time that was, the time that might have been
Find in this shell of stone a chance to kiss
Before they part eternally:
He feels a world without, a world within

Wrestle like old antagonists, until each is
Balancing each. Then, in a heavenly calm,

The lock gates open, and beyond
Appear the argent, swan-assemblied reaches.

>   (C. Day Lewis, 233)

Beside the bitter heft of Douglas, even the dry ironies of Stephen Spender's "Ultima Ratio Regum" (1939), his elegy for a soldier in the Spanish Civil War, look facile and indolent:

O too lightly he threw down his cap
One day when the breeze threw petals from the trees.
The unflowering wall sprouted with guns,
Machine-gun anger quickly scythed the grasses;
Flags and leaves fell from hands and branches;
The tweed cap rotted in the nettles.

Consider his life which was valueless
in terms of employment, hotel ledgers, news files.
Consider. One bullet in ten thousand kills a man.
Ask. Was so much expenditure justified
On the death of one so young and so silly
Lying under the olive trees, O world, O death?

>   (Spender, 69)

Until the very end, Douglas, like the young man that he was, who fell in love at every possible opportunity, never lost hope in the defeat of war by love. But in "Landscape with Figures," written in 1943 as three separate poems and then published by Desmond Graham in the 1966 *Complete Poems* as a single poem in parts, the repeating pieces work over the same possibilities without coming to poetic closure on any of them. The second poem openly positions Douglas as protagonist alongside the soundless writhing of the dead that he has witnessed, without any sign of relief to come. The section ends this desert scene:

The decor is terrible tracery
of iron. The eye and mouth of each figure
bear the cosmetic blood and hectic
colours death has the only list of.
A yard more, and my little finger

Inside the Whale   **143**

could trace the maquillage of these stony actors
I am the figure writhing on the backcloth.

> (Douglas, *Complete Poems*, 110)

For Keith Douglas, war may share the theatricality that Spender and C. Day Lewis find, but in these latter poems, war shows an unmistakably ugly suffering, an immobilized vulnerability swept by a sense of rupture and anomalous, incalculable loss.

"The glorious bran tub"

In poems and in his battle memoir, *Alamein to Zem Zem*, published posthumously in 1946, Keith Douglas recorded war death in various moods. In his memoir, however, war was something actively sought, not just helplessly evaded. In it, there is a residual exhilaration, a kind of "I dunnit!" in having achieved the coveted position of both witness and participant. The book swells with a visible, active desire, an almost careless spill of words and thoughts that means to get down everything that Douglas was feeling and seeing, wanting much more to chase life than to examine the hazard of death.

There is little of the elegiac sadness that conditions the opening of Edmund Blunden's memoir of 1914–1918, *Undertones of War* (1935). Blunden, later Douglas's tutor, mentor, and friend, begins: "I was not anxious to go." The paragraphs are full of a grave, rather ceremonious foreboding. Blunden, put in charge of soldiers recovering from wounds before he himself embarks for France, begins in valedictory mildness:

> I began to love these convalescent soldiers, and their distinguishing demeanor sank into me. They hid what daily grew plain enough—the knowledge that the war had released them only for a few moments, that the war would reclaim them, that the war was a jealous war and a long-lasting. 1914, 1915, 1916. . . . Occasionally I would ask the silly questions of nonrealization; they in their tolerance pardoned, smiled and hinted, knowing that I was learning, and should not escape the full lesson. (Blunden, *Undertones*, 21)

Blunden, whose service at the front was longer, at more than three years, than any of the other poets of his generation, subsequently reports of his recovered convalescents, "I never saw them again; they were hurried once more, fast as corks on a millstream, without complaint into the bondservice of destruction"

(*Undertones*, 23). The prose is somber, sonorous; only age and reflection can allow the speaker such a loving tolerance and tenderness for youthful ignorance or unfold with such acceptance of death, and with such serene respect for the bitter knowledge that he himself had moved forward to acquire.

Keith Douglas, however, shared none of Edmund Blunden's initial reluctance to serve. In 1942 in Egypt, he raced toward war, abandoning a desk job to catch up with his regiment. Having made a perpetual nuisance of himself through a fire of complaints and suggestions, his colonel had retaliated by sending him back to Divisional Headquarters, where he had been assigned to teach a camouflage course, keeping him well out of the way. Hearing that the engagement he was been spoiling for was now materializing, Douglas officially requested that he be reinserted into the regiment grinding towards Alamein; that effort failing, he bolted.

No doubt the unhappy conclusion of a romantic entanglement a few weeks earlier had spurred on his decision to leave; Douglas's initial enlistment in 1940 had been triggered in part by Britain's declaration of war against Germany, in part by news of a girlfriend's final desertion into marriage with someone else. Although there were other and stronger reasons to go to war that a lifetime had put in place, failing as a lover meant to Douglas that at least he could partially recover self-esteem by facing combat and seeking to "bloody well make my mark in this war" (Douglas, *Alamein*, 79). Now, at the onset of battle, he saw to it that he would not be denied the heroic role that would correct the imbalances of his bad luck with women.

Unlike Blunden's *Undertones of War*, which had been written a decade and more after the 1914–1918 war, Douglas began drafting *Alamein to Zem Zem* in 1943, only months after the campaign he describes took place. This is how he got to the front line:

> The battle of Alamein began on the 23rd of October, 1942. Six days afterwards I set out in direct disobedience of orders to rejoin my regiment. My batman was delighted with this maneuvre. 'I like you, sir,' he said. 'You're shit or bust, you are.' This praise gratified me a lot. (17)

As Douglas drove onward the Ford two-tonner that he had commandeered, he mentally rehearsed his next moves, determined to force his colonel's acceptance of his appearance on the spot; if refused, he would take his truck back to Alexandria, "and from there through Cairo and Ismalia and across the Sinai Desert to Palestine, to amuse myself until I was caught and courtmartialed."

But he was lucky in others' ill-luck: several officers having been lost in the previous days of fighting, he was needed, and taken back without questions. In contrast to Edmund Blunden's "I was not anxious to go," Douglas opens with another sort of limitation: "I am not writing about these battles as a soldier, nor trying to discuss them as military operations" (15). Keeping a writer's detachment about what he will make of his battle experience, he nonetheless hangs on to its significance:

> To say I thought of the battle of Alamein as an ordeal sounds pompous: but I did think of it as an important test I was interested in passing. I observed these battles partly as an exhibition—that is to say I went through them a little like a visitor from the country going to a great show, or like a child in a factory—a child who sees the brightness and efficiency of steel machines and endless belts slapping round and round, without caring or knowing what it is all there for. When I could order my thoughts I looked for more significant things than appearances; I still looked—I cannot avoid it—for something decorative, poetic or dramatic.

He makes himself responsible to literature rather than to patriotism, and above all, he presents himself as a naive amateur, as someone who did not identify with the army as an institution. Even as he names battle "an important test," it is still murky as to what will constitute a passing grade; nor does it ever emerge as to who might judge him, other than himself.

There is a cadenced smoothness to Edmund Blunden's *Undertones of War*. Framing the book is a steady contrast between pastoral France and Belgium, and the antipastoral trench war, as Blunden in the mode of memoir casts loving looks, full of muted anguish, at the violated farms and villages of his soldier years. There is also an iron distance maintained between the older and the younger self, however subtly tense and mood changes play with the gap between then and now, shifting our sense of audience to and from, now to the men with whom he fought, now to the general postwar audience, and now to the speaker himself, with his thoughtful view of the "harmless young shepherd in a soldier's coat" that he conceives himself to have been. The past is held at an irrevocable distance from Blunden's contemporary mind and increasingly middle-aged body, as Blunden mended his text several times, a veteran soldier wishing to keep the past ever more precisely alive beside him.

In comparison, Keith Douglas's almost pell-mell performance in *Alamein to Zem Zem* will be heterogeneous as to tone, focus, and genre. Where disillusion

FIGURE 7. Keith Douglas, Alexandria, 1942. Photo by "Milena." The Brotherton Collection, University of Leeds.

with the useless waste of the war creeps, or seeps, into Blunden's account, it's the incredulous wondering note of surprise at war's illogic, each little shock of Douglas's running encounter with dysfunction, that jolts his observation along. While the opening rather ingenuously claims to adopt the child's perspective, the book is full of learned allusion as well as scraps of colloquial dialogue, and the resulting composite is multilayered, tentative, lurching in pace. Almost as a notebook effort on how to write about war, or shape a text on human character, Douglas will do flat description, ironic juxtaposition, running commentary, and conversation. Yet in spite of announced intention, the mood always veers to the analytic and against the dramatic; in spite of not caring or knowing about "what it's all there for," there are improvisational bursts of ordering and a strong need to voice conclusions. The narrative brakes and wavers, full of ellipses and discontinuities, copying the anomalous structure of the war by which his senses were being flooded—while he wrote and as he felt it.

Much as Randall Jarrell had described his place in the army as a cog in the industrial military machine, Douglas described his own littleness in relation to the vastness of what he had joined, but in naturalistic metaphor:

Through areas as full of organization as a city of ants—it happened that two days before I had been reading Maeterlinck's descriptions of ant communities—I drove up the sign-posted tracks until, when I reached my own place in all this activity, I had seen the whole arrangement of the Army, almost too large to appreciate, as a body would look to a germ riding in its bloodstream. (*Alamein*, 17)

It is not too large for Douglas to appreciate nor to be glad of his berth in it, accepting, via the reading that never stopped, the almost organic irrationality of what engaged him.

With a pride close to apology Douglas explains:

> But it is exciting and amazing to see thousands of men, very few of whom have much idea why they are fighting, all enduring hardships, living in an unnatural, dangerous, but not wholly terrible world, having to kill and be killed, and yet at intervals moved by a feeling of comradeship with the men who kill them and whom they kill, because they are enduring and experiencing the same things. It is tremendously illogical—to read about it cannot convey the impression of having walked through the looking-glass which touches a man entering a battle. (16)

In spite of the continuities that he shows between his prewar and his wartime self, it is the uniqueness of battle that seizes his attention: "Whatever changes in the nature of warfare, the battlefield is the simple, central stage of war: it is there that the interesting things happen" (15)

Alamein to Zem Zem, quickly written and fairly quickly taken for publication, follows an adventure ideology with mostly offhand and understated commentary on tragic event. Keith Douglas seems to have lost no friends dear to him, and his campaign, one of the major engagements of the British forces in World War II, was one fought by unusually clean standards. There were no notable incidents of prisoner abuse or of harassment of civilian populations, who were, in any case, sparsely settled over this desert terrain. Writing to a friend about taking prisoners, Douglas says:

> But when they broke they broke properly, and the pursuit was very like hunting in England, except that instead of killing the fox when we found him, we gave him a tin of bully beef and searched him for souvenirs. (Douglas papers, British Library, Add 56355)

Had Douglas survived the war and had the time for reflection and revision that other combat survivors like Graves, Sassoon, and Blunden managed after

World War I, most probably he, too, would have darkened the lights in this text. Through Douglas's leaning for irony and satire, however, the likelihood is greater that this memoir would have moved closer to the kind of dark comedy that characterizes World War II in Joseph Heller's *Catch 22* and in Paul Fussell's Word War II memoir, *Doing Battle*, subtitled *The Making of a Skeptic*. But while Douglas's credentials as a skeptic were fairly good, the manner that Blunden called "cheerful and disputatious and affectionate" (in Douglas, *Prose Miscellany*, 155) gives a volatile touch to a short book in which Douglas's omnivorous curiosity crammed a very broad banquet of perception.

Nothing escaped his interest or need to record, from the stacked petrol tins which sheltered "comfortable" latrines dug on the way to Tripoli, to the way in which a fellow soldier was barbered—"he had the kind of mustache that can be seen from behind" (115). There is always the swing of follow-through in his detail: when a mate decorates his tank with the Eye of Horus, Douglas takes down that it's done with sump oil and the blacking off a brew-tin. When he picks up a German edition of Nietzsche's *Also Sprach Zarathustra*, he notes that the previous owner had underlined all the passages that boost National Socialism. He examines the first dead man he has ever seen meticulously:

> There were no signs of violence. As I looked at him, a fly crawled across his cheek and across the dry pupil of his unblinking right eye. I saw that a pocket of dust had collected in the trough of the lower lid. (*Alamein*, 38)

Passing a row of corpses pulled from burning tanks, he adds: "For some reason the feet and boots had nearly all escaped the flames" (54). The dead always have white faces painted on them by the ubiquitous desert dust.

His is a mind alert for reasons, for the clear logic that battle so obdurately refuses. In the absence of reason, he obviously delighted in the massing of absurdities, grappling within battle chaos for the pattern and style in which the brutal and the comic mixed themselves. An account of burning tanks and mutilated bodies offers a judgment on Italian soldiers' habit of booby-trapping corpses, which is then followed by the trouble he is having with the buttons of his fly, the sharp tin buttons of which "begin cutting themselves off as soon as they are sewn on" (54). He eventually loses all of his buttons, and tries to cinch his trousers with his belt. Called to dismount from his tank by his colonel,

> I tumbled out of the turret, forgetting the state of my trousers, which immediately fell around my ankles. I hauled them up with one hand and

staggered across to him. When I had told him all I knew I hobbled back and climbed on to my tank in time to hear Ken Tinker reporting the destruction of the last 88. (55)

The guns, buttons, and military intelligence gathering are narratively on a par.

The needs to station, to register, to contextualize, even in the absence of contextual logic, show themselves throughout *Alamein to Zem Zem* in the eye restless for literary parallel. While bits of literary reference were trimmed here and there in the portions of the manuscript that Douglas had a chance to edit, indicating that much more may have been deleted from a final cut, the habit was nonetheless irrepressible: a red aureole above an advancing tank makes it look as if the dead crew were bringing it in: "A very slim connection reminded me momentarily of Ambrose Bierce's Horseman in the Sky" (57). Looking at a tank just hit by high explosive fire, he remarks that "a shower of light and dark grey-blue smoke flew from the side of the leading Sherman's turret, like the goddess Sin springing from the left shoulder of Satan" (117). It is characteristic that Douglas works in not just the Miltonic echo, but the tint and saturation of the color.

The next observation records the physical gap between seeing and hearing: "The tank was in flames before the noise and impact of the explosion reached me." He was not only interested in mining his senses for what they were worth, but in gauging the kind and nature of their interplay, in discovering how battle crowded sensation and destroyed the ordinary connections between sense and feeling. Here is a passage tracking the flight of an enemy plane:

> Up above in the clear sky a solitary aeroplane moved, bright silver marking its unhurried course. The Bofors gunners on either side of us were running to their guns and soon opened a rapid, thumping fire, like a titanic workman hammering. The silver body of the aeroplane was surrounded by hundreds of little grey smudges, through which it sailed on serenely. From it there fell away, slowly and gracefully, an isolated shower of rain, a succession of glittering drops. I watched them descend a hundred feet before it occurred to me to consider their significance and forget their beauty. The column of tanks trundled forward imperturbably, but the heads of their crews no longer showed. I dropped down in the turret and shouted to Evans who was dozing in the gunner's seat: 'Someone's dropping some stuff.' He shouted back a question and adjusted his earphones. 'Bombs!' I said into the microphone. (27)

There's an odd slow motion, a double take going on, before the eerie beauty of the plane in flight gives way, and the aesthetic drops into the realistic mode, the passive to the active. It takes a whole delaying paragraph for antiaircraft fire to be realized as more than "smudges," and for "glittering drops" to become "bombs." More precisely, it takes a while for the connection between eye and mind to mend their battlefield disruption. In the distancing of mechanized warfare, the ground has a hard time catching up with the sky, and the ear fails to tune into the wireless, enacting the fatal gap between seeing and doing, between saying and hearing, that existed in Douglas's life as a tank commander, here registered with exactitude. The whole weight of the paragraph runs deliberately backward, suspending the dramatic thread as it does in "reality," where danger occurs but cannot be reacted to until it is named: "bombs," or trails away from "fire" into "smudges," as the work of "titans" supervenes over the work of small and soft-skinned human beings.

Battle renders the working of Douglas's senses preternaturally alert. The task of the memoir, though, is not only to understand the full range of their functioning, but also to note that their failure to function is an integral part of battle during the saturated hours or minutes when fear and paralysis seize the self both directly and indirectly. An original title for the book was "Anatomy of a Battle"; the primary urge was a totalizing description, and this drive steadily takes precedence over the creation of the heroic.

Alamein to Zem Zem is written in two parts, the first and longest of which begins with the flight towards Alamein and the preparation for that battle and ends with Douglas tripping a mine wire on the advance through Libya. There is a brief coda describing the term after his injury and his return to the regiment that brought him to the Wadi Zem Zem in Tunisia. The final paragraphs sums up the loss of several key officers, ending not in elegy, however, but with a celebration:

> And tomorrow, we said, we'll get into every vehicle we can find, and go out over the whole ground we beat them on, and bring in more loot than we've ever seen. (152)

After this tomorrow and its respite Douglas would face the Normandy beachhead.

Despite the refusal of military analysis at its opening, *Alamein to Zem Zem* offers an unrelenting inquiry into what goes askew in battle, which becomes part of the book's consistent deflation of conventional battle heroics. The first day's engagement provides the pattern for the much longer fight in the advance towards Tripoli. Douglas gives no maps, rarely names generals and ignores the code names like Crusader and Torch with which the military historian is inevitably saddled. Rommel and Montgomery receive a couple of mentions apiece in the entire memoir. But what happens in the Crusader tanks that Douglas inhabited along with his drivers and his gunners is covered minutely.

While Douglas's poem "How to Kill" projected himself as an aggressor, *Alamein to Zem Zem* disperses the connection to actual killing. People get killed, but Douglas's narrative is not interested in tracking agency because battle seems just too big, too noisy, and too confusing to do this correctly anyway. Finally, the tidal wave of destructive energy that war releases is too vast and overwhelming to keep straight what the sides do to each other or even themselves in the heat of the mutual barrage. Without comment, Douglas registers the occasions in which soldiers face injury from artillery blasts that fall short into their own troops.

On his first day in battle Douglas finally succeeds in getting his sulky gunner to direct a prolonged burst of artillery at what he thinks is a machine gun nest. But in the ensuing moments, the assault changes:

> A few yards from the left of the tank, two German soldiers were climbing out of a pit, grinning sheepishly as though they had been caught in a game of hide and seek. In their pit lay a Spandau machine-gun with its perforated jacket. So much, I thought with relief, for the machine-gun nest. But now men rose all around us. (38)

Eventually, forty men surrender, leading to a richly satisfactory haul of weapons, rations, coffee, and binoculars, the latter, in the most hostile action of the episode, are nicked by the English infantry patrol assisting Douglas's tank squadron. Douglas's references to German prisoners are neutral in emotional tone; while he quotes soldiers who talk about "Jerries" and "Nazis," his own nomenclature was an undeviating "German." He feels no particular animus; when he catches up with prisoners, he is happy to try out his German on them and is quite pleased to find it in working order.

Douglas is even happier to acquire German weapons, food, and clothing, superior to what has been issued to him in many instances. Scolded by a publisher's reader for his references to looting, which the home front was sure that British soldiers do not practice, his reply was firm and unequivocal:

> Loot is one of the most important things—and it is the thing that makes all that exhilaration in fighting. And believe it or not, our utmost thought at the end of the battle was loot. By that you must not understand—as I believe you do—pillaging or corpse robbing, but simply rummaging in the glorious bran tub provided by any battlefield. (*Prose Miscellany*, 153–54)

The bran tub, of course, is where the horses are fed; Douglas's choice of metaphor is quite interesting, given the contempt he shows in "Aristocrats" for the anachronistic idealism of the cavalry and all soldier-centaurs. Here he evinces a simple receptivity to horse values.

For this young man in his twenties, battle has become the test, the glass through which he must pass to gain Alice's knowledge of reversed perspectives. In this distorted mirror of the normal, the battlefield is the killing floor, but all soldiers on any side are alike subject to its hazards and exist together in fatal equilibrium. For Keith Douglas this meant not hating your enemy; your focus on killing him is diverted to making your impartial weaponry function and keeping yourself intact. In this description, there is a gap between defense and offense in which defense is everything and offense is solely concentrated on working your machines. Your direct designs on another soldier's person are limited to what is delectably portable and can be detached. As in a schoolboy contest, the real goal, other than your own survival, reads as the prize given out at game's end.

At Galal Station, Douglas once more observes the enemy dead. Climbing into a derelict Italian tank and hunting for more Birettas for his trading hoard, he finds only people and parts of people distributed about the turret: "About them clung that impenetrable silence . . . , by which I think the dead compel our reverence" (*Alamein*, 66). It brings him up short, and he chooses to look for Birettas in another tank. But he closes this episode with the most buoyant of his passages on that enormity, war:

> In the evening we closed into night leaguer, facing westwards again. Tom was in high spirits; he and Ken Tinker had found an Italian hospital, and their tanks were loaded inside and out with crates of cherries, Macedonian cigarettes, cigars and wine; some straw-jacketed Italian Chianti issue, some

champagne, and a bottle or two of brandy, even some Liebfraumilch. We shared out the plunder with the immemorial glee of conquerors, and beneath

the old star-eaten blanket of the sky
lay down to dream of victory.
    (66)

The moments matching this snugly cosmic content, the whole host sleeping together in brotherly safety, are fairly few. Reaching back to quote T. E. Hulme's best line from his World War I poem, "The Embankment," Douglas's hold on comfort is rooted in another of those unforeseeable literary ironies: neither Douglas nor Hulme survived the wars that so severely tested their embrace of what Hulme had termed "heroic values."

War and its terror make their appearance only briefly at the end of Douglas's first day of battle, in which twelve enemy tanks fire on his squadron. He writes of this concentrated terror, in which position is lost and only confusion seems paramount: "These were the intensest moments of physical fear, outside of dreams, I have ever experienced" (42). Even here, it should be noticed that reality is not allowed to trump the internal power of nightmare. But Douglas recovers the moment, shaping it in a clear narrative and dramatic trajectory, full of triumph and the relief of surviving danger:

> The turret was full of fumes and smoke. I coughed and sweated; fear had given place to exhilaration. Twilight increased to near-darkness, and the air all round us gleamed with the different coloured traces of shells and bullets, brilliant graceful curves travelling from us to the enemy and from him toward us. The din was tremendously exciting. Above us whistled the shells of the seventy-fives. Overhead the trace of enemy shells could be seen mounting to the top of their flight where, as the shell tilted towards us, it disappeared. Red and orange bursts leapt up beside and in front of us. (42)

Douglas rides invincibly through layers of fire—and like boys' mock battles in a schoolyard, this time nobody gets hurt. Next:

> Darkness ended the action as suddenly as it had begun; the petrol lorries alone blazed like beacons, answered by distant fires in the direction of the enemy. Gradually we found our way into leaguer, creeping past the dim shapes of our companions.

Peacefulness vibrates in that lying down together. The final account of battle that this baptismal experience precedes occurs after a long stretch of logistical maneuvering, in which analysis of officers, communications systems, and resupply and transport dominate. The description of the battle itself, which culminates in the injury that removes Douglas from the fighting, drops the exalted mode and focuses more nearly on war as a species of deadly fuckup, as seen by an impatient, clever, and hyperactive intelligence that thinks the people in charge are not doing it right: it is not the view of a rakish and triumphant cavalier-duelist. Finally, Keith Douglas joins all the other twentieth-century poets and memoirists who see war as a corporate blunder in which the emphasis falls on an incompetent, bloody, and disorderly use of human beings turned into inconsequent things.

The chapters leading up to the climactic final engagement are actually bullish on modern war. Chapter 16 reassures the reader that the supposed hardships of this desert campaign were not exiguous; Food, if limited, was nonetheless steady in supply, and the cookery of the troops was ingenious. Keeping clean was difficult but not impossible on the daily ration of a half gallon of water intended for all cooking, drinking, and washing. Harder, evidently, were the mental strains: for a man "so given to amusing himself with imaginative arrangements of the future" (*Alamein*, 105) to stop such forward speculation was frustrating; the difficulty of dealing with the general strain of living in the present entirely was also amplified by the tedium of living for months with the same randomly selected people. Yet even here, Douglas is surprised by "how agreeable we found each other's company" (105).

And there follows in chapter 17 an analysis of the superiorities of tank warfare:

> Anyone who takes part in a modern battle in a tank, which is equipped with a wireless, has an advantage over the infantrymen, and over all the soldiers and generals of earlier wars. Before his mind's eye the panorama of the battle is kept, more vividly even than before the general of other times who watched his soldiers from a vantage point, or was kept posted by telephones and runners. (107)

The tank officer is especially well informed, for

> before going into action he has listened to the scheme of orders for the whole army. He knows, or has had represented to him by a coloured diagram on a

map (the main outline of which is soon fixed by the skill of habit in his mind), the position, the route, the objectives, of each Division and Brigade. In his own Brigade he knows where the squadrons, the supply vehicles, the guns and infantry of his regimental group are, and their radio code names. Within his squadron . . . he knows the positions of the other troops and of his squadron leader, and finally of the tanks of his troop. As he moves forward, the coloured lines advance across the map of his mind. (108)

From here, the description glides gradually away from this idealized summary into the actualities of wireless exchange and tank maneuver, so that by the time we are well into the next battle, all the potentials for breakdown between men, equipment, and plans materialize, step by horrific step.

Everything sticks. Tanks break down, lose tracks. Gears and guns jam. Visibility is lost. Orders foul up in transmission between officers and men; terrain is misread; targets are mistaken; map bearings are lost; and group coherence crumbles. In the intense anxiety of battle, codes are confused, and the communal solidarity of advance is hopelessly, horribly scrambled. In one cruelly nightmarish moment, Douglas realizes that the comforting tanks that surround his foray against an enemy tank are not functional machines containing the support of friendly living men, but instead form the dead and abandoned hulks of a deserted position. He is alone, outgunned, and exposed in a machine that is dying on him. But what is more fundamentally exposed, in the darkest surreal comedy, is the irrationality and depthless vanity of the idea of war as order. Control is a mirage that evaporates in desert reality.

The battle in which Keith Douglas participated was a notable Allied success; he himself performed all of the acts that constitute merit in an officer. He reconnoitered in the face of opposition, took fire and aimed his own, scouted for advantage, and evaded the enemy. His initial command of four tanks reduced one by one to none, he was finally sidelined in his last tank by a direct hit, but he hung around long enough to retrieve the body of his driver and carry another wounded officer to safety.

If we extract the bald particulars, he followed his training and did all the right things—and in the end he was part of victory. Yet his own narrative subverts and undermines both the epic and the heroic. In one narrative maneuver, he stops his story cold, in the middle of a tight pursuit, to tell a story:

His voice recalled to me a description he once gave us at dinner of fighting a battle in a Grant tank: 'The "75" is firing, but it's traversing round the wrong way. The Browning is jammed. I am saying: "Driver advance" on the A set, and the driver who can't hear me, is reversing. And as I look over the top of the turret and see twelve enemy tanks fifty yards away, someone hands me a cheese sandwich.' At the moment this seemed just another true word spoken in jest. (*Alamein*, 120)

In Douglas's war, there is always a cheese sandwich—or something worse—stuck in the action.

In his war narrative, Keith Douglas stumbles on these conclusions by hunting out direct experience. Christopher Isherwood and W. H. Auden, however, in their tour of the battlefields that, as "foreign correspondents," they were barred from viewing too closely, emerged with the same idea. Isherwood, from beside the Sino-Japanese war in 1940 reports on the broken narrative as the story of war, where operations are truncated in fear and haste, in inundating circumstances. Decisively, they reject the official journalism:

> Everything was lucid and tidy and false—the flanks like neat little cubes, the pincer-movements working with mathematical precision, the reinforcements never failing to arrive punctual to the minute. But war, as Auden said later, is not like that. . . . War is untidy, inefficient, obscure, and largely a matter of chance. (Auden and Isherwood, 202)

Nothing that Keith Douglas encountered obliterates these conclusions, hardly unfamiliar to him or to us, and yet he was driven by the need to see for himself, to use his own flesh for the acquisition of discovery.

His own wounding follows the same discontinuities, the same refusal of cause and effect to line up. After a series of passages during which three men had been killed on ground from which Douglas had tried to warn them away, the last of the four tanks of his troop has been hit directly. Stunned but unhurt, he emerges from his tank to take cover, gets his wounded driver hauled out of the turret, searches his kit for morphia, finds he has none, and goes to get a syringe from a dazed soldier standing in front of another blazing tank about to explode; the soldier, headphones on, responds neither to shouts to move away from the blazing tank nor requests for a syringe. Twenty-four tons of metal then disintegrate from twelve yards away, while Douglas gets the morphia, which when injected does nothing to relieve his driver's pain because by mistake a preparation for waking people from anesthesia has been substituted in the soldier's kit.

"My mind was not working properly," Douglas writes, as he recalls making a run for it under heavy fire: "I did not care if they shot me but I was unnerved by the thought of capture" (*Alamein*, 127). Used to the motion of quick response, capture represents stall and stoppage. For Douglas risking death is preferable to being unable to move freely; capture will mean the encumbered will, or the effective cancellation of all versions of "shit or bust."

Encountering more wounded in the pit that he does succeed in reaching for shelter, Douglas looks at one of the wounded:

> Only his clothes distinguished him as a human being, and they were badly charred. His face had gone: in place of it was a huge yellow vegetable. The eyes blinked in it, eyes without lashes, and a grotesque huge mouth dribbled and moaned like a child exhausted with crying. (128)

As if one more horror, one more collapse were the straw on the camel's back, Douglas again opts for flight, saying that he will go for help, thereby justifying his leaving the scene. But he says to himself:

> Before I had gone a hundred yards I was ashamed: my own mind accused me of running to escape, rather than running for help. But I hurried on, determined to silence these accusations by getting a vehicle of some kind and bringing it back, in the face of the enemy if necessary. I knew that if only I could gain the cover of the ridge and stop to think, and if I could find where the regiment had gone, I should be able to organize myself and go back. (128)

He does regroup; he does get help; he manages a rescue. Yet the internal accusation that he panicked results in a characteristic response: to run, to move, is always better than to accept stasis. If he were ever to stop, going on would be impossible; paralysis and stupor lie in wait for those prone to waiting.

After rejoining his squadron, he moves again, to hail the car eventually set to bring the rescue. But as he advances, someone shouts, "'Look out. There's a trip wire.' I knew already. I had just tripped it. I should have thrown myself down at once, but a sort of resignation prevented me, and I walked on a few steps before the mine exploded" (129). It is in fact a series of mines; by the second, Douglas topples and sprawls. He explains that "It was a bright new wire strung through wooden pegs: I realized I had seen it and discounted it because of its newness, and because subconsciously I had come to expect such things to be cunningly hidden." Mines had been part of everyone's consciousness in this campaign. Once, an unlucky soldier casually swung a tree branch out of his way, only to discover that it had been mined. But Douglas is following one logic, the logic of the hidden, while the mine layer has followed another, the logic of the obvious.

Definitively downed, with injuries to face, torso, and legs, Douglas pulls himself through wounding and convalescence with the same need to observe, to record, to keep track of himself, that has served him well so far. As he is carried into a tent for the wounded, as if still trying to get his mind to work "properly," he says: "There was a great deal to watch in this tent." And again, orienting to the artist's life: "Cruikshank would have drawn this interior well, and Hogarth would have made a shot at it" (133). He wants two things, neither of which he gets: that the surgeon cutting his clothes off him preserve his suede leather waistcoat, of which he is quite fond; and above all, he wants his picture taken:

> Almost covered with dressings from head to foot and still wearing the filthy remnants of my clothes, I looked vainly round for someone from the Army Film and Photographic Unit. After my whiskey and hot tea I felt thoroughly cheerful and ready to produce a traditional grin to go with my costume. I could readily forgive the destruction of my clothes to achieve such an artistic whole as my appearance after treatment. (131)

It is hard to believe that this is all tongue in cheek. Later he dryly observes that the kind and scope of his injuries exactly match those of another soldier who, hundreds of miles *behind* the front line, merely went for a walk and tripped a mine. He closes his own battlefield phase by saying, "I must send a cable to Mother, and then write her a letter with a diagram of where the wounds were" (141). Just as he had sent off a letter to his mother when he was ten of a winning kick in football, with diagrams, where several earnestly scrawled pencil sketches gave in exact perspective the ball, the goalposts, and the playing field, from two sides and then frontally. Both battlefield and playing field are sites of honor; but on both occasions in his solidly structural details, Douglas is "stationing," much as an admiring Keats so many years earlier had described Milton's thoroughgoing poetic discipline.

"Bete Noire"

A handful of Keith Douglas's poems in major English and American anthologies of twentieth-century poetry, most notably "How to Kill," and

"Vergissmeinnicht," perpetuated the sense of him as an English soldier-poet. The irony of that assessment is that in his final poems, Douglas continued to expand his sense of personal isolation to include the fragmentation and alienation felt by all of those at or in war, leaving little to distinguish his work from that of the combatant or noncombatant observer. But for the timing of his death, Douglas would never have been given to literature as a war poet, but as a poet simply. Likely he would be remembered as a poet who was memorably an all-purpose man of letters, who wrote essays, stories, novels, memoir, and so on. Like the shark's eye in his poem "The Marvel," which, used as a lens, brought life to sharp focus for the sailors on deck of a ship, war focused the themes of Douglas's short life: had that life lengthened, war, too, would have been pitchforked onto the heap of all the other crucial experiences he would use to transform life into art.

Retrospectively, any measure of Keith Douglas's war poetry, the whole short, intense body of it, must allow for the extent to which it is not a poetry of battle, but largely a poetry of prelude and aftermath to war and an account of both civilians and soldiers within a vast, kaleidoscopic confusion, of which battle forms the smallest part. Randall Jarrell, with a conspicuously partial success, projected a comprehensive landscape of twentieth-century war from a snug niche on the home front. Keith Douglas's war poems, however, are in William Scammell's words, "curiously private," their action muted significantly by the literary politics of belatedness. For Douglas, war poetry, or what he was learning to pass beyond as his primary concern, had all been done before.

Even if, as readers, we first come upon this poet as an exemplar of the battle poet, the more useful and enduring task may be to understand how his insights into war fit within the larger mission of the lyric, which is generally to write elegy in the shadow of death. We tend to read Douglas—like Sidney Keyes, like Wilfred Owen, like Isaac Rosenberg—as a particular subspecies of poet, the Fated Boy, with his own heroic aureole stretching into the magnificent and misty Undone. In this scheme, Keith Douglas gets swept up as a minor object in literary history, making us settle for him as something lesser, a figure of pathos. Yet Douglas's tough, wiry poems shifted, before his life ended, from witnessing war as part of a doomed generation, among people who were entrepreneurs in the social project of war itself, to the separate and personal task of seeing himself as an isolate, someone condemned and apart yet tortured by the destructiveness of that self-assessment, and fighting it. Removing the "war poet" label from Douglas and his work should amplify the poems' real perspectives and let us hear how Douglas's thinking on war was thinking about death and how a man's bonds to community fray and tighten between his own and others' needs. Listening harder to the metaphysical content in Douglas's poems, and responding to the person and temperament in them, also clarifies the two-way traffic between "war poetry" and other genres and subgenres.

Douglas acknowledged to Edmund Blunden, in response to T. S. Eliot's observation of his poetry, that it was indeed changing and moving into a new phase not as yet mastered. But in June 1943, when Douglas admonishes John Hall for a failure to understand his swerve from a purer, more objective lyricism, Douglas defends himself against Hall's "precious" poetry. Such a lyricism is in Douglas's terms too "anti reportage and extrospective (if the word exists)"; the rougher sound and diction of his poems represents a style which seemed to him "the sort that has to be written just now, even if it is not attractive" (Douglas, *Prose Miscellany*, 121).

There is also an overwhelming sense of the provisional and the fleeting in Douglas's view of his use of language, caught in a few lines in the poem "Words," written in the General Hospital at El Ballah around January of 1943:

But I keep words only a breath of time
turning in the lightest of cages—uncover
and let them go: sometimes they escape for ever.
    (*Complete Poems*, 107)

This lightness may be part of his poetry's unique poise. The language of Douglas's poems hovers just above prosaic bluntness but still tenses within a mastery of traditional sound, in which a subtle, varied, and ingenious use of rhyme and stanzaic form keeps Douglas anchored in tradition but looking forward to the newer and broader innovations of English poetry happening in the century. In these happenings, common speech rhythms increasingly obliterate the search for songlike sound, moving against the formal music that will destroy the flyway between poetry and ordinary speech.

When Douglas takes up the subject of his current practice again with Hall on 10 August 1943, he winds up interestingly enough, with a defense of a deeply witnessing poetry by describing his own "extrospective poetry" as a talisman against the "sentimental" or "emotional," qualities recognizable of course as first cousin to Philip Larkin's feared "bathos":

But my object (and I don't give a damn about my duty as a poet) is to write true things, significant things in words each of which works for its place in a line. My rhythms, which you find enervated, are carefully chosen to enable the poems to be *read* as significant speech: I see no reason to be either musical or sonorous about things at present. When I do, I shall be so again, and glad to. I suppose I reflect the cynicism and the careful absence of expectation (it is not quite the same as apathy) with which I view the world. As many others to whom I have spoken, not only civilians and British soldiers, but Germans and Italians, are in the same state of mind, it is a true reflection. I never tried to write about war (that is battles and things, not London can Take it), with the exception of a satiric picture of some soldiers frozen to death, until I had experienced it. Now I will write of it, and perhaps one day cynic and lyric will meet and make me a balanced style. (*Prose Miscellany*, 127)

Once readers stop expecting him to sound like the previous generation, his poetry sounds nearer to that balanced style, with its acceptance of the cadences of ordinary speech, than he or John Hall thought. But for Douglas, the justification for a style both economic and authoritative, one closer to the demotic, is not a simple revolt against the primacy of beautiful sound; his counter to the argument that a too ardent or meticulous realism destroys universality of meaning seeks to defend a grittier realism as in the final service of truth, a dedication that wartime demands.

Yet while his own confidence in writing about war may have increased the brilliance with which he tackled it, with the experience of battle behind him the mature poems that followed from that dose of blood, fire, and death differ little in rhetorical intention from the notable noncombatant poetry of the period. War focused, narrowed, clipped, and intensified Douglas's style, but his insights into combat are not hugely different or more extensive than those found, for instance, in Roy Fuller's or Alun Lewis's poems on war, both of whom saw considerably less of it than did Keith Douglas. Douglas's war poems entirely lack Hamish Henderson's breaks into sentimental fondness for regimental glory in his *Elegies for the Dead in Cyrenaica*. Douglas is also free of the intermittent clank of Henderson's rhetoric for the fallen. A reading of Henderson, a soldier writing from experience in the same theater of war, provides a quick measure of Douglas's originality.

In Keith Douglas's mind, his friend John Hall, the defending champion of tradition, lines himself up as a lover of beauty, while Douglas, the knight-errant of contemporaneity, puts up ugliness or the starkly direct as his weapon of choice. In wartime, Keats's truth, beauty, and poetry are separable, or, at

least, beauty gets to wear a face without the cosmetic of lush rhythms and aureate diction. Where readers like Philip Larkin see the violent particular dis-
serving the reader by diminishing imaginative range and broad cultural possession, soldier-poets like Douglas, and Isaac Rosenberg and Siegfried
Sassoon before him, see war with an urgency that is wary of suffocating
painful fact through preoccupation with a caging prosodic necessity or a crip-
pling deference to the noncomprehension of civilians. Ultimately, the great
soldier-poets fit their tragic subject within the universal and recognizable domain of human suffering, but, like any experience brought into poetry, war
comes trailing its own stubbornly indissoluble colors.

For Douglas, the truth of war in the twentieth century cannot be contained
within the old language; for form to enact subject, a contemporary poetry was
bound to disrupt the old rhythms and cadences, nor could honor be paid to
death in war through the old conventions of mourning. To memorialize the
heaped dead without falsity meant bearing the most transparent witness possible to war's reality. Isaac Rosenberg and Keith Douglas follow one impera-
tive, to plunge headlong into the free practice dedicated first to fullness and ac-
curacy. In the autumn of 1916, Rosenberg wrote to Laurence Binyon:

> I am determined that this war, with all its powers for devastation, shall not
> master my poeting; that is, if I am lucky enough to come through all right.
> I will not leave a corner of my consciousness covered up, but saturate my-
> self with the strange and extraordinary new conditions of this life, and it
> will all refine itself into poetry later on. (Rosenberg, 248)

Both he and Douglas trusted poetry to tumble into the right grooves laid down
first by experience.

Half the terrible poignance of both poets' poetry and prose is still saturated with our knowledge of their early death. For Keith Douglas, the troubling
question that intrudes may be the degree to which he fatalistically sought
death, rather than, in Ted Hughes's words, "foresuffered" it. What did the
"sort of resignation" with which he yielded to the mine's trip wire really mean
about his life as a soldier and a man? When he enlisted, friends recall his saying, with a certain amount of adolescent bravado it should be noted, that he
would "bloody well make my mark in the war. For I will not come back"
(quoted in Graham, 79). Over the remaining four years, this premonition was
repeated to many. To a girlfriend he wrote in more qualified terms: "I can't
help thinking that I haven't got an awful long time before I leave this lazy life,

possibly for good" (quoted in Graham, 88). Under the circumstances, this was a foreseeable outcome.

But combat seems to have diminished these fears, which do not appear again until months after his Middle Eastern service, when he returned to England. At this point, he was again reiterating his conviction to one girl or another, that she should marry him for the pension that would fall to her in the event of his death. In the Middle East, he was busy making plans for the future: inquiring after a job as lecturer at the British Council, making jokes about being around to write posthumous reviews of his rivals, and planning not on death, but a less permanent exile: Tunisia looked good to him. Besides, he was not all that fond of the English, commenting that "England will never be my home country. I must make my life extend across at least half the world, to be happy." And again, "I can't stop among more or less undiluted English people for long, much as I like a few of them" (Douglas papers, British Library, Add 56355).

Perhaps a better explanation than fatalism for his headlong rush to combat lies in a self-description. In a letter to an early fiancée, he wrote that he had a "terror of perishing into an ordinary existence"; this, while another part of him wanted settling down, and a partner "to whom I can give all my love without fear of being hurt" (quoted in Graham, 82). Like the good stoic who expects to lessen hurt by preparing for it, Douglas rigorously anticipated all forms of loss, including death. Yet each sharp reversal in his fortune as a lover sent him racing into danger. Unlike Wilfred Owen, who in returning to his regiment was returning to men whom he loved and saw himself caring for supremely, so that death, love, the society of men, and masochistic sacrifice were inextricably entangled, for Keith Douglas war represented the antiworld of emotional defeat. While initially, that antiworld bore a gloss of heroics, by the time he got back to England and had had about a year to absorb the shocks administered to his system in North Africa, the gloss had worn thin: a kind of numbing and repetitive defeat that he was beginning to acknowledge as personal and psychological rather than cultural was taking over.

By the time he returned to England, other factors altered his mental preparation for death. In all probability more retroactively affected by his battle experience than he admits, and certainly more disillusioned by his experience of irrational and uncompensated loss in war, he writes to Edmund Blunden sometime before leaving for France in 1944:

As you will see from my cryptic address I've been fattened up for more slaughter and am simply waiting for it to start. . . . I am not much perturbed at the thought of never seeing England again, because a country which can allow her army to be used to the last gasp and paid like skivvies isn't worth fighting for. For me, it is simply a case of fighting *against* the Nazi regime. After that, unless there is a revolution in England, I hope to depart for sunnier and less hypocritical climates. (Douglas, *Prose Miscellany*, 152–53)

Yet Douglas could not allow himself complete cynicism:

To be sentimental or emotional now is dangerous to oneself and to others. To trust anyone or to admit any hope of a better world is criminally foolish, as foolish as it is to stop working for it. It sounds silly to say work without hope, but it can be done; it's only a form of insurance; it doesn't mean work hopelessly.

Negation forms a kind of defense here, as "insurance"; but there was also an increasingly sharp limit to what he felt that war could teach. He writes to John Hall:

Did you ever receive the poems I wrote in hospital? I am not likely to produce anything but virtual repetitions of these, until the war is cleared up now, because I doubt if I shall be confronted with any new horrors or any worse pain, short of being burnt up, which I am not likely to survive. (*Prose Miscellany*, 123)

This time it was not because of his hunger for battle experience that he made little effort for a staff job behind the lines, but for bleak adherence to a code of duty prescribing that he remain in union with his regiment facing battle.

The fragments of the poem "Bête Noire" indicate how war began to lose ground as Douglas's preoccupation in the last months of his life, as the more personal theme of a man with a fatally riven consciousness comes forward. "Bête Noire" rounds and completes his earlier understanding of himself as facing a force, now described as part of himself, that is bent on his harm. It was not possible for Douglas to complete the poem. His notes refer to "Bête Noire" as "the poem I can't write; a protracted failure, which is also a protracted success I suppose" (*Complete Poems*, 129 n) Success or failure, these fragments proved to Douglas the very intractability of the theme, which he drew in pictures intended for the cover of his next book of poems, and which he singled out as its title. The notes say:

The beast, which I have drawn as black care sitting behind the horseman, is indefinable: sitting down to try and describe it, I have sensations of physical combat, and after five hours of writing last night, which resulted in failure, all my muscles were tired. But if he is not caught, at least I can see his tracks (anyone may see them), in some of the other poems. My failure is that I know so little about him, beyond his existence and the infinite patience and extent of his malignity. (Douglas, *Complete Poems*, 129)

In bald, unmusical lines, the kind that usually stay hidden in desks after the "real" poem is published, Douglas writes:

He is a jailer.
Allows me out on parole.
brings me back by telepathy
is inside my mind
breaks into my conversation with his own words
speaking out of my mouth
can overthrow me in a moment
can be overthrown, if I have help
writes with my hand, and censors what I write
takes a dislike to my friends and sets me against them
can take away pleasure
is absent for long periods, shows up without notice
employs disguise.
If this is a game, it's past half-time and the beast is winning.
    (*Complete Poems*, 129)

As a piece of psychological self-analysis, rather than as poetry, the passage could be said to work. Douglas sees all that sours the natural breadth of his responses to life, that shrinks his love of people and squeezes his hopes; yet like his discouragement, the anguish will not dissipate. The continuity is sketchy and undramatic, and the words do not fly: "the beast is winning."

It seems unfortunate, however, that the poem receives the narrow attention that seeks to make Douglas a poster boy for battle stress. Ben Shephard quotes lines from "Bête Noire" in his 2001 study to show the "beast on my back" that Douglas "quietly carried after his experiences in the desert campaign":

Yes, I too have a particular monster
a toad or worm curled in the belly

stirring, eating at times I cannot foretell, he
is the thing I can admit only once to
anyone, never to those who have not their own.

(Shephard, xxiii)

To anyone reading the whole of Keith Douglas's work, Desmond Graham's biography, or Douglas's correspondence, drafts of poems, and miscellaneous prose, it should seem clear that in this poem, in its broken forms, Douglas's beast materialized from a wider understanding of himself beyond the ideologies of masculinity and character formation to which his fascination with military combat had led him.

But this record of self-discovery was abruptly terminated. We learn from the remaining manuscripts not the simpler lesson of how a young man was indelibly imprinted by war, but rather what the cost is in terms of the loss of whole persons, whole lives, and the chance to do the work in maturity, which societies cut off through war. In the handful of poems left from the year in the Middle East and from the months of waiting for the invasion of France in England, Douglas is haunted by a self in suspense, a flickering self living on the edges of posthumousness or purgatory. Most of all, this is a self driven by irreconcilable dualisms. The war that concerns him is the one inside himself, as shown in "Landscape with Figures 3":

I am the figure burning in hell
and the figure of the grave priest
observing everyone who passed
and that of the lover. I am all
the aimless pilgrims, the pedants and courtiers
more easily you believe me a pioneer
and a murdering villain without fear
without remorse hacking in the throat. Yes
I am all these and I am the craven
the remorseful the distressed
penitent: not passing from life to life
but all these angels and devils are driven
into my mind like beasts. I am possessed,
the house whose wall contains the dark strife
the arguments of hell with heaven.

(*Complete Poems*, 111)

The memory of high explosive and its abrupt and pitiless powers of cancel-lation enters personal and impersonal experience. In "Tel Aviv," Douglas writes:

> Do not laugh because I made a poem
> it is to use what then we couldn't handle—
> words of which we know the explosive
> or poisonous tendency when we are too close. If
> I had said this to you then, BANG will
> have gone our walls of indifference in flame.
>> (*Complete Poems*, 113)

In "This is the Dream," another poem with another concluding "BANG," Douglas desperately strives to cling to some hope of love, but whitened by the ellipses of the unknown and fearfully imagined future, he writes:

> I see myself dance happiness and pain
> (each as illusory as rain)
> in silence.   Silence.   Break it with the small
>
> tinkle;   apathetic buzz buzz
> pirouetting into a crescendo, BANG.
>> (*Complete Poems*, 120)

It is a life in which the spectator not only leaves the stage, but enters a posthu-mous existence, as in "Actors Waiting in the Wings of Europe," who, even be-fore completion of their turn on stage, morph into ghosts:

> Everyone, I suppose, will use these minutes
> to look back, to hear music and recall
> what we were doing and saying that year
> during our last months as people, near
> the sucking mouth of the day that swallowed us all
> into the stomach of a war. Now we are in it
>
> and no more people, just little pieces of food
> swirling in an uncomfortable digestive journey,
> what we said and did then has a slightly

fairytale quality. There is an excitement
in seeing our ghosts wandering

(*Complete Poems*, 125)

The preoccupation with death and deadness is not new to Douglas; surprisingly, however, the personal image that gains ground in the last poems is not that of the soldier, but that of an isolated and increasingly deracinated self, several times seen as the Wandering Jew.

This image surfaces in "The Hand," where the mind wanders "as the Jew wanders the world" and in "Saturday Evening in Jerusalem":

But among these Jews I am the Jew
outcast, wandering down the steep road
into the hostile dark square:
and standing in the unlit corner here
know I am alone and cursed by God
like the boy lost on his first morning at school.

(*Complete Poems*, 112)

In an early draft of "Actors Waiting in the Wings of Europe," one of a number of tentative conclusions to the poem reads:

tomorrow I set out across Europe to find
these islands, this land behind the mountains
there are three things [will happen] which may happen to me
to find them suddenly or at the end of years
to continue to death like the Jew
to trip suddenly and fall in the earth, disintegrating.

(Douglas papers, British Library, Add 53773)

Here, of course, he is also realizing how narrow his escape was from Wadi Zem Zem.

Geoffrey Hill recognized that Douglas played with themes, possessing "the kind of creative imagination that approached an idea again and again in terms of metaphor, changing position slightly, seeking the most precise hold" (Hill, 10). Here, powerful feelings of persecution, abandonment, and despair coalesce around the figure of the Jew. Had Douglas lived, he might have achieved some synthesis in the theme of the wandering Jew, just as he was beginning to do with his dual fascination with and repulsion by military energy and war. In the case of militarism, he seems to move towards an understanding that the attraction to the violent excitement of war represents his own conflicted energies, his will to live and love exerted against the hurt that the world offers, most notably and immediately, in the literal exercise of war facing off against death. Yet the persecuted Jew offered Keith Douglas a shape for problems more deeply and explosively buried, and far less accessible, beneath his own skin.

Arriving in Palestine, he wrote off to his mother for addresses of people to contact. Finding that his English aunt knew only other English people, he was annoyed: "Addresses came. But I was hoping for Jewish ones—should have known better—fancy living in a country for years and only knowing English people!" (Douglas papers, British Library, Add 56355). He was very clear about the need to widen his knowledge of the world's people, but in negative terms:

> I try to avoid English people for two or three reasons such as A) they frequent all the most expensive & uninteresting places B) once abroad, they become more insular & unintelligent than ever. C) One can meet quite enough of them in England while there are interesting people out here whom I'd never have met otherwise.

Then follows a hateful and cruel passage:

> The Jews en masse are horrible and I can sympathize with anyone who feels an urge to exterminate them. They are like rabbits but not so pretty. Every other rabbit characteristic, promiscuous breeding, dirtiness, lousiness, cowardice, they have in abundance. They are filthy, sullen, slovenly swine, and I can't be more accurate than that. We should have done much better to put our money on the Arabs who apart from having a slightly villainous inclination & being very dirty & uncivilized, are very pleasant amiable people. If the Jews are educated they only learn how to profit from people. But the Arabs work without being so keen on returns, and are very eager to learn. (British Library, Add 56355)

Yet after this ugly outburst resembling the kind of anti-Semitism typical for the English of those years, Douglas speculates at a later point that he will probably marry a Jew. To Olga Meiersons he wrote:

> I don't like, almost hate and fear many Jews—yet I feel more and more that in the end it will be a Jewess I will marry. Probably from suffering

some real or fancied injustice I have acquired something of a Jewish mentality myself. (Quoted in Graham, 159)

Earlier he fussed about his "Jewish" nose. Yet the time never came for him in which he could more wholly resolve the contractions and suspicions of victimization with his own more generous awareness of the nature and necessities of justice.

He did know better than to allow personal pique an exit into anti-Semitic ranting. An exam book that Douglas wrote as a seventeen year old at Christ's Hospital offers a mock history of his old school, lashing out at the school's snobbish hypocrisy, its latent and militarist fascism, and its festering anti-Semitism. His parody runs, in oily self-congratulation:

> You may ask, what is it which gives to these boys that unique character, the perfect addition to a complete education? At school they have been brought up with wide interests, and as a result every boy has a great admiration for German methods & for the FUEHRER in particular.

After some bumptious fooling, the piece continues:

> The chapel is a beautiful building, filled with artistic pictures and stained glass windows. A scheme is at present underway to allot Herr Hitler a place next to King Henry VIII. . . . In the afternoon games are played, rugger, football, cricket, & five, and each boy learns to use his muscles in emulation of his athletic German cousin. The youth organisations are many, and the few Jews who, by underhand methods, worm their way into the school, are rigidly banned from them. In this way Christ's Hospital carries on fitly the tradition of progress & broadmindedness so dear to the heart of every Nordic youth. (Douglas papers, British Library, Add 56359)

There is something so intemperately splenetic about the later outburst against Jews that it sounds out of character, as if it burst forth from some fetid and momentary personal grudge or disappointment.

In later letters Douglas records making friends with Jewish women; he willingly chooses to stay with a Jewish family rather than his regiment for a month in Palestine, where he allowed himself to be cosseted by everyone: laundry done, meals cooked, clothes ironed and mended, and so on. His stay included an attempt to romance the daughter. Of another refugee Jewish friend he commented:

Vera Nova, who is from Germany, offered to give up her room and sleep with friends so that I should have somewhere to sleep over the weekend—this is the first time she ever met me. I can't help thinking that there are very few people who would do that in England even for someone English. (Douglas papers, British Library, Add 56355)

Alamein to Zem Zem adverts to a day spent at Givat Brenner, a kibbutz where Douglas, who had known little of nuclear family life himself, was struck by the apparent happiness of the children in this communal setting. If Keith Douglas was an anti-Semite, he was a mixed one. His early homelessness was clearly made to resonate with the cultural stereotypes and caricatures, favorable and unfavorable, that he had absorbed about Jews, and made them into an icon that both repelled and attracted him, and onto which he could project a number of his own vague discontents.

But by the end of his service in the Middle East, it seems fair to suppose that the cultural baggage strapped to him in England was in any case beginning to fall away. Like W. H. Auden, Christopher Isherwood, and Stephen Spender before him, Douglas rejected English parochialism. In good moments, he no doubt saw leaving England as a splendid adventure and a grand leap that war had forwarded; in bad, he became the defiant or desolate figure leaving with curses on his lips for the unworthy and unappreciative homeland behind him, sending him on to his death. That there was a residual anger and sense of ill-usage seems palpable; he was finally ready to quit the style of war that he had encountered, but from which he saw no honorable way to withdraw. It is not difficult to see how, for an ambitious, energetic, and resourceful young man, these feelings coalesced into the figure of fate as a black beast pressing him hard.

The narrative of Keith Douglas's final day recoups him for literary history as a war hero. John Bethell-Fox went out on patrol with Douglas on 9 June, and he tells how Douglas had insisted on coming along. After driving their tanks through an orchard, and arriving at the river-bank, they both got out of their tanks, taking grenades and a German submachine gun that Douglas had collected somewhere, waded the river, and then crawled toward a church, where a machine gun opened fire on them after their brief sortie. They ran back to the cover of the river bank. Desmond Graham summarizes:

Douglas had been grazed by one of the bullets, and for a moment crouched under the bank, unwilling to move. Bethell-Fox was perplexed by the momentary failure of nerve, for Douglas, though often unconventional in action, had been well known for his courage; hardly had he noticed it before Douglas quite normally suggested they should swim a hundred yards up stream so as to appear where the enemy was not expecting them. (Graham, 256)

They did this, it worked, and they started back to report on their reconnaissance. As they got to the crest of a hill, they returned to their tanks and took heavy mortar fire. Douglas had climbed out of his tank to make his report, and "as he ran along the ditch one of the shells exploded in a tree above him. He must have been hit by a tiny fragment, for although no mark was found on his body, he was instantly killed" (Graham, 256). Both the final hesitation, the final going forward, and then the instantaneous death by invisible wound seem emblematic. In Robert Lowell's terms from "For the Union Dead," in going forward Douglas could rejoice "in man's lovely, / peculiar power to choose life and die—" (Lowell, *Life Studies*, 71) The death he had been growing met the life, and life and death closed with terrible simplicity around the poetry, making it difficult ever to separate them. Like the two halves of a Platonic lover, reader and poet can not seem to avoid the locking radiance in which the death of the life slides over to encase the poems.

Every reader of this strong, vital, and original poet feels the sucking intake of a real vacuum, of a window in a storm left permanently open, with no chance for the spirit to reenter, take hold, and complete the promise so acutely there. But the last stanza of "On a Return from Egypt," written in March and April of 1944, a month before Douglas's death, gives the sensation of a cutoff, of abrupt departure that leaves the after-swing of presence still vibrating in its unanswered and unanswerable state:

> The next month, then, is a window
> and with a crash I'll split the glass.
> Behind it stands one I must kiss,
> person of love or death
> a person or a wraith,
> I fear what I shall find.
>   (Douglas, *Complete Poems*, 132)

All of us have death to fear. *King Lear* tells us that ripeness is all; surely the tensions of this message, in all of its ambiguity, are peculiarly and unforgettably Keith Douglas's to entertain.

5

Randall Jarrell's War

WHEN readers have a mind to name Randall Jarrell's best work, they often pick the war poems, by far the biggest group he wrote on any subject, or they light on the poems about childhood, found throughout Jarrell's poetry, but consummately contained in the last book, *The Lost World*. You can see why the choice is made: some favor the one subject over the other—and each subject probably represents either a higher or a lower tolerance for history or autobiography on the part of the chooser. *Why* and *how* Jarrell's war should connect with Jarrell's children is, of course, an irresistible question.

Hayden Carruth, reviewing Jarrell's *Complete Poems* for *The Nation* in 1969, undercounts the actual number of poems given over to living or dying soldiers, pilots, battered civilians, prisoners of war, and the lost or dead orphan, but he still finds that "Jarrell's war poems are his best in every sense. They are the most alive poetically, the most consistent thematically" (Carruth, 158). War, written about by Jarrell in uniform, but as a wholly stateside soldier, still removed him "to a certain distance from the complexity of the ordinary world" (Carruth, 158), and wonderfully concentrated his powers.

These are not only Randall Jarrell's strongest poems, they are the largest and most singularly vivid group of American poems that we have on World War II, and Carruth is joined in this judgment, although with a dismissive nod at the overall quality of World War II poetry, by Stanley Kunitz. Kunitz, Jarrell's elder by nine years, overlapped Jarrell's term in the army, serving from 1943–45. On the way to praising Michael Casey's Vietnam War poems as the most "significant" for that generation, Kunitz writes "In fact, no poet—American or British—was to achieve superlative distinction or special identity from a distillation of his World War II experiences." Comparing Jarrell to Keith Douglas, Kunitz adds that "Randall Jarrell's war poems of the period were more vital and clever—he had the curious gift of making the whole grim business sound like a sinister fairy tale—but the irony, I fear, begins to wear a bit thin in places" (Kunitz, 277–88).

Carruth answers strongly for both Jarrell and his epoch:

> Nowadays we commonly hear critics declare that World War II produced no memorable poetry. Even a critic as astute as George Steiner has said that the poetry of 1940–1945 is without "the control of remembrance achieved by Robert Graves or Sassoon" in 1914–1918 (see Steiner's *The Death of Tragedy*). To this I can only reply that if I know what "control of remembrance" means, in my experience the poems of Jarrell have it, and they have it preeminently. (Carruth, 159)

Carruth's bringing up George Steiner is interesting because Steiner was really after bigger critical game than a mere "control of remembrance." Before the passage Carruth cites, Steiner says: "The political inhumanity of our time, moreover, has demeaned and brutalized language beyond any precedent." As language is corrupted by an inhuman politics, and we become numbed and accustomed to that debasement; cruelty is no longer "commensurate to the scope or response of the imagination." In that faltering of the imagination, tragedy dies, and "Language seems to choke on the facts. The only array of words still able to get near the quick of feeling is the kind of naked and prosaic record set down in *The Diary of Ann Frank* (Steiner, 316). But while Carruth's review avoids Steiner's larger meaning, balking at giving Jarrell the status of a tragedian, he still wants to defend Jarrell's language as more than "naked and prosaic record," and to point to his ability to touch evil and make us shiver, reaching in us and himself that "quick of feeling."

In this piece, Hayden Carruth lets us know that he is a veteran of World War II, and thereby qualified to gauge the literal truths of a war poem. At the same time, he means us to subsume personal witness and autobiography within something larger and distinctly visionary. Carruth takes up the word "truth" unflinchingly to describe what he means:

> I am certain that other readers of my age, those who were there, find in these poems of soldiers and civilians, the dead, wounded, and displaced, the same truth that I do. And it is not merely the truth of Friday night at the VFW; old dogfaces may use their memory to corroborate the materials of Jarrell's poems, but the *truth* is in the poems—it is an esthetic presence.

Carruth continues:

> Warfare gave Jarrell the antagonist he needed; not fate, not history, not the
> state, not metaphysical anxiety, but these all rolled into one—The War—
> that brute momentous force sweeping a bewildered generation into pathos,
> horror, and death. . . . The irresistibility of the war, the historical inexora-
> bility of it, the suffering of all its victims, Americans, Germans, Japanese—
> Jarrell wrote it down with equal understanding, equal sympathy. And he
> wrote it then, there, at that time and in those places, with power, spon-
> taneity, and perfect conviction. (Carruth, 160)

At the end of Carruth's encomium, however, the affirmation of Jarrell's imaginative vision comes to share honor with the quality of the lived experience
that he also employed in making these war poems. In this generous acknowledgment from someone six years younger than Jarrell, but still a member of
that wartime generation, Hayden Carruth sets Jarrell's range and authenticity,
alongside his capacious intelligence and widely receptive feeling.

The war poems, more than forty of them, that Jarrell plucked from his first
four books of poetry, annotated, and then isolated and rearranged according
to subject headings in his *Selected Poems* of 1955, clearly represent a major offering in his own eyes. These seven roomy and elastic headings, which gather
up nearly half of his republished poems, represent his comprehensive ambition: "Bombers," "The Carriers," "Prisoners," "Camps and Fields," "The
Trades," "Children and Civilians," and, last and simplest in its sweep, "Soldiers." As Hayden Carruth points out, these headings comprise nearly all bat-
tlefronts and various home fronts, and they move psychologically across generations and nationalities, into friend and foe, civilian and soldier.

What did Jarrell not make himself cover about the war? And what cost did
this inclusiveness exact: because while the war poems may be the most prominent feature of Jarrell's poetic landscape, only those readers concentrating on
its general contours manage to leave unmentioned the dogged flatness and
willed elevation that mark many of these poems individually. Even friendly
testimony like William Pritchard's notes that "Burning the Letters" and
"Siegfried" are poems in which "Each teeters on the edge of the lugubri-
ous. . . . These are poems which in their reiterated insistence never let up, but
purchase their intensity at the cost, perhaps, of wearing out the reader—for all
the vividness of individual passages." Pritchard reminds us, "it is to passages
or stanzas that one responds, rather than to the poems in their entirety"

FIGURE 8. Randall Jarrell at Chanute Field, Illinois, 1943. Referring to his appearance in June 1943, Jarrell wrote to Mackie Langham Jarrell from Chanute: "I have that fresh-in-from-the-wilderness-with-locusts-and-wild-honey look." Berg Collection, New York Public Library.

(Pritchard, 120–21). And often enough, thickly worded passages, stanzas, or images within the longer, less successful poems do become enormously seductive. Read patiently, carefully, and with sympathy for the ideas they represent, a dense, forbidding block of lines yields up its intelligence, its supple, subtle, and easily overlooked wit.

As war poetry, this work does occupy a different ground from that of the World War I soldier-poet, which Karl Shapiro was one of many poets to define. Feeling the same burden of belatedness, and responding to the same need for proof of heroic masculinity that haunted Keith Douglas's generation, but spelling out the American twist on the problem, Shapiro says:

> There is a salient difference between our war poetry such as Jarrell's and that first great war poetry written in our fathers' war by Wilfred Owen and Rosenberg and Blunden and so on. The British war poets who showed everyone how to write antiwar poetry were themselves all outstanding warriors and heroes. They cried out against war but were as conversant

with blood as Lawrence of Arabia. None of my generation was a war hero, that I remember, or even an outstanding soldier. It says in a note in one of Jarrell's books that he "washed out" as a combat pilot and became a celestial navigator, a much more suitable classification for a poet. In a sense, we waited out the war in uniform. (Shapiro, 221)

The new feature of this work, Randall Jarrell's broad compassion for the soldier as both victim and victimizer, may well come from his position of suspension within the army and within the war but, unlike the earlier soldier-poets, outside combat. Besides this, all the conflicts and liminalities of life and person in Randall Jarrell helped to tauten and intensify the natural dialectic of his work. Like Emily Dickinson, a poet with a mind inhabiting borderlands between life, death, and dream, Randall Jarrell was also a borderer living between battle and battle support and a romantic pacifist with an eye for the glory of the airborne. Crucially, an androgynous sensibility who held himself between the usual intersections dividing men and women, Jarrell was also inhabited by a mercurial comic sense whose penetration was both merciless and childlike. But much that Randall Jarrell most truthfully wrote about war *did* stem from personal experience of the profound loneliness of being a member, both infantilized and imprisoned within the twentieth-century mass army, and *did* bind the intelligence of his poems to the politics and history that he knew kept war in motion.

Driven by his large doubts about the ethics of twentieth-century industrial war making, Randall Jarrell stands stylistically, substantively, and historically between Wilfred Owen and Siegfried Sassoon, who came before him, and the American poets of the Vietnam War, who came after, in his accounts of soldier culpability within war's violence. Sassoon and Owen memorialized the Great War soldier by counterpointing his agony against the callousness and indifference of the chateau generals who sacrificed him. Middle-level officers who had actually inhabited the no-man's-land that, by policy, was emptied of the presence of high-level command, Owen and Sassoon, the one by fate and the other by inclination, stopped short of any real reconception of the functions of militarism.

Sassoon, while surviving the war, did not allow his early antiwar feeling to grow beyond the park borders of his gentleman's socialism. In 1917, Sassoon's statement against the war had been read aloud in the House of Commons; the clarion eloquence of the lines brought Sassoon a tidal fame lasting long beyond the war itself:

I am making this statement as an act of wilful defiance of military authority, because I believe that the War is being deliberately prolonged by those who have the power to end it.

This preamble led to the famous sentence, "I believe that this War, upon which I entered as a war of defence and liberation, has now become a war of aggression and conquest" (Sassoon, *Sherston*, 496). But by 1945, Sassoon had effectively doused the 1917 pacifism that had brought him to Craiglockhart, the military mental hospital. An older Sassoon, in explaining his repeated returns to the Western Front for active service, wrote that "in spite of my hatred of war and 'Empery's insatiate lust for power,' there was an awful attraction in its hold over my mind" (Sassoon, *Siegfried's Journey*, 69). Not the least of these attractions was not only going back to war, but to the front, with his idea of courage intact. His alter ego, Sherston, reports: "I would rather be killed than survive as one who had 'wangled' his way through by saying that the War ought to stop. Better to be in the trenches with those whose experience I had shared and understood" (*Sherston*, 549).

Finally, each earlier poet merely shifted glory away from the generals and onto the shoulders of the bloodied brotherhood of the combat soldier: they lay their chief devotion   literally, during the famous foot inspections of World War I—at the feet of Other Ranks.

Randall Jarrell, owing to the vagaries of American service classification in World War II, began as an enlisted man, moving gradually from private first class to corporal and then, at the war's end, up to sergeant, never belonging to the officer class. Army service was for Jarrell a long and tedious humiliation, an exile of the clever bee among the drones; it is a tribute to his character and sympathies that so much of his poetry remained elegiac about the men he served among. It may have been partly an effect of the interwar cynicism of the Auden generation, as well as Jarrell's position nearly at the bottom of the heap, that prevented some of the greater gilding of war narrative that belonged to an officer-poet like Wilfred Owen, along with his depiction of its horrors. But Jarrell's perspective as a stateside flight instructor forced him away from the brutalizing immediacies of war and from the agonies of later poets like Bruce Weigl and Yusef Komunyakaa, the veterans of the Vietnam conflict who report on a soldiers' brotherhood in a troubled bonding over rape, pillage, and arson, in addition to the pity and terror of combat.

Nonetheless, unlike these soldier-poets, Randall Jarrell, mute on wartime sexuality but soberly articulate on military destructiveness, wrote both shame and glory into his view of his mates. Perhaps only an airman with an outlook both cerebral and idiosyncratic could maintain the contrary measures of distance and intimacy to the soldier clans that would produce Jarrell's tender celebrations of murderous innocence. In Great War poetry, the soldier is dominantly the victim, hostage to the plans of others. But in World War II, Jarrell finally makes a significant alteration, asking the soldier to hold himself as agent as well as pawn of his society, although inexorably he also makes the responsibility for prosecuting and accepting war spread over all of us, combatant and noncombatant. It is Jarrell's accomplishment—before, during, and after World War II—to stretch the war poem to accommodate the larger civilian politics gestating it.

One more of the customary binaries to dissolve in Jarrell's analysis is certainly that of the divide between war and peace. Karl Shapiro describes this melding of war and postwar that Jarrell understood and participated in:

Unlike the poets of World War I, who never recovered from the experience, our generation did. We inherited a historical perspective which was denied our fathers. We foresaw and witnessed the whole world turning into the state. The war was of secondary importance to us even while we were part of it. When we came home there was grass growing on all the highways of the forty-eight states, but not for long. Our army went from demobilization to college or television school; our poets became the university poets. But the tragedy of our generation—and I believe it is the tragedy—was that our army never melted away. It remained, it grew bigger, it was more and more all over the world. It became the way of life, the state—if not the garrison state itself, then something resembling it mightily. The war never came to a stop; only the protocols of armistice were suspended. (Shapiro, 222)

Besides exploring how Randall Jarrell illuminates the ethics of war within his poems, set at the distance where temperament and circumstance installed him, I will briefly pose other responses, draw on Jarrell's own review of Marianne Moore's war poetry, and follow that with an antimilitarist poem by Elizabeth Bishop, whom Jarrell admired, and with whose outlook he felt in harmony. Two poems, Elizabeth Bishop's "Roosters" and Marianne Moore's "In Distrust of Merits," contrast what noncombatant status, kept further back from war by gender and not encased in uniform, might produce as support for either the heroic elegiac (Moore) or as antimilitarist myth making (Bishop).

The Particulars of the Poem

His nearly fifty war poems did not come smoothly or evenly to Randall Jarrell. The least successful of them approach battle directly, in dramatic settings concentrating not on character but on dilemma. As an instance of what I mean, consider the opening of "A Pilot from the Carrier," where all the war words wind up tight to boost the protagonist into an atmosphere commensurate with ennobling elegy. This is the second poem of Jarrell's *Little Friend, Little Friend*, a book written during the war but published at its end. In the opening lines of "A Pilot from the Carrier," a fine image is nearly brought down by the weight of detail choking it:

> Strapped at the center of the blazing wheel,
> His flesh ice-white against the shattered mask,
> He tears at the easy clasp, his sobbing breaths
> Misting the fresh blood lightening to flame,
> Darkening to smoke; trapped there in pain
> And fire and breathlessness, he struggles free
> Into the sunlight of the upper sky—
> And falls, a quiet bundle in the sky,
> The miles to warmth, to air, to waking:
> To the great flowering of his life, the hemisphere
> That holds his dangling years.
>
> (Jarrell, *Little Friend*, 13)

It is an image Jarrell will use again: an airman-fetus who will be born into the new life of death into which danger, injury, and extremes of suffering have catapulted him.

Even the fussy overqualification, the straining to get flight details and all the mechanics of carrier combat right, cannot destroy the sweep of the poem's initial conception. That the pilot should be centered on that wheel, that the sky at that altitude is not lower but upper, that the clasp should be easy, the cycling precise by which the blood lightens, fires, then smokes—the multiplying touches do not manage to blunt the image, as the description finally clears and steadies:

> a lonely eye
> Reading a child's first scrawl, the carrier's wake—
> The travelling milk-like circle of a miss

Besides the plant-like genius of the smoke
That shades, on the little deck, the little blaze
Toy-like as the glitter of the wing-guns,

Swung between immensities of sky and water and high above the sharply miniaturized landscape of his launching point, the hurt pilot is reduced to a child's helplessness. At just that invocation of the child, the bite of description becomes direct, accurate and simple. Yet the finish never meets the initial stake raised by the beginning, and the terminal couplet settles for an elegant but aestheticized irony:

Shining as the fragile sun-marked plane
That grows to him, rubbed silver tipped with flame.

Later poems like "Pilots, Man your Planes," and "The Dead Wingman" share the same faltering and stalling out. Even in the 1950s, other war poems similarly struggle for altitude, as Jarrell wavers between two antithetical attitudes towards soldiers' deaths. In the heroic economy, death is a large but justifiable expense, affirming our belief in bravery and existential daring, although Jarrell consistently shows the bitterness of the sacrificed in preference to any resigned pride and acceptance. But in the unheroic economy of the war-resistant, soldier death is horrifying waste and a reimmersion in the blood mesh of violence that the armed state perpetuates.

Starting with the political ironies of "The Emancipators," Jarrell makes the unheroic point clearly. It is western "progress" and the rise of the mercantile society that have brought us the ravages of the capitalist state. Addressing the Emancipators, he revises Rousseau, "Man is born free, but everywhere lives in chains," to say:

Man is born in chains, yet everywhere we see him dead.
On your earth they sell nothing but our lives.
    (*Little Friend*, 14)

To make sure that we understand the political and economic connections between the generations of violence, the prose poem "1914," as well as "The Soldier" and "The Sick Nought," all ascribe the death of soldiers not merely to some generalized and ineradicable bloodlust in the human character, but to the systems that have bred and empowered the modern state. "1914" was the genesis of World War II; as we flash through an album of the earlier war what we see is "everybody's future, how could any of it seem old-fashioned to us?—it was our death." The present wasteful crop of "our death," not exactly a new idea, but put with freshness, originates in 1914–1918:

> the innocent armies, marching over the meadows to three haystacks, a mill-dam, and a hedge, dig a trench for their dead and vanish there. Over them the machine-guns hammer, like presses, the speeches into a common tongue: the object-language of the Old Man of Laputa; here is the fetishism of one commodity, all the values translated into a piece of meat.

In a brilliant compression, Randall Jarrell fuses Jonathan Swift and Karl Marx into one cross-national and terrifying view of commodification. On Swift's island of Laputa, language, or symbolic reference, has been replaced by the things themselves, which the Laputans lug around for communication, by-passing words. In Marxist terms, human beings, and human values, are similarly bypassed, reified, and traded for money, rendering the living flesh a thing of meat. Jarrell goes on:

> A wire-coiled Uhlan, pressing to his lips a handkerchief dampened with chlorine, looks timidly into the great blaze of the flame-thrower his supply sergeant hands to him; the sergeant takes away the haystacks, one by one, the hedge, the mill-dam, and puts in their places the craters of the moon. The winter comes now, flake by flake; the snowflakes or soldiers (it is impossible to distinguish—under the microscope each one is individual) are numbered by accountants, who trace with their fingers, in black trenches filled by the dancing snow, the unlikely figures of the dead. (*Little Friend*, 44)

The natural universe disappears under machine-gun fire: snowflake or soldier, the only count that registers now is the body count, in which the individuality of the soldier, as indisputable as that of the snowflake, is nonetheless as evanescent as snow. "1914" ends with a view of a dead soldier, and under his picture we find written, "*Es war ein Traum*" ("It was a dream"), and Jarrell concludes: "It is the dream from which no one wakes."

Once more the victim of this nightmare of history turns up in "The Soldier":

In the first year of the first war called the *World*
I watched a world blaze skyward into States,

And faced across the trenches of a continent
The customers whom I was shipped to kill.

. . . .

All integers alike—the young and old, the poor and poor—
Were shadowed past distinction by the deaths
The States sowed over continents like salt.
Those years the flesh was levered from our bones.
> (*Little Friend*, 50)

And so on, in the wars that Jarrell sees generated by the pitiless buying and selling of global capital.

Much as he may have been tempted, Jarrell knew that he could not fill *Little Friend, Little Friend*, published in 1945, only with poems written during and about his army service and manifesting what he called his "new style." The vigorous thump of the rhetoric, however, and the stark imagery may have roused and consoled him for the small, numbing miseries, the crushing boredom, of his life in the army, suspended from all of his usual occupations and thrown into intimate and unavoidable contact with uncongenial strangers, just at the point when his professional life had begun to take wing. When, in April and May of 1943, he wrote to his first wife, Mackie Langham, enclosing poems like "The Emancipators" and "The Wide Prospect," he responds to her decrying his "neo-Hegelian doctrines"; then he acknowledges his "political economy style an unlikely thing"—and teases her: "Aren't you sorry? I'm building up quite a pile of such poems" (Jarrell to Mackie Langham Jarrell, Berg Collection, New York Public Library) Sometime in June 1943 (Jarrell rarely dated the war letters to Mackie) he wrote to her about "The Emancipators": "Pretty soon they'll be calling me the 18th century Marx, eh? Seriously, I can see now . . . some of the 18th Cent. practices you naturally fall into when you're writing with hatred and generality about politics, the world, and such" (Jarrell, Berg Collection).

Jarrell knew that this style could only partially serve him. In July 1943, he wrote wryly to Mackie:

In the future they'll say: 'It is difficult to understand what induced this talented poet to introduce into his works, often at elevated moments, rhymed paraphrases of what are today political or economic commonplaces.' (Jarrell, Berg Collection)

Yet the "rhymed paraphrases" or "commonplaces" were a necessary and not negligible part of his developing thought; there is a traceable exhilaration, too, in being able to make them work in poetry as well as they do.

Mostly, poems like "1914" and "The Soldier" are interesting for the ideology that can be extracted from them; they set the context and provide thematic launching pads for other and better work. "The Sick Nought" tries harder to attach flesh and local dramatic color to the earlier, more generalized propositions about the dehumanized soldier. Writing at odd moments in barracks also brought him compression: he joked to Mackie about the short poems that short spells of leisure necessitated. "The Sick Nought" begins in an army infirmary, where a soldier with a "sick worried face" receives a visit from wife and baby: "in the crowded room you rubbed your cheek / Against your wife's thin elbow like a pony."

But now Jarrell reverts to a more impersonal, hortatory mode:

But you are something there are millions of.
How can I care about you much, or pick you out
From all the others other people loved
And sent away to die for them? You are a ticket
Someone bought and lost on, a stray animal:
You have lost even the right to be condemned.

Jarrell initially worried about the "mild-mannered insincerity" of "How can I care about you much," but what seems to have worried him more was the possibility of losing his poem in sentimental pathos, so off we go into an ironic hypostatizing, as the soldier takes form again in "my Army or political style" (Jarrell, Berg Collection):

I see you looking helplessly around, in histories,
Bewildered with your terrible companions, Pain
and Death and Empire: what have you understood, to die?

And begins his conclusion in the Marxist vein familiar to this period of his life:

What is demanded in the trade of states
But lives, but lives?—the one commodity.
To sell the lives we were too poor to use,

To lose the lives we were too weak to keep—
This was our peace, this was our war.
  (*Little Friend*, 51)

But the last three lines drop Marx for a moral reflection: if the nought is a
nought, his weakness must be sternly regarded; finally, in true Auden style,
his weakness has become our weakness, our infirm progression from peace
to war.

Jarrell perceived the danger of either ironic or sentimental reduction.
Writing to Mackie about Allen Tate's "Ode to Our Young Pro-Consuls of
the Air," he said scornfully, "I feel like quoting when I read such poems, 'Because you saw, and were not indignant . . . 'The evil of the universe is a poor
thing to be ironic about" (Jarrell, *Letters*, 81). Jarrell flexed to gain other perspectives, finding them in the details and duties of the young pilots who surrounded him and who afforded other possible mutations of theme on the difficult relation of heroic and antiheroic. The balancing need to see the soldier
as something other than a passive victim is reflected in the composition of *Little Friend, Little Friend*, published in October 1945, at the war's end. Although
many of the poems appeared earlier in wartime journals, Jarrell reordered this
collection against chronological composition, heavily concentrating the poems
of war and wartime. This order, different from his thematic arrangements in
the *Selected Poems* of 1955, allows an approximate measure of how Jarrell's
treatment of public and political themes altered through the pressure of his
years in the army.

Little Friend, Little Friend experiments with different mixes of impersonal
rhetoric and direct, intimate focus; the familiar and conversational tone
worked against the elegiac and elevated. Never again in his life would Randall
Jarrell be hammered so bluntly by the divide between his ongoing and defining intellectual and emotional preoccupations and the chafing harness of his
ordinary, hourly existence—a life in which he would step out after hours of
dishing up macaroni and cheese to lines of recruits, to retreat to barracks for
the mail telling him of his latest acceptance in *The Nation* or *The Partisan Review*, periodicals which were not stocked in army libraries. *Little Friend, Little
Friend* opens with "2nd Air Force," moves to the "great flowering" of death in
"A Pilot from the Carrier," passes through poems like "1914," "The Soldier,"
and "The Sick Nought," and, closing the book with a reverberating denial of
both the glory and the necessity of heroic economy, ends with "The Death of
the Ball Turret Gunner."

"2nd Air Force," or "Second Air Force," as it came to be known later, is the first war poem that only Jarrell could have written; it bears the singular tone and diction, the peculiar edged tenderness, that characterizes all of his best poems about soldiers. The mood is elegiac, but the world is palpably shabby and somehow too homely for the fully heroic. Everything is oddly diminished; somehow the natural joins the powerfully mechanical in being antithetical to the human. "2nd Air Force" begins with a mother who comes to an air base to see her son:

> Far off, above the plain the summer dries,
> The great loops of the hangars sway like hills.

The music of the opening lines sets up a certain expectancy, suggesting both suspension and inexorable process, which, quietly and carefully, the poem works to deflect.

The only dulling note in "2nd Air Force" is struck by Jarrell's awkward handling of the mother, through whose eyes the air base is ostensibly seen. Tom Sleigh represents many when he says: "When Jarrell thinks discursively in his poems (dramatic monologues generally in women's voices like "Next Day" or "The Woman at the Washington Zoo"), he feels and talks like a woman who feels and talks like Randall Jarrell" (Sleigh, 148). "2nd Air Force" is fortunately not a first person dramatic monologue, so Jarrell has less need than usual to make the character sound like somebody's mother. After all, whole poems, whole novels, have been successfully written in indirect discourse without a word resembling what ordinary people actually say. In Jarrell's "Burning the Letters," for instance, the speech of the poem emanates from the mind of the wife of a dead pilot, and Jarrell manages to carry it off with a consistent if stagy conviction. In "2nd Air Force," however, he would have done well to have kept even more of this lady in his own voice. When the nameless mother is given a shot at speech, it lumbers into the maudlin: "she thinks heavily: My son is grown"; Well yes; but the heaviness is not entirely hers.

In the next lines, to our relief, Jarrell kneads her words back into his own style:

> She sees a world: sand roads, tar-paper barracks,
> The bubbling asphalt of the runways, sage,
> The dunes rising to the interminable ranges,
> The dim flights moving over clouds like clouds.

The armorers in their patched faded green,
Sweat-stiffened, banded with brass cartridges,
Walk to the line; their Fortresses, all tail,
Stand wrong and clumsy on their skinny legs,
And the crews climb to them as clumsily as bears.
The head withdraws into its hatch (a boy's),
The engines rise to their blind laboring roar,
And the green, made beasts run home to air.
Now in each aspect death is pure.

Something curious, and unique to Randall Jarrell happens here. In Tom Sleigh's perception:

> A lost child's search for Mother or Father—the clear, homely simplicity of Jarrell's loneliness lies at the heart of the war poems. . . . This loneliness haunts the lost bomber-pilot children who search for the Mother-Carrier strafed and torpedoed into flames. They find instead the ghostly Father incarnated in the weapons themselves.

Sleigh's reading is too sketchy to work in every instance; but the root idea of the lost child's search shows how projection allows Jarrell an authentic undertow of personal emotion to build a fictional and more generally convincing reality.

It is not just the fathers who get to be weapons; the planes themselves in this poem *are* the pilots. They displace them: in "2nd Air Force" the bombers stand in prominently for the awkward adolescents flying them. The machines become more real, more powerful, than the people and take over the description quite startlingly: those "Fortresses, all tail" standing "wrong and flimsy on their skinny legs." The pilot is a decapitated head withdrawing to a hatch—only a parenthesis with a boy inside—and then the engines rev, "pure death," olive drab, "green, made beasts" running home to air, a kind of metal leviathan, although in the air instead of water, and, like Jonah, the pilots are getting a good run inside.

The first stanza is the truly memorable one, climbing into a time and a place, a gleaming terrible pathos of men and machines. What they have become lost in is so large and final it cannot be seen, although hour after hour the signs and portents drift in:

(At twilight they wink over men like stars
And hour by hour, through the night, some see
The great lights floating in—from Mars, from Mars.)
    (11)

By this time, the woman and her son have retreated to the shadows, joining the
familiar dumb-beast passivity of other Jarrell soldiers: "In the last dreaming
light, so fresh, so old, / The soldiers pass like beasts, unquestioning," and the
poem taxis on to a generalized vision of combat, in which the newspaper-
reading woman "hears" a bomber calling, "*Little Friend*" to its fighter escort.
To explain that hearing, Jarrell invokes the epigraph with its quoted response
that has given him his title:

> *Then I heard the bomber call me in: "Little friend, Little Friend, I got two en-
> gines on fire. Can you see me, Little Friend?"*
>   *I said "I'm crossing right over you. Let's go home."*

Poems and pilots are an odd mix of celluloid heroism and children limping to
shelter in a grim fairy tale, as their streaming, blossoming, floating lives flame
"like stars above the lands of men." In Jarrell's backdrop to "2nd Air Force,"
people come home in a starburst of death.

    This poem, however, will not end in the stratosphere. As in all of his more
successful war poetry, Jarrell adopts a tone both particular and familiar, literally grounding the poem in details drawn from the real air bases on which he
served. The woman sees:

> A section shipping, in its last parade—
> Its dogs run by it, barking at the band—
> A gunner walking to his barracks, half asleep,
> Starting at something, stumbling (above, invisible,
> The crews in the steady winter of the sky
> Tremble in their wired fur); and feels for them
> The love of life for life.
>   (*Little Friend*, 12)

The force of this description, the pulse of its bewildered, unwilling, only half-
believing love of life for life amounts to Jarrell's own running sense of loss, of

nostalgia, or home pain, here come together as a masque of maternal grief. In his poems, Jarrell can finesse the emotional trauma of having been unmothered by a mother who betrayed him both with a divorce and with a displacing younger brother, by now *being* the mother in the domain of his poetry, wholly on his own terms. Jarrell's mother is made to sorrow (how fine it is to make a mother cry for you!); although for the pilots, the Lost Boys in an adventure to Never Never Land, "the bombers answer everything." And as they do, this first poem of Jarrell's most wholly wartime book is beautiful, terrible, and oddly shaded with somnambulism.

The poem with which Jarrell ends *Little Friend, Little Friend* is "The Death of the Ball Turret Gunner," and in it the mother is not a guiltless bystander, nor is the bleak homescape offered that of the bombers of "Second Air Force." In the poem's last bald, antiheroic, and utterly unforgettable fetal image, the gunner flowers only as a corpse born into meaningless death:

From my mother's sleep I fell into the State,
And I hunched in its belly till my wet fur froze.
Six miles from earth, loosed from its dream of life,
I woke to black flak and the nightmare fighters.
When I died they washed me out of the turret with a hose.

Blind and helpless, part child-warrior, part neglected pet, he is the whelp of a cowed nature colonized by totalitarian politics.

From "The Death of The Ball Turret Gunner" to the writing of "Losses" and "Eighth Air Force," Jarrell made a still bigger leap away from glorifying heroic sacrifice to projecting killers as killed and writing about boy-pilots who were both victims and makers of victims. From the 1940s on, Jarrell labors for an ethical reconciliation with a war that his reason regarded as justly anti-Nazi and antifascist, while his principles showed him it led to the murderous Allied bombing campaigns of industrialized war. Often it is the jar of stateliness against individual rage and suffering, the smack of the aureate against the vernacular diction, that clues us into Jarrell's ambivalence about this war. The best poems reject the solemn, high-minded style, costive with unuttered reference, and take on a diction capable of the ingenious and striking fusion of formal and colloquial that served Jarrell so expressively from *Little Friend, Little Friend* on. While the anxious masculinity of the older homefront soldier whom combat had bypassed may have pushed him towards a celebration of the glory and suffering of the combatant, ultimately Jarrell's own life as a soldier began to adjust that view, supplying more and more data for work that kicked free of reflex patriotism. War linked him to larger communities, and gave him an immense and fruitful subject away from what he called "that short disease, myself" (*Letters*, 152), even if war did not, however, lead him immediately to the autobiographical preoccupation of his last decade.

Two poems from *Little Friend, Little Friend*, "Losses" and "The Dream of Waking," illustrate the complexities of dipping selectively into the witness of autobiography to feed a convincing emotion to the wartime risk and grief that Jarrell wanted his poems to embody. In a long letter to Robert Lowell, Jarrell begins with a discussion on determinism and free will, which he follows with an analysis of soldier choice:

> In a war like ours most of the soldiers are, if not completely, at least virtually, ignorant of the choices they make; besides this, they are pretty well determined in the passive sense—even if they should choose not to do a bad thing (and they usually do not have the information and training to make it possible for them to make a really reasonable decision about it), they will be forced to do it by the state (which has already misled them about it by giving them as much misleading determining information as it could). Also, most of the things suffered in war are entirely determined, the person has no choice to make: who in Tokyo or Hamburg or London chose to be burned to death?

Characteristically, he names the consequences of both allied and axis bombing campaigns, refusing the oversimplifications of the patriot. His conclusion was not to relinquish personal choice, or personal feeling, but to see what a huge irrelevancy these were in the war that was flooding him:

> I've never written a poem about myself in the army or war; unless you're vain or silly you realize that you, except insofar as you're in exactly the same boat as the others, aren't the primary subject of any sensible writing about the war.

It is an attractive modesty that Jarrell draws on; it is also the wellspring of the pitying comprehensiveness that so notably marks his work. In sum, he writes to Lowell:

> The main feeling you have about most people in the army—and in the war, too—is that you're sorry for them; everything else comes after. But the

next feeling, I imagine, is one of wonder: the size and impossible lunacy of everything in the war and army are beyond anything. (*Letters*, 151–52)

Pity and wonder brought Randall Jarrell very far; his intellectual and emotional grasp of what he and his world were facing brings his work its lasting gravitas. But a keen general insight did not prevent him from the occasionally useless borrowing from newspaper anecdote or newsreel symbol to anchor or inflate the significance of his poems. Nor did it help when he took his species membership too much for granted in scattered poems throughout the war, relying fruitlessly and indiscriminately on the universality of idiosyncratic bits of his own feeling and memory to stuff into his reading about war victims. These blendings of his life and his reading may have given him practice in the more successful uses of autobiography in the later poems of *The Lost World*, but in World War II, his enthusiasm for his ability to impersonate dead pilots, downed navigators, and pilot's wives may have been overextended. The better poems are the ones more frankly detached, or those that work identification with less conscious purpose.

Both "Losses" and "The Dream of Waking" inhabit the interval between life and death. But "Losses," one of a dozen of Jarrell's most frequently anthologized poems, has a muscular conceptual or ideological orientation that moves it out of the haze of dream territory, and away from the blurring subjectivity with its personal overtones that actually limits the dramatic or rhetorical impact of a poem like "The Dream of Waking." "Losses" does not merely report on the slurring distance between life and death; it declares the metaphysical interconnectedness of both and offers otherworldly vantage as the prop of its wisdom. In the safely distant and untouchable dream of death from which the boy-pilots of "Losses" speak, error is washed from them by suffering. Throughout this poem, the governing pathos of the poet's realization of the pilot's expendability is perfectly balanced against his knowledge of the pilot's reign of fire. As in "2nd Air Force," the stamp of "Losses" is the remote tenderness of its bitter beholding, within an evenly weighed-out drama of guilt and innocence.

Randall Jarrell titles this war poem "Losses":

It was not dying; everybody died.
It was not dying: we had died before
In the routine crashes—and our fields
Called up the papers, wrote home to our folks,

And the rates rose, all because of us.
We died on the wrong page of the almanac,
Scattered on mountains fifty miles away;
Diving on haystacks, fighting with a friend,
We blazed up on the lines we never saw.
We died like ants or pets or foreigners.
(When we left high school nothing else had died
For us to figure we had died like.)
    (*Little Friend*, 15)

It is second nature for Jarrell to set aside the usual stock divisions—into us and them, soldier and civilian—and even to blend notice of battlefront and home-front casualty. These young pilots die by accident and by friendly fire as well as in battle hostilities because Jarrell saw from his own posting at air bases that industrial war preparation inevitably means a high proportion of random and indiscriminate death.

When Jarrell had enlisted in October 1942, he was twenty-eight, a year past eligibility as a combat pilot, and for the length of his service, he found himself cast as elder observer. While he was irked and bored by military mis-use and misdeployment of manpower, his discomfort did not alter his instruc-tions to himself to transcend cynicism, stay cheerful, and evade the distortions of personal grievance as well as he could.

Being in the army erased the civilian hierarchy he knew. Marching and drilling with other soldiers, most of whom were nearly a decade younger, he would occasionally encounter former students. He wrote a little diffidently to Mackie, "I'm surprisingly good at getting myself treated respectfully" (Jarrell, Berg Collection). Yet he writes of fervent preparation for tests that might bet-ter his work assignments. The whole immersion must have been profoundly disorienting; Jarrell was once again the student, rather than the teacher. Worse yet, his teachers were awful: "we learn in a very long day what could be learned in two hours at most; it's crazy, even the dumb ones think something's wrong" (*Letters*, 77). Regressively plunged among student-age soldiers, rather than separated from them by a desk or lectern, Jarrell's dominant tones were incredulous indignation or amusement at their ignorance and, finally, pity for the waste of their youth.

"Losses" is full of that pity, but Jarrell sees that it is the same young life, crisp and vulnerable, that eradicates other innocent life:

We read our mail and counted up our missions—
In bombers named for girls, we burned
The cities we had learned about in school—
Till our lives wore out; our bodies lay among
The people we had killed and never seen.
When we lasted long enough they gave us medals;
When we died they said, "Our casualties were low."
They said, "Here are the maps"; we burned the cities.

The end point of this is pity and wonder; in some unframeable calculus, the poem has begun with dying that is not dying, and ends so:

It was not dying—no, not ever dying;
But the night I died I dreamed that I was dead,
And the cities said to me: "Why are you dying?
We are satisfied, if you are; but why did I die?"
    (15)

Not dying, but dying; not dreaming, but dying, not dying but dreaming—a repetitive welter in which all forms of the verb "to die" tail into inaccessible negation, unanswerable interrogatory. How can there be an answer to such a why, the poem asks, except with another why, and so on, in an infinite regress attempting to blunt, delay, deny, or dismiss the inescapable conclusions.

"The Dream of Waking" is deliberately less focussed on externals; the poem gambles on its manipulation, its simulated broken consciousness, to represent the wartime moment of crossover states between surviving and dying, which are made parallel to sleeping and waking. In John Donne's great Christian paradox, "one short sleep past, we wake eternally" (Donne, 342) But a twentieth-century poet like Randall Jarrell concentrates far more on the sleep of life, than on the religious triumph over death.

I wish I knew where the epigraph to "The Dream of Waking" comes from—very likely, contemporary journalism. It runs:

. . . in the bottom of a boat, badly wounded, crying and stroking the face of the other, who was dying; and saying, "Come on now, you'll be all right. You'll be all right."

Little in the loose poem that follows adds to the poignance and sweetness of the battle brotherhood that Jarrell took as the poem's given. But he dutifully puts himself there in the bottom of the boat, one of the caring brothers, to say in italics:

> *Something is there. And teacher here at home*
> *Curled fast on the quilt like Kitten, saying Come*
> *You'll be all right, you'll be all right—is gone,*
> *And the water trembles upward into light,*
> *And the light's smile breaks; is laughter—it is me*
> *And the room and the tree: oh, morning, morning.*
>
>   (*Little Friend*, 17)

Trying and trying, Jarrell says that "it is me" there in the boat, but it is not. In fact, there is not a believable anybody. There is instead a respectful, decorous trimming by Nature ("the water trembles upward into light") to waft the poem and its inhabitants Over There, into the big Eternity, or at least into the reasonable facsimile that Jarrell has recognized all his life as the connective tissues of sleep with the otherworldly. But even infusing the poem with his pet cat, Kitten, won't quite do the job of making the poem feel real. In fact, most of the time that Kitten shows up in one of Jarrell's war poems, it is a signal that Jarrell is marking time, and imagination has gone off duty to be temporarily replaced with the outward props of the poet's life.

The whorelessness of "The Dream of Waking" is painfully acute in its middle stanza:

> *And the frost is starry, like the sun between my eyes*
> *In my lashes so they open: and the white*
> *Is the breath the night breathed, there like mine;*
> *My clouds are cover and my nightgown and the breath*
> *That prints me on the window; and my sun*
> *Is gold all mixed with air, is my own life—*

More desperately yet, "*my*" clouds, "*my*" childish nightgown, "*my*" breath, and "*my*" very own boyhood life prove such a dead end that Jarrell can do little more with this waif than to end the poem with the reiterated contents of the borrowed epigraph, and a return to the moaned refrain invoking morning:

And he is back for good: the boat is bodies
And the body broken in his broken arms
And the voice, the old voice: *Please don't die—*
His life and their death: oh, morning, morning.

For Jarrell at this stage, it is his thinking about war, his general knowledge, and—as he certainly recognized in the laboratory of war in which he knew himself to be one of the guinea pigs—only the slimmest, but deepest, pieces of his life in the army that will make effective poems.

Tom Sleigh writes on death in Jarrell's war poems, a shade too emphatically denying the visceral impact of a well-constructed abstraction:

Jarrell displaces death onto machines; or he sees it as the unconsciousness of sleep; or as an abstraction synonymous with the authority of the State. Death never comes to Jarrell's soldiers with the brute, bitter finality displayed in Wilfred Owen's poem, "Asleep." (Sleigh, 150)

Sleigh quotes from Owen's poem, with its suggestively parallel title:

Death took him by the heart. There was a quaking
Of the aborted life within him leaping . . .
Then chest and sleepy arms once more fell slack.

The judgment is intriguing. If we take just the lines Sleigh selects, it does seem true that Owen has zeroed in on a moment in which, unlike Jarrell, he acknowledges death both arriving and being abrupt and irrevocable. Even the human obliteration in "The Death of the Ball Turret Gunner" is softened by posthumous voice-over. And yet, so much in Owen's poem shares even more of the zest for mechanical and sentimental ornamentation than Jarrell's "The Dream of Waking." "Asleep" ends in a full-throttle High Romantic commemoration:

Whether his deeper sleep lie shaded by the shaking
Of great wings, and the thoughts that hung the stars,
High pillowed on calm pillows of God's making
Above these clouds, these rains, these sheets of lead,
And these winds' scimitars;
—Or whether yet his thin and sodden head
Confuses more and more with the low mould,

His hair being one with the grey grass
And finished fields of autumns that are old . . .
Who knows? Who hopes? Who troubles? Let it pass!
He sleeps. He sleeps less tremulous, less cold
Than we who must awake, and waking, say Alas!

(Owen, *Complete Poems*, 1:152)

Owen, too, plays with the parallel accordances and discordances of sleep and waking, of life and death, that haunt Jarrell. In Owen's lines, bitterness is fairly smothered, and as for "brute finality," that seems even harder to dig out from under the thick blanketing of Owen's sentimental irony. Each of these pieces offers an example of poetic misfire, in which once again death is wrestled to frustrated abstraction.

The three known manuscript versions of "Asleep," including the fair copy, reveal the uncertainty governing Owen's choices. A canceled title suggests explicit circumstances prompting the poem: "Lines on a soldier killed asleep by a shrapnel bullet." But whether one agrees with editors Blunden and Stallworthy on how to shuffle the existing lines of Owen's poem, Sleigh's argument seems to imply that Wilfred Owen, the veteran of battlefield death, says it better than the unblooded Randall Jarrell. And yet what is lacking in both of these poems to anchor them to reality, or even to a compelling discourse, is not authentic, verifying personal experience, but solid, substantive focus and stylistic restraint.

In a notebook that was evidently part of his preparation for a 1942 lecture, recently published from a later typescript as "Levels and Opposites: Structure in Poetry," Randall Jarrell wrote about concrete particulars in poetry. In opposition to the contemporary aesthetic that, in imagined deference to William Blake, demanded concrete particulars over idiotic generalizing,[1] Jarrell protests:

> The *particulars* of the poem are no more *real* particulars for all the purposes of the poem than the colors, ink, paper of the map are *real* particulars . . . , for all the relations between particulars are always universals and it is these which are being asserted, *not* the particulars.

And he avers that

> of course none of Tate's or Ransom's particulars are *really* particulars, but moderately high degrees of abstraction. . . . it seems an extraordinary superstition to hold that certain levels of abstraction are uniquely valuable for

poetry and not higher ones. Sometimes higher levels have effectiveness more in proper context, vanity vanity ripeness, etc.

[These allusions are a little fuller in Jarrell's typescript]

Actually there is no limit—Time is the Mercy of Eternity. The unique "particular" the poem carries is a unique collection of universal relations— and is like a "particular," like a person, in this sense. (Jarrell, unpublished draft, Jarrell papers, Berg Collection)

While Randall Jarrell may have benefited from the experiential substrate of concrete particulars that underlay his choice of materials for poetry, he would not yield a theoretical inch of the mind's abstracting power to organize or consolidate a poem.

Jarrell refused to submit to American nominalism or to accept naively what became William Carlos Williams's elevation of the thing in the doctrine, "No ideas but in things." In 1942, Jarrell sees that as soon as a thing enters a poem as a word, it surrenders its thingness to become abstraction or, inevitably, an idea about a thing. Proceeding from this recognition, poetic practice becomes a question not of avoiding abstractions, but of timing and varying their range and deployment, so as not to gut the poem of ideational structure or, more simply, meaning. In this notebook, Randall Jarrell reinstates the power and necessity of abstractions.

In sum, it is not merely memory, or mimesis, but also a tenacious and receptive intelligence that makes poems; and it is not merely intelligence, but the explosion or simultaneous detonation of all possible perceptions that governs the inexhaustible and often inconclusive dialectic that Jarrell saw as the good poem. Poetry is not a static thing, he reminded us in the published version of his Princeton lecture, "Levels and Opposites": "But the poem is completely temporal, about as static as an explosion; there are no things in a poem, only processes" (Jarrell, "Levels," 697). Protecting the poem's dynamism, he distinguished between a ruling generality encasing the poem, and rejected "those views which regard it as a sugar-coated generalization, something in which the stone of universality is masked by the ivy of particularity" in the working out of these essential relationships:

Poetry exhibits a constant struggle between the general and particular: if the general overpowers the particular, we get the abstract intolerable didacticism of the worst eighteenth-century poems; if the particular over-powers the general, we get doctrinaire imagism or surrealism. (701)

So, we might say, runs the tension between self and the world, which also exists in the poem in struggle. So, too, most of Jarrell's war poems exhibit the dialectic he names between "abstract intolerable didacticism" and, if not a doctrinaire, then a murky or surreal imagism, with a dozen or more like "Losses" and "2nd Air Force" occupying fortunate and memorable midground. The particulars of self, its gritty urgencies, may be the inevitable clay lumping to-gether for a poem, but Randall Jarrell knew in theory, if not always in prac-tice, that the walls of the vessel are raised, shaped, and finessed by the mental art of the potter. If "2nd Air Force" remains one of the memorable poems of World War II, and "The Dream of Waking" lives on as a poem for special-ists, it is because the first poem possesses more than formal excellence and of-fers more than personal testimony, while the second poem, an immiscible con-glomeration, collapses into extracts, atmospheric haze, and self-conscious recollection. Still, from the very beginning, character in Jarrell's poetry tend-ed to flatten, and abstraction had a tendency to get out of hand. Delmore Schwartz complained that Jarrell saw his people from the distance of an opera glass (Schwartz, 184). It is certainly true that the force of the image in which the dead tail gunner is flushed out of his ball turret by a hose does not lie in the memorable particulars of the gunner's person. He, and the other child-warriors subject to the greater and lesser injustices of the state are merely vessels to the poem's thought. But that thought, neither boring nor irrelevant, is very much an evolving part of Jarrell's politics of the war poem.

"He learns to fight for freedom and the State"

From the outset of his service in 1943, Randall Jarrell built from his own experience in barracks to imply a larger war, nested within a larger history. "A Lullaby" croons:

He learns to fight for freedom and the State;
He sleeps with seven men within six feet.

He picks up matches and he cleans out plates;
Is lied to like a child, cursed like a beast.

And the poem finishes with: "his dull torment mottles like a fly's / The lying amber of the histories."

All of these poems generated by Jarrell's enlistment share a sense of the army and the state fusing to produce an inherently totalitarian institution. Within it, individual identity and moral agency are torn away by mass crowding within narrow space, demeaning labor, institutional clothing, and control by a command hierarchy indistinguishable from prison, also an experience of doing time. Within such a prison, a terrible longing grows to waken beyond the nightmare, only then to feel disconsolately that the endless doldrums of the military sentence makes civilian life the dream into which one escapes.

Unlike his friend Robert Lowell, Jarrell was not a pacifist and chose to enlist. But as a poet whose memory clung to the helplessness of childhood fears and losses, Jarrell fits with predetermined ease within the antimilitarist recognition that industrial, mechanized warfare returns the soldier to a child's fatal dependency. In the army's rigid hierarchy, the tiny cog moves within the wheels of a giant engine, itself only remotely, if murderously, connected to field operations. The passive, suffering figures that rise from Jarrell's poems are first orphans within the family then orphans within the maw of the army. Eventually, however, even such a child, so negligently reared, must awaken to the consequences of his own moral choices. Jarrell's sensitivity to the position of the abandoned child, his lifelong attunement to feelings that never left the core of his response to the world, and then his projection of that child's feeling into what undergirds his understanding of the mass army turns out to be his most creative adaptation of the use of personal circumstance in his war poetry. In the laboratory of experience that war afforded, and in the exercise of empathy, Jarrell tried out various matches of the particulars of his life to the life of the many men surrounding him. What he did in the best of these poems was to make canny use of personal memory and sensation, of that deepest listening to the self, both child and adult, as he transformed any potential self-pity into his own uniquely cogent exploration of the moral dangers of infantilization for a person, an institution, and a society.

As a three-year part of the great predatory mechanism of the army, Jarrell was not silent about being pinioned within it. In the same years, Keith Douglas described the view from inside a tank column as what "a body would look to a germ riding in its bloodstream" (Douglas *Alamein*, 17). Jarrell used a similar figure in a more disgruntled tone: "Being in the army is like being involved in the digestive process of an immense worm or slug or something— . . . it doesn't seem terribly stupid or at all malicious, just too big to have any sense or meaning—a mess rather" (Jarrell to Mackie Langham Jarrell, Berg Collection). In a letter to his wife written during the last frantic months of his army career, trying to expedite his reentry into civilian life, he was less temperate:

> the atmosphere was entirely one of lying, meaningless brutality and officiousness, stupidity not beyond belief but conception—the word for everything in the army is *petty*. (*Letters*, 120)

Jarrell's impatience with military regimentation fits what the English historian Michael Howard marks as a difference between European and American perspectives on war. In the pre–World War I literature of Britain and Europe, cultural roots are sunk in "a bellicist past" little eroded. It is a tradition "at once terrible and comforting" (Howard, 184–85); in it lies the European idea "that in the endurance and overcoming of suffering there is something that is ennobling, an idea that had reconciled the Christian and warrior ethic since the end of the Dark Ages." Disapproving of the American lack of stoicism, Howard notes that "together with the yet older tradition of the classics that man should maintain dignity and serenity in spite of the wildest caprice of the gods—all this has disappeared" (186).

Indeed Jarrell did not identify the state with the gods. Toward the end of the war, and during the postwar years, like everyone learning more about the realities of Nazi atrocity, he moved towards a greater acceptance of the necessity of the war—everybody's war—but struggled to find the dignity of a sacrifice called for by a grinding industrial mechanism devaluing and degrading the process of rendering it.

Randall Jarrell and his contemporaries, including Elizabeth Bishop and Marianne Moore, show the raw ends of war logic as it played out for American poets who flourished or came to maturity during World War II. The historical reality penetrating discussion of World War II poetry names an enlarged theater of war that elides the boundaries between civilian and soldier, as soldiers bombed and civilian populations worked—and survived or died—within the arc of their missions. Inside the circle of that mobilization, the customary distinctions between what men and women do also shifted. Women, still in defeat treated as sexual booty, nevertheless slid out from under protected, neutral status to active defense work.[2] While total civilian fatalities in World War I were fifteen percent of the whole of what Wellington called "the butcher's bill," in World War II civilian fatalities, including Holocaust victims, shot up to sixty-five percent (Ehrenreich, 206). As a commentary on this difference, Samuel Hynes could say:

> Stephen Spender once remarked that bombed cities were to the Second World War what the Western Front was to the First—the essential image of the war. One can see what he meant: the fact that in the Second War historic cities of Europe and Asia were attacked and destroyed from the air made that war unique, and the memorable records in films and photographs of those ruined cities—the shells of buildings, the unidentifiable streets, the landscape of ashes—are images of that uniqueness. (Hynes, *Soldiers' Tale*, 228)

It is worth mentioning that it is attack by high-flying airmen that left this distinguishing image; war, or the tactic of devastating the soft civilian underbelly is not new, and constituted an important part of medieval warfare, as Clifford J. Rogers informs us.[3] Nevertheless, battle, or the core definition of war making, is supposed to engage only men, yet in the total war of industrial civilizations, women, children, the elderly, and the infirm go down in greater numbers than soldiers, although their narratives are rarely what is meant when we tell the orthodox "war story."

Correspondingly, as more civilians were threatened, more soldiers were not: the majority of soldiers—like Jarrell, like many soldier-poets—who were posted in increasingly extended rear echelons, or even stationed in occupied countries, rarely or never saw actual combat. Yet as soldiers in uniform, poets like Jarrell have the imaginative authority to speak of war that women and children, only the victim of the soldier, lack. This authority sustains the administration of pathos as a terrible temptation for the noncombatant soldier writing about the war experienced by others.

In fact, in the gathered armies of England and America, large numbers of soldiers suffered comparatively little but the irksomeness of their constricted and suspended lives. In Charles Carrington's memorable phrase, "The teeth of a modern army are more formidable than they were in 1916 but the tail is much longer" (Carrington, 15). Paul Fussell's acerbically elaborates on that judgment:

> In 1943 the Army of the United States grew by two million men, but only about 365,000 of those went to combat units, and an even smaller number

ended in the rifle companies. The bizarre size and weight of the administrative tail dragged across Europe by the American forces is implied by statistics: between 1941 and 1945, the number of troops whose job was fighting increased by only 100,000. If by the end there were 11 million men in the American army, only 2 million were in the 90 combat divisions, and of those, fewer than 700,000 were in the infantry. (*Wartime*, 283)

Two million out of the eleven that dressed for war actually fought, but all the millions are called soldiers. As John Ellis evaluates and analyzes these statistics, it means that in both the American and British armies fewer men saw combat because of the "tail," but for those that did, casualty ratios were generally and surprisingly as high and damaging as they had been in World War I (Ellis, *The Sharp End*, 159). But World War II poetry, both English and American, represents the majority, noncombatant, experience.

The World War II poems of soldier-poets like Roy Fuller and Randall Jarrell—still within the category that we commonly and mistakenly recognize as the only authentic witness to war—tend to be as much about life in uniform as life in battle. Writing to Mackie Jarrell in 1943, Jarrell remarks with some surprise, that he has come to realize "how much I write about the Army, and how little about the War" (Jarrell to Mackie Langham Jarrell, Berg Collection). Yet his imaginings of battle are also printed and treated with an unconscious deference beyond that assumed or given by women either within or without the circle of battle.

World Wars I and II saw significant alteration in the class and status of the soldier. While combat still fell disproportionately to the lot of the poorer and less educated soldier in both wars, as Paul Fussell has observed, the writing and fighting classes were no longer separate, as mass conscription took over modern armies (Fussell, *Thank God*, 237), and conspicuously civilian points of view began sounding from soldiers only temporarily in uniform, with independent loyalties transcending their term of service. Literate representation of soldiering emerged for a broad reading public, even if it may have taken decades for the more controversial opinions to be heard or accepted, for Wilfred Owen to be read and listened to above Rupert Brooke or Alan Seeger. Still, the main record of war in poetry stayed in uniform; no American or English woman in either war—and I include Muriel Rukeyser, Edna St. Vincent Millay, H. D., or Edith Sitwell in this assessment—either attempted or, better yet, succeeded, in writing a large-scale and visionary poetry of war. That this is *not* the outcome in fiction and memoir should intrigue us all.

Randall Jarrell had dropped his burgeoning career as a writer and cultural journalist for a life in the army that for the duration bumped along from one relatively low-level position to another. At least in part, the distinctive features of his antimilitarism emerged in response to his subsequent military experience, alongside an ingrained skepticism mostly denying the heroic. Nonetheless, Jarrell finished his army service as a flight instructor and trainer in celestial navigation, by then persuaded of the modest, practical utility of his service. Living at the edge of combat operations, Jarrell was never a Luddite opposed to the machine. In 1938, he startled Robert Lowell by discoursing with contemporary glibness on the superiority of British planes to German equivalents and showed Lowell how a bombing attack might plausibly work over Kenyon College (Lowell, "Randall Jarrell," 107). In the army, his letters to his wife contain diagrams explaining the Link trainers and celestial navigation towers with which he worked; another correspondent is directed to the April 1943 issue of *Popular Mechanics* for a full, clear explanation of the work of these towers. Late in life his passion turned toward sleek, expensive racing cars. In a 1954 piece written for *Vogue* both comic and fervent, he detailed his passion for races and racing cars and praised the driver Phil Hill in a warmth of tone he normally reserved for favorite poems ("The Little Cars"). A 1957 issue of *Mademoiselle* found him, with equal amounts of precision and passion, detailing the pleasures of buying a Mercedes 300SL with fuel injection, gull-wing doors, and a high-speed axle that will do 167: "It's not that I *want* to do 167, but it'd be a nice thing to have in reserve for Judgment Day" (Jarrell, "Go, Man, Go," 283).

Mary Kinzie writes persuasively of Jarrell's poetic program, and his sustained use of dreamwork. Jarrell produces

> a deliberate dreaming-back, a relatively conscious act. It is further significant that the dream of early years to which his poetic dreams recur is principally the period of latency, not the earlier precognitive period. It is as if the two great periods of libidinal and aggressive energy, infancy and adolescence, had been erased by their very violence, and what remained were the states among which Jarrell holds his dialogue, childhood and maturity, two periods of achieved quiescence that do not know their real histories or their real names. (Kinzie, "The Man Who Painted Bulls," 834)

Quoting "The Difficult Resolution" in support of her argument, Kinzie suggests that in Jarrell's exclamations and questions, it is "as if each version, child and adult, of the self-in-arrest were asking about its dark, forgotten, torrential years, suspecting that there is a link, a point of passage between them, but unable to prove anything" (Kinzie, "The Man Who Painted Bulls," 834).

Mary Kinzie's perceptive, brilliant analysis can be brought next to Jarrell's war poems to suggest that Jarrell recognized the same "self-in-arrest," the same suspensions, repressions, or erasures of development and libidinal energy in his own life, as parallel events in the life of the mass conscript. His own and the soldier-nought's dreaming-back coincided fruitfully in his war poems and helped to produce Jarrell's profoundly original and thoroughly modern work about army life. In the suspended life of the recruit, and by his own moral qualifications rejecting the heroic code, Jarrell sensed that his own unconventional masculinity, something at issue throughout his life, was compromised by a militarist institution. Penned among other men with similarly arrested and shrunken individuality, Jarrell repressed any active erotic expression, along with all the other repressions of his civilian self; yet he kept as the one remaining, not wholly manageable outlet for uninhibited maleness a residual romancing of flight and of the mechanics of flight.

Jarrell's appreciation for the heroics of high speed and soaring elevation was not negligible, although his army experience with the airplane actively brought to light both disabilities and ambivalence. As he explained to a young acquaintance in 1943:

> For about two months, back around Christmas, I flew all the time, sometimes twice a day; then I got washed out because the chief pilot thought I did some maneuvers badly. (I guess he was right, too.) I didn't like flying much because it isn't very thrilling—instead of seeming to move fast you just seem to stand still, with the world moving around you very slowly, as if it were a motion picture. Besides, we always had to fly at *just* so many miles an hour, at *just* such an altitude, in *just* such a direction—it was too much like one long examination. (*Letters*, 100)

To Lambert Davis in 1943, Jarrell wrote: "I was washed out (I got into a spin in a check ride and the chief pilot, as he said, decided I wasn't a safe flyer)" (*Letters*, 68).

Unlike James Dickey, who lied about every possible aspect of his wartime career as a pilot and clung to the grandeurs of participating in wartime rituals of masculinity, Randall Jarrell represented the complicated range of his acts and feelings fairly. In actuality, flying large planes in formation more closely resembles bus-driving in traffic than the soaring of birds, one more restriction of the self's powers, imaginative or otherwise. To Allen Tate, Jarrell said he had had "a pretty good time when I was flying," but then went on to speak of the navy combat pilot he was close to who had been killed and frankly acknowledged his relief at not being a pilot: "I'd flown about thirty hours, most of them solo, when I was washed out. It was a very great piece of luck for me." When he got to Sheppard Field, his luck continued: "I was lucky to get there when I did—six weeks later and I'd have been made a gunner" (*Letters*, 119). Jarrell has made clear to us the undesirable fate of gunners.

Clearly, the army brought sobriety about what was central and deadly and not for Jarrell in the experience of planes and flying, yet it could not wholly eradicate the thrill associated with planes and flying; a thrill there, even in the most sorrowing of the poems he wrote about men, planes, and carriers. On 25 June 1943, he wrote to Mackie about a moment after getting out of the drudgery of KP:

> just as I got out, at 8, twenty or thirty flying fortresses landed on the field, in a wonderful clockwork procedure that took about thirty minutes—there were so many that lined up, they stretched from one end of the big airport to the other. I said to my fellow KP'ers, "this isn't *my* Air Corps." And it wasn't. Every single pilot made a beautiful landing. The crews looked so young—they had on all sorts of non-G.I. clothes, straw hats (like cowboy hats) were very common. Thousands of students, instructors, nurses from the field swarmed around the planes; the sun was just setting. It was really lovely. (Jarrell to Mackie Langham Jarrell, Berg Collection)

Jarrell had just had leave he badly wanted taken away from him, and he had been punished for wearing nonregulation clothing, which helps explain how wistful this is, how much the observer (at KP, a domestic slavey of diminished masculinity), is segregated from this youthful male aristocracy of risk, how layered his feelings of pity, envy, and wonder.

Jarrell's first, early fascination with the airman is in perfect harmony with the visionary-ecstatic mode about flight familiar in American poetry since Hart Crane on the Wright brothers in *The Bridge* (1930) or Muriel Rukeyser's celebration of them in *The Outer Banks* (1967). Poems like "Losses," "Siegfried," "A Pilot from the Carrier," and "Pilots, Man Your Planes" quicken to say what it means to send earth-hugging flesh upward in the exhilaration of flight, but they also move toward understanding the Faustian daemonic inherent in those planes and engines. In *Fields of Battle*, the military historian John Keegan divides America's romance with the airborne into one strain of boyish exaltation, lifting Americans skyward, and another and darker in which the lift holds a payload of destruction, that lift constituting a bargain always tinged with our least-confessable urges for dominion:

> The madness which seized Europe in 1940–42, the madness of nihilism, ultimately seized the U.S. Army Air Force also, and at the end of the war it bombed and bombed as if bombing were an industrial process, a form of work, the human activity at which America excels above all other nations. (332)

But beside his penchant for the elegiac, Jarrell shared the leftward politics of the journals in which he published. In 1941, Jarrell's view of "The war aim," or what he paraphrased as the newspapers' idea of "Great Britain and the United States as the armed police force of the world—" struck him as something "surely beyond any parodist's talents or dreams" (*Letters*, 49). While opinions about capitalist excess initially ruled Jarrell, his life in the Air Force grounded his tendencies to apostrophize or abstract. In the titles alone of certain poems—"The Sick Nought," "Mail Call," "The Lines," and "Absent with Official Leave"—one can see the growth of a homely, deflationary realism about army life, at variance with, as well as sometimes complementing, what Jarrell had called his "new political style." "Absent with Official Leave," as strange and haunting a poem as "The Black Swan" or "The Eland"—two later signature Jarrell pieces—like them plays with an odd swooping consciousness, a body at the edge of a space full of graphic apparitions and displaced temporality, in and out of sleep and dreaming. It begins, "The lights are beginning to go out in the barracks." In that instant, the almost-sleeper drifts to war, to childhood, to states of danger, to doze finally in the helplessness of a child in a bathtub, presided over by women. Other machinations happen, and then

> He moans like a bear in his enchanted sleep,
> And the grave mysterious beings of his years—
>
> The causes that mourn above his agony like trees—
> Are moved for their child, and bend across his limbs
> The one face opening for his life, the eyes
> That look without shame even into his.

And the child awakes, and sees around his life
The night that is never silent—broken with the sighs
And patient breathing of the dark companions
With whom he labors, sleeps, and dies.
>   (*Little Friend*, 33)

There is a marvelous element of the magical and grandly mysterious in this poem, a surge of feeling beyond Jarrell's more pedestrian attempts at synthesizing borrowed, invented, and remembered experience like "The Dream of Waking." He had written to Mackie:

> Sometimes in flying an orientation problem (finding the beam and then flying into the station) you get hopelessly lost, and so childishly confused and exhausted (mentally, mentally) that you can't think out the simplest thing. It amuses me, because it brings home to me what a wonderful mixture of grown-up and childish entirely unchanged layers one is. (Jarrell to Mackie Langham Jarrell, Berg Collection)

But with what joy and relief that child could be greeted. In these poems whose writing was stuffed into crevices of army time, Jarrell dives deep down to embrace a submersion into states resembling sleep, and along the way he encounters the lost, primary continuities of self in the soldier-prisoner. Both sleep and childhood fuse in the altered past, and his task is to find the whole adult male hidden in the uniform, among all the serial beds.

For whatever reasons, there is a heartfelt candor about what it means to go to sleep in a crowd, with someone breathing or coughing or sighing audibly around you all night long. An early experience of sleepless displacement bothered Jarrell enough that he wrote about it. In a folder of unfinished drafts for poems at the Berg Collection, there is a sketch of a poem about being put in the same bed at night with his younger brother:

> When I was a child I slept with my brother, who moved continually enough, Pascal's point, to take up most of the bed; I lay narrowly constrained at the verge, like a sleep-walker moving along the gutter of a roof[.] Sometimes I would not fall asleep for a long time, and sooner or later I thought about a tablet. (Jarrell papers, Berg Collection)

A drawing of this tablet follows, the "One Pound Wonder Tablet," which has one of those images of infinite regress: on the cover, a scale contains a tablet with a picture of a scale on its cover, and inside the tiny picture with its tinier tablet, you make out yet another drawing, with yet another tablet with yet another scale on its cover, and so on. The image of a painful wakefulness, of its teetery and dizzying spaces, now clinging to the bed, now clinging to the roof, about to fall from a great height—taking Jarrell back down into the pit of absolute helplessness.

In letters to Mackie, the issue of sleeping in a herd rose again and again: he drew her diagrams of his quarters, how his bed stood in relation to others. He analyzed their snoring and, evidently wakeful, described how morning broke at 4:30, with "a *very* queer sound: somebody is running down the street as fast as he can blowing a whistle—the whistle gets louder and louder (accompanied by footsteps) and then vanishes away" (Jarrell to Mackie Langham Jarrell, 1943, Berg Collection).

The whistler got put into "Soldier [T.P.]," as did Jarrell's wistful reference to the civilian world as the place where "they marry and live in houses" (*Little Friend*, 25) Jarrell served for a time as the interviewer who would classify soldiers for assignment, as in "Title Pending"; when he assumes the character of the interviewee in the poem, however, he knows that he speaks for those both in front of and behind the desk:

> But his house and wife are—pending; and the life
> That was his to starve in, to waste as he chose,
> Has no option now: the iron unchanging
> Chance that had governed his price like a plate's
> Is smashed for an instant, as the atoms' wills
> Are fused in the grim solicitude of State.

But the poem blinks in its denunciation of history, ending:

> You must live or die as the dice are thrown on a blanket;
> As the leaf chars or is kindled; as the bough burns.
> (*Little Friend*, 25)

In contrast to these quasi-biblical dispositions of fate with which "Soldier [T.P.]" effectively enough concludes, "Mail Call" makes its point with an attractively consistent simplicity of means and tone. Jarrell relished what in letters he called "a pretty ceremony"; in the patter he developed for public readings, he described how mail delivery meant calling out the name of the soldier and then shying each letter by hand to the recipient soldier in a graceful arc, perhaps producing the one entirely innocent instance of flight in the war:

> The letters always just evade the hand.
> One skates like a stone into a beam, falls like a bird.
> Surely the past from which the letters rise
> Is waiting in the future past the graves?
> The soldiers are all haunted by their lives.

And then the ache for simple recognition and integrated selfhood with which the poem has the great sense to conclude:

> In letters and in dreams they see the world.
> They are waiting: and the years contract
> To an empty hand, to one unuttered sound—

> The soldier simply wishes for his name.
> > (*Little Friend.* 35)

Losses, published in 1948, continues the mix of subjects that the war years bred for Randall Jarrell. But where *Little Friend, Little Friend* had been prolific with barracks life, prisoners, and children, *Losses* begins to trek away from the war, making wider and wider circles as it does so, until Jarrell takes in other theaters like the Pacific and ends this phase with a vision of postatomic war in "1945: The Death of the Gods." The poem uncoils ominously, in one large thundering sentence linked by unrelenting dashes and colons and ends small: here is a portion.

> you who determine
> Men's last obedience, yourselves determined
> In the first unjudged obedience of greed
> And senseless power: you eternal States
> Beneath whose shadows men have found the stars
> And graves of men: O warring Deities,
> Tomorrow when the rockets rise like stars
> And earth is blazing with a thousand suns
> That set up there within your realms a realm
> Whose laws are ecumenical, whose life

Exacts from men a prior obedience—
Must you learn from your makers how to die?

> (*Losses*, 48)

Many of these poems labor heavily, clad in a deep rhetoric favored, I fear, by only the most hardened readers of poetry. As in the previous book, the memorable poems work with an amalgam of what Jarrell was familiar with, and what, from the basis of that familiarity, he could then imagine, and speak for, with authority.

Being in the Air Force and reading Ernie Pyle instead of Allen Tate brought Jarrell a more supple balance between image and discourse, between the general and the particular. Even if a civilian like Ezra Pound saw World War I fought "For a botched civilization, / . . . For two gross of broken statues, / For a few thousand battered books" in *Hugh Selwyn Mauberley*, a soldier-poet like Ivor Gurney preferred to see "England the Mother" in leafy embrace; Gurney's motherland

Will leave unblotted in the soldier-soul
Gold of the daffodil, the sunset streak,
The innocence and joy of England's blue.

> (Gurney, 51)

But Jarrell hung onto his 1930s sense of the overmastering "State." Working beside the many other men shipping out for active duty in Europe, the familiar pieties of soldiers as honorable ransom for the continuities of civilized life withered for him, and doubts grew about the necessity or value of their sacrifice.

Jarrell's distance from and compassion for these men and the "commodity" of their lives are visible in a score of these poems. Living within a sense of his own life as suspended for the duration of the war, Jarrell saw the soldier's life as an otherness, a dream of being in which glimpses of different and better realities were intermittently and achingly present. Jarrell was inordinately attuned to liminal being, and a remarkable number of his poems rest in the turn between sleep and waking, night and day, where palpable and impalpable merge and drift. It is not surprising, then, that his war poems on airmen, prisoners, and concentration camp inmates should follow the contours of these states, adding a sense of the fantastic against the commoner drive towards naturalistic representation.

FIGURE 9. Randall Jarrell with Kitten in the 1940s. Jarrell wrote to Mackie in 1943, "I wish it were possible for Kitten to make a noise over the phone—maybe you could hold him upside down to make him growl." Berg Collection, New York Public Library.

A Poetic and Semifeminine Mind

Randall Jarrell did not see his gift in poetry as necessarily discursive, and while he appreciated scientific accomplishment, he gendered himself and his work to Allen Tate in 1939 as "poetic and semi-feminine" (Jarrell, *Letters*, 19). In the army by 1943, Jarrell's letters to his wife defy the styles of manliness at large in the culture or imposed on the military recruit. While he was only able to keep his mustache and longer hair for a short time, here and there

Jarrell bespeaks his resistance to a conventional masculinity by referring to himself in female terms: in March 1943, he jokes that next war he will join the Campfire Girls; a little later, speaking of his alienation he says, "I feel as if I were the Faraway Princess daydreaming or something"; and at another point, he refers to himself as "old Pollyanna" (Jarrell to Mackie Langham Jarrell, Berg Collection). One of his requests in a letter home was for a hand mirror. Something of a dandy, it was not difficult for him to cast himself in what he chose to recognize as female roles. I am reminded by Ellen Bryant Voigt of how remarkable it is that a southern male in these years would be so little interested in promoting any sign of himself as hypermasculine; Jarrell took a pliant and labile masculinity very much for granted. He wrote to Amy de Blasio that "As long as I can remember I'd been so different from everybody else that even trying to be like them couldn't occur to me" (*Letters*, 64).

Yet his appropriation of women's ways of thinking hardly escaped a conventional gendering in his poems, in which women become expressive outlets for feelings of vulnerability, vanity, and impotence of one sort or another. After the war, he convincingly imagined himself as Richard Strauss's glamorous Marschallin and as the "aging machine part" of "The Woman at the Washington Zoo." In the 1940s, however, the wife of the pilot who burns her dead husband's letters in "Burning the Letters" remains a narrative convenience, a threshing floor for some of Jarrell's most contorted thinking about war and Christian sacrifice, a subject to which he brought a much greater and more genuine anguish in "Eighth Air Force." Perhaps what Jarrell felt to be feminine in himself, and which received vital expression in his war poetry, was not only the pity and wonder that he wrote of to Robert Lowell as being evoked by war, but a charged tenderness.

Any reader of Randall Jarrell ought to be careful not to make simplistic arguments about repressed homosexuality. It is as if Jarrell retreated to being a woman, or being maternal at any rate, not so much because he really wanted to be a woman or give up any of the powerful prerogatives assigned to the male gender, but because he did not wish to be a certain kind of man. If that meant appropriating feminine character and poaching on emotions normally thought to belong to women alone, then that would be what he would do. Like all of his strategies that avoided splitting into the predictable binaries, this assumption of femininity also had the double benefit of allowing Jarrell to replace and internalize the disappointing mother of his memory with an imagined self, triumphant, both mothered and mothering. In his poetry, this becomes not a cancellation of male identity but an enlargement of it.

In Jarrell's work, there is little room for the adult heterosexual male. All of the many wartime letters to his first wife, Mackie Langham, have something of the quality of a boy's communications from sleep-away camp: He rarely inquires about her life apart from him. He lavishes endearments, looks forward, with an edge of desperation, to phone calls and meetings, but asks for no detailed portrait, such as he gives of himself, of how she fills her hours. His interest in her is oddly impersonal; it is as if she exists only as a trusted repository of his own reflections on life. Her letters in return are currently in no public archive, but in Jarrell's existing letters there is little sense of a reciprocal, conjugal narrative. Like his poems, his letters represent exchanges between men and women in an asexual, parental mode.

At the edge of war, both within and without it, Jarrell found in himself the womanly loving kindness which he denied first to government and then to nature itself. Ascribing all feminine forgiveness to his disembodied speaker, Jarrell's poems either exclude or diminish wives and mothers, although a brooding, maternal tenderness for boy pilots is matched by his tenderness for the cities that went up in flames under them. When women appear in poems like "The Sick Nought" or "Protocols," they, and other adult, civilian survivors, with a few conspicuous exceptions like the Jews of Haifa, present a featureless passivity.

If Randall Jarrell's semifeminine poetic mind directed feeling, it was not only to let feeling grow away from women, but to sidestep the sexual lives of adults, effecting a lopsided concentration on parenting, where nurture is withheld by an undifferentiating universe. In counterpoint, a flow of caring is made to exude from the disembodied voice of an impersonal narrator. Poems like "The Death of the Ball Turret Gunner" use the myth of a morally abdicating maternal State, while others cultivate a grieving receptivity towards prisoners and orphaned children.

Gathered up and read one poem after the other as they are given to us in the section "Children and Civilians" in his *Selected Poems* of 1955 and in *The Complete Poems* of 1969, Randall Jarrell's poems about dead children present an excess of compassion, which Richard Fein reacts to as "a kind of intellectual sentimentality" (Fein, 152); Mary Kinzie labels this "a narcissism out of which was drawn an inordinate sympathy for others" (Kinzie, "New Sweetness," 69). Why is that "inordinate"? In the aggregate of these poems, it might be a peculiar relishing of horror, an otherworldly dwelling on extinction that smothers the actual hideousness of what overtook war orphans because the perspective held is so rigidly postmortem. For reader and writer, the poems can become too orderly a containment; the removal of a fearful obscenity to something a little too beautifully borne.

And yet administered in the small, complete dose of a single poem, as readers most often encounter "Protocols" or "Come to the Stone . . ." or "The Angels at Hamburg," each poem has a power beyond the simple pathos of their stories of wretched abandonment. In moving to secure a space some respectful distance from the subject, the formal grace and the poem's dignity and beauty are allowed to rest on the vulnerable little people who lacked all of that in their passing; it is not clear that we should always resent these properties or recoil from what might seem an insulting effort of the elegist to lay dignity and beauty over the unspeakable truths of atrocity in some ultimate denial of their suffering. Is Jarrell gilding these deaths, superimposing poetry on them, or is he genuinely retrieving or uncovering a humanity that has been there all along? Why should we not assume that it is the latter?

When we pursue the details of torture and murder, when we unfold them close to the bones of their happening, there is a suspicion that we are not merely recording cruelty, but repeating it—and that such a recall cannot help but participate in its re-creation and perpetuation. Then too, the repetition of facts has a tendency to numb and blunt impact: the timing of reiteration becomes part of the aesthetic tact of poems dealing with extremes of suffering.

The children in "Protocols," said to speak alternately from Birkenau and Odessa, allow Randall Jarrell to restate the unthinkable in the bleakest and most stripped of rhythms and linguistic resources. Diction, description, all the pointed monosyllables in their rough pentameter are compressed and focused so that we narrow to the essence of the horrendous events being evoked. In the first stanza the children say:

> We went there on the train. *They had big barges that they towed,*
> *We stood up, there were so many I was squashed.*
> There was a smoke-stack, then they made me wash.
> It was a factory, I think. *My mother held me up*
> *And I could see the ship that made the smoke.*

In the first five-line stanza, the little ping of the rhyme "squashed / wash," with its slight trace of the Seussical, holds the ghost of laughter up to oncoming death: for which "my" mother holds me up and which "I" am able to see, if not understand. Whether or not this was ever so, there is the suggestion of an obedient, jaunty, childish stoicism sketched for us; even in an unremitting hell there are peaks and valleys, where the children's language clings to normalcy no matter how their circumstances subvert it. And as the poem progresses, the child's even tone becomes more terrible:

> When I was tired my mother carried me.
> She said, "Don't be afraid." But I was only tired.
> *Where we went there is no more Odessa.*
> They had water in a pipe—like rain, but hot;
> *The water there is deeper than the world*
>
> *And I was tired and fell in in my sleep*
> *And the water drank me. That is what I think.*
> And I said to my mother, "Now I'm washed and dried,"
> My mother hugged me, and it smelled like hay
> *And that is how you die.* And that is how you die.
> (*Little Friend*, 38)

The orderly mechanics of the world of things does not stop pumping. The poem becomes more regularly iambic; the five-line sequencing does not give way. And the pattern of one punctuating off-rhyme per stanza continues— "tired / world"; "dried / die." Nor do children stop being children because they are reversing their and your life cycle by dying; in helpless and hopeless irony everything contributes to the unstoppable and unthinkable function.

We ask ourselves if Jarrell has gotten the difficult balance of loving and grieving for these children in the face of the annihilation to which our minds are implacably held; we should feel the sinking terror, the obliterating numbness overtaking them, as if we were breaking into their presence. And yet other parts of the reader-writer contract ask that we, altogether too safe outside the text, not be made voyeurs of pain and that we not turn too expeditiously away from the children to examine ourselves and our own feelings of fright and horror. To feel often seems the most evanescent of states that a poem may confer; granting that evanescence, however, still does not seem enough of a warrant to stop the imperfect solution of the poem from being made. In these stupefying circumstances, there is a graspable sufficiency in Randall Jarrell's accomplishment for which we should and can be grateful, a fragile purchase extended to us from a reality which, for most of us, is entirely too easy to elude.

"A Camp in the Prussian Forest," a poem transiting between Jarrell's familiar categories of children, prisoners, and soldiers, is made with the same quiet and understated regard for the impact of measured and rhymed syllables, for shapely line extensions and regularly irregular pauses in rhythmic effect to carry its grim meaning. It does not concern children alone and does not make use of the ready-made pathos that they afford, but the same symbolic and terrifying eating and drinking stand for a gorging on human beings, as they are put not in a place where they eat, but where they are eaten:

> Here men were drunk like water, burnt like wood.
> The fat of good
> And evil, the breast's star of hope
> Were rendered into soap.
>
> I paint the star I sawed from yellow pine—
> And plant the sign
> In soil that does not yet refuse
> Its usual Jews
>
> Their first asylum. But the white, dwarfed star
> This dead white star—
> Hides nothing, pays for nothing; smoke
> Fouls it, a yellow joke,
>
> The needles of the wreath are chalked with ash,
> A filmy trash
> Litters the black woods with the death
> Of men; and one last breath
>
> Curls from the monstrous chimney. . . .

But now the first-person narration that began his poem—"I walk beside the prisoners to the road"—forces Jarrell to conclude his poem with that same "I"; after the ellipsis, he goes on to interpose a fantastic self busily full of judgment and a stagy bitterness:

> I laugh aloud
> Again and again;
> The star laughs from its rotting shroud
> Of flesh. O star of men!
>> (*Losses*, 7)

This conclusion with its openly ironic laughter is not quite so genuinely and effectively disturbing as the troubling hint of a child's laughter in "Protocols." "A Camp in the Prussian Forest" switches too quickly to the rendition of the speaker's reaction and trusts us too little to find feeling without a narrator's help.

In Samuel Hynes's *The Soldier's Tale*, he observes a change in war narrative toward inclusion of more stories of sufferers than of agents:

> War stories have been traditionally told by the *agents*—the men of power who fight and kill; the *sufferers*—the helpless, the unarmed, the captive, the weak—all those human beings caught up in war and killed or maimed or imprisoned or starved simply because they were powerless and were there—these have had no voice.
>
> In our century this has changed; for the first time, narratives of suffering have been written by the sufferers. (Hynes, *Soldiers' Tale*, 223)

As passive suffering enters the annals, accounts of atrocity, accounts of imprisonment become more numerous in the twentieth century, even though the initial feeling in World War I was to mute the experience of the prisoner because it denigrates the soldier and the soldier's occupation. Imprisoned, the readiness for combat that defines the soldier ceases or goes underground in muted form: "All imprisonment diminishes, but a prisoner of war is especially deprived; disarmed, denied freedom of action, stripped of his signs of rank and his duties, he is dispossessed of what defines him—his soldiership" (Hynes, *Soldiers' Tale*, 233).

But Jarrell's poetry, characteristically rejecting conventional binaries of agency, amends these assumptions, first by splitting off "the men of power who fight and kill" from the soldiers that do the actual shooting, killing, and waiting and serving in the twentieth-century army. Jarrell allowed his poems to straddle the line between combatant and noncombatant and revise distinctions between civilians and soldiers, friend and foe.

And he wrote about prisoners on both Axis and Allied sides. In *Little Friend, Little Friend*, he includes two poems, facing each other in sequence, "Prisoners" and "An Officers' Prison Camp Seen from a Troop Train." When the first poem was republished in 1955, a note informed readers that its three military prisoners are American. But the earlier publication makes no important distinction between these Americans and the German officer prisoners of the second poem. Both sets belong to kindred worlds of force and oppression.

In "Prisoners," under the rifle of the yawning guards, the three prisoners

> Go on all day being punished, go on all month, all year
> Loading, unloading; give their child's, beast's sigh—of despair,
> Of endurance and of existence; look unexpectingly
> At the big guard, dark in his khaki, at the dust of the blazing plain,
> At the running or crawling soldiers in their soiled and shapeless green.

> The prisoners, the guards, the soldiers—they are all, in their way, being
>   trained.
> From these moments, repeated forever, our own new world will be made.
>   (*Little Friend*, 52)

In "An Officers' Prison Camp Seen from a Troop Train," the guards are still yawning; it is a soldier leaning from a train full of other soldiers that sees the scene taking place in a converted school. In the time of armies present and future, all men live in a convict world.

Even before his soldier life, Jarrell's civilian imagination took in refugees. *Blood for a Stranger*, published in 1942, has poems that haunt the railway carriages and stations of the dispossessed in an Auden-induced profusion. But the sense and movement of "The Refugees" make an awkward sestina, whose six diffused repeat words, "vacant, mask, waste, extravagant, possessed," and the handily blank "this" fail to assemble; the lines rotate with ever-increasing centrifugal force.

In the remaining two books of the war years—*Little Friend, Little Friend* (1945) and *Losses* (1948)—however, Jarrell came much nearer to poems that matter. The near-obsessive poems that linked soldiers, prisoners, children, and pets in dream states either on or over the border of death and sleep—some successful, some not so successful—gave way in 1948 to a last war-and-childhood poem written in the aftermath of war, "The Truth." This dramatic monologue flashes with vivid circumstance and a subtle and rich interplay between its principals, profiting greatly from Jarrell's reading and writing about Robert Frost's dramatic poems, which he carried on at roughly the same time. In "The Truth," a displaced, fatherless boy calls up Jarrell's acute empathy for a childhood of denial and adult betrayal. Jarrell's bibliographer, Stuart Wright, excerpts this letter to Elizabeth Eisler, where Jarrell explains that "The Truth" was based on readings in Anna Freud. The poem is said initially by a little girl, a child most of whose family has been killed in the London air-raids early in the war—she has been evacuated to a sort of institution for children, and hysterically alienated from her mother's lies about what has happened. I read a number of such case histories in a book by Anna Freud. One child in the book said, "I'm nobody's nothing." (Wright, 280)

In its final form, the poem, which drew on the case history of a little boy as well, may also have been too close to Jarrell's own family dynamics for him to resist changing the sex of the child.

As Richard Flynn quotes and summarizes the initial material from Anna Freud and Dorothy Burlingham's *War and Children*, the main issue is the child's insistence on the truth of her father's death against the potential comfort of believing her mother's lie about his survival, which the mother insists the girl accept. Freud and Burlingham say of this exchange between mother and child:

> The little girl repeated the words after her with a sullen expression and had to promise never to say or think it otherwise. The children of this family show the effects of this discrepancy between the truth they know and feel and the legend they are forced to adopt in wild and unruly behavior and general contempt for the adult world. (Quoted in Flynn, 47)

Perhaps Jarrell's poem, with its poignant reversal of the original outcome—in which the child is forced to cooperate with the lie, and child and parent remain estranged and unreconciled—came as a result of Jarrell's own gradual postwar accommodation to the facts of his childhood betrayal and the movements that he saw as emotional abandonment by both his parents and his beloved paternal grandparents. But whatever the autobiographical facts forming the substrate of the poem may have been, "The Truth" is unique among Jarrell's work on childhood until the late work of *The Lost World*; in its diamond-sharp, direct handling of relations between children and adults, the poem is in strong contrast with the earlier wartime poetry that Jarrell wrote: it is a poem of aftermath. Also, in the teeth of wartime loss and destruction, open acknowledgment of irremediable loss and terror becomes a route to healing, as the boy, like the poet seeing him, struggles with the definitions of what is said to be true, what is true, and the conflict between what one dreams and what one knows. The boy in "The Truth" begins:

When I was four my father went to Scotland.
They said he went to Scotland.

When I woke up I think I thought that I was dreaming—
I was so little then that I thought dreams
Are in the room with you, like the cinema.
That's why you don't dream when it's still light—
They pull the shades down when it is, so you can sleep.
I thought that then, but that's not right.
Really it's in your head.

And it was light then—light at *night*.
I heard Stalky bark outside.
But really it was Mother crying—
She coughed so hard she cried.
She kept shaking Sister,
She shook her and shook her.
I thought Sister had had her nightmare.
But he wasn't barking, he had died.
There was dirt all over Sister.
It was all streaks, like mud. I cried.
She didn't, but she was older.
I thought she didn't
Because she was older, I thought Stalky had just gone.
I got *everything* wrong.
I didn't get one single thing right.

The confusions are heaping—night that is day, dreaming that is waking, and
what is in your head or out there: does your mother cough or cry? Is the dog
barking or dying, and why is your sister silent?

And, furthermore, the one remaining parent lies to you, leaves you, comes
suspiciously back, and then tries to buy off your truculent questions and bad
memories with a new dog that isn't even real:

She never said one thing my father said, or Sister.
Sometimes she did,
Sometimes she was the same, but that was when I dreamed it.
I could tell I was dreaming, she was just the same.

That Christmas she bought me a toy dog.

I asked her what was its name, and when she didn't know
I asked her over, and when she didn't know
I said, "You're not my mother, you're not my mother.
She *hasn't* gone to Scotland, she is dead!"
And she said, "Yes, he's dead, he's dead!"
And cried and cried; she *was* my mother,
She put her arms around me and we cried.

(Jarrell, Complete Poems, 195–96)

The pronouns wander, are jarringly reunited, and the questions repeat with the same destabilizing confusion, until finally a truth emerges to make at least the mother return, the child able to establish a self as a part of a "we" who now can mourn.

In Ellen Bryant Voigt's account of Jarrell's tactics of repetition, by which a repeating sound and a syntax make the emotion shine transparently through the language on the page, she sees, then hears "the heartrending paratactic stutter that constitutes the whole of 'The Truth'" (Voigt, 390), a poem that leaped ahead to the styles and truths of a much later Randall Jarrell, whose final return to the themes of childhood would take up his own past.

But in a return to the traditional war lyric of the soldier, it is usually Jarrell's young airman who flares in memory, as Christ and hero, damaged, damaging, and consecrated.

"Men wash their hands, in blood, as best they can"

Throughout *Little Friend, Little Friend* and *Losses*, published in 1945 and 1948, respectively, as postwar books, Jarrell blends compassion and keen insight into the confusing distributions of guilt and innocence that characterize everyone drawn into wartime event. Even if the political views embedded in these books—indeed in all of Jarrell's books—are fairly abstract and general, he still sustains a critical distinction between the victim-soldiers and victim-civilians. Nowhere is this so clearly evident as in "Eighth Air Force," the World War II poem in which Jarrell balances equally pity for both bombed and bombing.

From another kind of tenderness, stemming from traits temperamentally, historically, and psychologically different, Wilfred Owen in an earlier war drew the parallel between Christ's and the soldier's sacrifice in ways that later soldiers were bound to modify. Dominic Hibberd in *Owen The Poet* documents in Owen's art his fin de siècle despair and its fatalistic resignation; Paul Fussell in *The Great War and Modern Memory* comments as well on the theme of the love-death, or Liebestod, for which Owen's tender views of his soldier-charges provided the psychological underpinning. In so many of his poems, the themes of the betrayed young and the noble, eroticized death of the handsome soldier demonstrably have their roots in the underground Uranian, or homosexual, literature that Owen had discovered before the war.

This apotheosis of the doomed youth becomes the broader story of the holy company of the dead, which living women enter only as mourners of a more and more masochistic and death-driven Christian hero. But when Christ appears as soldier in World War II, as he does in Randall Jarrell's "Eighth Air Force," the ambivalence and ambiguities of the parallels knot them with ironies of a lesser splendor. Here is the first stanza:

> If in an odd angle of the hutment,
> A puppy laps the water from a can
> Of flowers, and the drunk sergeant shaving
> Whistles *O Paradiso!* —shall I say that man
> Is not as men have said: a wolf to man?

In four lines, Jarrell sets a deliberately and cozily domestic scene. The puppy laps water from the flower can in one of the minor indiscretions of the dog world, and the sergeant drunk in his own minor indiscretion whistles "*O Paradiso!*"[4] The whole setup undercuts the major darkness of the poet's query, meant to vibrate throughout, posing animal innocence in answer to animal brutality. At this still innocuous moment, these bomber pilots stationed in England are by implication not so very wolflike. And yet, by the second stanza:

> The other murderers troop in yawning;
> Three of them play Pitch, one sleeps, and one
> Lies counting missions, lies there sweating
> Till even his heart beats: One; One; One.
> *O murderers!* . . . Still, this is how it's done:

Jarrell puts us exactly where he wants us: confronting "murderers" who troop in yawning not like soldiers but like Boy Scouts playing games back at the den, until the poem slews around finally to the sweating insomniac turning over and over on his cot, who counts the missions left that he has to fly. (Jarrell's note explains that this man has "one to go before being sent home.")[5] It is as if a deeper brass were replacing the piccolo notes in the score, as guilt and distress occupy the remaining lines about these exiled playfellows. In the final stanzas,

> This is a war. . . . But since these play, before they die,
> Like puppies with their puppy; since, a man,
> I did as these have done, but did not die—
> I will content the people as I can
> And give up these to them: Behold the man!
>
> I have suffered in a dream, because of him,
> Many things; for this last saviour, man,
> I have lied as I lie now. But what is lying?
> Men wash their hands, in blood, as best they can:
> I find no fault in this just man.
>   (*Losses*, 20)

For both Wilfred Owen and Randall Jarrell, the boy status of the soldiers is held in mitigation of their blood guilt, but for Jarrell's distressed, lying, and complicit speaker, boyishness inevitably becomes a property of infantilization, a retarded sense of responsible agency.

Jarrell never resolved—as if it could be resolved—the morality of our behavior in the bombing firestorms of Dresden and Tokyo with his own sense of the larger justice of the Allied position in World War II, a justice which he acknowledged directly and simply in 1961 at a reading of "Eighth Air Force" at Pfeiffer College in North Carolina.[6] Speaking with immense sympathy for the pilots, he says quietly: "These people were our saviours. I mean if people like this hadn't murdered other people and died why we would be under a Nazi government and there would be a concentration camp over at High Point and so on."[7] By this time, Jarrell appears to have switched wholly to thinking of World War II as the good war, but what soldiers do, whether infantilized or not, still stands under the name of "murder."

Always for Jarrell, infantilization, or the morally numb consciousness of the soldier-nought, has been the clear outgrowth of the menacing control that the superstate imposes on a diminished, Orwellian citizenry. But "Eighth Air Force" allows a critique of boyhood, part of a larger critique of the impact of cultural codes of masculinity, wholly absent from Owen's work.[8] For Jarrell, much more frankly than for Owen, blood guilt appears as an issue both for the primary actors, *and* for the witnesses and pledges of that action: "This is a war." And still resembling Owen's tender and tormented officer who sells out his charges to their time on Golgotha, the poet of World War II steps inside Pilate, washing his hands of, and sending on his way, the murderous God-man to be crucified and killed. Quite differently from Owen's passage, Jarrell's final lines, with a terrible irony, echo Christ's presentation to the people, unsoftened by Jarrell's own explanation of what he intends. In *The Complete Poems*, Jarrell's note for "Eighth Air Force" reads: "The phrases from the Gospels compare such criminals and scapegoats as these with that earlier criminal and scapegoat about whom the Gospels were written" (8). The complicated set of synoptic references render the bomber pilots as one with Christ.

And yet in "Eighth Air Force," there is no denying that men's hands are washed in blood, not water; or that Pilate's hand washing in the Biblical text symbolizes a cowardly evasion of judgment; no denying the premise that whatever justification for murder that there is lands in human courts, not holy ones, and erupts there with undermining force. If Christ and man are one, and spilled blood and the water of absolution and abandonment are one, crime and sacrifice still join, reverberating in hopelessly dissonant chords of meaning. "Wolf / dog / man" and "soldier / Christ," the triplet and the pair, balance in a tense mix of elements that the poem asks us to question and pleads with us to resolve. Jarrell's poem echoes the query about man's wolfish behavior that he found in Moore's "In Distrust of Merits," although his reading of her poem in "Poetry in War and Peace" was both trenchant and cruel. Wilfred Owen, writing "Dulce et Decorum Est" and scolding Jessie Pope for her patriotic invocations, assaulted her with his irony. Dealing a similar blow, Jarrell seems to punish Moore for being a sheltered bystander daring to write about war at all. Moore charges herself in these lines:

> I must
> fight till I have conquered in myself what
> causes war, but I would not believe it.
> I inwardly did nothing.
> O Iscariotlike crime!
> Beauty is everlasting
> and dust is for a time.

What seems to have angered Jarrell is this passage:

> O
> quiet form upon the dust, I cannot
> look and yet I must. If these great patient
> dyings—all these agonies
> and woundbearings and blood shed—
> can teach us how to live, these
> dyings were not wasted.

(Moore, 138)

For Moore, indirectly honoring a brother on active duty in the Navy, soldiers hold their ground in acts of "beauty." Like Owen, Jarrell takes particular offense at ascriptions of nobility in war, of "beauty," and a too-ready civilian acceptance of wasteful dying. The question of waste, of course, has been particularly burdensome. Thundering at Moore that "passive misery" is the sum "of that great activity, War," he says:

> she distrusts her own merits, but trusts, accepts almost as if she were afraid to question, those of the heroic soldiers of her poem. She does not understand that they are heroes in the sense that the chimney sweeps, the factory children in the blue books, were heroes: routine loss in the routine business of the world. She sees them . . . *fighting fighting fighting*; she does not remember that most of the people in a war never fight for even a minute—though they bear for years and die forever. (Jarrell, "Poetry in War and Peace," 129; emphasis in original)

Indignantly, with a confidence born of his army veteran status, Jarrell annuls the distinction between front line and rear line and shoos Moore away from war and back to her animal Baedekers, pointing to her morality as a weakness of her politics: "We are surprised to find Nature, in Miss Moore's poll of it, so strongly in favor of Morality; but all the results are implicit in the sampling—like the Literary Digest, she sent postcards only to the nicer animals." He ends crushingly:

> Both her economic practice and moral theory repeat wistfully, *Laissez faire, laissez aller.* Poor private-spirited citizen, wandering timidly but obliviously among the monoliths of a deadlier age, will they never let you

alone? To us, as we look skyward to the bombers, this urban Frost, the frequenter of zoos, calls *Culture and morals and Nature still have truth, seek shelter there*; and this is true; but we forget it beside the cultured, moral, and natural corpse . . . At Maidanek the mice had holes, but a million and a half people had none.

Moore's "private spirit" blinds her to the complex drives of the universal warfare state, in which victory continues to maintain bombers overhead. Under Jarrell's basilisk stare, nature, partner to culture and morals, remains pure only to those who limit their intercourse with animal ferocity to the zoo.

Unlike Owen, but closer to W. H. Auden's perspective in the thirties and forties, Jarrell faced a war in which censorship could not wholly conceal the impact of bombing and tank campaigns on nonmilitary targets. The blind, averted gaze of noncombatants of World War I, which had so outraged Wilfred Owen and Siegfried Sassoon, was, for many, made aware and redirected in World War II, painfully or knowingly or both. Besides the journals for which Jarrell wrote, like *The Nation* and *The New Republic*, he had reading access to various official materials. To Lowell he wrote in August 1945: "You should see a diagram of the latest type incendiary (it's literally impossible to put *it* out) they use, on the Japanese cities. What a nightmare! . . . I wrote this about two weeks ago, before the atom bomb and the peace. You can guess how I feel about both—especially about Nagasaki, which was bombed simply to test out the second type of bomb" (*Letters*, 129).

Finally, unlike Auden's eventual retirement from a poetry inflected by politics, Jarrell's boil of indignation rested less on spectatorial futility, perhaps a reflection of the differing, and changing, relations to world power of each poet's nation.

But Randall Jarrell's postwar reaction to Marianne Moore's "In Distrust of Merits" only heightens the spectacle of his unqualified and enduring admiration for Elizabeth Bishop. In writing "Roosters," Bishop evinced an antimilitarism like Jarrell's, yet her poem acknowledges more extensively than Jarrell's war poetry ever did the social injury that a pure worship of heroic masculinity engenders. A ripe decade into their acquaintance, Randall Jarrell wrote to Elizabeth Bishop, warmly but deferentially merging their poetic enterprises:

I like your poetry better than anybody's since the Frost-Stevens-Eliot-Moore generation, so I looked with awed wonder at some phrases feeling to me a little like some of my phrases, in your poems; I felt as if, so to speak, some of my wash-cloths were part of a Modigliani collage, or as if my cat had got into a Vuillard. (*Letters*, 420)

There's no indication that Bishop reciprocated these feelings. In 1948 she remarked to Carley Dawson that "Jarrell at his best has a remarkable dark, creepy Grimm-Wagnerian quality" (Bishop, *One Art*, 173). In the same letter, she notes that his interest in the French poet Tristan Corbiere brings out "more and more of his rather maudlin, morbid streak." To Robert Lowell and others she is often picky and grudging about Jarrell's poems, in the early years especially offering the rapid fire of disapproval with which one sibling might spray another too close to treading on his feet. To Lowell she says: "Have you ever read Capt. Slocum's books? They are wonderful—but please don't breathe a word to Randall because I'm sure he'd like them, too, and immediately write a poem about Slocum, and I really think I'd like to try one myself" (Bishop to Robert Lowell, Houghton Library, Harvard University).

The same uneasy, jokey competitiveness governed her estimate of Jarrell's war poetry, with which in 1956 she saw herself in unfortunate collision for the Pulitzer Prize, which she went on to win. In June she wrote to Lowell again, saying "I honestly feel from the bottom of my heart that it should have gone to Randall, for some of his war poems, and I don't know why it didn't" (*One Art*, 319). The "honest" note, with its self-conscious protest creeps in to Jarrell himself on 7 October of the same year. Again lamenting the disposition of the Pulitzer, she says, "I really cannot for the life of me understand why they did-n't give it to you." She adds: "Some of the war poems are surely the best ever written on the subject, honestly—and as far as our wars go, the only ones. But re-reading them I began to think that perhaps that's just why; that's why they settled on someone innocuous like me. The war is out of style now and they want to forget it?" (*One Art*, 324). Bishop attempts to be soothing here—"surely" she never considered her own poetry "innocuous"—and to patch over, at least with Jarrell personally, the ongoing discomfort of valuing high-ly his praise of her work—from the very first always given generously—which rubbed continually against her private judgment of many of his poems.

Other reservations might stem from her settled dislike of his representation of women and from her own suspicion of anything resembling a public rheto-ric or a capitulation to conventional sentimentality about war, a subject invit-ing from so many the "maudlin" and the "morbid." It is worth noting that in her consolatory message to Jarrell, she merely notes that war is now unfashionable, refusing to sort out the complexity of what exactly his poems in their singularity do with war.

Bishop ranked her own responses to war with Virginia Woolf's antiwar themes in *Three Guineas*. With Woolf Bishop shares what she characterizes as a distaste for war's "terrible *generalizing* of every emotion"(*One Art*, 113) For Bishop, one of war's corruptions is the rhetorical reduction and oversimplification of experience, and an appropriate resistance to war seems to extend even to allowing it house room in the life of the imagination—so susceptible is art to its deformations.

Unlike many European, Latino, Asian, and African women, but very like most North Americans, Elizabeth Bishop's direct experience of war was marginal. When she found herself in the middle of insurrection in Brazil in 1956, and then again more sharply in 1964, Robert Lowell first worried about her safety and then in letters could not resist egging her on to write the war that clearly his mouth was watering to digest: "I am still reeling as I try to imagine the stir of the last few days and surely the last weeks or months" (Lowell to Elizabeth Bishop, Special Collections, Vassar College). Indeed, his mind already leaps ahead to possess her conflict:

As I flew home, there was a clear sky across the Atlantic when we reached it, and I pictured the same moon, thousands of miles south, shining on the same ocean, everything strangely nearer because the sandy shore led like a road to you, and in the mind one might walk it, and be lost as I then thought in conflicting knots of thin helmeted soldiers.

Bishop's amused response deliberately undercuts these dreamings and imaginings in cool and domestic detail; "thin helmeted soldiers" are replaced by an incongruously childlike image of Brazilian marines in military regalia:

Another division of marines held the sort of park where Goulart's "palace" is, protecting him—but there are also big apartment houses in it where several of our friends live. They couldn't go out at all for a couple of days. There's a small playground in the middle, and at 2 AM the friend looked out and saw marines (they're the ones that wear the pretty uniforms and Scotch bonnets with streamers) swinging in the swings, "pumping away," he said to swing as high as possible. (Bishop to Lowell, Houghton Library, Harvard)

She sidelines combat, and derides a show of "pretty uniforms."

Similarly, her vision of "thin helmeted soldiers" in "Brazil, January 1, 1502" ends not with the men in creaking armor, but with those "maddening" women in tormenting retreat before them. Her reworking of Civil War extracts "From Trollope's Journal" again dismisses imperial glory, focussing on a shabby Washington, "The White House in a sad, unhealthy spot," and poxy cattle for the Army quartered deep in mud. She ends with a croaking surgeon, himself diseased:

"Sir, I do declare
everyone's sick! The soldiers poison the air.
      (Bishop, *The Complete Poems*, 132)

Infection and disease, the domestic realities for massed armies that up until the moment of penicillin always accounted for as many or more deaths and casualties as direct battlefield hits (Cowdrey, 3), come to the forefront in Bishop's poem, but the final line suggests the contagion of militarism itself.

But "Roosters" provided the most open feminism of Elizabeth Bishop's career. Although she swept away Marianne Moore and Moore's mother's improving suggestions with as much dispatch as an affectionate and genuine respect for these ladies would allow, she sounds quite firm about the slant of her poem. With unusual defensiveness she wrote to Moore: "I cherish my 'water-closet' and the other sordidities because I want to emphasize the essential baseness of militarism" (*One Art*, 96). Much later, when she spoke to George Starbuck in 1977 about the poem's tendency towards "feminist tract"—a tendency that "history" has shown her—she intuitively distrusts such abstractions. Admirable or not, poems centering on war stir her ambivalence.

Tardily, in a letter to Moore she acknowledges receipt of a copy of "In Distrust of Merits," saying that it

overawed me into another two months' silence. Oh Marianne, all my congratulations. It seems to me so intricately impressive, with a kind of grinding caterpillar tread that is almost too upsetting. (*One Art*, 113)

This intricate impressiveness indeed weighed heavily. The caterpillar tread of a tank shadows her reality only in metaphor, as Bishop refuses to give an inch to any open acknowledgment of martial necessity. Her reaction is full of self-conflict. Bishop's prepublication letter in January 1945 to her editor, Ferris Greenslet, taken up with other last minute details about her first book of poems, says anxiously: "The fact that none of these poems deal directly with the war, at a time when so much war poetry is being published, will, I am afraid, leave me open to reproach" (*One Art*, 125).

In 1945, not to write about war appeared unpatriotic or, worse, obtuse, yet for any woman not in nurse's or war-worker's shoes, and not being bombed or interned or on the run as a refugee in the dominant narrative of the time, the literary options are dubious: from a woman sensitive to her position as beyond the reach of combat, a wary response was requisite. An American woman could play a latter-day Jessie Pope and cheer on the soldier laddies aggressively from her sheltered corner, cry for an absent lover, or, employed, single and unencumbered, bank the swollen checks drawn from a booming war economy. In any case, as war spread more and more deeply into a working and thinking life, it could have brought Bishop a deeply troubling sense of her own irrelevance at the site of others' pain, grief, and confusion. But while the proliferating war struck her as the responsibility of masculine others, female anger and frustration at being unable to change the river in its bed and send it elsewhere brought her to stinging protest of the whole gendered system.

In "Roosters," written in 1940 in response to Axis bombing, war is inextinguishably the territory of the male, and in this poem, war for Bishop becomes the always compromised subject of the heroic, in which strutting cocks

brace their cruel feet and glare

with stupid eyes
while from their beaks there rise
the uncontrolled, traditional cries.
   (Bishop, *Complete Poems*, 35)

In "Roosters," whose "sordidities" were so stoutly defended by Bishop, tradition, roused in "the gun-metal dark," becomes a fouled (certainly fowled) presence rising from "the water-closet door, / from the dropping-plastered henhouse floor," and the allegorized male ego thrusts "Deep from protruding chests / in green-gold medals dressed, / planned to command and terrorize the rest." Each "'Very combative'" rooster is "an active / displacement in perspective"; one rooster flies "with raging heroism defying / even the sensation of dying." Yet another "lies in dung / with his dead wives" (Bishop, *Complete Poems*, 37). In this poem, war is a fundamentally dirty enterprise, and the hero takes the women dumb enough to constitute a compliant harem along with him. "Virile presence" is a comic grotesque, and any civilians submissive to its appeal go down in terror and ignominy with it. Significantly for feminists claiming a special female innoculation from the vice of war, when men can be brutal, women can be weakly complicit.

By concentrating on civilians, Bishop shares a subject with both early and late Jarrell. But while she grapples allegorically with the gender economy that produces rooster fighters and hen supporters and causes suffering to both, her poems do not attempt the comprehensive scope with which Jarrell is both so partially and strikingly successful. Jarrell's war poems gather breadth of reference from his removed status as a noncombatant, in weaker poems translating this into clunky description and exhortation. Both Bishop and Jarrell sit out the war in American safety. But dressed in soldier's khaki, Jarrell did identify the potential for damage within the boyish shallowness tainting martial ideology, while Bishop, unable to change the deeper dress of her gender, from the sidelines still perfected a parallel strike against the drape of masculinity itself.

From Jarrell's first to almost his last book, his opinions about war and society nonetheless match Bishop's antimilitarist assessments in many particulars. Even in the war poems most addicted to the grandiose or Bishop's dreaded *"generalizing,"* Jarrell's work takes surprising turns. The greatest temptation, to surrender to the blind patriotism that inflates friend and degrades enemy, that moves to flat binarism and cartoon or posterboard motivation, never compromised his choices. By 1940, Jarrell had found his stride, and his chameleon sensitivity—however incomplete—was born, with which he slipped inside the skin of refugee children, the wife of a dead pilot, the mother of a returning airman, and other assorted wartime identities of all genders, ages and geographic stages of wartime posting.

"A fresh visionary tension"

That Randall Jarrell, as man and soldier, had a soldier's ticket of admission as an authentic war witness did not prevent various critics from dismissing his war poetry on the grounds of either sentimentality or bad style. While poets and critics like R. W. Flint and Karl Shapiro were strong in their praises, others like James Dickey and Donald Hall were doubting or hostile (See Dickey, "Randall Jarrell"; Hall had an essay in the same volume).

It seems to me that R. W. Flint, during World War II a gunner on a carrier himself, might have the last word for this generation's war poet: "There was no other poet, none who came within shouting distance of Jarrell." Flint generously rejects his own expectations for a more familiar kind of war poetry and goes on to say:

> That he had been, like Whitman, very lucky in his circumstances, neither too far in the fighting nor too far out, a true airman in every figurative sense, and even better prepared by genius and training to render the particulars of war by diffraction from a radically civilized and simple philosophy. . . . all this was obscured from some of us who had been closer to the action and wore a veteran's foolish pride not quite lightly enough, forgetting that the civilian Whitman and Melville had been the Civil War poets, resisting a repetition of the mud-soaked griefs of Wilfred Owen and Isaac Rosenberg in World War I, looking perhaps for poetry more in the jaunty style of Howard Nemerov in America or Keith Douglas in England; something abrupt and hard-bitten, steeped in romantic disillusion and military slang; brief, sweeping, dismissive ironies, like the crushing out of a last cigarette before take-off. (Flint, 77–78)

Ultimately, Flint looks at Jarrell's work as an advance in the subject matter and thinking of the war lyric. In his useful writing on these poems, Flint considers what Jarrell did in his "long patience of outfacing a worn-out myth of heroism"; in Flint's word, Jarrell enlarges both subject and point of view in war writing:

> He moves beyond the avuncular-idyllic manner of Whitman's *Drum Taps*, beyond the lovable Kipling fantasy of marching, campfires, and taverns, beyond even the comradeliness of Owen, to a place that mixes pity and philosophy, exact knowledge of war and sympathy for its victims, on a grand scale; a fresh visionary tension. (Flint, 83)

Randall Jarrell grasped the implications of late-twentieth-century industrial war making, but in the best of his work he also tucked his conclusions inside a language as homey and direct as a couch pillow. The poems construct an encircling map of twentieth-century consciousness in wildly ambitious categories moving from "The Graves in the Forest" to "Bombers" to "Carriers" to "Prisoners" to "Camps and Fields" to "Children and Civilians," and so on. In perhaps the least persuasive of Jarrell's rhetorics, many of the poems, especially the midwar poems like "A Pilot from the Carrier," try to fly. In the manner of the traditional elegiac and transformational heroic, they want to soar, leaving material death behind or beyond in some ether of the poet's coruscating and embalming language.

But poems like "Losses" and "The Death of the Ball Turret Gunner," acknowledging a truth about the youth and expendability of airman and soldiers by a ruthless state, also link the resemblance of pilots and gunners to the postwar existence of the "aging machine part," Jarrell's name for the anonymous speaker of "The Woman at the Washington Zoo." The aureate diction of some of his poems creates a dignity for wartime sacrifice in keen opposition to what Bishop evaluates as war's impact, a dignity suspiciously close to what Jarrell condemned in Marianne Moore's poem. Jarrell's poems encompass lager and prison camp and the whole horrifying, global reach of burning city, fortified desert, and mined atoll. One man, he could not load all that pain and terror onto his poetry and manage unwavering insight and investment in reality, too. Is it that lyric particulars must break under epic necessity, pining for a genre of greater mass? Or is it the larger need to acknowledge that even the ambition to represent war's range gives play to suffering that should stay unspeakable and unaffirmable in depiction? At the least, the reverse side of Jarrell's coin provides a tough and bitter antidote to Moore's parochialism: the evil that created World War II recurs in the fret of postwar life.

No judgment of Jarrell's war poetry is complete that does not account for his difficult mix of irony and elegy or the magnitude of his vision, one having the further intelligence to settle war itself within the disquieting borders of the modern peace. When Jarrell scolds Moore he says: "she should have distrusted the peace of which our war is only the extrapolation. It is the peace of which we were guilty." War/peace, remembrance/forgetting, and most potently, innocence/guilt—these are only some of the binaries which Jarrell's brilliance exploded in a war poetry not quite like any other.

6

American Poets of the Vietnam War

with an M-16
I broke their little stick bodies in that ditch. . . .
Cry for us all, for learning our lessons well.
Sentence me where you will; I've been to hell.
—Lowell Jaeger, "The Trial"

"Cry for us all, for learning our lessons well"

In Hemingway's *A Farewell to Arms*, when Frederick Henry finds himself "embarrassed by the words sacred, glorious, and sacrifice and the expression in vain" (185) in the mouths of contemporary orators, he is poised at the outbreak of rebellion to the militarism that has swallowed nine million lives in World War 1. At that moment, the modern war lyric, smashed by industrial war making, lost the old ways of commemorating and enduring sacrifice and was reborn into another kind of bearing witness and another set of aesthetic demands.

Besides the changes in warfare itself, immense change in the style and genre of poetry came about because of shifts in who spoke and to what audience. In England, as mass recruiting transformed the professional army, a literate soldiery began to write its own elegies, its own reflections on war. No one should underestimate the impact of the convergence of mass education with mass conscription or the paradigm shift that occurred when, to paraphrase Paul Fussell, the poetry-writing and the war-fighting classes became one and the same (*Thank God*, 237).

As early as 1915, the language of war poetry switched its loyalty from the chivalric code, from what Edmund Blunden once called "the gonfalon and aureole world to that of the platoon and the forlorn hope" (Blunden, *War Poets*, 27). Yet war poetry was still poised between the old and durable need to honor the dead and acknowledge with both regret and proper gratitude the dire nature of their civic contribution, and the second and more unsettling need to voice the sometimes dishonored and sometimes dishonoring terms of that sacrifice. Pressed by these needs, new forms, new language, new cadences must still meet the old styles and genre preoccupations and also face the battering need to justify the increasingly hurtful collisions that occur between people and modern weaponry. By the second half of the last century, war poetry came to embody an antiwar ideology, and judgments about politics and history have thoroughly rearranged the conventions of the war poem. Who could still write the equivalent of "my valiant sword, my noble steed, my trusty companions" in the face of napalm, helicopter gunships, and service rotation? And yet even in the poetry of the Vietnam War these fossil tropes still appear.

Winning Hearts and Minds

Any reader can follow the curve of what changes and what stays the same in the four anthologies of poetry from the Vietnam War dating from 1972 to 1998. In 1972 came *Winning Hearts and Minds: War Poems By Vietnam Veterans*, edited by Larry Rottmann, Jan Barry, and Basil Paquet. W. D. Ehrhart copyrighted his anthology, *Carrying the Darkness: The Poetry of the Vietnam War*, in 1985; in 1991, the first anthology to solicit poems from the women of that war was published, *Visions of War, Dreams of Peace*, edited by Lynda Van Devanter and Joan Furey. Phillip Mahony published the most recent anthology, *From Both Sides Now: The Poetry of the Vietnam War and its Aftermath*, in 1998. Mahony's title, in fact all the titles, signal the stages of concern.

In the first, *Winning Hearts and Minds: War Poems by Vietnam Veterans*, the title's ironic reference to the American propaganda war, nudged along by the subtitle, gives us fair warning of editorial intentions. One of the anthology's editors, Jan Barry, was the founding member of Vietnam Veterans Against the War, and both Jan Barry and Larry Rottmann were activists in that movement. The contents of the anthology originated in the climate that produced the Winter Soldier Investigation, the 1971 forum for political protest in which Rottmann and Barry testified. A quick flip to the index of *Winning Hearts and Minds* yields not only each poet's name, but his hometown and state, as well as military rank and specialty—and in every case, a list of the medals, badges, and ribbons earned.[1]

Thrown into the mix for seasoning, there is a corporal from the People's Army of Vietnam, a woman who served with the American Friends Service Committee in Danang, and the high school student who ends these selections, writing: "I am a Veteran of Vietnam." Not quite in the style of World War I, she represents Jane Q. Public, frozen in front of her TV set, the tiny scenes of metal and flesh racing and coming apart a few yards from her gaping jaw. A voyeur of war, she, like everyone else in the volume, adds a contribution heavy with self-accusation, its authenticity unmarred by retouched spelling:

I've seen people
Tortured.
Bombed.
Burned.
Destroyed.
Beyond hope of recovery
While I
sit contently
watching . . .
and let it
go on
           (Rottmann, Barry, and Paquet, *Winning*, 113)

Unlike the people at home in World War I, she cannot claim ignorance of frontline horrors, yet the implied guilt immersing her resembles the complicity and assent for war death, that shadowed the earlier generation of noncombatant patriots so ardently accused by Wilfred Owen and Siegfried Sassoon in England. In this later American war, both confessional soldiers and morally passive civilians feel continuing responsibility for what happens. While displaying considerably more skill, however, few American civilian poets in the sixties and seventies went much beyond the content given above; so far, it is the soldier-poets, in their perspective as both criminal and perpetrator in what they felt to be the long crime scene of the war, who wound up with the most to say.

When Larry Rottmann, Basil T. Paquet, and Jan Barry introduced their veteran-poets in 1972 in *Winning Hearts and Minds*, they carefully marked the difference between the poems they chose and earlier antiwar efforts. The editors wrote:

Previous war poets have traditionally placed the blame directly on others. What distinguishes the voices in this volume is their progression toward an active identification of themselves as agents of pain and war—as "agent-victims" of their own atrocities. This recognition came quickly to some and haltingly to others, but it always came with pain and the conviction that there is no return to innocence. (Rottmann, Barry, and Paquet, *Winning*, v)

In 1971, in his closing statement for the two days of testimony that was organized by the Vietnam Veterans Against the War in Detroit, Michigan, and subsequently published as *The Winter Soldier Investigation: An Inquiry into American War Crimes*, Lieutenant, and later editor, Larry Rottmann said:

> There is a question in many people's minds here. They say, "Well, why do you talk now? Why do you come here and tell us these things that happened maybe two, three, maybe four, five years ago? What is your motivation behind it? You want to get on the boob tube? You're on some kind of ego trip?" You know, why are you here? I'm here, speaking personally, because I can't *not* be here. I'm here because, like, I have nightmares about things that happened to me and my friends. I'm here because my conscience will not let me forget what I want to forget. (Vietnam Veterans, 163–64)

The raw intensity and dangers of this first-person witness mark all of the poems in this first anthology.

The editors' intention is to share the rankling conclusions of their war and, in counterwitness, to correct official and prevailing disinformation. In a step only lightly linked to the politicized poets of the 1930s and 1940s, they intend the thrust of their collection to come from what the poems say, who says it, and with what urgent burden of experience. The poems have been sifted from a much larger collection of writing, but in this initial anthology, the question of literary merit does not come up, and we can forget about ties to "tradition"—the word itself bearing the smell of a suavely conservative politics alien to the collectors and collected alike. Ultimately, their book aims at history rather than literature, at ethics rather than aesthetics.

In these American poems, the operating distance between civilian and soldier shortens severely, and among the soldiers allowed to report, other boundaries, other fixities of literary production dissolve. Vietnam war poets bring all the traits of W. H. Auden's Democratic Principle forward—a broad scouring of all possible topics of war along with a complete disregard for traditional proprieties of subject and a fondness for the didactic and journalistic. But above all, the customary hierarchies collapse, as distinctions of class and rank loosen; there are many fewer officers among those writing—even as ethnic awareness grows and grows, its functions more acutely at issue than in any other war poetry.

World War I Poets like Wilfred Owen and Siegfried Sassoon generally lay the burden of guilt for war at the feet of their leaders and their homefront supporters, and not at their own. In poems like the familiar "Dulce et Decorum Est" and in Owen's "Parable of the Old Man and The Young," soldiers are victims of the grotesque and foolish commands of their elders and superiors, and if wrath attaches, it attaches to this older generation. Siegfried Sassoon's "On Passing the New Menin Gate" stands for the feelings of his age group when he decries the civilian impulse to commit monuments glorifying the massacre of troops:

> Here was the world's worst wound. And here with pride
> "Their name liveth for ever," the Gateway claims.
> Was ever an immolation so belied
> As these intolerably nameless names?
> Well might the Dead who struggled in the slime
> Rise and deride this sepulchre of crime.
>
> (Sassoon, *The War Poems*, 153)

There is little doubt in this elegy as to who has committed the crime, which is certainly not the blameless victims. Yet Edmund Blunden, one of the quietest of that war's voices, in one poem juxtaposed a wartime concert party with "men in the tunnels," unidentified men of either army, brutally kicking other men to death. In Blunden's "The Concert Party," and even in Owen's "Strange Meeting," there are unmistakable glimpses of soldiers at their trade of killing, and not just being killed.

The poets of World War II also acknowledged this trade; self-doubt and retrospective guilt were not unknown to them. Randall Jarrell kept a Walt Whitman–like tenderness for the postadolescents in uniform beside him but never flinched, in poems like "Losses" and "Eighth Air Force," at naming the paradox of murderous innocence. And for Keith Douglas, who saw soldiers immolated in tank battles from El Alamein to Zem Zem, the perspective from which he writes is most conspicuously not how to die but "How to Kill"; in this poem, discussed at length earlier, the protagonist sees his target through "my dial of glass," as he notes "How easy it is to make a ghost."

The candid acceptance of complicity in death at the heart of war in Douglas's poem seems at no terrific distance from W. D. Ehrhart's poem "Hunting," written more than a quarter of a century later about Vietnam. Ehrhart's forceful and blunt simplicity of language, however, lacks the formal torque of Douglas's onionskin rhyme and the elegance of his metaphor. Ehrhart writes:

Sighting down the long black barrel,
I wait till front and rear sights
form a perfect line on his body,
then slowly squeeze the trigger.

The thought occurs
that I have never hunted anything in my whole life
except other men.

(Rottmann, Barry, and Paquet, Winning, 33)

The similarity of these two poems written by men in their early twenties may simply be the unsayable dread at the loss of innocence. The tone of amazed outrage, however, that fuses and sustains the larger blaze of anger marking all of these later poems, seems specifically American. Keith Douglas's poetry, born of the uneasy and anxious conscience of those following the Auden generation, carries a greater fatalism, a more subdued acceptance of war itself.

Amending the editorial absolutism of Rottmann, Paquet, and Barry, we might assert that the real difference between the soldier-poets of World Wars I and II and those of the Vietnam War is the acknowledgment of an evolution in the line of soldier duty from killing each other to indiscriminate killing of combatants and noncombatants alike in the name of defense of country. Both Douglas and Ehrhart hunt men, but before Ehrhart completes his tour of duty, darker admissions, darker necessities, than the hunting of men will rule him and his fellows. He writes in his memoir, *Busted*:

> When I first arrived in Vietnam, I had expected to be greeted by thankful peasants lining the roads, waving and cheering like the newsreels I'd seen as a kid of American GIs liberating French villages from the Nazis. The peace-loving people of South Vietnam were being invaded by cruel communists from the north. I was going to defend them. . . . What I found in Vietnam bore no resemblance to what I had been led to expect by Lyndon Johnson and *Time* Magazine and my high school history teachers. The peasants of Vietnam had greeted me with an opaque silence that looked for all the world like indifference or hostility. And the cruel communists were indistinguishable from the people I thought I had been sent to Vietnam to defend. And the premier of South Vietnam was a French-trained pilot who wore tailored purple flight suits and admired Adolph Hitler.
> (Ehrhart, *Busted*, 13)

The politics or the war goals of the Vietnam War rarely aided the moral functioning of its participants a did the broadly popular politics and goals of World War II. As the Vietnam War went on and on, the general threat that the Vietnamese represented got foggier and foggier: from what were Americans being saved; against what were all Americans being defended? The long arm of Victor Charlie never reached across the oceans to dislodge a stone or break a pane of glass from an American building. Broken heads and property damage only occurred on American ground in skirmishes between Americans over American politics, in police riots and in the proxy rage of dissidents and war veterans objecting to the bloody manipulation of their patriotism by their own government.

By the postwar nineties and on, of course, Americans and Vietnamese would eventually move to become partners in trade, in the bewildering switches of alliance characterizing the moves of international capital. Paving the way for this rapprochement, the migrating South Vietnamese have created "Little Saigon," a hub for the approximately 135,000 ethnic Vietnamese who live in Orange County, California. This enclave blooms forty-five miles south of Los Angeles, and in 2002 Seth Mydans can write of it:

There are miles of pastel mini-malls where all the shops have Vietnamese names. The sales pitches on billboards are in Vietnamese. Quavering Asian melodies float from storefronts. A woman power-walks through a park wearing the conical straw hat of a rice farmer.

Everything looks clean, new and well-to-do, from the polished cars that jam the parking lots to the grocery stores with exotic foods wrapped in plastic.

It is like an episode of "The Twilight Zone," a slice of alternative reality: this is what Saigon might have looked like if America had won the war in 1975. . . .

There is nothing like it in Vietnam, in the struggling communist society produced by the people who won the war, where private enterprise is still a new toy to play with and where there is still no such thing as a parking lot.

Meanwhile, in the 1960s and 1970s, the Vietnamese struggle for national liberation, while brutally conducted on both sides, never persuasively brushed U.S. soldiers with the chill of Cold War menace or made them feel that the Vietnamese were about to spearhead attacks across continents. Nor did the doctored threat that produced the Tonkin Gulf resolution and only de facto declaration of war ever resemble in any way the true geopolitical gut reach of Japanese bombs in Pearl Harbor.

Even as the fundamental mistake of conceiving an ultimate unity of purpose between China, Russia, and Vietnam led us to misread the Vietnamese-American conflict, Americans eventually had to assess correctly the collision between Cold War territorial imperatives and the facts of Third World guerrilla nationalism. The unpleasant surprise for so many political innocents who put on uniforms was the realization that Americans, inheritors of a nationalist and anticolonial revolution, were in this war funding and training the regressive forces that had supported a corrupt French colonialism. For David Connolly, "we became the hated Black and Tan, / and we shamed our ancestry" ("To the Irish Americans Who Fought the Last War," Connolly, 39). Queerly enough, at the point where America had achieved superpower status and the English were in political decline, American war poets advanced the genre of war poetry by being forced through circumstance to relate, with honesty and literary inventiveness, not a full praise of the armed righteousness of American might, but our blundering inability to wage war either creditably or effectively.

Tennyson, Hardy, Kipling—even Rupert Brooke—had all had their chance at the confident sonorities of the imperial bard, but in the American tradition of the barbaric yawp, only Whitman, confined to the nineteenth century, would come close to any similar matching of war and majesty. Yet even in the rubble of empire, English World War II poets like Alun Lewis, planted within a war that most found just, could use the global nature of their conflict to meditate with a dignified abstraction on the clash of cultures. A disinterested observer, trained in history, in 1944 Lewis could write about wartime India that

> Across scorched hills and trampled crops
> The soldiers straggle by,
> History staggers in their wake.
> The peasants watch them die.
>   (A. Lewis, 120)

For Lewis, war is still an amphitheater of death in which soldiers die, *not* peasants, even though peasant crops are trampled, and probably peasant homes are burning, too, in those scorched hills, with the odd farm animal thrown in. But the similarity of what peasants and soldiers suffer has not quite registered; in

Lewis's poem, the main show is still military. Most of the egalitarian spin of his liberal politics, achieved in the short span of his life, looks to the class warfare within his own army.

Lewis was aware of the bad bits in British imperialism. In his journals, he could write about South Africa and about the obvious injustices of the racial problem, saying of the English, "To equip and humiliate people seems to be our general policy" (A. Lewis, 42). But he still had faith in civilizing missions. Ian Hamilton describes Lewis's politics as suffused with "dazed, unhappy contradiction"; in his analysis,

> The personal life is both clutched at, and rejected, democracy is both the enemy of art and its single goal, the war can both corrupt and ennoble; and beneath this 'series of violent reactions' there is the thought of 'Death, the ultimate response that he, despite himself, desired.' (in A. Lewis, 26)

A recipient of neither an Oxbridge education nor of an upper-middle-class childhood, Alun Lewis does not shake free of the elitist separation of the observer class from the observed that the act of making "art" confers, creating Hamilton's "dazed, unhappy contradiction" between art as the enemy of democracy as well as its single goal. There is also, in spite of his acknowledgement of "the racial problem," an uncomfortable but persistent sense of racial distance. In "Port of Call: Brazil" (1942), Lewis wrote:

We, who thought the negroes were debased

This morning when they scrambled on the quay
For what we threw, and from their dugout boats
Haggled cigars and melons raucously
Lifting their bleating faces like old goats.

But now the white-faced tourist must translate
His old unsated longing to adventure
Beyond the European's measured hate
Into the dangerous oceans of past and future.
    (A. Lewis, 104)

In "To Rilke," Alun Lewis still confidently writes that in spite of ill-assorted risk, adventure ideology could take him and his fellow European soldiers and bureaucrats to a place of renewal: "I knew that unknown lands / Were near and real, like an act of birth" (A. Lewis, 105).

For American poets of the Vietnam War, the possible future and the immersing present were squalid and dangerous. Civilians were neither bystanders nor enablers, and any interest in peasants could not bypass the bitterness of inevitable and immediate ironic contrast between the official U.S. rhetoric of helping peasants, and the reality of destroying them. The soldiers put this reality into the language nearest and most natural to them. Michael Casey laconically acknowledges that reality in "A Bummer," where a rice farmer hits an American military vehicle with his rake for attempting to cross his paddy; in consequence, this peasant is taunted by watching a year's food supply methodically destroyed in front of him:

> So the tracks went sideways
> side by side
> Through the guy's fields
> Instead of single file
> Hard On, Proud Mary
> Bummer, Wallace, Rosemary's Baby
> The Rutgers Road Runner
> And
> Go Get Em—Done Got Em
> Went side by side
> Through the fields
>> If you have a farm in Vietnam
> And a house in hell
> Sell the farm
> And go home
>> (Rottmann, Barry, and Paquet, *Winning*, 7)

Casey's version of hell is in line with M.Sgt. Don Duncan's closing statement in *The Winter Soldier Investigation*; soldiers were going berserk with cruelty in a country where they were told to risk their lives for policies that, over and over again, proved hardly rational. In Duncan's instance: "We built forts in Vietnam to protect villages, or so we told the Vietnamese. And at the first shot fired at Tet in 1968 we destroyed the villages to protect the fort" (Vietnam Veterans, 166).

If in a closed circuit of destruction the material policies made no sense, the only accounting system remaining was that of the human body itself; in a country with very little left to destroy, the infamy of the daily body count dominated. For M.Sgt. Duncan:

We have brought wondrous tons of ordinance—hundreds of thousands of men—Dr. Strangelove weaponry. We have used an air force against a country that has none. We have used a navy against a country that has none. And it still wasn't enough, and still the war goes on, and still the Vietnamese fight. It has been called a war of attrition. A war of attrition in an industrial society means, in fact, destroying the means of waging war—the factories, communication lines, the roadways, bridges, the iron factories, and so on. In a non-industrial society—in an agrarian society such as Vietnam—when you talk of a war of attrition, you're only talking of one thing. You're talking about destroying the means to resist—that is, killing people.

Our country has set out very systematically to kill whatever number of people are necessary in Vietnam to stop them from resisting whatever it is we are trying to impose on that country. This, I think is policy. (Vietnam Veterans, 167)

This amounted to inadmissible terror and devastation as the chief military tactic; worse yet, this technological instrument of uncertain precision was applied to friend and enemy alike. W. D. Ehrhart's "Guerilla War" (1975) pinpoints this with bleak simplicity:

They all talk
the same language,
(and you couldn't understand them
even if they didn't)

They tape grenades
inside their clothes,
and carry satchel charges
in their market baskets.

Even their women fight;
and young boys,
and girls.

It's practically impossible
to tell civilians
from the Vietcong;

After a while,
you quit trying.
                    (Ehrhart, *Carrying*, 93)

Poems witnessing, if not confessing to performing, acts of random cruelty exist as a subgenre of American Vietnam War poetry. Basil Paquet's
"Mourning The Death, By Hemorrhage, Of a Child from Honai" (9172)
marks the place where even soldiers of good will had to face the results of the
tactical erasure of the line between combatant and noncombatant. Here, Paquet cannot permit himself the elegiac heights of Dylan Thomas's World
War II style of mourning civilian casualties, in which a grandiose rhetoric of
indomitability led Thomas to "A Refusal to Mourn the death, by Fire, of a
Child in London":

Never . . .

. . . .
Shall I let pray the shadow of a sound
Or sow my salt seed
In the least valley of sackcloth to mourn

The majesty and burning of the child's death.
I shall not murder
The mankind of her going with a grave truth
Nor blaspheme down the stations of the breath
With any further
Elegy of innocence and youth.

His heart nonetheless permanently blasted, and his conscience quite free of
blame for the violation of any child, Thomas concludes: "After the first death
there is no other" (Thomas, 112).

More clumsily and without the enlarging biblical resonance, but with a
feeling whose numbed but furious immediacy registers wholly, Paquet says
instead:

I could only wonder what ideology
The child carried in her left arm—necessity
Must have dictated an M-16 round
Should cut it off, and her gaining the role of martyrology.

Her dying in my arms, this daughter
Weaned on war, was for the greater
Glory of all concerned.
There was no time to mourn your slaughter
Small, denuded, one-armed thing, I too was violator,
And after the first death, the many must go unmourned.

(Rottmann, Barry, and Paquet, *Winning*, 77)

In this war, a bitter and helpless shame takes over the rhetoric of mourning, as Paquet, a medic who must implicate himself in the wounding, is left to work an impossible healing.

Angry, savage, satiric, and openly polemical in tone, the poems of *Winning Hearts and Minds* are caught up in resistance to the Vietnam War. On the ground, these soldiers knew at firsthand the most devastating reasons for halting the war, as their minds and bodies lived its contradictions. Their anthology offered to continue the war over the terrain of consciousness; they knew and trusted the importance of their witness. For them, despair and impotence were luxuries; in the curious bulletin of the short poem, they held the weapon of the insurgent word, and through it, released their need to speak.

In explaining the genesis of soldier atrocities in the Vietnam War, Sergeant Jamie Henry said:

You are trained "gook, gook, gook," and once the military has got the idea implanted in your mind that these people are not humans, they are subhumans, it makes it a little bit easier to kill 'em. One barrier is removed, and this is intentional, because obviously, the purpose of the military is to kill people. . . . the second reason for atrocities that occur is because it doesn't take very long for an infantryman in the field to realize that he is fighting for nobody's freedom. You can ask any of the men here. They may have thought they were fighting to protect their mother when they got there, but they sure didn't believe that for very long. And this isn't just the grunt. It's the lieutenants, it's the officers in the field. Our captain believed it.

It takes only a few months to be subjugated to the circumstances of Vietnam when you come to the realization that you are not fighting for Ky's freedom; you are not fighting for Thieu's freedom; you are not fighting for your mother's freedom or anybody's freedom. You're just getting your asses shot up and all you want to do is go home. (Vietnam Veterans, 45)

In part answer to the bewildering flood of atrocities from people who did not seem to be moral degenerates in their other lives, Cpl. William Hatton could only say: "You know, if Vietnam is not violently painful then it's such a crashing bore that you can't stand it" (Vietnam Veterans, 72). Beyond the questions of sheer survival, these were not often soldiers who, their peacetime lives swiped from them, were able to take an interest in their surroundings. A violent and dangerous boredom, however, seems to belong to military life: the boredom seems to amplify, as dedication to soldiering is hobbled, in states that depend on universal conscription rather than on standing, professional forces, which might have, or could have, a better developed drill of restraint in killing. Awash in the sense of rupture, within the aching suspension from ordinary life that springs from an existence bound by systematic coercion, adolescent and postadolescent servicemen evince the boredom that dulls perception and response, from World War II onwards. On naval duty in World War II, Roy Fuller wrote in "What Is Terrible":

> I
> Must first be moved across two oceans, then
> Bored, systematically and sickeningly,
> In a place where war is news. And constantly
>
> I must be threatened with what is certainly worse:
> Peril and death, but no less boring.
>   (Fuller, 79)

His boredom looks like the universal mischief-breeding hazard of young men bound into dangerous and coercive circumstance.

In *Winning Hearts and Minds*, Rottmann, Barry, and Paquet's acknowledgment of the poetry's ties to the teller's own experience of war is an homage to the belief that war itself, for men, as childbirth for women, constitutes an experience only to be understood by those who have undergone it—like the messenger to Job, "I only am escaped alone to tell thee" (Job 1:17 AV). The primary urgency is that of witness, as if the unbelief, the extraordinary inhumanity of what is reported needs verification to a world at large, unable either to measure or comprehend its magnitude or extremity. At the outermost reaches of experience, in those painful and deadly places where sensation fails to meet an adequate match in language, mystery supervenes: seized by those vibrating, supplicating arcs of intensity, often no better impulse exists than to make a poem, a story, a play, encasing speechlessness and framing it. When that work of art emerges, with its source bindingly imprinted, some other element infuses its hearing whose force will not be suppressed.

Even decades later, when the drive to witness and to bespeak one's own complicity has passed beyond the drive to stop the war, a retrospective and pervasive anguish still controls the poetry. In "Infantry Assault," published by Doug Anderson in 1994, the apocalyptic burn of Vietnam still flames in the bones:

> the way they dragged that guy out of the stream,
> cut him to pieces, the stream running red
> with all the bodies in it, and the way the captain
> didn't try to stop them, his silence saying *No Prisoners* and
>
> the way when all the Cong were dead, lined up in rows,
> thirty-nine in all, our boys went to work on all the pigs
> and chickens in the village until
> there was no place that was not red, and
>
> finally, how the thatch was lit, the village burned,
> and afterwards we were quiet riding back
> on the tracks, watching the ancestral serpent rise
> over the village in black coils, and
> how our bones knew what we'd done.
>> (Anderson, 4)

The quiet of that self-implicating witness travels light years away from the soldier-poet of World War II. The dropped innocence that Rottmann, Paquet, and Barry name is of another kind from what Louis Simpson gives us in a soldier strung out with fatigue after the Battle of the Bulge in "The Battle" (1955):

> At dawn the first shell landed with a crack.
> Then shells and bullets swept the icy woods.

This lasted many days. The snow was black.
The corpses stiffened in their scarlet hoods.

Most clearly of that battle I remember
The tiredness in eyes, how hands looked thin
Around a cigarette, and the bright ember
Would pulse with all the life there was within.
        (Simpson, 53)

The cigarette is not a joint, and the soldier is traumatized, not traumatized and stoned. The numbness of this soldier's shock has only a cousinly relation to the scorch of memory that Anderson's soldiers feel after combat, and as the Vietnam veteran might point out, in the earlier poem, soldiers are the only corpses in view.

But there is nothing in Vietnam War poetry quite like the cool and precise music of Simpson's "Memories of a Lost War" (1955):

Hot lightnings stitch the blind eye of the moon,
The thunder's blunt.
We sleep. Our dreams pass in a faint platoon
Toward the front.

Sleep well, for you are young. Each tree and bush
Drips with sweet dew,
And earlier than morning June's cool hush
Will waken you.

The riflemen will wake and hold their breath.
Though they may bleed
They will be proud awhile of something
Death still seems to need.
        (Simpson, 52)

Very little of that conscious pride stiffens any Vietnam War poetry. And with perhaps a half-dozen exceptions, the polished control of rhyme, meter, and diction in these stanzas is beyond either the talent or the interest of most of the poets publishing about the Vietnam War. Following W. H. Auden's Aristocratic Principle, Simpson's war poem is well defended against "barbaric vagueness," and its bloody detail is tailored closely to fit within what the classic tropes of war will allow. Yet while it is necessary to observe that Simpson retrieved his memories of World War II only after a period in a mental hospital after the war, it is also true that his poem roots itself in a stoic acceptance of the necessity of that war, a faith not granted the later American soldier-poets. Perhaps one could say that the unfettered expressivity of the Vietnam War poet had to boil and break past tradition in order to arrive at all.

At an even greater distance from self-recrimination, when Alun Lewis dispassionately observes collateral war damage and Keith Douglas inserts commentary on the war greed and exploitative politics of Cairo civilians or Roy Fuller in full equanimity writes loving details of the zebras and gazelles that he watches from a rear posting in the green hills of Africa, they are all experiencing a moral comfort in relation to their theater of war quite different from what propelled the witness in Vietnam.

The sense of literary belatedness that weighed down the English poet in World War II hardly touched the American poets of the Vietnam War; the ennobling tragic gloss of a Wilfred Owen or a Siegfried Sassoon was too culturally and historically remote to be seductive. As a younger generation, they were also free of the stylistic dominance that through the 1950s had left both English and American poets lashed to the same traditions, the same respect for rhyme and meter, which were poised and in enervating place again after the High Modernist attack on those conventions in the earlier part of the century. But in Vietnam, the self-accusative turn that moved American poets in directions quite different from that of the miseries chronicled by World War I poets, nevertheless helped them to produce a literature of comparable intensity and urgency. In the hammering trap of their war, and in their refusal of Wilfred Owen's "pity"—for themselves, especially—they were not hindered by a sense of the possible staleness of what they had to say against war itself. If the opening poems of this American phase are rougher and cruder than those of other generations of English speakers, they are committed to a deeper delving into the ethics of war, and their gain is in the freshness and wide impact of a poetry far more egalitarian in scope.

Finally, these poems restore narrative as a lyric force. In their late-twentieth-century positioning, down go the walls of genre, and poets are free to plunder the richness of the novelist's range of detail. We see them draw, from a realism that stretched from Émile Zola to Tim O'Brien, the body and all the soldier body's acts: its sweats, its nightmares, as the body goes from the harrying of peasants to the shit-burning details of latrines and all the exigencies of its sexual needs; in fact, these poems cover transport from wheel to nerve ending.

While the war poets of Vietnam were as tied to vers libre as poets of the 1950s were lashed to rhyme and meter, in their wildly different aesthetic practice and in their need to speak of a world from whose actions the homefront witness was decisively barred, the poets of Vietnam do eventually rival the poets of World War I in their emotional impact. Little soars in their poetry; only occasionally can one dwell on a complex music or a recognizable and familiar technical brilliance. Yet in its occasional tenderness, in its knifing directness, and within the explosive coil of the best of its compressed forms, this is a poetry that need not be shrugged aside as merely political expressivity, although this is surely and powerfully there. The politics of Vietnam War poets, by way of their confident focus on the self, and the acts and feelings of the self in war's maelstrom, eventually bring their poems away from narcissism and somberly toward the self's responsibilities to others.

In their greater articulation of soldier cruelties, voluntary and involuntary, the Vietnam veterans explore more solidly than any other historical grouping of poets how a retreat to the use of force subverts any cause advanced by its means. George Gascoigne points at the general problem in the sixteenth century, when he writes of his experience in the lowland wars:

Search all thy bookes, and thou shalt finde therein,
That honour is more harde to holde than winne.
  (Gascoigne, 150)

Vietnam War poets took this, in detail, as their main text, and in doing so, they made significantly different war poetry. In Wallace Stevens's "Adagia," "A change of style is a change of subject" (Stevens, 171). Surely we can plunge ahead and say that the converse of this is also true. Stevens also said that "Poetry is a renovation of experience" (177). Maybe that gives the further license to find that a renovated experience exposes the root properties of poetry.

In an age of autobiography, brought upon us as the personal life bleeds increasingly into the public, we favor the fading, endangered, and increasingly self-conscious personal over the imagined in all literary genres. On war especially, American audiences, for decades weaned on openly autobiographical free verse, have been schooled to prefer the "I have seen" of the scarred visionary, of the tempted one. In the late twentieth and the early twenty-first centuries, audience and practitioner alike in America have redefined craft, overturning with abandon the formal bias that rules in favor of imaginative reconstruction over literalist copy of event. In Vietnam war poetry, for both the more and less skillful, rhythmic and metrical conventions have largely become outmoded or a culturally irrelevant artifice. Truth, a truth avidly sought, was in any case no better off in the hands of rhymers than those of nonrhymers. But in poetry's apparently inconsequential and culturally marginal haven, soldier-poets of the Vietnam War, who had endured the experience of guilt and atrocity and were dodging the appropriation of their experience by either mass culture or governmental disinformation, found a place for their feelings that was both portable and tenable.

Burdensomely, however, direct witness installs an aesthetic that constricts or oversimplifies many poems. Artless inexperience, for instance, masking itself as economy, telegraphs meaning through monotonously short, breathy lines, a surfeit of abbreviations, and a collaging of acronyms and technical jargon. And yet the texture of "Saigon tea," "triple canopy jungle," "Willy Peter," "*dien cai dao*," "LZ," "LRRP," "BAR," and so on, define the usable language. Poets back into their subject by means of their war's drugs, weathers, weapons and operations—and probably a dozen poems about the firefight or the ambush or the siege would be unable to assemble their effects without them. Names, terms, abbreviations, and slang, depending on a reader's tolerance for a spread of diction, work either just hard enough or too hard to preserve texture and physicality, as the poem also mimes the extent to which the consequences of many acts were hidden or masked from the participants by an official language that evaded feeling and judgment with a quite sinister Orwellian purpose.

Jonathan Shay, in defense of jargon, suggests other reasons for its dominance in soldiers' language, shaping that language as it does toward an initiated listener. Shay describes a veteran, representing the feelings of many, who "speaks of his most painful war memories as 'sacred stuff.'" But access to the sacred is by way of soldier lore. Shay continues: "There is also a pleasurable side to the use of jargon, speech rhythms, tones of voice that combat veterans take in talking to each other about their experiences." And he names the hours on end in which bewildered or bored family members hear veterans talk together exclusively and excludingly about the details of weaponry. Yet that pleasure has its healing function: "the technical minutiae are sometimes the only doorway a veteran finds into the rooms full of pain that they carry" (Shay, *Odysseus*, 89–90). Therapeutic or not, the practice is widely present in Vietnam War poetry.

In the best of these poems, the effectiveness of a masking jargon frequently lies in how the poet manages to expose the feelings nonetheless flooding it. Basil Paquet's "Morning—A Death" (1972) is a countererotic ballet, built in three mimic parts, with a Pindaric turn, counterturn, and stand; the first turn starts with a medic:

> I've blown up your chest for thirty minutes
> And crushed it down an equal time,
> And still you won't warm to my kisses.
> I've sucked and puffed on your
> Metal No. 8 throat for so long,
> And twice you've moaned under my thrusts
> On your breastbone.

But the poem ends:

> The bullet barks apocalyptic
> And you don't unzip your sepulchral
> Canvas bag in three days.
> No articulation of nucleics, no pheonix,
> No novae, just an arbitrary of one-way bangs
> Flowing out to interstitial calms.
> The required canonical wait for demotion
> To lower order, and you wash out pure chemical.
> You are dead just as finally
> As your mucosity dries on my lips
> In this morning sun.
> I have thumped and blown into your kind too often,
> I grow tired of kissing the dead.
>
> (In Rottmann, Barry, and Paquet, 22–23; also in Ehrhart, *Carrying*, 218–19)

Again, the chief stylistic virtue is an ironized compression, as poems take the strength of anecdote, joke, epithet, and epigram to ram their points home. Many poems by Rottmann, Barry, and Paquet are edged by difference or metaphors of awakening and conversion. They take Hemingway in *A Farewell to Arms* to heart:

> I had seen nothing sacred, and the things that were glorious had no glory
> and the sacrifices were like the stockyards at Chicago if nothing was done

with the meat except to bury it. There were many words that you could not stand to hear and finally only the names of places had dignity. Certain numbers were the same way and certain dates and these with the names of places were all you could say and have them mean anything. Abstract words such as glory, honor, courage or hallow were obscene beside the concrete names of villages, the number of roads, the names of rivers, the numbers of regiments and the dates. (185)

The titles of these poems are filled with names, places, and dates: "Vietnam— February 1967"; "Fragment: 5 September 1967"; "Saigon on Christmas Eve"; "An Outpost Near Cambodia, July 1969"; "Phu Cat, 3 Dec 1969," and so on.

Seasons are marked. Perhaps because of the intense counting down that went on for people recruited for a fixed term, or to note the different values of danger and risk, many poems post the time as day or night, notice the moon, or add the weather. *Winning Hearts and Minds*, a book charged with deaths and woundings also includes two poems on graves registration. Innumerable poems are haunted by body bags; innumerable poems repeat again and again that death in war is violent, explosive, rending—above all, unpredictable and unfair.

I was struck, too, at the large number of writers with service backgrounds as medics; the contrast between the healing function and the massive wounding and mutilation over which they struggled for control must have been part of what propelled them into speech. Basil Paquet writes through the wrath and mortifying helplessness that the experience of a child victim dying in his arms wrung from him. Yet he and other medic poets who write of the war's brutality towards civilians either have not observed or make no direct comment on the medical care consistently withheld by the Americans to the Vietnamese, either ally or enemy. These bald truths are laid open in *The Winter Soldier Investigation: An Inquiry into American War Crimes*.

At this public forum, at least half a dozen voices condemned the indifference or malice, or both, of numerous medics and doctors in treating the Vietnamese, southern or northern, soldier or civilian. From SP/5. Michael Erard, of the 173rd Airborne Brigade, a senior medic at Fire Base Abby:

In regard to medical treatment of wounded Vietnamese, and this involves not only captured prisoners, but also any Vietnamese, when we went out into the field we were issued a small bottle of serum albumin, about 500 cc's. Our platoon sergeant said, "This is worth $25. Never use it on a gook." There were many occasions where a wounded Vietnamese was sent back or dusted off with only a bandage to stop the bleeding when the man needed

IV fluids to make it. He was not given that aid. We had to account for our bottles of serum albumin just as we had to account for our morphine. We were, we were not allowed to waste it on a Vietnamese. (Vietnam Veterans, 89)

In a final, uncomfortable stutter, the denial of care emerges. Captain Ernie Sachs, 1st Marine Division: "I flew probably 500 Medivac missions in the course of 13 months. I can't recall ever evacuating a Vietnamese civilian" (Vietnam Veterans, 17). Sergeant Michael McCusker spoke to "the systematic destruction of village hospitals, by mortars, by air, by artillery, believing that if these hospitals were destroyed the Viet Cong could not use them" (Vietnam Veterans, 32).

This shameful triage of men and resources stumbled out of the darkness mainly for memoirists, journalists, and historians, while poets and novelists, with whatever deficits of experience, recorded the more usual and benign versions of the healer. The picture of the Vietnam War medic that does come up is dominantly wary and endangered. In the lasting confusions of his time and space, D. F. Brown, in "When I Am 19 I Was A Medic" (1984), reports:

All day I always want to know
the angle, the safest approach.
I want to know the right time
to go in. Who is in front
of me, who is behind.
When the last shots were fired,
what azimuth will get me out,
the nearest landing zone.

Each night I lay out all my stuff:
morphine, bandages at my shoulder,
just below, parallel, my rifle.
I sleep strapped to a .45,
bleached into my fear.
I do this under the biggest tree,
some nights I dig
in saying my wife's name
over and over.

(In Ehrhart. *Carrying*, 51)

For this medic, the war is on repeat mode.

But even when poets took on the moral burden of openly detailing their brutality in a fierce and merciless war, the old World War I fury against the fathers and leaders who put them in their dilemma continues to ruffle the verbal surface, ameliorate the sons' guilt, and qualify the editors' theme of change. As a final example of this 1972 anthology's choices, I quote from "Bedtime Story," written by Gustav Hasford "during the storming of the Citadel, Hue City, Vietnam, February 12th, 1968," which begins:

Sleep, America
Silence is a warm bed.
Sleep your nightmares of small
cries cut open now
in the secret places of
Black Land, Bamboo City.

And ends:

Bad dreams are something you ate,
So sleep, you mother.
(In Rottmann, Barry, and Paquet, 41; also in Ehrhart, *Carrying*, 125)

Hasford's wording here echoes what he will pick up again for his novel *The Short-Timers*, a half dozen years later (Hasford, 144). In these poems, fathers (America) are indeed motherfuckers, and the split in generational thinking, like the split endured in World War I, becomes a discontinuity in experience of sex and gender as well. Yet a poem like Bruce Weigl's "The Kiss," written in the eighties about his father, will trace other feelings:

All the goodbyes said and done
I climbed into the plane and sat down.
From the cold I was shaking and ached
to be away from the love
of those waving through the frozen window . . .

and it ends:

that day on the plane
he appeared to me,

my forgotten orders in his hands.
He bent down to put the envelope in my lap,
on my lips he kissed me hard
and without a word he was gone
into the cold again.
Through the jungle, through the highlands,
through all that green dying
I touched my fingers to my lips.

> (Weigl, *Song*, 68)

Samuel Hynes establishes convincingly that the break in the confident transmission of knowledge from generation to generation began in the literature of the Great War. For him, and for other literary historians, this break, or rupture in the weaving of history, is the dual predicament of both industrial war and modernity. But the break between civilian and soldier experience, between wartime and peacetime, persisted as a literary subject, not just a generational problem, for American veterans of the Vietnam War. While former soldiers like Siegfried Sassoon and Edmund Blunden carried their scarring memories deep into civilian life, wearing them through a second global conflagration, the persistent and painful lingering of war into civilian life was not their major subject.

Vietnam War literature, on the other hand, becomes as much a literature of aftermath as a literature of recall, where poetry massively demonstrates the atemporal fluency of combat experience, as the dissonant tenses in D. F. Brown's "When I Am 19 I Was a Medic" demonstrate. Noncombatant poets of earlier American wars left oblivion as the taste of war in the public mouth, dedicating monuments to unknown soldiers. "Pile the bodies high at Austerlitz and Waterloo," said Carl Sandburg in the familiar poem "Grass"; "And pile them high at Ypres and Verdun" (Sandburg, 136). All will be forgotten, because the grass, or imperial nature, covers all. But in "The Dead at Quang Tri," published in W. D. Ehrhart's *Carrying the Darkness*, Vietnam veteran Yusef Komunyakaa speaks for many when he writes:

The one kneeling beside the pagoda,
remember him? Captain, we won't
talk about that. The Buddhist boy
at the gate with the shaven head
we rubbed for luck

glides by like a white moon.
He won't stay dead, dammit!
Blades aim for the family jewels,
the grass we walk on
won't stay down.

       (In Ehrhart, *Carrying*, 153)

It is not the covering grass, but the corrosive flame that lingers. Even more acutely, war maintains itself as a vicious probe into the nature of a vulnerable masculinity.

When Yusef Komunyakaa published "'You and I Are Disappearing,'" he chanted a litany for the burned, beginning:

The cry I bring down from the hills
belongs to a girl still burning
inside my head. At daybreak
she burns like a piece of paper.

She continues to burn "like a sack of dry ice," "like oil on water," "like a cattail torch / dipped in gasoline," and finally, in echo of a Judeo-Christian divine retribution, "like a burning bush / driven by a godawful wind" (Komunyakaa, *Dien*, 17). There is no end to the burning—literal, figurative, and eschatological. By 1998, these memories have gained such momentum in print that Bill Jones, in "The Body Burning Detail" can report:

Three soldiers from the North
Burned for reasons of sanitation

. . . .

They burned for five days.
It was hard to swallow
Difficult to eat
With the sweet smoke of seared
Flesh, like fog,
Everywhere.

Twenty-five years later
They burn still.

       (In Mahony, 144)

American Poets of the Vietnam War   **259**

Even the ordinary maintenance of animal human life meant burning: *From Both Sides Now*, edited by Philip Mahony, records the particular disposal of human waste at army camps in several poems. In "Shitbirds," Jon Forrest Glade writes, "I always thought of the contents / of those flaming barrels / as burned offerings / to the gods / of that particular war" (in Mahony, 131). Bruce Weigl ends "Burning Shit at An Khe,"

> I lay down in it
> and fingerprint the words of who I am
>   across my chest
> until I'm covered and there's only one smell,
>   one word.
>
>   (In Ehrhart, *Carrying*, 263–64)

At the finish of this war, ordure and ash, the leavings of the body, indelible and lingering, sear the senses. Haunted by the greased, skin-eating fires of napalm and white phosphorus, survivors themselves still burn in memory. Bruce Weigl, home from the wars to a loving wife, ends "Song of Napalm" like this:

> And the girl runs only as far
> As the napalm allows
> Until her burning tendons and crackling
> Muscles draw her up
> Into that final position
> Burning bodies so perfectly assume. Nothing
> Can change that; she is burned behind my eyes
> And not your good love and not the rain-swept air
> And not the jungle green
> Pasture unfolding before us can deny it.
>
>   (In Ehrhart, *Carrying*, 273–74)

Carrying the Darkness

Even for poets gripped by the need for revisionist content, awareness of historical continuities in the lives of soldiers is hard to squelch completely, and as more decades wind past us, other collections of Vietnam War poetry add new preoccupations and more formal mastery. Although there is some overlap in these anthologies, W. D. Ehrhart's *Carrying the Darkness* is technically a lot smoother and more sophisticated in style than *Winning Hearts and Minds*; *Carrying the Darkness*, appearing originally in 1985 and reissued in 1989, includes work by civilians and apologetically adds a few women, who offer a little sauce of stateside perspective to what remains largely a main dish of male combat experience. Ehrhart's preface explains that he was just looking for good poems— "the best work by the best poets of the Vietnam generation" (xxvi). Only the passage of further years will test how close he comes to this mark, but he does cull the better poems from those printed earlier. Because his principles of selection consciously include literary merit, he gives more than mere historical documentation or partisan argument. By 1985, there was not only more time for sifting, but also more combat poetry to sift. Over the decades, Ehrhart's editorial acumen would lead him to prod new poets, Jim Nye and Dale Ritterbusch among others, to publish their own compelling collections.

The boldest of the contrasts between Vietnam War poets and the poets of World Wars I and II is the large admission of civilians and women to the texture of what is later reported. Great War poets left the doings of civilians to practitioners of the novel and the memoir. In World War II, with its far-flung theaters of engagement, ordinary civilian lives were more open to access by footloose soldier-poets, who were intellectually curious and often university-educated, usually young, and newly abroad in cultures for which they had been taught forms of respect. In the European theater especially, soldiers were not dismissive or in contempt of what they found. But in the main, the soldiers in Vietnam were only occasionally college boys or members of the ruling class loaned out for a tour of an empire's outposts and eager for knowledge of foreign culture. Lucky, affluent, or intellectually inquisitive students during the Vietnam era who managed to keep up their grades usually avoided the draft or strutted their stuff safely at home in the National Guard. But the overwhelming upgrade of firepower achieved in Vietnam, palpable to all, with its acceleration of civilian casualties and its proliferation of indiscriminate cruelty, eventually drew horrified and helpless response from the war poets unlucky enough to be there, or within earshot of those who had been.

In "Sergeant Brandon Just. U.S.M.C.," Brian Alec Floyd, not a combat veteran himself, but in Marine uniform from 1966 to 1968, lays out the dilemma for others:

> By slightest mistake of degrees
> on an artillery azimuth,
> he had called for rockets and napalm.

Their wild wizardry of firepower
expired her mistake of a village,
killing everyone except her,
and napalm made her look
like she was dead among the dead,
she alone alive among their upturned corpses
burning toward the sky.

The poem does not end here, in a pure fire of pathetic effect. The protagonist visits the surviving child every day:

Sung, knowing it was him,
would turn toward the sound of his feet,
her own, seared beyond being feet,

. . . .
And as he would come in,
Sung would hobble up to him
in her therapeutic cart,
smiling even when she did not smile, lipless,
her chin melted to her chest
that would never become breasts.

Floyd's sergeant details the extent of the damage to this child's body, and then concludes:

Sung was child-happy
that he came and cared,
and when he would start to leave,
she would agonize her words
out of the hollow that was her mouth.
Her tongue, bitten in two while she had burned,
strafing his ears,
saying, without mercy,
I love you.
                (In Ehrhart, *Carrying*, 108–10)

For such acts of war, penance carries no absolution. Even the merciful could not avoid corruption, nor could the honest witness excuse himself through abstention from action. When Bruce Weigl returned to America after serving in Vietnam, he wrote: "I felt wholly unworthy of any human kindness, not because of anything I'd done in the war, but because of what I'd seen" (Weigl, *Circle*, 152). Even the barest, lightest telling of experience that felt unclean to that degree exerts an intolerable and presumptuous weight of interpretation, and the strength of many Vietnam poems is the poet's refusal to add a syllable more than necessary. In agonizing fullness, he gives the amoral darkness that this war's prosecution largely prevented even decent American men and women from palliating.

In one of his poems not immediately anthologized, David Huddle's "Work" (1988) presents us with bald, painful understatement:

> I am a white, Episcopal-raised, almost
> college-educated, North American male.
> Sergeant Tri, my interpreter, is engrossed
> in questioning our detainee, a small,
> bad-smelling man in rags who claims to be
> a farmer. I am filling in the blanks
> of a form, writing down what Sergeant Tri
> tells me. This is dull. Suddenly Tri yanks
>
> our detainee to his feet, slaps him twice
> across the bridge of his nose. The farmer
> whimpers. Tri says the farmer has lied and waits
> for orders. Where I grew up my father
> waits at the door while my mother finishes
> packing his lunch. I must tell Tri what next.
>
> (In Mahony, 95)

Much is subtly timed and condensed here. In the sonnet's fourteen concise lines, the traditional *volta*, or turn, occurs at the yank of the detainee to his feet. In the poem's tight compass, Huddle presents the dilemma of abetting the brutality of a subordinate whose ethnicity and presumable awareness of enemy intention outstrips your own, in a place where the various charades of control by which service rank and political and linguistic utility manifest themselves are all joltingly counterpointed in the innocence—half a world away, and by another clock—of the father's wait for his lunch. In this dissonance, the speaker complicitly suspends himself and Sergeant Tri, waiting for orders. Within this

FIGURE 10. David Huddle in Germany, 1965.

poem, too, the ubiquitous boredom of a postheroic age is punctuated an equally ubiquitous violence.

Wrongs done to children form an oppressive subtheme in Vietnam war poetry. Here the burden of guilt may have been especially intolerable because so much of the popular imagery of World War II stressed the insouciant generosity and open temperament of the American GIs, who in the national memory distributed not bullets or blows but Hershey bars to war's gaunt and malnourished orphans. In Vietnam, the grunts found other uses for the rations issued them, as the children they met became the recipients of a fairly sour philanthropy. Whether the appalling meanness of so many was born from all the other betrayals of the American ideologies of help that the war engendered can only be guessed at. Bruce Weigl's "The Last Lie" details a common practice:

> Some guy in the miserable convoy
> raised up in the back of our open truck
> and threw a can of C rations at a child
> who called into the rumble for food.
> He didn't toss the can, he wound up and hung it
> on the child's forehead and she was stunned
> backwards into the dust of our trucks.

The child, who expects nothing better from soldiers, laughs, and with hand to bleeding head, fights off others to keep the C rats; the throwing soldier also laughs

> and fingered the edge of another can
> like it was the seam of a baseball
> until his rage ripped
> again into the faces of children
> who called to us for food.
>
> (Weigl, *Song*, 18)

The tidal rage, the horribly inappropriate laughter is as startling here as the flat, telling lack of tears in Jim Nye's "It's Too Late" (1991):

> The dumpy, toothless woman
> > Mouth and gums red from betel nut
> Screamed and cried
> > Kneeling over the body
> The kid got caught in a cross fire
> > Spun around and dropped
> Other villagers joined the keening
> > And the wailing
> And I thought,
> > Lady, it won't help
> > It won't bring him back
> > If I thought it would
> > I would kneel beside you
> > And weep

But it's too late
There is nothing in this world
    As dead as a dead child.
        (In Mahony, 164)

But glum and morally inert as this soldier narrator is, the honest record of his numbed reflection is perhaps preferable to the elevated histrionics of Dylan Thomas's strange elegy.

Without comment, Doug Anderson's "Two Boys" describes an American marine sighting in a machine gun by training it on a group of children. The first rounds hit high, and all but two boys get away. As the gunner sights in on a remaining boy,

this eight year old, with wisdom perhaps
from the dead, yanks off his red shirt, becomes
the same color as the fields, the gunner lowering
the muzzle now, whispering a wistful, *damn.*
        (Anderson, 17)

The two veterans retelling these stories know that even as bystanders they are implicated in these unnervingly casual cruelties, so that guilt pairs with impotence as part of the bleak aftertaste, even for people like John Balaban and Lady Borton, who were in country explicitly to help the Vietnamese injured. The same deadening futility that Nye records in "It's Too Late" registers in another poem of Doug Anderson's, "Xin Loi," which he notes means "I am sorry" in Vietnamese:

The man and woman, Vietnamese,
come up the hill,
carry something slung between them on a bamboo mat,
unroll it at my feet:
the child, iron gray, long dead,
flies have made him home.
His wounds are from artillery shrapnel.
The man and the woman look as if they are cast
from the same iron as their dead son,
so rooted are they in the mud
There is nothing to say,

nothing in my medical bag, nothing in my mind.
A monsoon cloud hangs above,
its belly torn open on a mountain.

(Anderson, 163)

There is "nothing in my mind," but the final image of the cloud with its torn belly leaves the future slashed open and hinting of what will come due for the soldier himself, or anyone caught in that landscape.

Ultimately, the inability to feel will catch up with these medics and soldiers, also changing the consciousness of the society to which they return: one of the lasting aftereffects of the Vietnam War will be a heightened attention to what is now so glibly referred to as "collateral damage." Most of the American public in World War II was little troubled by the wounding or death of women, children, and the elderly in the fire-bombing raids over Tokyo and other Japanese cities: air war historians Michael C. Sherry and Conrad C. Crane show at length the relative indifference of most military and government officials, as well as the general public, to the question of the civilian casualties that accompanied the horrific firebombing campaigns. But by the Vietnam War, media coverage and literature sensitized at least a growing minority of observers of war, not only to the limits of precision in technologically advanced killing instruments, but to the wide devastation of their use. Mindful of the civilian dead swelling the background and foreground in these pictures of a war, the poems of noncombatant suffering which populate Vietnam War literature surely intensify the questions, even for those not essentially pacifists, about war and the policing of its connections to unrestrained retribution.

The Vietnam War left literal and figurative trackmarks over all of its survivors. In *Busted* (1995), one of several memoirs narrating his experience in Vietnam, W. D. Ehrhart writes:

At first appalled by the brutality and callousness of my brother Marines, in a few short months I found myself splitting an old man's foot to the bone with the flash suppressor of my M-16 because he would not or could not tell us where the mines and boobytraps were planted in his village, blowing up a family's house with dynamite because we'd found a hundred pounds of rice that might be used to feed the Viet Cong, throwing C-ration cans from a speeding truck at the heads of begging children just for laughs.

I had become something evil, but I did not know what it was or how it had happened or why. (13)

Elsewhere, Ehrhart remarks that "ethics and war are mutually exclusive. You can have one or you can have the other, but you can't have both. . . . And my poetry is an ongoing attempt to atone for the unethical, for my loss of a moral compass when I was a young man" ("War, Poetry, and Ethics," 31).

Most of these poets strip image and story to the basic and stingingly artless details that keep the emotional charge tightly coiled, with as little authorial intervention as possible. Many poems illuminate atrocity; others are about bad luck and carry the incendiary excitement that we conventionally expect of the war story. But by the 1980s, when *Carrying the Darkness* was first published, poets found the wider context within which the Vietnam War lay embedded, and the historical and literary parallels through which its experience might be variously filtered began to show more clearly. A rough dozen of years after the war lurched to a close, the whole body of work dealing with this epoch oscillates with different densities of language and allusion, tracking complexities of feeling that defy our accumulating stereotypes.

Nevertheless, W. D. Ehrhart's alphabetical listing of poets suggests a less than accidental framing when he opens *Carrying the Darkness* with Philip Appleman's "Peace with Honor." This poem skillfully blends the dark country into which Caesar's legionnaires spread—in which "The outer provinces are never secure"—with that darkness of the unknown into which our own ground troops advanced in southeast Asia. There is a real frisson here, as we lean down to recognize the parallel and converging tracks of these imperial adventures:

The enemy seethed everywhere, like a field
of wind-blown grasses.
There were the usual
harangues, the native leaders boasting
their vast numbers, screaming
freedom or death;

. . . .

and every man remembered
the shame of Eagles fallen, comrades' bones
unburied: there was that curious thing,
men in bronze and steel, weeping.
And then the charge, the clash of arms,
cavalry with lances fixed, the glorious
victory: a hundred thousand tons of TNT
vaporized their villages, their forests were

defoliated, farmland poisoned forever,
the ditches full of screaming children,
target practice for our infantry.

(In Ehrhart, *Carrying*, 4–5)

Such parallels deny the originality of American war guilt and confirm the passive sagging of our minds towards fatalistic acceptance of war and vengeance, but they also fix our thoughts on the stubborn knotting of all human history within violence. The quick of our attraction toward war poetry may be this perpetually unresolved tension where the brilliant feat, the mesmerizing, imaginative command of courage and defensive resourcefulness, practiced in the throes of war, can always be found, even during war's prodigal reductions of glorious act to dead meat and wrecked real estate. If only in our enduring need for the dramas of the heroic, we could find "the moral equivalent of war," as William James described the search a long time ago, when we were doing what we called defending "our little brown brothers," the Filipinos, in yet another war against Asians.

Carrying the Darkness opens with this affirmation of historical connection then rolls on through Bruce Weigl, Deborah Woodard, and Ray Young Bear to close with poems of aftermath. Although most of the poems Ehrhart chose to anthologize tilt towards veterans' experience, Frank Stewart's "Black Winter" nevertheless chronicles his flight as a draft resister to Stockholm. By the poem's end, however, Stewart shifts abruptly from his own chilling experience of exile to that of the soldiers trapped in an equally remote Vietnam. A decade ago, and as far away and cold as Sweden, the triple canopy of the Vietnamese jungles still spreads over this whole generation:

Out by the reef a low fire is burning on the sea,
and in the silent dark a color like old roses
is shining on the swells. When they'd burn off
the cover in those green jungles, the suffocating
small hills would crouch there beyond the flames
like these waves. Ten years beyond the war on this
wharf, I can justify almost nothing so simply as this
fire. The smell of petroleum burning and brine slams
me like a fist that strikes on a cold morning
and strikes again, insists and strikes until there's only
blood and burning through the nostrils. A black

mirror: "One should watch and not speak. And patriotism has run the world through so many blood-lakes: and we always fall in . . ."

(In Ehrhart, *Carrying*, 244–46)

Beautiful Wreckage

Aftermath and its stubbornly recursive arc play out in Vietnam War poetry in three ways. First, through a spatial and temporal strike of the past flooding into the present in poem after poem, in the familiar form of the flashback, shaping what has become a defining symptom of post–traumatic stress disorder. The term itself is a signal of the high proportion of war veterans who came home and were officially counted as wounded by war, during the seventies showing up in hospitals and prisons as a prominent statistical bulge. A second mass of poems deals with the derealizing impact of the war, in which profound feeling is balked and war representation retreats into theater or numbed and dimensionless spectacle. Third, poems of return accrue for veterans like W. D. Ehrhart, Yusef Komunyakaa, and Bruce Weigl, as they revisit the sites of war, their poems in reverse symmetry to those that come to be written about the emigration of Vietnamese people to the United States. Eventually the flow of peoples effects a kind of equilibrium, a new stasis of peaceful relation. W. D. Ehrhart describes what he sees after a fall from a rock gashes his daughter's face in "How it All Comes Back":

The bullet entered between the eyes,
a hole like a punctuation mark
from an AK-47 or M-16,
white at the edges but glistening black,
a tunnel straight to the brain.

The hole that is his daughter's cut takes only three stitches to close, but the poem ends:

I couldn't look at my daughter
for months without seeing that hole:
I'd seen holes like that before,
but never on someone alive.

(Ehrhart, *Distance*, 9)

Vietnam veterans came home mostly alone, and they were not debriefed. In his memoir *The Circle of Hanh* Bruce Weigl writes: "One day I was squatting down in a bunker, stoned on Vietnamese dope so rich that it stained my fingers with its resin, waiting out a rocket attack, and two days later I was standing in the knickknacked living room of my parent's house, breathing the old air." Coming home from the airport in San Francisco had been a bump down: "I suppose I was jumpy. Standing in line before the ticket counter, I fell to the carpeted floor when some kid threw an empty soda can a few feet from where he sat into a metal trash can." People looked him up and down, but nobody said anything. Weigl adds: "I picked myself up from the airport carpet unashamed, happy that the soda can's bang hadn't been small-arms fire, or mortar rounds that the VC walked in on us as we slept under guard of the trees" (Weigl, *Circle*, 126).

The veterans' memories are there, wanted or not. For Dale Ritterbusch in "Canoe Trip" (1987), a flooded farm landscape and a slaughter pit filled with dead pigs brings back a village massacre in Vietnam. For Walter McDonald in "Hauling Over Wolf Creek Pass in Winter" (1984), a trucker takes his rig past wolves as he takes a load of pigs into Pagosa Springs, Colorado. Imitating the stampede of the Gadarene swine, these pigs seem destined for disaster, as they squeal in fear:

I let them squeal, their pig hearts
exploding like grenades.
The wolves are dark and silent.
Kneeling, I watch them split up
like sappers, some in the tree lines,
some gliding from shadow to shadow,
red eyes flashing in moonlight,
some farther off, guarding the flanks.
Each time, they know they have me.

. . . .
    I crank the diesel,
release the air brakes
like a rocket launcher.
Wolves run in circles. I hit the lights.
Wolves plunge through deep snow
to the trees, the whole pack starving.

Revving up, the truck rolls down the highway
faster, the last flight out of Da Nang.
I shove into third gear, fourth,
the herd of pigs screaming, the load
lurching and banging on every turn,
almost delivered, almost airborne.

> (In Ehrhart, *Carrying*, 194–95)

In parallel lives, the frustrating lurching and banging goes on and on, the cargo of memory containing the dead of the lost war and its abandoned refugees never quite delivered, never quite airborne to safety.

For so many, combat results in a boomerang of delayed reaction, an erosion of feeling audible in the ubiquitous catchphrase of this war, "It don't mean nuthin'," which inevitably diminishes within those who rely on its comfort. "It Don't Mean Nuthin" is also the title of a poem by Jim Nye in which, between beers, a soldier recites,

> "Death is nuthin' he said
> I've killed, what, 20, 30
> Don't mean nuthin.
>
> . . . .
> We're all gonna die anyway, right
> Some now, some later
> Me, I give a shit," he said.
> > (Nye, 30)

David Connolly also has a poem called "It Don't Mean Nothin," which shows the same proposition, but for his protagonist, "It" cuts a little deeper:

> He puzzled at their leader,
> the nineteen year old veteran
> with the pale, yellow skin,
> bleached rotting fatigues,
> and crazy, crazy eyes,
> who hawked brown phlegm
> on each dead American saying,
> "That don't mean nothin;
> y'hear me, meat?"

And everywhere he went,
there were more,
down all the days and nights,
all kinds of bodies,
ours, theirs, his,
until nothin meant nothin.

(In Mahony, 49)

In Gerald McCarthy's "Untitled," the corpse is not a friendly, but the effect is by now familiar:

We found him
his chest torn open,
shirt sticky brown.
A corporal with a bayonet
cut off his ears,
and kicked the body
in passing.

(In Mahony, 69)

Finally the reiteration of nothing into nothing hits bottom and begins an unavoidable ascent into something. "Ours, theirs, his": the flicked pronouns asserting dominion over the dead return everybody—every body—to the same grim kingdom, from which the living fly, needing to claim their difference.

This motion does not produce another poem like Wilfred Owen's "Strange Meeting," about a confrontation with a double in enemy uniform down in hell, nor does it call up Keith Douglas's enemy-as-twin in "How to Kill," where a mirror-soldier is visualized in cool amity and recognition through the sights of a combat rifle. For the Vietnam-era poet, the brotherhood of war cracks into feelings closer to Hamish Henderson's words for the North African desert of World War II, where the essential conflict is seen to lie not between friend and foe, but "between 'the dead, the innocent'—that eternally wronged proletariat of levelling death in which all the fallen are comrades—and ourselves, the living" (Hamish, 11). Succinctly put, the conflict is between the innocent dead and the guilty living. The mirror most commonly found in Vietnam War poetry glints from the black polished granite of Maya Lin's memorial wall, which is ubiquitous in poems after its dedication in 1982.

It is the dead friend or the dead beloved whose lettered name is carved on the wall and then indelibly viewed in the shine of their own reflected faces, with whom the living survivors must make their troubled encounter.

The brotherhood of battle changes in the Vietnam War. This war passed its brothers through a revolving door, a year of individual service rotation, spitting survivors in and out in bewildering and bitter disconnection. Because the practice of mustering conscripts in groups was scrapped for Vietnam, soldiers entered and exited from their wartime term of service largely as isolated persons, dislocating the customary bonding. Bonding is still inevitable, given battle interdependencies, but in the white heat of these war poems, buddying or wartime unity brings up sharply divided, often angry and agonized emotions, which are as much about betraying as being betrayed.

Even saving or trying to save the wounded erupts in small, scattershot bursts of anger. Jim Nye's "Dead Weight" enacts the rapid, rocketing transition from living to wounded to dead that is war's subject, as, in the perilous combat fraternity, soldiers accelerate the self-protective process of adjusting their loyalties. Battlefields enforce a swift triaging of the affections. In "Dead Weight," Brown has been disabled by rifle fire, and Jordan elects to carry him to safety:

> Jordan knew him from home
> Wouldn't let anyone carry him.
>   It was 16 klicks to a clearing
> Up the ridge line.
>   We carried Jordan's ruck, weapon and gear
> He carried Brown
>   It took a very long time—
> Stopping for Jordan to rest.
>   But we made it.
> The choppers picked up Brown,
>   Jordan sat exhausted,
> Looked at me and said,
>   "I'm finally done with that
> Son of a bitch,
>   Don't have to carry him no more."
>   (Nye, 20)

For the time-servers in this unpopular war, individual survival took the place of victory or patriotic fulfillment or homeland defense as the dominant goal. The emotional price of substituting this narrower end and the psychic burdens of its adaptation keep bleeding over into language. The unity of an invading force at the friction point of a battle shreds into the simplest terms: death to the others and life to our guys. The only binding thread that seems to keep a force from splitting into the chaos of every man for himself is still what unites each side into this common assertion of sides. Yet the question for so many students of war remains: what, in the face of overwhelming peril, makes an army stand and not run away? In situations of weakened motivation, why do soldiers still keep to their groups, so many choosing the survival of the group over their own annihilation?

In the large professional armies that mushroomed with the advent of gunpowder, to fear your sergeant more than your enemy kept many soldiers in line, but in the democratic, not necessarily god-fearing or brutalized twentieth-century American army after World War II, besides the drill for obedience, commanders were taught that the best glue was the buddy system. But if "buddies" are all that you have left to stiffen men for Captain Fluellen's "discipline of the warres," the system provides a slender buttress. In John Keegan's analysis from the commander's perspective, "Inside every army is a crowd struggling to get out—and the strongest fear with which every commander lives—stronger than his fear of defeat or even mutiny—is that of his army reverting to a crowd through some error of his making"(*Face*, 173). From the bottom of the military hierarchy, caught in the antiauthoritarian bent of the Vietnam War, these poems explore all the difficult edges, all the potent fraying and tightening of soldier bonds.

In Vietnam, if we put aside some sense of what soldier-poets construed as the original injustice that transported them to Vietnam and kept them there, their reactions still read, at least in part, as the rage of living men at the injustice of having to adapt to an aroused universe of death and dying, and as a hapless, impotent rage at their dead fellows for abandoning them and surrendering to it. Running under this anger, there is another displaced rage against being called out for risk and sacrifice: the eternal "why me?" David Connolly's "A Goodbye" is dedicated to a medic:

Gallant, the medic,
moved toward him
through worse
than what had brought Gracie down
while we silenced the gun.
Gallant worked on Gracie

for ten minutes, then ten minutes more,
mumbling, "Live, you bastard,"
between breaths,
while Bugs and I
plugged Gracie's bullet holes.
When Gallant gave up
he kicked Gracie's slack jaw.

We understood.
    (Connolly, 16)

"We" understand; but what is it "we" understand? That Gallant kicked
Gracie's jaw, furious because he had risked his own life for a life only now re-
vealed as beyond saving? Furious because his own passage through severe fire
was nothing, in the calculus of saves through which any risk must be comput-
ed in order to be understood and absorbed? Or is Gallant furious at Gracie for
not cooperating and now becoming the insensate matter that *can* be kicked, in
a dislocated rage at everything else that cannot be kicked away? "Gallant" and
"Gracie"; *gallantry* and *grace*: the names are suggestive of ironic allegory. In
all the gaps between desire and act within this poem, how act is mocked; even
under this mockery, how powerful the sense of duty.

These poems are written not from a simple point of view as speaker-
participant, but from the point of view of a man of the combat brotherhood,
who hears and understands and then interprets subvocally to those others listening in on what the speaker is saying. Think how this poem would change if
it were only a first-person recounting, failing to allow for the gap in which a
message is conveyed, and then instantly processed. Suppose the poem merely
read, "*I* kicked Gracie's jaw in passing"? As readers, we need the remove, the
distancing ricochet from subject to object and back, or the speaker is merely
psychotic, as the speaker at the moment of the poem may well be. But "we"
are not: the hearer of these words pleads with us, the overhearers of the combat gnostic, to shade in the whole story, to bridge the mysterious segregations
of experience and put boundaries to the desperate cry.

Back at home, "we" become "I," and say as Gerald McCarthy does in
"The Sound of Guns" (1977): "Never in anything have I found a way to throw
off the dead" (in Ehrhart, *Carrying*, 180–81). And then the sticky dead begin
their slide toward all those connected to the survivor. In his prose poem, "The
Little Man," Connolly remembers:

this stringy, little brown rice-propelled killing machine, floppy hat, black shirt and shorts, his folding stock AK held close to him in his left hand. He's facing away from me, aiming at my brothers' backs, so I can't see his face. I notice the cover of his spider hole as he kicks it away; his head swivels. He's lining up his run through our hasty defensive position and his targets on the way out. The brothers are all facing outboard, away from him, intent on the jungle, the fire coming from it and their own outgoing.

But Connolly is weaponless, wounded, and voiceless before the men who are about to die. Years later, he brings himself back from nightmare, "gagging on the choke of cordite and coppery blood, and find my wife has heard." She soothes him, as he concludes:

> But you see it will never be OK. That little man will make his run in my head as I helplessly watch and neither time nor tears will make him stop. It is not my fault I couldn't stop him. I know that. I've always known that.
> But now she thinks it's her fault because she can't. (Connolly, 66–67)

The labile guilt flows and spreads, no resting place for its containment.

In the last paragraph of his prose poem, "Tet, Plus Twenty Four," which Connolly dedicates to Bill Ehrhart as one combat veteran to another, a single concluding sentence tallies the painful equation by which all the bodies come to nothing and look so perilously close to nothing even twenty-four years after a battle:

> Speak for the dead we didn't have time to stand and weep over, for all the dead on all the trails, in all the paddies, from both sides, for my friends killed or cooked in ACAVs, for your friends atomized by the big guns aimed at Con Thien, but especially for those dead boonierats and grunts whose bodies, looted by our allies, still lie in our minds, looking like so much garbage on the streets of Bien Hoa and Hue. (Connolly, 41)

If war memorials of polished, reflective stone exist, they do not compete with the remembering locked behind the eyes of survivors. If there is a surge of genuine antiwar feeling in this generation's war poetry, it exists in often contradictory acknowledgment of the witness of war memorials, sometimes perceived as healing and consoling, sometimes as woefully false and incomplete. Poems like David Connolly's reach back all the way to Siegfried Sassoon's condemnation of the Menin Gate, to the sense of war itself as an inevitably criminal and contagious despoliation.

As the grip of the dead does not lift in glory, the field of the remembered also undergoes remodeling. The other battle-inflected revision of battle bonding visible in Vietnam War poetry reworks not only the lateral ties between men, but the vertical and hierarchical ones between officers and enlisted men, the source of so much welling tenderness in the officer poetry of Wilfred Owen. It is potentially a much more bristly relation in Vietnam, seen more from the bottom up than from the top down.

When David Connolly remembers "Our Fourth LT," it is simply to praise his devotion to his men's survival, and of course the title itself comments on the survival rate of lieutenants in relation to the men they lead. When receiving his Silver Star, the fourth Lt. says to the general awarding him the medal:

> "Sir, I have come to consider
> my primary mission
> in Vietnam to be
> to get my own young ass
> and those of my men
> the fuck out of here, alive.
> It just happened
> that this time
> the Army's mission
> and mine, coincided."
>
> He had smartly snapped
> one beaut of a salute
> and spun on his heel.
>   (Connolly, 25)

In other situations, when young first and second lieutenants rank mission and men in a different order of priority, the outcome changes. Yusef Komunyakaa retells a common story in "Fragging":

> Five men pull straws
> under a tree on a hillside.
> Damp smoke & mist halo them
> as they single out each other,

pretending they're not there.
"We won't be wasting a real man.
That lieutenant's too gung ho.
Think, man, 'bout how Turk
got blown away; next time
it's you or me. Hell,
the truth is the truth."

(Komunyakaa, *Dien*, 16)

In *Back Fire*, Geoffrey Regan comments: "Statistics for this form of assassination are unavailable for the First World War, yet it remains an open question as to what proportion of the extremely heavy casualties among junior officers were caused by their own men" (Regan, 231–32). Christian Appy sets the context for fragging deaths in Vietnam within the larger category of friendly fire. Describing the ambivalence that the average grunt felt toward supporting fire, he notes that it was both "protector and destroyer, welcome ally and terrible threat" (Appy, 184). Because grunts needed bombs and artillery to save their lives, they called in "air and arty"; yet they knew that "if mistakes were made by pilots or artillerymen, or if equipment malfunctioned, the bombs could land on American positions. The grunts could be killed by 'friendly fire.'" Appy cites a Pentagon study conducted in early 1968 that concluded that 15 to 20 percent of all U.S. casualties were caused by friendly fire and adds:

> Most Americans killed by their own side died from misdirected bombs, artillery, and strafing fire. Others died from accidentally discharged grenades or weapons on the ground. In the confusion of battle some men were shot by their own troops. The intentional murder or "fragging" of U.S. troops by other American soldiers may have accounted for 5 to 10 percent of friendly fire deaths. (185)

Vulnerable to all, grunts, who in Appy's persuasive analysis were often used as bait by other American field forces to draw and locate enemy fire, had their loyalties severely tested.

In the steady scaling down of the heroic, in a terrain where the strongest mission is to outlast missions, obedience loses its appeal as military discipline or virtue, and one more restraint against anarchic individualism erodes. Ronald J. Glasser's story "Bosum" from *365 Days* illuminates facets of both David Connolly's and Yusef Komunyakaa's poems. Bosum, the eponymous hero, is a lifer and World War II veteran who, as an operations adviser, sets out to shape up South Vietnamese and American troops. He's amazed by his soldiers:

> He had never seen troops so fatalistic. Even at the worst in Burma, when the only thing between the Japanese and India were 15,000 poorly equipped United States and British troops, there was nothing close to the soporific fatalism he found gripping the G.I.'s in Vietnam. The troops knew that if they made it 365 days without getting killed or wounded they were done. (Glasser, 183)

And then they could go home, whole. They didn't believe in the war anyway.

Unlike the postwar military theorists who ascribe American defeat to a deficiency of backup firepower, Bosum makes his troopers "push" for military gain:

> from now on, after making contact with the enemy, they were not to have their units pull back in order to call in artillery or gunships; instead, they were to keep pushing with all they had. He was sure the techniques of making contact, pulling back, and calling in support strikes gave the enemy forces a chance either to regroup or filter out of the area. It also tended to keep his men battle-shy. (Glasser, 183)

"Pushing," and "All they had" meant increased American casualties, over 60 percent more within a recombined, beefed-up combat unit. The tighter discipline on the trail and in patrols meant a reduction in American casualties by land mines and booby traps, but it also meant costly engagement with Vietcong and, finally, with NVA regulars. "There was less rest for everyone, but the brigade started getting 80-percent kills. They began to hurt Charlie" (Glasser, 186). Militarily, Bosum's campaign is a success. At the point, however, where he begins to see a full-scale enemy retreat from his district, Bosum is killed by a grenade thrown into his tent by an American soldier.

All hierarchies wobbled in this war. Conventional belief in the sanctity of patriotic death was sharply challenged as the pathway from the living to the dead soldier demanded a sharper definition. An anxiety spread about the ceremonies of matter, in which the flesh of the warrior hero passes into spirit. In retrospect, memory of those who died festers into a worry-point: at what instant do flesh and spirit part? Does spirit really then go it alone into the never-never? What does the crossover really represent, when someone deadens into nothing, an instant witnessed over and over with so much fear and confusion?

Painfully, carefully, repetitively, like a man prodding a barely-formed scab, Jim Nye and so many others pick away at the place where the fabulous transition from life to death occurs. At the unfixable junction when infinity takes over, and just-now life becomes death, the war poet's after-hours job becomes the regeneration of the war lament as a view into the intersection of the mortal with the eternal.

Plain-spoken, seemingly artless, these poems reflect the contemporary coercions of social structure that define the extreme duty of killing for an able-bodied male citizen. But the poems also find their unerring way back to a central task of Romantic poetry, which is to wrestle with death's relation to life and to question the passing of the self closed in its body of matter. In a sequence of poems from a book called *After Shock*, Nye in "Aftershock 1" tracks the course of a grenade exploding, during which time a man died in front of him.[2] The speaker sees the man fall,

> Then lift off the trail.
> A glimpse of eternity
> Suspended.
> . . . .
> The shock wave hit.
> I took a piece of shrapnel
> In the thigh and heard afterward
> The thump of the explosion.
>
> He dropped heavily—
> The debris and dirt pattered down,
> My ears rang,
> But I still heard his voice
>
> From an instant ago.
>   (Nye, 15)

Where does the voice go, and how does it manage to sound again in memory? What is the placeless place, the irresolvable aporia, the "neither this nor that," that both holds and releases the voice, the poem sets itself to ask. And it asks again and again, as one soldier or another unaccountably makes the passage from being alive to being inert. Back in the world, the sights and sounds refuse to go away; they destroy the sequencing of past and present, as soldiers carry the signals of the deadly crossing from the one condition to the other with them. Yusef Komunyakaa's "Ambush" starts from a pause before an attack, so quiet the birds begin again, as a waiting platoon listens hard for the enemy:

> & then a sound that makes you jump
> in your sleep years later,
> the cough of a mortar tube.
>> (Komunyakaa, *Neon*, 129)

In Walter McDonald's "Rocket Attack," he prays:

> Daughter, oh God, my daughter
> may she never
> safe at home
> never hear the horrible
> sucking sound a rocket makes when it
>> (In Ehrhart, *Carrying*, 190–91)

which is the poem's last line, entire. The opening is awkward, even sentimental, but the space McDonald opens to make our ears hear this unspeakable sound is more than effective. In this land of the unsayable and unbearable, in which soldiers deliberately misrepresent a good half of what they feel in order to protect the decaying remnants of their sensitivities, war itself hardly stays real; they begin to do what they can to make thoughts or objects from back home lock it out. There is always another and more consoling arena available behind the forehead, in Yusef Komunyakaa's words from "Camouflaging the Chimera," where "a world revolved / under each man's eyelids" (*Dien*, 9). Concentration splits between the demands of the self and the war, yet the self remains, knowing that "The real interrogator is a voice within." Even as that voice is for a moment successfully quelled: for Komunyakaa, a voice in "Jungle Surrender" winces to recall "how I helped ambush two Viet Cong / while plugged into the Grateful Dead" (Komunyakaa, *Dien*, 37).

His is not a division of mind foreign to other war poetry. Of trench warfare decades earlier, E. E. Cummings wrote:

> meanwhile my
> self etcetera lay quietly
> in the deep mud et

cetera
(dreaming,
et
cetera, of
Your smile
eyes knees and of your Etcetera
(Cummings, 193)

In Vietnam, however, the splits in soldier consciousness are not just escape or coping mechanisms, but an inundation by the mental leavings of other wars, as even the soldier's sense of his own soldiering is loosened and destabilized. As to the historical continuum within which the Vietnam War was perceived by Americans, William Kendrick startles us by saying:

When the war finally broke into the American living room it seemed as unreal as the rest of television fare. It had to vie with the other war still being portrayed on the screen in *Combat*, *Twelve O'Clock High* and *Hogan's Heroes*. . . . In the shank of the evening, receiving the highest audience ratings, were seen the film epics of World War II: *The Bridge on the River Kwai*, *The Longest Day*, *Anzio* and *The Sands of Iwo Jima*. Which was the real war and which was the movie? (Kendrick, 5)

He goes on to note that "Not only for those at home but for many in combat in Vietnam the war had a feeling of fantasy about it. Young conscripts risked their lives daily in a kind of trance and one of them won the Medal of Honor for valor while under the influence of drugs."

D. F. Brown, in a poem from *Returning Fire* called "Still Later There Are War Stories," writes:

Another buddy dead.
There is enough dying—
Gary Cooper will
ride up, slow and easy
slide off his horse
without firing a shot
save us all.

It is a matter of waiting.
(Brown, 45)

One cannot demand rescue from reality itself; it seems one can ask only for the grace of bankrupt myth, a myth infiltrating Vietnam through the pounding music and movie memory from home that all soldiers carried in their heads and headsets. It became a deflationary grace, too, paying off in a perpetual and demoralizing self-consciousness. In "Proofs," Brown writes, "if this were moving / I would be singing / in frames 10 and 23," but the possibility of singing cuts off, and Brown's speaker is left

> posing as myself
> in another war story
> the way it gets done
> until something different
> happens. I can think
> of all the reasons in the world.

The pose of "myself" will break: even as Brown ends "Proofs" in thrall to self-consciousness, the derealized mental world of war can only decay and shrivel the heroic identity:

> there is smoke in every frame
> in 29
> my hands blur
> catching my friends
> as they fall into their stories
> pulling on the dead
> to tell it
> down to scale
> (Brown, 32)

Brown's remnant of the heroic self lands stateside; in "First Person—1981" it declares, "there are days I have to pretend / I am someone else to get out of bed" (Brown, 35).

In Gerald McCarthy's title poem from his 1977 collection *War Story*, being wounded touches off the reduction of the self to an automaton, his body given over to the crude cartoon handling of the "war story," as the soldier gags on the actual and lets fantasy explode his sense of connection:

> We wait for the word
> to move out

and nobody changes the reel,
we don't get time for intermission.

Everyone's up
moving across the rice paddy,
the lieutenant gets his face blown off.

We make the ridge
and there's nothing there,
except a hundred and fifty naked women,
all ex-playboy club bunnies
all nymphomaniacs,
who say to us in one voice:
"Ford has a better idea."

When the narrator is hit, he says:

Knocked backward, rolling to one side
it happens all at once.
He's got me.
The arrow sticks in my chest
and in the distance I can hear the bugles,
the pounding hooves.

Light blinds me,
I lie hands and feet tied
feeling the heat.
Jesus Christ, somebody pull the switch.
              (McCarthy, 22)

Somebody stop the projector, change the cowboys-and-Indians film trapping this soldier. Tell him he is not John Wayne, that irrepressible phantom making its derisive appearances throughout Vietnam War literature. Earlier in this sequence of poems, McCarthy writes: "Wading through streams / rifles overhead, / they photograph us for LOOK / and some idiot smiles" (17). "Some idiot" is capable of forgetting the difference between a war on the idiot box and a war for real. As in the Freudian logic of dream language, where the mental life of images and the lives of other bodies in time exist and touch like crossed wires, displacement, denial, and reversal serve these soldier-poets, sometimes as kit for survival, and sometimes not.

When McCarthy's speaker returns home, "I stand in the bus station, / hoping someone / will notice the ribbons / pinned above the pocket / of my shirt" (23). But for the most part, nobody clapped at the end of this show. Soldiers went home, many going back to school, and the subsequent pour of veterans' books showed the divergence in their opinions of what, finally, to make of the uncertain and perpetuating boundaries of this war. For Jim Nye, who took a double tour, one in the 101st Airborne and one in the Special Forces, his interest in "the discipline of the warres" makes itself felt: in his conviction, it is an honorable, exacting, and uncompromising profession. Performing its duties with learnable skills, and walking its line, Nye teases the gap between life and death. Nye's "Chimaera," or "*fabulous fire-breathing monster*" makes no bones about loving war; "There is something dark in my soul," he announces:

> Its heart pulses heavily
> As it inhales deliciously the
> Bitter cordite, coppery smell of blood.
> That revels in the fear,
> Watching the tracers stitch
> Across into the brush,
> The body dropping, heavily, limp.
> Jamming home another magazine,
> Panting, gasping,
> Nourished and feeding,
>
> My God, I love it.
>   (Nye, 45)

Clearly, many soldiers are caught in the drag of this fascination, the pull of its heroic movies. And yet, Nye's "Career Choice" announces that there is no "need to wrap myself in the flag, / Make a career of being a veteran" (Nye, 69). Dale Ritterbusch in " Friends, " refuses to let memory be a consolation or to let "a few stories" become "recompense" and "titillation" (Ritterbush, 68). But again, something, in "What There Is," yanks him back to the heroic narrative still radioactively at work in war:

About the only thing that matters,
caught back of the eye,
downed like a chopper
slammed into the side of the hill,
burning orange into the trees,
is this strange recollection—
true or not—seeing death
as a man you beat at cards,
as your childhood, as history,
as part of the landscape,
as beauty
terrible and fulfilling.

> (Ritterbush, 76)

The beauty of the attempt to master death that Ritterbush remembers as his active exercise does not enter these lines, but it exists somewhere off the page, a frightening, enduring compulsion not only for the man, but for the culture.

W. D. Ehrhart's evocation of aftermath is characteristically far more wary of the beauties of war's conflagrations. In the title poem of *Beautiful Wreckage*, he starts to build a poem out of "what ifs"; what if, for instance:

Gaffney didn't get hit in the knee,
Ames didn't die in the river, Ski
didn't die in a medevac chopper
between Con Thien and Da Nang.
In Vietnamese, Con Thien means
place of angels. What if it really was
instead of the place of rotting sandbags,
incoming artillery, rats and mud.

What if the angels were Ames and Ski,
or the lady, the man, and the boy,
and they lifted Gaffney out of the mud
and healed his shattered knee?

The poem ends:

FIGURE 11. Cpl. W. D. Ehrhart, First Battalion, First Marine Regiment, Con Thien, August 1967. In "Beautiful Wreckage," Ehrhart notes that Con Thien means "place of angels" in Vietnamese. To him it was, "the place of rotting sandbags, / incoming artillery. Rats and mud."

What if none of it happened the way I said?
Would it all be a lie?
Would the wreckage be suddenly beautiful?
Would the dead rise up and walk?
     (Ehrhart, *Beautiful*, 206)

The force of this poem lies in its terrible admission that there were and are no miracles and, above all, in its denial of beauty in war. In the allowing this thought of angelic status for all the dead, there is such a wish that extremes of suffering be seen as conferring a holy exaltation to the sacrifice, yet the inter-rogatives of this poem—heroic in their postheroic mode—consider, but ulti-mately reject, the uplift of that resolution. Ehrhart knows that he saw what he saw, that memory has not betrayed him; only in the denial of those truths can myths of the beauty of war prevail, and yet the desire—his desire and that of so many others—that the myths prevail is so intense that it still trails on into the ambivalent title bannering the poem and festooning the latest, longest, and summary collection of Ehrhart's work in 1999: *Beautiful Wreckage*.

"Brothers in the Nam"

The divided loyalties of black and minority soldiers were articulated in poems well before the Vietnam War. In Gwendolyn Brooks's "Negro Hero," published in 1945, the bitter taste of an ambivalent black patriotism is clear:

> I loved. And a man will guard when he loves.
> Their white-gowned democracy was my fair lady.
> With her knife lying cold, straight, in the softness of her sweet-flowing
>   sleeve.
> But for the sake of the dear smiling mouth and the stuttered promise I
>   toyed with my life.

That "stuttered promise" left the "Negro Hero" wondering about his actual place in a white war:

> Am I clean enough to kill for them, do they wish me to kill
> For them or is my place while death licks his lips and strides to them
> In the galley still?

Can a black soldier be a hero if he is made to stay behind the lines as the cook and driver? But even so, or even if, he says,

> I helped to save them, them and a part of their democracy.
> Even if I had to kick their law into their teeth in order to do that for them.
>   (Brooks, 48)

But by the late 1960s, as large numbers of eligible middle-class white men continued to take their college draft exemptions, black soldiers made up a much larger part of American combat forces than they had in World War II, and attitudes, both official and unofficial, shifted. As Horace Coleman renders a bar scene in Khanh Hoi in his poem "OK Corral East Brothers in the Nam," the balance of power tilts to favor black:

> the grunts in the corner raise undisturbed hell
> the timid white MP has his freckles pale
> as he walks past the high dude
> in the doorway in his lavender jump-suit
> to remind the mama-san quietly of curfew
> he chokes on the weed smoke
> he sees nothing his color here
> and he fingers his army rosary his .45
>
> but this is not Cleveland or Chicago
> he can't cringe any one here and our
> gazes like brown punji stakes impale him
>
> we have all killed something recently
> we know who owns the night
> and carry darkness with us
>
> (In Ehrhart, *Carrying*, 71)

These black soldiers are armed and dangerous; the white power that prevails stateside pivots differently in Vietnam.

But the black American soldier, if he experienced new status within the army's front lines, and even in rear overseas postings, had his class and ethnic loyalties tweaked by what he came to know of the Vietnamese style of nationalism. In Yusef Komunyakaa's "Report from the Skull's Diorama," a platoon of black soldiers comes back with five dead; the fire base to which they return has just been blitzed with leaflets that say, "VC didn't kill / Dr. Martin Luther King" (in Mahony, 150). In Komunyakaa's "Hanoi Hannah," the taunting, elusive voice of Vietcong radio comes to say:

> "You know you're dead men,
> don't you? You're dead
> as King today in Memphis.
> Boys, you're surrounded by

General Tran Do's division."
Her knife-edge song cuts
deep as a sniper's bullet.
"Soul Brothers, what you dying for?"
            (Komunyakaa, *Dien*, 13)

Whatever they die for, the risks are shared, but the pleasures are still segregated. Komunyakaa's narrator in "Tu Do Street" tries and fails to get a beer
in an effectively "Whites Only" bar and says:

We have played Judas where
only machine-gun fire brings us
together. Down the street
black GIs hold to their turf also.

And he concludes:

Back in the bush at Dak To
& Khe Sanh, we fought
the brothers of these women
we now run to hold in our arms.
There's more than a nation
inside us, as black & white
soldiers touch the same lovers
minutes apart, tasting
each other's breath,
without knowing these rooms
run into each other like tunnels
leading to the underworld.
            (*Dien*, 29)

In that underworld, all lovers, soldiers, and siblings meet. But in this incisive
probe into the tense and volatile layering of his allegiances, Komunyakaa's
soldier accepts the grip by which language and nationhood still trump the loyalties of skin color.

  Throughout Yusef Komunyakaa's *Dien Cai Dau*, published in 1988 and
dedicated to a brother who served in Vietnam before him, he, like the other
poets of his battle fraternity, makes "Brother" a term to fit both enemy and

friend. There is room to notice, however, the extent to which his vulnerable position as a black man serving in a white-controlled army opens his vision with special acuity to the conflicts inflecting the ethnicity, race, class, and gender of all soldiers. Komunyakaa, who went to Vietnam as a combat reporter for the Army, spoke in a 1998 interview about the background of his Vietnam poems:

> I was quite aware of Vietnam's history. . . . A crucial bond was the concept of the Vietnamese "peasant." I, myself, came from a peasant society of mostly field workers, and my father always believed if one worked hard enough, he or she could rise to a certain plateau—a black Calvinism. So I saw the Vietnamese as familiar peasants because that's what they are, and consequently, I could have easily placed many of the individuals I'd grown up with in that same situation—especially the sharecroppers. (Komunyakaa, *Blue Notes*, 94–95)

Komunyakaa was not alienated by Vietnam; he had grown up in a lushly fertile, subtropical Louisiana nearly as vibrant as what surrounded his senses in southeast Asia. It is not simple race oppression that is operative, nor will race alone be the cleaver which Hanoi Hannah wields to split a black soldier's loyalty.

Asked, however, if he were affected by the civil rights struggle at home, Komunyakaa, his pronouns standing at a diplomatic distance from his answer, replied:

> You were keenly sensitive to surviving, and you knew that you had to connect to the other American soldiers. But when you saw friends getting killed or wounded, all kinds of anger would flare up, but let's face it, if you're placed in that kind of situation—and you've been trained—you're going to fire your weapons. You are going to try to stay alive. You're going to try and protect your fellow soldiers, black or white. But at the same time, there were those vicious arguments with oneself. One would feel divided. (*Blue Notes*, 96)

Safety means bonding between combatants; whatever species glue gets unstuck enough to divide people into murderous antagonists, once at war, the cast-off solidarity reagglutinates between partisans. In 1990, when Komunyakaa returned to Vietnam with five other war veterans, he was surprised at how "forgiving" the Vietnamese were to former enemies. Yet even in what was written before that visit, his poems leap to see the fraternal ties beneath the feral conflict. "Sappers" marvels at the dedication of the Vietcong:

> Opium, horse, nothing
> sends anybody through concertina
> this way. What is it in the brain
> that so totally propels a man?

The Americans, "Caught with women in our heads," fire back, but:

> They fall
> & rise again like torchbearers,
> with their naked bodies
> greased so moonlight dances
> off their skin. They run
> with explosives strapped
> around their waists,
> & try to fling themselves
> into our arms.
>> (*Dien*, 24)

The Vietcong extend a deadly but erotic embrace that includes all. As Randall Jarrell's poems embraced the contradictions of a uniformed adolescent both lethal and innocent, Yusef Komunyakaa surrenders his feelings to a respected foe, acknowledging an intensity that includes a sexualized flooding of the aggressive instincts underpinning war. In "We Never Know," the poem takes a moment when "Our gun barrels / glowed white-hot." A stricken soldier dances with the tall grass "like he was swaying with a woman"; then:

> When I got to him,
> a blue halo
> of flies had already claimed him.
> I pulled the crumbled photograph
> from his fingers.
> There's no other way
> to say this: I fell in love.
> . . . .

I slid the wallet into his pocket
& turned him over, so he wouldn't be
kissing the ground.
>   (*Dien*, 26)

This yearning to nullify antagonism, let some kind of love seep into enmity, spreads into other poems. Komunyakaa says of his Vietnam work: "These poems were prompted by a need; they had fought to get out. I hadn't forgotten a single thread of evidence against myself" (*Blue Notes*, 14). Like Keith Douglas and W. D. Ehrhart, Yusef Komunyakaa in "Starlight Scope Myopia" is peering down the sights of his M16 at the enemy to be killed; but instead of Douglas's fatalism or Ehrhart's rue, Komunyakaa approximates Randall Jarrell's tenderness:

Viet Cong
move under our eyelids,

lords over loneliness
winding like coral vine through
sandalwood & lotus,

inside our lowered heads
years after this scene

ends. The brain closes
down. What looks like
one step into the trees,

they're lifting crates of ammo
& sacks of rice, swaying

under their shared weight.
Caught in the infra red,
what are they saying?
. . . .
> They say
"up-up we go," lifting as one.
This one, old, bowlegged,

you feel you could reach out
& take him into your arms.

(In Ehrhart, Carrying, 150–51)

This tonality and its appreciation of an enemy's communally-shared effort are probably not accessible, however, right up against moments when your own life is in danger.

Maybe this feeling for connection emerges only for a former enemy, surfacing in aftermath and retrospect. Komunyakaa slips past the now familiar image of the enemy double, intent on his own war, his own perception. In the loops of his imagery, the tunnels that undercut the war he remembers are ubiquitous, and their underground presence gives shape to the elusive parallels worming into the consciousness of soldiers on both sides, beneath the layers of difference. Like a good soldier on either side in any war, the tunnel rat in "Tunnels" wriggles forward:

Through silver
lice, shit, maggots, & vapor of pestilence,
he goes, the good soldier
on hands & knees, tunneling past
death sacked into a blind corner,
loving the weight of the shotgun
that will someday dig his grave.

(In Mahony, 77)

"Jungle Surrender" is written for prisoners of war; here, what heals each prisoner has to mutate beyond the taking of sides, in the rooms which, in yet another poem, "run into each other like tunnels / leading to the underworld." In "Jungle Surrender," the prisoner knows we're all connected, but, in another burrowing metaphor, he touches "fraying edges of things, to feel hope break // like the worm that rejoins itself / under the soil . . . head to tail" (Komunyakaa, *Dien*, 37). What ties this underground imagery to Wilfred Owen's "Strange Meeting" may be the ongoing sense that all this connection will only happen in hell.

More underground connections dug by the war show up in the complex network resulting from interracial sexual contact. As in *Winning Hearts and Minds* and *Carrying the Darkness*, Philip Mahony reprints poems in *From Both Sides Now* by Horace Coleman and Yusef Komunyakaa that show each black soldier's ambivalent feelings for children fathered in Vietnam and for the more literal blood ties of the war. Horace Coleman's "A Black Soldier Remembers" begins: "My Saigon daughter I saw only once / standing in the dusty square," and apparently without making any attempt to approach her, the soldier finishes:

> The amputee beggars watch us.
> The same color and the same eyes.
> She does not offer me one of the
> silly hats she sells Americans and
> I have nothing she needs but
> the sad smile she already has.
>> (In Mahony, 156)

We wonder about that elastic space, the uncrossed distance between father and daughter, and the nature of what has been silently assented to in that sad smile: What is it that has been abandoned, or denied. The poem is bursting with things seen but unsaid. In "Dui Boi, Dust of Life," Yusef Komunyakaa says to a child, "Come here, son, let's see / if they castrated you." He ends:

> With only your mother's name,
> you've inherited the inchworm's
> foot of earth. *Dui boi.*
> I blow the dust off my hands
> but it flies back in my face.
>> (In Mahony, 263)

"*Bui doi,*" or dust of life: either Yusef Komunyakaa or the editor, Philip Mahony, has here given the right meaning but inadvertently reversed the initial consonants of the Vietnamese phrase into "*dui boi.*" On the opposite page, facing Komunyakaa's "Dui Boi, Dust of Life," R. A. Streitmatter correctly transliterates Tran Trong Dat's "worthless dust" into "Bui Doi"; two other poems by Tran Trong Dat, taking as their subject the self as abandoned orphan, are titled "Bui Doi 7" and "Bui Doi" (in Mahony, 261–62). In any case, a clash of hope and anger has come to dust the poems by American and Vietnamese alike.

Men and Women and Women

There are missing voices in the early books and anthologies—a large silence, for instance, is produced by the absent Vietnamese, and a curiously reverberant silence is created by the general omission of women's first-person voices. Women, sparse in the tables of contents of the initial anthologies, are nevertheless all over the place in Vietnam War poems, whether flashing out as a thirteen year-old vendor selling herself and her mangoes from a Saigon doorway or as a straight-backed nurse gunning her Honda 50 through traffic or as black-toothed, betel-chewing farm adolescents or crones.

With an almost sadomasochistic purity, a beautiful woman, an avenging angel, turns up repeatedly as a Vietcong fighter. Disguising death in love's shape, she becomes the sign of the satanic exchange that war performs with love, where death must trade places with life as the goal. It is as if a fateful mother acknowledges that a deadly return to the womb of earth is now ritually intended as the natural inverse or completion of birth, however much young soldiers far from home and their mothers may fear that return. Sometimes, as in Yusef Komunyakaa's "Night Muse & Mortar Round," the compelling woman is just the angel of death passing over, skimming the heads below.

But whatever she amounts to as symbol or propaganda for either Americans or Vietnamese, the woman soldier was a reality for North Vietnam, where she and her companions were dubbed "The long-haired warriors" by Ho Chi Minh. In 1986, Carol Lynn Mithers reported that the North Vietnamese government had recorded the deaths of 250,000 female fighters (Mithers, 81). In 1999, Sandra C. Taylor examined other statistics: "From 1914 to 1965, according to one Communist Vietnamese source, female revolutionaries in the South suffered 250,000 deaths, 40,000 disabilities as the result of torture, and 36,000 imprisonments" (Taylor, 58–59). Taylor questions the reliability of any of these figures but follows up on the huge role of women in armed resistance from the fight to overthrow the French through the American War. Taylor's study, *Vietnamese Women at War*, is based on interviews with northern women who fired weapons, provided intelligence, and toted loads of up to two hundred pounds of war supplies on the Ho Chi Minh Trail. In the south, Taylor interviewed women who went to prison and were tortured, beaten, and starved in the infamous tiger cages for their efforts. In any case, she demonstrates that the reality of their existence is not debatable. Armed resistance was not confined to the north, however:

As the war progressed, women increasingly participated in militia and guerilla units. In a South Vietnamese NLF publication, probably written in 1970, the anonymous author stated that "women made up the greater part in the militia units." (Taylor, 61)

Rand Corporation interviews during the war show both prisoners and defectors among these women soldiers; Vietnamese documents occasionally complain about the quality of recruits; propaganda documents undoubtedly move towards stylization and exaggeration. Nevertheless, women throughout Vietnam were an integral part of the actual fighting forces.

Lady Borton, who served in Quang Ngai province from 1969–1971 as a hospital worker for Vietnamese civilians, quotes a Vietnamese woman she meets after the war, in her memoir, *After Sorrow*:

"We did everything!" Second Harvest said. "We climbed mountains, we hid under rivers. We captured prisoners. We carried ammunition. We trained ourselves to use weapons. We guided the soldiers when they wanted to attack the American base at Binh Duc. We were the guides, *we* were the spies. Don't you see? Ours was a citizens' war. *We* were the women fighters." (29)

In this conflict, "the long-haired warrior" was a fertile source of mythic amazement to the American soldiers. In Jim Nye's brief prose sketch, "Water Detail," the protagonist is the deadly one, meeting Her. A soldier blunders up to a stream to fill the squad's canteens, the sound of water covering his movements. He comes upon a person in black, and freezes, still out of sight. Encounters of this kind are always a blend of risk and eros:

The person was in black with a brown headband, an AK47 and a small pack. He saw that it was a young woman who sat on her heels, still as a stone, as her eyes swept back and forth.

He had his hand on the M-16 across his legs. He wanted for her to sense his presence in the shadows. But she didn't. She finally leaned the AK against a branch and as she filled her water bottle he slid the safety to single fire. The movement of the water bottle covered the tiny click. (Nye, 27–29)

In Stanley Kubrick's scene of soldiers converging on a Vietnamese woman sniper in *Full Metal Jacket* (screenplay by Kubrick, Michael Herr, and Gustav

Hasford), the woman, captured and wounded, begs at hideous length to be shot. And she is. The whole scene, in the film that the scriptwriters Kubrick, Herr, and Hasford have eased from the carcass of Marine combat correspondent Hasford's novel, *The Short-Timers*, on which the movie is said to be "based," reworks and repositions this scene as the final episode of the film. In the climax of Hasford's novel, it is an unknown sniper of unidentified gender who picks off a squad one by one. There is an earlier chapter in which Joker, the central character, kills a female sniper at the Citadel in Hue:

> The sniper is the first Victor Charlie I've seen who was not dead, captured, or far, far away. She is a child, no more than fifteen years old, a slender Eurasian angel with dark, beautiful eyes, which, at the same time are the hard eyes of a grunt. She's not quite five feet tall. Her hair is long and black and shiny, held together by a rawhide cord tied in a bow. Her shirt and shorts are mustard-colored khaki and look new. Slung diagonally across her chest, separating her small breasts, is a white cloth tube fat with sticky reddish rice. Her B. F. Goodrich sandals have been cut from discarded tires. Around her tiny waist hangs a web belt from which dangle home-made hand grenades with hollow wooden handles, made by stuffing black powder into Coca-Cola cans, a knife for cleaning fish, and six canvas pouches containing banana clips for the AK-47 assault rifle slung on her back. (Hasford, 116–17)

Even more than Jim Nye's Vietcong woman, the controlled pathos of Hasford's description echoes the tone of an anthropologist sighting a rare and glorious species, one whose quaintly primitive but deadly equipment evokes irony, respect, and pity. But after another of his buddies shoots this girl without killing her, Joker says, boiling down all the previous description of the novel's inner/over voice to one dismissive noun, "we can't leave the gook like this." Animal Mother, another squad member, tells Joker to waste her, which Joker does, proving his status as "hard," as a real hard-core Marine and a real grunt.

In the following chapter, the novel concludes in a scene with a sniper, which focuses on whether Joker will sacrifice the whole squad to retrieve their wounded: the unseen sniper of the novel clearly intends to suck each member of the squad into range, killing them off one by one as they attempt rescue. Hasford's novel climaxes not with women and mercy, but with the relations among men. Animal Mother has said to Joker: "Marines never abandon their dead or wounded, Mr. Squad Leader, *Sir*." And when Joker gives the order to move on, abandoning the wounded, Animal Mother growls at him, pointing his M60 waist-high, "Stand down or I will cut you in half" (Hasford, 173).

Hasford's Joker's devastating response to Animal Mother and the U.S. Marine code is to turn instead and shoot Cowboy dead, their mate who is pinned down, audibly, visibly dying in the unreachable jungle in front of them. He moves the remnant of the squad on to safety, leaving the unknown sniper in undisputed possession of the field. After the initial disabling shots by the sniper, Cowboy kills off two of the dying men, and then before Animal Mother can kill Joker, Joker kills Cowboy, his buddy since Parris Island. A lot of bodies litter the final pages, and guns are turned on Marines by Marines.

Unlike Gustav Hasford the novelist, Stanley Kubrick the filmmaker maintains a triumphant enactment of the heroic myth and assembles "a Hollywood movie": even if the novel, in the voice of Animal Mother, growls deep in its throat, "'This ain't no Hollywood movie, Joker'" (Hasford, 177). It is a curious symmetry, too, that Kubrick chooses a downed woman sniper over one unknown and victorious. But the pivotal issue, and Joker's rite of passage, whether to carry out the suicidal rescue attempt, is what Hollywood, in the person of Kubrick, refused. Kubrick elevates the death of the woman *and* secures the safety of the squad *and* denies the drama of insubordination *and* fudges the retrieving of the dead. For Kubrick and for Hollywood, heroic masculinity demands the presence of a subjugated female to displace the center of quarreling warrior brothers and, if not the confirmation of heroic rescue, than at least its elision. And once again the most unpleasant realization is dodged: that the Vietnamese enemy, undertechnologized and frequently feminine, won over superior American force.

Hollywood and Kubrick represent wishes for an alternate reality that dies hard. In a similarly mythic mode, and with the same feverish sense of hyperrealism, in Nye's "Water Detail," whatever happens, the narrator must persuade us that his movements are orderly, soldierly, necessitous. Nye's soldier

> slowly raised the M-16 until she was in its sights and as he began to squeeze the trigger she took off her headband, dipped it in the water, unbuttoned her shirt and began wiping herself with the cool, wet rag. He watched as she rinsed herself, her small breasts moving from the pressure of her hand. (Nye, 27)

We might be preparing for a rape; here, however, the little death is neatly exchanged for the big one, and there is no "double veteran," the Vietnam soldier's term for someone who both murders and rapes. The narrator sees his own girlfriend in the Vietcong soldier's movements, and flashes back atavistically to other smells: "of sex, perfume, Coors—he closed his mind." And the poem goes on to an unrelenting and obliterating fire.

The death is followed by his buddies' disapproval; conflict again erupts between soldiers in the settling of soldier ethics, and women literally embody the conflict. Nye's squad members think his protagonist should have raped the Vietcong woman and let her go. His response:

> He stopped and turned to Johnson. As he did he lifted his M-16 with his right hand and slapped the safety to automatic with his thumb. He put the muzzle under Johnson's jaw and pulled him close with his left hand. Johnson couldn't move.
>
> "You dumb, fucking asshole. You been here three months you're still a cherry. You think she see you, she fall in love? Sneak in through the perimeter and fuck you? Fuck you to death, man. You stay outta my sights. I got 15 days left—just stay away from me." (Nye, 28)

The residual message of both *The Short-Timers* and "Water Detail" is of survival in impotent, unhappy isolation. The whole mixed, confused code—protect women, have sex with them and don't kill them, or have sex with them *and* kill them, with eternal loyalty not to women but to men, and save your buddies whatever you do—goes up in bang-bang. For Hasford's Joker: "*Semper Fi*, Mom and Dad, *Semper Fi*, my werewolf children. Payback is a motherfucker" (179). When Nye's narrator returns home, sexual response to his girlfriend has been arrested by emasculating memory of what he has made of reality. The simpler wartime assent to the displacement of sexual pleasure by killing proves irreversible, making repatriation problematic. Nye's piece ends with any guilt for the death of the Vietnamese woman being sublated into inconsolable mourning for the death, hitherto unmentioned, of male friends: "he was alive and his friends were dead. His life stretched before him like a long, straight river, all upstream, and he was very, very tired." In any case, masculine potency and masculine bonding crumble within war's corrosive agreements, and women are their indeterminate sign.

Rape, injury, and death are intermittently audible and visible; nor do the poems fail to show the moves by which women, through silence or withholding, maintain the upper hand. In Walter McDonald's "New Guy," kneeling washerwomen silently but obdurately refuse to move aside for the naked

American male about to shower (in Mahony, 41). Within the strict measures of the sonnet "Vermont" (1988), years later David Huddle's speaker still feels the sting of an old rebuff:

> I'm forty-one. I was twenty-three then.
> I'm here with what I've dreamed or remembered.
> I spent some time with the most delicate
> sixteen-year-old girl who ever delivered
> casual heartbreak to a moon-eyed GI.
> I am trying to make it balance, but I
> can't. Believe me, I've weighed it out:
>
> rising that morning up to the cool air where
> the green land moved in its own dream there,
> and I was seeing, the whole flight back to Cu Chi,
> a girl turning her elegant face away
> after I'd said all I had to say.
> This was in VietNam. Who didn't love me.
>
> (Huddle, 11)

In a country hallucinatorily beautiful and full of danger, young men could buy and plead for love, comfort, and respect and get about as much of it as they no doubt deserved.

In painful retrospect, former soldiers continue mentally to exhume their earlier contact with Vietnamese women, belatedly enlarging the meanings they have begun to understand, as memory of efforts at love twine murkily and inseparably around memories of hostility, the blind, boyish quotient of unconscious egotism embarrassingly naked to the older, remembering eye. Bruce Weigl writes in "Short":

> There's a bar girl on Trung Hung Do who has half a ten-piaster note I tore in my drunken relief to be leaving the country. She has half and I have half, if I can find it. If I lost it, it wasn't on purpose, it's all I have to remember her. She has a wet sheet, a PX fan, PX radio, and half a ten-piaster note, as if she cared to remember me. She thought it was stupid to tear money and when I handed it to her she turned to another soldier, new in country, who needed a girl. I hope I burn in hell. (Weigl, *Song*, 17)

The short-timer's drunken sentimental ritual has given away to a sober realization of exactly what he has transacted and not transacted with this woman,
what he has left behind, and what he has not been able to leave behind. Nye,
Huddle, and Weigl's stark little pieces, crossbreeding the tones and rhythms
of prose and poetry, condense the tangential, incommunicable miseries, the
self-deceptions and mutual exploitations of race and gender opposition that
power is powerless to dissolve.

The final stanza of Wilfred Owen's "The Last Laugh" makes a *liebestod*, a
love-death, that only illustrates war's pitiless ironies of destruction:

> 'My Love!' one moaned. Love-languid seemed his mood,
> Till, slowly lowered, his whole face kissed the mud.
> And the Bayonets' long teeth grinned;
> Rabbles of Shells hooted and groaned;
> And the Gas hissed.
>
> (Owen, *Complete Poems*, 1:168)

But decades later, Bruce Weigl's "What Saves Us" explores the rivering underground of erotic climax and where its onset touches or joins love, death,
and dissolution in war. This war poem looks with less passivity and less fatalism at the eroticized bond between a company of men dedicated to death.

In more sharply heterosexual terms, Bruce Weigl prods the mysterious
junction where the self leaves the body and dies—and lets his poem vault into
something else. "What Saves Us" begins:

> We are wrapped around each other
> in the back of my father's car parked
> in the empty lot of the high school
> of our failures, sweat on her neck
> like oil. The next morning I would leave
> for the war and I thought I had something
> coming for that, I thought to myself
> that I would not die never having
> been inside her body.

In the midst of this urgent scrambling, the protagonist's girlfriend reaches for
a crucifix:

FIGURE 12. Bruce Weigl (*left*) and Doug Anderson (*right*) in the village of Nui Kim Son, south of Da Nang, January 2000. Photo by Kevin Bowen.

> She put it around my neck and held me
> so long that my heart's black wings were calmed.
> We are not always right
> about what we think will save us.
> I thought that dragging the angel down that night
> would save me, but I carried the crucifix in my pocket
> and rubbed it on my face and lips
> nights the rockets roared in.

All of this part so far is ordinary: holy love wins out over profane, and the woman is reduced to her guardian or mother function. But in the very next and closing lines:

> People die sometimes so near you,
> you feel them struggling to cross over,
> the deep untangling, of one body from another.
>   (Weigl, *What Saves Us*, 21; also in Mahony, 31)

It is the winding and rubbing of crucifix and car-closed bodies together, of love, sex, and faith, that constitutes what saves us. The "save" is the abrasion of our senses and our ordinary identities and their breaking down within the extremity of love and death. Where love and death heighten and shorten all the moments into timelessness, we are released from one body of space to an unknown other, crossing over and out from the deep and desperate tangle of limbs and creased consciousness that war brings about. Or maybe, in some place of absolute terror and resignation, some place inexplicably resembling the ones we are brought to by love and faith, we are able to hear the soul struggling to be free of the body, or the body in its last struggle to be free of the soul.

While their presences illuminate poem after poem, "woman" or "girl" time and again look like signifiers emptying out their signified. Because the jostle of conflicted content makes stable signification impossible, or because the content of the sign is too fluid and fast, "woman" and "girl" are the constant sources of painfully labile dread, guilt, confusion, and desire.

In the oldest, most exiguous form of male definition, women exist not as women, but as the other half of the excluding binary that the male imagination so often constructs, in which gender consists not of men and women, but of men and not-men. Carol Lynn Mithers shows how war only strengthens this thinking:

> Although women require the presence and attention of men to "prove" their femininity, men cannot become men except in the *absence* of women. If combat is to "make" men, women cannot be included. "War," said General Robert H. Barrow, Commander of the U.S. Marines, in 1980, "is man's work." (Mithers, 82–83)

In the Freudian logic of the eternal return of the repressed, women as not-men therefore turn up everywhere in the armed forces. Even in basic training, McAvoy Lane tells us in "On the Yellow Footprints" (1973) how the drill sergeant introduces himself:

> "Well now, look at this unsightly herd,
> Standin' there passin' the crud to one another
> Without even movin.'
> My name is Briant, girls.
> I'm your mother now,
> And I'm going to give you some motherly advice,
> Quit on me,

And I'll show you a short cut back to the old
Neighborhood,
Right through your ass.
Is that clear?"

(In Ehrhart, *Carrying*, 164)

Women treacherously materialize in all male precincts as the soldierly universe struggles to complete its human self, even if only by a parodic inclusion
of female roles and traits, to be etched with fear and loathing. Here is Gloria
Emerson on feminized soldiers:

> a mountain boy tell[s] me what he thought of "lifers." The enlisted men
> called the career officers "lifers," . . . The boy was in a mortar crew; he was
> saying that he thought lifers didn't really like women or want them around
> much. And then he said something startling and wise: "We are their
> women. They've got us."
>
> He meant the enlisted men and he was right. I had always known how
> women were leashed, confined, made so small and uncertain. But in Viet-
> nam, among the most helpless and humiliated were the soldiers themselves.
> (Emerson, 7)

In the parodic family of wartime masculinity, at the bottom of the heap, the
untrained grunt is sweated down to the dangerous feminine, a quality for these
largely unmarried and untested adolescents that is unnervingly and uncontrol-
lably everywhere as a threatening position of changefulness and vulnerability.
Given the prominence of women as regular and irregular soldiers in the Vietnamese army, the gender alignment in the American soldier's experience of either enemy or friend in this world must have been profoundly disorienting.

In 1962, at the very beginning of U.S. involvement in Vietnam, Jan Barry
catches a horrified glimpse of a nun burning herself in a street demonstration:
"flames and a smoke plume her terrible costume" (in Ehrhart, *Carrying*, 27).
Toward the end, millions can remember a naked prepubescent girl running
down a street, her clothes burned from her body by napalm, her round mouth
making a sound that the photograph fortunately prevents us from hearing. In
Phillip Mahony's anthology *From Both Sides Now*, no fewer than three poems
re-evoke this photograph; there must have been many more. But the sudden,
silent, and uninterpretable in woman's shape remains a running subject, literally and metaphorically.

In Doug Anderson's "Ambush" (1991) the confusion is literal:

There is a woman running past
tripping on her ao dai, but no, it's not.
Before I can shout a warning the garment comes unsashed,
instead of womanflesh, an automatic rifle
flashes in an arc, and firing from the hip,
the man runs for his life.

     (In Mahony, 84)

In Elliott Richman's "The Woman He Killed" (1994), it is indeed an armed woman that a door gunner in a Huey faces:

Black hair waving in Laotian wind,
blouse rustling in updraft
she looked so young and beautiful
even as she attempted to blow me
away with a handgun,
the only weapon she had.

     (In Mahony, 71)

In a dance under tracer light his machine gun saws her in half. Whether or not Richman's poem draws from actual experience, he plays out a deadly encounter in language close to sadomasochistic fantasy. But in reality or in fantasy, the complicated gender politics of Vietnam were usually beyond a nineteen year old's comprehension. More than war poems of any other era, Vietnam war poems try to tell the individual stories at the flashpoints clustering around gender and violence, within the flammable arenas of power, desire, fear, and sex.

But the codes of behavior are bewildering beyond what any of us might have been prepared to face. Jon Forrest Glade's "Blood Trail" (1998) tells another of those terse stories, the specialty of Vietnam War free verse, that reads like a parable. The speaker holds a man in his sights, shoots, but sees the man get up and run away:

We followed the blood trail
and found only an abandoned pack.
The lieutenant took the cash,

the men divided the food,
Intelligence was sent the love letters
and I got the credit
for a probable kill.

There are still further consequences. From the contents of the abandoned love letters, intelligence identifies the woman who wrote them as living in the southern provinces:

Which meant she was arrested,
beaten, raped, locked in a tiger cage,
forced to eat her own excrement
and beaten again.

If she confessed, she was executed.
If she refused to confess, she was executed.
It was a funny war.
I shot a man.
I killed a woman.
(In Mahony, 67)

Again, it is the enemy body, with its deadly and frustrating shape shifting, in which an invisible male corpse metamorphoses into an unseen woman victim. Whatever the elusive gender, each amorphous body produces terror and shame, explosive frustration, and, in the test of masculinity that war continuously imposes, frequent exposure of the impotent, wartime will.

The average soldier in Vietnam was nineteen years old, not the twenty-six of World War II. As poets look back on their adolescent selves encountering women in the opening passages of their adult lives, their poems record with a soul-scraping honesty how the tables could be turned in the power relation between American men and Asian women. Even under duress, women keep the power to mock and reject, flaunt indifference, or shrug at need with incomprehension. At times, the predictable and ubiquitous abuse could be deflected or unexpectedly altered or reversed in the complex drift of relationships.

Even the terror of the ultimate sexual wound did not escape articulation, becoming one more item of threatening impotence to list and fear. Basil Paquet's "Basket Case" (1972) goes a nightmare step beyond Wilfred Owen's "Disabled" to spell out the furthest range of sexual trouble. In "Basket Case," the phallic anger of the mine not only emasculates its victim, but reverses the usual course of wartime rape:

> I waited eighteen years to become a man.
> My first woman was a whore off Tu Do Street,
> But I wish I never felt the first wild
> Gliding lust, because the rage and thrust
> Of a mine caught me hip high.
> I felt the rip at the walls of my thighs,
> A thousand metal scythes cut me open,
> My little fish shot twenty yards
> Into a swamp canal.
> I fathered only this—the genderless bitterness
> Of two stumps, and an unwanted pity
> That births the faces of all
> Who will see me till I die deliriously
> From the spreading sepsis that was once my balls.
>   (In Rottmann, Barry, and Paquet, 20)

No other war poetry explores the rage, grief, fear, and misdirected potencies of wartime sexuality with quite the same range and density.

Other boundaries involving race as well as gender blurred, like the boundaries between children and adults, between cross-cultural norms of sexual encounter, between conquest and service. Doug Anderson's poem, which bears the ambiguous title "Purification," from *The Moon Reflected Fire*, a book published in 1994 and dedicated to "the Vietnamese and Americans who knew this war," was published many years after the period which produced it. The poem runs:

> In Taiwan, a child washes me in a tub
> as if I were hers.
> At fifteen she has tried to conceal
> her age with makeup, says her name is *Cher*.
> Across the room,
> her dresser has become an altar.
> Looming largest,
> photos of her three children, one black,
> one with green eyes, one she still nurses,
> then a row of red votive candles, and in front,

a Buddha, a Christ, a Mary.
She holds my face to her breasts, rocks me.
There is blood still under my fingernails
from the last man who died in my arms.
I press her nipple in my lips,
feel a warm stream of sweetness.
I want to be this child's child.
I will sleep for the first time in days.

> (Anderson, 11)

The poem opens itself to the shattered moralities of the narrator's position. He allows himself no easy forgiveness. In the explicit words of the poem, it is a violated child from whom the soldier-medic receives sexual and emotional comfort, and he makes us all peer under her layers of makeup to find this child. But the chain of responsibility extends from him, the one who displaces the true suckling, to the other men of presumably American and multiethnic background who have been his predecessors.

The integrity of the "fifteen year-old" is not taken away from her: this child mother is adult enough to offer a genuine comfort and purification; she has a sturdy identity, taken even from the soldiers and the war who have robbed her of her own traditional culture, in which she may have received other kinds of serenity or violation than the ones recorded here. Nor is the ritual of cleansing debased through its varied dispersal of the presiding sacred images. It is too complicated to explain these two people, to finger every edgy possibility: only the gestures, like names, dates, and places, can give us the flash compression or the leaky dignities of the poem, a poem that very likely could not be written until years of reflection went into the consciousness that eventually uttered it.

Many of the poems that Phillip Mahony reprints in *From Both Sides Now* enlarge the scope of the previous anthologies by adding Vietnamese voices. Published in 1998, at a point when American defeat and Vietnamese victory had been established as facts long enough for both sides to get used to them, Mahony includes poems that make stabs at reconciliation, or at least at bridging the raw and festering oppositions. There is a generous selection of poems in translation from North and South Vietnamese soldiers and survivors and many that describe the troubled fusion of races created by the war. Mahony's collection is the first to deal extensively with the war's intergenerational, cross-national impact.

In the English of Vietnamese Americans like Barbara Tran, Bao-Long Chu, and Christian Nguyen Langworthy, Mahony lets us hear the emigrant and orphaned children's voices, strained and anxious. There are many prostitutes in Vietnam War poems, but from Barbara Tran's angle in "The Women Next Door" (1996), we are made to feel what it was like for the Vietnamese under American rule. Tran describes a curious child watching the neighbor whores perform:

> their cries
> always seemed pained and they were always
> on the bottom as if hiding their bodies
> under the large, pale American men.
>> (In Mahony, 153)

Until the war's aftermath, there was no broad publication by Vietnamese in English spelling out the trashing of women that is war's first wound. Not all the rapists were American. In the voice of a boat person who made it to the other side, Bao-Long Chu writes of her bond to her raped mother in "This Is the House I Pass through Daily" (1995):

> on that boat we were flesh
>> to flesh, because my mother
>>> breathed hard, clutched my hand
>
> every time
> a man came to her. Her body saved me. Not milk.
>> Not food. And not my father,
>>> who came after us,
>
> not knowing
> how my mother wanders from him, how I stand guard
>> over this house she has made
>>> smooth from such sharp stones.
>>>> (In Mahony, 257)

Still other poems tune in on the parental generation left on the home front, or replanted in Paris or California or Minnesota. In these later collections, a huge story is wheeling into place and completing itself—healing, or not healing, the survivors.

In their 1991 anthology of women's writing on the Vietnam War, *Visions of War, Dreams of Peace*, Lynda Van Devanter and Joan A. Furey add a sampling of the voices of the nearly 15,000 American women, largely nurses and medical personnel, who served their own memory-bruising tours of duty, and who barely register in the books we've scanned so far.[3] According to Mithers (81), eight women of that nearly 15,000 died in or near combat duty.

Why were they ignored for so long? Is it because the jobs performed by these women were so much within the convention of what women in wartime are expected to provide? The shock and dangerous allure of the Vietnamese women was unexpected, so little in conformity with what American troops had imagined in advance, and worth recording; perhaps when women of their own class and race moved forward into risk and trauma, they merely presented the known, the too-familiar. Or is it simply, as W. D. Ehrhart later suggested to me in conversation, that because their numbers were relatively small in comparison to the huge number of American men mustered up for war, that American women who were there hardly made a dent in consciousness? Most men who were wounded saw male medics exclusively.

The reports of wartime nursing experience that Van Devanter and Furey collect, themselves veteran nurses, are scalding. A nurse identified only as Dusty writes: "I went to Vietnam to heal / and came home silently wounded." Later she adds in an epigraph:

There is nothing more intimate than sharing someone's dying with them. When you've got to do that with someone and give that person, at the age of nineteen, a chance to say the last things they are ever going to get to say, that act of helping someone die is more intimate than sex, it is more intimate than childbirth, and once you have done that you can never be ordinary again. (In Van Devanter and Furey, 121)

In these writings, for women as for men, the sense of battlefield experience as indelible and distinguishing persists, but the offices and duties have been notably different—even as the impact bears the same weight.

The core of pain, loss, and neglect embedded in these artless, sleeve-tugging narratives cannot and should not be resisted or denied. But as poetry, most of *Visions of War, Dreams of Peace*, with its forced rhythms, taste for the neat moral finish, and general flatness of language and blunt unimaginative-ness about its uses, disappoints. Half a dozen poems by Vietnamese women, who in translation never quite manage to cross the language barrier, add little and integrate the collection awkwardly. In the poems by nurses, there is a hopeful quality of women newly licensed to speak—but in most of the poems, technique founders under the stimulus set. The editors say plainly:

> Some of the works contained in this anthology may not be what is referred to as great literature, but first writings rarely are. We believe the poems and thoughts in this book have great value beyond their literary quality. They help people to understand the reality of war from a perspective rarely seen or acknowledged. (Van Devanter and Furey, xxiii)

If "great literature" simply meant greater ornamentation, the assessment of these poems would be correct. But in settling for too much of the flat reportorial over too little of the timely edit, the writers cede the possibilities of literature; the witness given suffers within its overly modest ambition. But for the experience in poetry of American women in and next to combat in this war, this volume is still all that we have. Next to the copious and already winnowed production of poems by men, produced by the approximately 2.5 million American men who enlisted for service in Vietnam, maybe we should bear in mind that the subset of at most 55,000 American women who went along necessarily makes for a smaller talent pool by comparison.

Enlarging on their habitual reticence, an inner check whereby army and navy nurses and Red Cross workers govern themselves not to complain and certainly not to be angry at anybody—which does not appear to be the best training for revelation in poetry—Kathryn Marshall explores other reasons for why women's writing took longer to surface:

> Another explanation for both their invisibility and their silence is that, by and large, women in Vietnam were caretakers and helpmates. They had been trained to take care of people, sick people, children. And they "did" for men because, in the military and elsewhere, that's what women did. By training and by habit they downplayed their own feelings and denied their own needs. The men's experiences, or the patient's or the child's feelings, came first. They were used to being minor characters in their own lives. (Marshall, 12)

In another of W. D. Ehrhart's anthologies, the novelist James Crumley is cited, saying that the average American's picture of war was framed by "millions of comic books and B movies" (in Ehrhart, *Unaccustomed Mercy*, vii). An error corresponding to the comic-book model may be to think that, like physical violence, deep feeling can be lifted from the diary entry and easily cropped and trimmed into a poem. With some of the picks in *Visions of War, Dreams of Peace*, you wish wistfully that the poem had stopped here, or here, or here. In too many, a stream of powerful, urgent data assembles itself, but the writer fishes from it only too randomly to draw out the final "poem."

Generally, women veterans have been more comfortable in prose, and it is to memoir, diary, and interview that we have to turn for amplification of what happened to them. Lynda Van Devanter publishes five of Lady Borton's poems with their tight-lipped little summaries in *Visions of War, Dreams of Peace*. It is impossible to forget the knifing facts of "Vo Thi Truong," in which a three year old sleeps in the spilled urine under her paraplegic mother's hospital bed. The mother, who took a bullet in her spinal cord while planting rice, may live another month, but in the meantime, before Borton picks Truong up to take her to a nearby day care center, it is Truong's job to bring her mother tea, fix her intravenous feed, and empty her catheter. There is no one else to do this: no other family member is still alive and all others are overwhelmed with other cares (Van Devanter and Furey, 21).

Only in the amplitude of Lady Borton's memoirs, however, in *Sensing the Enemy*, drawn from a six-month experience in 1980 as a director of a refugee camp for Vietnamese boat people in Malaysia, and in *After Sorrow*, written after a series of visits to a recovering postwar Vietnam, does the harrowing totality of her experience, along with the quirky richness of her reflections on it, emerge. Her poems clip the human exchanges she has observed, caging and blunting them within unnatural line breaks; but in her prose, those apparently inconsequential moments that define the observed Vietnamese as well as the American observing them, pulse within the complex collisions and contradictions of the life spreading open before her eyes.

Many Americans note the size inequality between Americans and Vietnamese; Lady Borton ("Lady" is her given name, not a title) makes one aware of the operation of this difference when, as a tall woman, she stoops to fit feet and legs to the cramped steps of an Asian latrine or puts even a slender American rump, still beamy by Vietnamese measure, on a cyclo. Many Americans wrote in passing of the blackened teeth of Vietnamese country women, but Lady Borton, characteristically wanting to know more, finds that on some women it is lacquering, a traditional cosmetic practice. She drinks everything, tastes everything, and notices everything with detached, affectionate curiosity. Unlike nearly all of the Americans currently writing about Vietnam, she learns the language, her ear grappling with the six tones of spoken Vietnamese. What does living as an administrator in a tropical refugee camp in 1980 mean?

> The dietary change from vegetables and goat's milk to rice and black tea made me constipated, and although I drank and drank, I urinated at most once a day. For those six months my menstrual cycles stopped. But my sweat glands worked overtime. Perspiration slid down my arms and back and legs even if I stood in the shade of a palm tree. My hair remained damp during the day though it dried at night, stiffened by my own salt. (Borton, *Sensing*, 40)

She sees herself through Vietnamese eyes: "a freak with white skin and copper-colored hair, which was kinky at that—a monster who loomed a head taller than everyone else, even the men" (*Sensing*, 8). The daily terrors—like the rats at Pulau Bidong that overrun her pillow at night and "turn her blood gray"—are succinctly noted. Then the rats return, flaring up in a whole chapter describing the unsuccessful campaign against the rats' evolutionary resourcefulness.

Confronted by one child's horrifying wound, memories of another child from ten years before in Quang Ngai province slip through. We learn a lot about Lady Borton in small, pungent doses: "I never voluntarily hold a baby. Infants bore me when they're contented; they terrify when they're squalling." At six or seven, she had announced to her family: "the world already had too many people and that they could make more if they wanted to, but I'd look after the ones who needed extra tending" (*Sensing*, 18).

Not everything makes it through a reticence partly ideological, partly temperamental. Lady Borton first went to Vietnam in 1969 and stayed until 1971, working for the American Friends Service Committee at the Friends' hospital for civilian and military casualties in Quang Ngai during periods of heavy fighting. Like the poet John Balaban, who performed similar services in Vietnam, Lady Borton did not shake the memories easily. The introduction to *Sensing the Enemy* takes paragraphs later published in poem form as "Row Upon Endless Row" in *Visions of War, Dreams of Peace* (53). In an earlier version, in prose tempo, however, Borton fills in slightly more of circumstance: in this effort, the words, like tired feet in shoes that finally fit them, are freed from line breaks to let us feel their full, sorrowing weight. Stretching before Borton, driving from Washington to Boston in 1971, and newly discharged from the war, is the vista of a graveyard:

> Rain started to fall and I slowed down. Thunder shook the air and with each crack like an exploding mortar, a sense of panic welled up from somewhere deep inside my chest. The tombstones went on and on like rows of parading soldiers. It rained harder and I turned up the radio. On the news, the President advocated more funding for the war in Vietnam.
>
> The rain pounded with the savagery of a monsoon, the wake from each passing truck breaking over my VW Bug thrusting it toward the guardrail. For a split second the wipers flicked the waves away and once again I saw gravestones, row upon endless row. The radio announcer listed the body count for American soldiers but disregarded Vietnamese. The tombstones and spires and mausoleums darkened, closing in; the road and the water grayed until panic washed over me.
>
> I pulled off onto the shoulder of the road and wept. (Borton, *Sensing*, 1–2)

This introduction does not lead tidily backwards in time toward an account of the hospital and day care center in Quang Ngai from 1969–1971. Instead, *Sensing the Enemy* fast-forwards to 14 February 1980. Lady Borton's wartime experience in Vietnam is still a huge elision, inaccessible to language and nameable only to other workers who have shared its tumults with her. A couple of introductory chapters, one titled "A Volcano," for the volcanic island set in the South China Sea on which she eventually landed, and a second titled "Madness," which once again returns to her immediate postwar life, grope kaleidoscopically for an explanation for what has pulled this seeker forward to what became a lifetime of involvement with the Vietnamese people. In all of these wartime poems, heroism and glory have been scarce commodities. Sacrifice, born from pain, has been even more agonizingly in question, with the direction and point of the sacrifice hopelessly obscure. Loving war, loving risk itself, proves to be a grudging admission that a professional soldier like Jim Nye can make, but the role of the patriotic soldier sustains itself largely for the deluded or co-opted. The political indecencies of the Vietnam War meant that, filtered through illegitimate purpose, the only positive action left to American soldiers was to endure and survive; the only positive actions remaining for backup personnel was to assist that survival and to adopt rescue as the best mission. And yet, unslaked within the massive scope of war, and within severely straitened limits, people's desire for ethical conduct could not be wholly repressed.

What seems most hopeful in Lady Borton's career lies exposed in the dignity of what she pulled from the trauma of futility and shock that Vietnam left in her. Having gone to Vietnam originally as a conscientious objector, she chose an organization independent of American military money for her field of action. After her term as assistant director of refugee programs in Quang Ngai, she came home and tried to summarize her life in Vietnam in a novel. But fiction failed to serve her: late at night she throws her papers on the bed, asking herself "Why bother? Who cares?" And then a familiar kind of flashback intervenes:

> I heard gunshots and looked across the brown fields to the far ridge. Men carrying shotguns against orange vests appeared over the hilltop. They were dragging a carcass. Hunters, I told myself, but then I heard the *chop-chop* of a helicopter, saw it graze the hill, watched it unload men in green fatigues. They carried M-16 rifles. Other choppers landed, disgorging men. I could see the soldiers' faces: high school boys I'd taught, toddlers from Quang Ngai, neighborhood kids, the riders on my school bus. They began shooting. I saw a face blown away. I saw a body spin and tumble. (*Sensing*, 14)

After this, Borton "lived in a stupor for four or five days"; then, staring at the photographs of Vietnamese in her living room, she reminds herself of each fate, including "Toi, the thirty-year-old quadruple amputee prima donna of the Quaker Rehabilitation Center." She knows the end of Toi's story. Initially she was shot by Americans during the My Lai massacre;[4] assisted by other Americans who rehabilitate her with artificial legs, Toi returned to My Lai only to be wounded again in crossfire during an attack by the Vietcong. Once more treated at Quang Ngai and released again by Americans, Toi finally dies during an American bombing raid over her village.

Reviewing all this, Borton writes, "as I sat there rocking, gazing at the faces which for years had haunted me, I gradually abandoned the need to create fictional characters" (*Sensing*, 15). Keeping her income low enough so that it cannot be taxed and put in support of the war, Borton has taken on a job as a school bus driver for retarded children in a rural district in Ohio. Gradually, she accepts that her involvement will be direct intervention, that novels and poems will give way to memoir, and that for her, language will have only fractional power to heal a life split by war wounds.

The visions of unending war in *Sensing the Enemy* are very brief. The memories from the war are scattered blips, brief paragraphs: in one episode in the refugee camp on Pulau Bidong, she helps to quiet a hysterical patient and plunges us into her memory of an earlier period in Vietnam, when she visited Quang Ngai Prison. Because she speaks Vietnamese, Borton served the Quaker doctor on his weekly medical visit as an interpreter. During the visit, Borton wrestles another hysterical woman, a prisoner who has become frightened at the introduction of an instrument unknown to her, an otoscope. Borton's re-creation of both events fills with the tactile, aural detail that marks a close struggle:

> The woman jerks and moans, throwing herself back and forth, knocking her skull against the bed frame with a sound like a dull axe against wood. Quickly I scoot around on the cot, throwing my legs over her so that they surround her torso. Her head slaps against my thighs. Holding her wrists, I lean over her. The muscles down my back and legs stretch as she rips me from one side to the other, pulling my arms tight over her breasts then shrieking and hurling me away. Her mouth contorts with terror. Perspiration seeps from her body as she twists. Sweat runs down my forehead and cheeks; it slips off my chin and drops onto her twisted face.
>
> "*Thoi!*—Enough!" She screams, her eyes widening in horror as sheer as razors. Grimacing, she twists, throwing me and the prisoner holding her feet off balance.
>
> "*Thoi. Thoi,*" we each say softly.
>
> "*Thoi!*" she shrieks, letting forth a scream that slices our ears.

Eventually, they inject and subdue the woman. Lady Borton is told that she has just come from "down the street":

> "The new building?" I say in a low voice. American Seabees have recently completed an interrogation center. It's surrounded by barbed wire coils and protected with corner watch towers like a World War II concentration camp. American officers enter it every morning as I'm driving children to the Day Care Center. (*Sensing*, 131–33)

The prisoner, after making sure no one is around to overhear, reports: "They attached electrodes to her nipples." Lady Borton is part of the American team that helps put together one human being tortured and torn apart physically and mentally by another American team. The contradictions of her loyalties and missions never do make it together into one story. What we are allowed to see of Lady Borton's war emerges in layered scraps during the account of yet another mission after the war, when the only answer to the war's scarring is not to make words, but to take on further rescue. She says, as she finally heads for home: "I felt as if Bidong had cured me of a long, painful illness." Yet Borton acknowledges that the cure will never heal permanent rifts of consciousness. A refugee, Bach, who is waiting for a reply from his American sponsor to complete his departure, tells Borton,

> "You're half Vietnamese, I think."
> "Perhaps," I replied in Vietnamese, "just as you're half American. And neither of us will ever feel whole in either country." (*Sensing*, 174)

The point that the poems in *Visions of War, Dreams of Peace* make movingly again and again is the violation of healthworkers' ability to feel; after a traumatizing exposure to the deep and ugly wounds that modern warfare drew these medics and nurses in to treat, they received little notice or help from anyone. As much on the front lines of pain and injury as combat troops, and occasionally directly within artillery range, their job was to put back together the men, women, and children that men in uniform were busy taking apart: the skill in either operation was almost equal. Of the women in service, Carol Lynn Mithers observes :

> The vast majority were nurses, low-ranking officers, but there were also enlisted women working as communications, intelligence, and language specialists, air-traffic controllers, and aerial reconnaissance photographers. As a group they were different from the men who carried the guns, on the average several years older and more educated. They were overwhelmingly white and middle-class, idealistic, often deeply religious "good girls" for whom the admonition to "ask what you can do for your country" was not political rhetoric but a moral imperative. All had volunteered to join the military; many specifically requested assignment to Vietnam. (Mithers, 75–77)

When they left Vietnam for home, they did not style themselves as victims. Many felt that "Vietnam became what almost every nurse would recall as the absolute peak of her professional career," yet as Mithers indicates:

The war's massive number of casualties—some 58,000 dead and at least 300,000 wounded—and one of the best medical evacuation systems in history (bringing men from combat to emergency room in half an hour) brought nurses an endless horror show of death and mutilation. Seventy-hour operating room shifts were spent patching bodies blown apart by mines, ripped by bullets and shrapnel and burned by napalm; helicopters came in "filled with hundreds and hundreds of body parts, arms, legs, heads." (Mithers here cites her interview with Pamela White; 76–77)

These "horror shows" had inevitable consequences. Penny Kettlewell, in "The Coffee Room Soldier" (1990), describes walking in for a coffee break to regroup from a "push" and stepping casually over a dead soldier about to be bagged for delivery home:

> I turned with cup in hand and ascertained the damage.
> His chest wall blown away, exposing his internal organs
> An anatomical drawing.
> Dispassionately I assessed his wounds
> and sipped from my cup.
>
> I then saw his face
> that of a child in terror
> and only hours ago
> alive as I
> or maybe I was dead as he,
> because with another sip, a cigarette and a detached analysis,
> I knew I could no longer feel.
>
> (In Van Devanter and Furey, 47)

There is more than one casualty in this room. Home from Vietnam, nurses disturbed by the same post–traumatic stress disorder that shook male veterans, within the same Vietnam veteran organizations that offered support to men, were once again expected to be not the tended victims but the tending caregivers. When Lynda Van Devanter, one of the editors of *Visions of War, Dreams of Peace*, enlisted for service in Vietnam, she was living out a dream of heroic adventure for both herself and her father. Her memoir, *Home Before Morning*, opens with a classic rush of adrenalin-fueled nightmare. Postwar sleeplessness brings her to traumatic memory, and in quick strokes, she details three separate occasions. Each of these instances moves her by blood-filled increments along to the climactic last: an extended account of a three A.M. call to service in the evacuation hospital at Pleiku in which Van Devanter has been working. Her narrative is classic war theater; danger threatens: rifles, artillery and mortars off in the distance. For protection, she has been asleep under her bed. But there are incoming wounded, and all the medical personnel rally. If nothing else, the sounds and breaking lights push one to respond with the urgency of the protagonists:

> I throw my flak jacket over one shoulder, my helmet onto my head, and race to the doorway of the hooch, my untied bootlaces dragging on the floor. By the time I reach the outside steps, my fatigue shirt is buttoned and the flak jacket is hoisted onto my other shoulder, one snap fastened to keep it from flapping.

Details of the clothing here are male and remind us that this is a soldier-nurse.

> Others are running ahead of me to the emergency room, their silhouettes sharply outlined by the flashing light of flares, exploding artillery rounds, and rockets. My heart is beating wildly.

But the scale of the scene in which the heart beats its thrilling strokes is monumental, the sound operatic in range, the whole thing also palpably beautiful:

> Miles away, red tracers rain down from Cobra gunships. The ARVN tanks are moving around the edges of our compound. Overhead, a helicopter begins its descent with more wounded as doctors, nurses, and medics push gurneys to the landing pad. The roar of the rotor blades becomes deafening.

The effects are all large. This is probably description that her cowriter, Christopher Morgan, could have arranged without Van Devanter's detailed memory because the scenes are now so familiar to all of us from countless war films and news footage. Van Devanter continues: the helicopter pilot is wounded but insists on going back for his next load: "It is the last time I will ever see him alive." Then there are more wounded, and finally, in the climax of the memory, Van Devanter turns in the ER to find a fellow medic—a good buddy she's partied with—lying on a gurney. She says:

Almost every man in his platoon has been killed or wounded tonight. Bennie has a gaping hole in his left side, exposing half his chest, another in his belly, and a bloody stump where his left leg used to be. Around the stump is a tourniquet that he probably applied by himself. (Van Devanter and Morgan, 16–19)

Van Devanter explains that Bennie's voice as he gives medical instructions for his surviving platoon members is "calm and well modulated, sounding like that of a precise and highly trained medic, and not that of a man with half of his body blown away." Bennie asks for an extra IV for someone going into shock, tells her to make sure to turn over another man for fragments in his back, and cautions the gas passer to go easy with "the crazy fucker who just finished eating six cans of beans and dicks before we got hit." She rushes off. But before she completes the night's work she passes a colleague pushing a dead body to the morgue, and in the logic that governs the war story we know that it is Bennie. But she tells us there is no time to feel, no time to mourn, because too many others are depending on her to keep them alive.

Van Devanter describes the "pushes," or mass casualty surgeries in evacuation centers to stabilize people before stateside attention as often lasting thirty-six, forty-eight, or on some occasions even seventy-two hours. Many times they never found out whether the people they were working over survived or not. Sleep deprivation was so severe that once "a surgical tech had fallen asleep and fell into an open belly while the doctor was repairing a kidney." In another case, through the quick astuteness of a surgeon moving his hands over the spread-out intestines of a wounded soldier, the bowel is run through yet a fifth time, and a fatality averted as the probing hands discover a new frag. On another night, because of incoming artillery they lower the operating table, and surgeon and scrub nurse bend over the patient on their knees. But over and over, Van Devanter discovers that the human body is made of damageable meat: on burn cases, nurses routinely cut away "entire chunks of flesh that was so crisp it could be broken in half."

As Kathryn Marshall notes:

In the Vietnam War, the small arms used by both sides were specifically designed to inflict massive, multiple injuries, as were the Americans' napalm, white phosphorous and "antipersonnel" bombs. Furthermore, because the country was small, because Americans had an enormous number of hospitals, and because helicopters—those ubiquitous symbols of the American military presence in Vietnam—could transport the wounded to base camps in a matter of minutes, soldiers lived who, in earlier wars, would have died en route. Even nurses with backgrounds in trauma surgery were unprepared for the kinds of injuries they saw. (Marshall, 6)

After seven months of steady exposure to these wounds and mutilations, what boundaries between life and death were being transgressed, and at what cost to those crossing them? What Faustian knowledge is truly possible to those breaking into the living body without enduring psychic penalty? And what needs do we ourselves bring to the reading of such accounts?

Much about Van Devanter's rocky road back to civilian life, marked by all the symptoms of post–traumatic stress disorder, matches what male soldiers have reported. In 1970 the Army dumped her, without much debriefing, back in San Francisco and failed to arrange further transport to her hometown. When the airport at which she found herself was shut down by strikes, she stepped out in her uniform, as she had for the past two years in similar predicaments in Vietnam, to hitch a ride. Unlike the friendly helicopters of American base life, the cars whizzed past for hours. Finally, one slowed down as though to stop for her, and as she ran alongside with her duffel, the driver, a college-age kid, leaned over, shouted, "Nazi bitch!" and spat on her. Someone else yelled out, "Welcome home, asshole!" (Van Devanter and Morgan, 211)

The most hurtful part of Van Devanter's account of this devastating period begins with her perception of herself as a nonperson even within the ranks of veterans themselves. As she walks through Washington, someone gives her a handbill for a Vietnam Veterans Against the War meeting. After much inner and outer consultation, partly because she is still in the Army and based at a military hospital and does not know if she is allowed to protest publicly, she goes to the meeting, and as the others start to line up outside for a parade, she takes a place up near the front. Van Devanter's memoir continues:

However, one of the leaders approached me. "This demonstration is only for vets," he said apologetically.

"I am a vet," I said. "I was in Pleiku and in Qui Nhon."

"Pleiku!" he exclaimed. "No shit! I used to be with the 4th infantry. You must have been at the 71st Evac."

"I worked in the OR."

"You people did a hell of a job," he said. "You folks saved my best friend's life." He smiled at me for a few moments while I shifted awkwardly under his praise.

"Do you have a sign or something I can hold?" I asked.

"Well," he said uncomfortably, "I . . . uh . . . don't think you're supposed to march."

"But you told me it was for vets."

"It is," he said. "But you're not a vet."

"I don't understand."

"You don't look like a vet," he said. "If we have women marching, Nixon and the network news reporters might think we're swelling the ranks with nonvets."

"I can prove I was in Vietnam."

"I believe you," he said. "But you can't be a member of our group. I'm sorry." (Van Devanter and Morgan, 31)

How were the handmaidens to cure themselves of the distresses imposed by wartime when their service could not be recognized even by the people whom they had accompanied and aided? The struggle simply to find a voice at all in that suffocating climate for what was happening to one's feelings must have superseded any attempt to produce literature.

Contrary to the assertions of all the anthologists whose selections stress sincerity or unique authenticity, and who claim to exclude literary reference, some literary modeling still clings to the poetry of the Vietnam War written by men. And if we study the brief biographical notice given for the male poets stocking the anthologies, we notice a large number now teaching in universities or lawyering or writing for newspapers or journals. Many, like Yusef Komunyakaa, John Balaban, Bruce Weigl, Doug Anderson, W. D. Ehrhart, Walter MacDonald, and David Huddle, were notably and permanently called to poetry. What Van Devanter's or Furey's women are doing now is neither given nor glimpsed, but what underlies this may be both gender and class differences in the education and aspirations of soldiers and soldier-nurses. It is certainly true, however, that all of these collections dedicated to the war include poems that are dogged by faltering meters, bland diction, and a lumbering style, and in many cases, wooden and inept-sounding translation. Certainly, the dip toward clumsy framing or sentimentalized pain in some women's writing is matched by a descent in their male counterparts to a comparably ineffective fusion of anguish and swagger, like "Coming Home" (1989), by Bill Shields:

it was real nice
to take a shit
& not watch
the worms
crawl out
my ass

If there is a debased romance of risk in the boys' adventure version of war, as Sandra Gilbert and Susan Gubar point out, there lives an equivalent romance of the feminine, as the nurse, the desexualized mother/sister, looms over an infantilized and incapacitated soldier (Gilbert and Gubar, 287). The secret of the lasting fascination with the theme of the dying comrade, or that of the dying soldier tended by the faithful nurse, may be that both allow for virtue in war by excising the moral discomfort of the murder at war's base with a sacralizing substitution of martyrdom and myths of fidelity instead. Accepting the stoic view that death in war is inevitable, we keep stubbornly turning glory not into the killing of enemies, but into the sacrifice of brothers and, in the armies of the future, of sisters as well.

But this is a set of values in tension with others. It seems the righting of a necessary balance of typologies and creeds that makes each of the anthologies return to the Vietnam Veterans Memorial Wall. One of the symbolically freighted accidents of the war's history saw a very young Asian American woman designated, through open competition, to bring her fitting memorial for the dead into being. If rape, pillage, and murder are war's not so very subterranean content, the side above ground has to be grief openly expressed and reconciliation effected, as we admit new vectors to our social rites, even if the residual feelings of bitterness and betrayal match Siegfried Sassoon's cold anger over the Menin Gate.

After Maya Lin provided the hands and eyes to configure earth, sky, and stone to make her brilliant and exalted locus of painful memory, she said of her monument:

I always saw the wall as pure surface, an interface between light and dark, where I cut the earth and polished its open edge. The wall dematerializes as a form and allows the names to become the object, a pure and reflective surface that would allow visitors the chance to see themselves with the names. I do not think I thought of the color black as a color, more as the idea of a dark mirror into a shadowed mirror image of the space, a space we cannot enter and from which the names separate us, an interface between the world of the living and the world of the dead. (Lin, 35)

That dark mirror is meant to counter what W. D. Ehrhart, standing before the memorial, calls "this / smell of rotting dreams" (in Mahony, 233).

Yet as a species, we are stalled in that smell. Back and forth, forth and back, Phillip Mahony's *From Both Sides Now* rocks between signs of healing—with accelerating commercial and emotional traffic between America and Vietnam—regret, remorse, and signals of forgiveness—the lot. Fifteen years after his war and his term as a conscientious objector, John Balaban goes back to Vietnam:

> Wandering the city that had suffered so much at American hands, it seemed to me that *it is only Americans who dwell on the war*, that the Vietnamese have undergone a "change of season," that they look to their futures not to their pasts, even though their present lives, marked by extreme poverty, are of course burdened by the past. (Balaban, *Remembering*, 309; italics in original)

But camping out, on the penultimate page, Greg Kuzma sets up "Peace, So That" (1972) as a series of furious epithets:

> every stinking son of a bitch
> can come home
> to his lawn mower and rice paddy,
> every punished son of a bitch
> can return to his father's bedside,
> every child of every bastard
> every child of every hero of peace
> of war
> can talk it over with the man he blames,

and then his rising assault on the angers of peace collapses in a glum finale: "And we be a long time at this" (in Mahony, 274). Yet Mahony cannot bring himself to stop here, and he ends the anthology with John Balaban's "In Celebration of Spring," a 1991 poem that opens, "Our Asian wars are over" and ends:

FIGURE 13. Lady Borton in 1990. Lo Thi Pua (*right*), president of the Women's Union in highland Son La Province, wrapped her headdress around Borton in the style traditionally worn by minority Black Thai women. Ha Thi Cham (*left*) was then the vice president of the Women's Union. Photo by Linda Marsella, 1990.

Swear by the locust, by dragonflies on ferns,
by the minnow's flash, the tremble of a breast,
by the new earth spongy under our feet:
that as we grow old, we will not grow evil,
that although our garden seeps with sewage,
and our elders think it's up for auction—swear
by this dazzle that does not wish to leave us—
that we will be keepers of a garden, nonetheless.

     (275)

I appreciate Balaban's necessary hopefulness, but Kuzma's angry despair seems nearer the truth; there is still no real closure in this subject.

For a glimpse at the possible shapes of closure, I would like to return to one of the final chapters of Lady Borton's *Sensing the Enemy*. She focuses steadily not on the American War or the conflicts between Vietnamese and Vietnamese that created the plight of the boat people she serves on Pulau Bidong, but in her last pages a potentially deadly conflict erupts. In "The Riot," Borton describes her struggle with a Vietnamese mob, consisting of boat people, who want to destroy other boat people accused of murder on the desperate voyage in which, from a group of 370 who set out, 28 were known to have died en route.

Watching the gathering mob at the shore, Borton is "paralyzed with fear." A reluctant swimmer, eventually she overcomes her terror of both people and water, and, moving toward the knots of men kicking and beating other men,

> I dashed to the group farthest out. Water swirled above my waist, everyone splashing, flailing, the victim moaning. The men pushed the prisoner under the water and held him there while they beat, beat. Grabbing at arms, I elbowed the assailants aside and yanked the man from the sea bottom. I shook him.

This rescue continues uncompromisingly as a bald first-person narrative: it is an "I" who dashes, grabs, yanks, and shakes. Later, "I dragged the bloodied man to the beach where I stood holding him up while the mob seethed around us." The outcome of Borton's predicament is *not* paralysis, is *not* passive or shamed immobility, but unabashed activism.

There is time enough to discover that the guilt of the victims is shakily established. There is more confabulation among Borton and two colleagues and with the Malaysian guard force; "I wouldn't run in that scrimmage," the guard's commander comments. And yet, one colleague mutters, "We'll do it." Borton continues:

> Leaving the others, I started to push the crowd back down the beach, which was jammed from the guards' compound past the fresh-water tanks and the hospital to the supply warehouse. Arms outstretched, my voice low and even, I paced slowly up and down in front of the crowd.
> "Move on back, now," I said in Vietnamese. "Move on back."
> "But they're VC!" the men protested. One tried to run past me. I grabbed his forearm and spun him around.
> The little boy named Vu, his masklike face contorted, yanked my shirt. He hardly came to my waist. "They killed my father!" He yelled over the mob's angry shouts.
> "If you kill your brothers," I answered, "whom will you live with?"

The mob boils over, roaring "Kill them!" Jim and Neville, Borton's colleagues, manage to get a wounded man on a stretcher and, fending off blows with feet and elbows, get man and stretcher behind the gate, which Borton slams in the face of the mob.

But they are not done yet. The mob drags two people back to the shore. Borton jumps off the jetty; she lifts a man up; squatting down and grabbing him around the buttocks she hauls him like a sack of oats to safety. She loses flip-flops, head scarf, pen. She's sopping. Her trousers are ripped across her thighs, hanging down in the back, and she is furious. Later, someone apologizes. At the market she buys new flip-flops with her damp ringgit, Malaysian money, and a stall owner fixes her watchband. The riot of the title has changed to an "incident" as the high feeling of the narrative subsides. As strangers stop her on the path, they say, "'The VC are cruel.'" "We are all cruel,'" Lady Borton responds (*Sensing*, 150–56). Moral indignation lends her words acts, her acts words.

All that lifting, yanking, hauling, pushing, climbing, dragging, and the frantic bodies churning in water! What keeps this heroic facing-down of a mob from boastfulness, though, is the clear burn of anger propelling a frightened Borton into righteous action. What has been missing from one guilt-soaked narrative after the other in this war has been the sound of that conviction driving the action. It seems a useful portent for future relations that the force of that anger, openly owned in a first-person telling, derives from a true mission of rescue, something massively, tellingly absent in the overall design and conduct of the American war itself.

Raids on Homer

All the bitter poetry that keeps pumping from the wounds of this war continues to churn up new speakers, new positions, new loyalties, and new hopes among the old griefs. In sharp contrast to the traditional rhyme and meter of so many earlier war poems, this work is enormously heterogeneous in style and literary orientation. The first soldier poems of the Vietnam War locate the range, with their flat colloquial diction, their forms close to joke, savage anecdote, and prose collage. Later poems from the 1980s and 1990s, by veterans like Bruce Weigl, Yusef Komunyakaa, and Doug Anderson, uncoil a whip lash of lyric intensity. Their poetry, tuned in the writing workshops that have flourished since the 1950s, draws energy from the post-Beat release from traditional forms, the cultural increase in sexual and personal candor, and the impact of feminist awareness. More recent Vietnam War poetry softens to admit a greater subtlety and a denser verbal music.

Other poets have begun to interpret their own wars in the light of Vietnam. Keith Wilson's *Graves Registry and Other Poems*, published in 1969, but based on his Korean War experience, and Rolando Hinojosa's *Korean Love Songs* (1978), for instance, make points about racism, imperial politics, and war guilt that only demonstrate how the wisdom gained in literature about the Vietnam War has come to shape our understanding of other wars, past or future. In one notable instance of this widening of reference, the title of Thomas McGrath's poem, "Ode for the American Dead in Korea," originally published in 1972 was emended to read "Ode for the American Dead in Asia" (McGrath, vii). When Andrew Hudgins published *After the Lost War* in 1988, he made the figure in his book, "Sidney Lanier," speak not as the nineteenth-century American poet who really did fight in the Civil War, but in the textures and sensibility of later veterans, closer kin to the voices surrounding Hudgins in the wake of the Vietnam War. Much as World War I came to encroach on the English presentation of World War II, American war poetry will continue to be similarly shadowed by the subjects and the cast of mind that made up war in the decade and a half of the Vietnamese-American conflict.

Since that war's end in 1975, poetry in English has come to include Vietnamese refugees publishing in America and children of former soldiers, former nurses, and medical workers. Veteran groups keep returning to Vietnam; Vietnamese keep coming here; the story expands, its style always more richly and riskily various. On into the millennium, many veteran poets, home again, begin to reclaim their ties with poetic tradition. Poets salt their poems ever more heavily with reference to earlier war poems. After publishing *Song of Napalm* (1988), Bruce Weigl collaborated with Thanh T. Nguyen to produce *Poems from Captured Documents* (1994). By 1980, John Balaban had already edited and translated Vietnamese folk poetry in *Ca Dao Vietnam*. R. L. Barth draws parallels with classical Greek and Latin texts in *Forced Marching to the Styx* (1983), and Doug Anderson, in his 1994 "Raids on Homer," a sequence of poems included in *The Moon Reflected Fire*, brilliantly interlaces archaic Greek and contemporary American war experience.

When art historian Peter Paret lucidly summarizes the visual representation of war over the centuries, he denies a common developmental line, wishing to emphasize "the general tendencies of the age," which are so likely to affect and bend specifics. Skeptically, with seductive common sense, he says:

Nor can we point to a single line of development in the representation of war in art from the Renaissance to our own day. The reflections in art of the great themes of life do not come together in orderly patterns, let alone coalesce into a clear line of development over centuries. (Paret, 112–15)

The line "broadens and fades," "is subject to sharp breaks." Yet war, in Paret's evocative words, a violent spectacle fascinating for "its closeness to fantasies of crime and punishment," as well as for its resistance to summary, still draws the artist to treat the common soldier as a pivotal concern, in fact, as "a principle regulating device." In older art, the common soldier appears and disappears in relation to those who call him out and lead him on, but in the twentieth century we are given "increasingly the images that are drawn and painted from perspectives that seek to be his." Goya, Callot, even the Renaissance masters, were fully aware of what war did to people, yet even Paret, the persuasive critic of theories of change, concludes: "But the frequency and openness of sorrow over war and criticism of war in modern art are new" (Paret, 112–15).

As with the graphic arts, so literature: these traits became true of poetry from World War I on, well past the matter of Yeats's deploring the unmanly and unimaginative decadence of Wilfred Owen's version of realism, all the way to the guilt-soaked poetry of the Vietnam veteran. Yet while R. L. Barth's *Forced Marching to the Styx* and Doug Anderson's sequence of poems "Raids on Homer" both respond to the propaedeutic in Homer's *Iliad*, each relates to past literature differently: each swerving within one camp of interest or the other, left and right, forward and back, in the press of ideology and culture.

There is a straight line between the Homer of veteran soldier R. L. Barth, who served three years in the Marine Corps and for thirteen months as a LRRP, or long range reconnaissance patrol leader, in Vietnam, and that of Edwin Muir, a decidedly noncombatant member of the World War I generation. Muir's "Ballad of Hector in Hades" (1925) lives in a heroic world of omniscient terror, where a vast, superhuman Achilles beats down a merely human Hector:

> I run. If I turned back again
>   The earth must turn with me,
> The mountains planted on the plain,
>   The sky clamped to the sea.

In the little space of Hector's fear-filled remaining life, he sees Achilles closing in:

> Two shadows racing on the grass,
>   Silent and so near,
> Until his shadow falls on mine.
>   And I am rid of fear.
>
> The race is ended. Far away
>   I hang and do not care,
> While round bright Troy Achilles whirls
>   A corpse with streaming hair.
>   (Muir, 24)

Hector's life and fear end simultaneously; if Muir's poem has one central mood and focus, it is to hold pathos and turn on the issue of a brave and manly death. In the whole of the poem, that is what we are made to care for, doubt, and dread with Hector.

R. L. Barth's "Prologue: Reading *The Iliad*," gives us a former soldier reading at his desk, coffee and cigarette forgotten:

> Stunned by the clamor under smoky skies,
> Boastings and tauntings, he looks up to see—
> Not the god-harried plain where Hector tries
>
> His destiny, not the room—but a mountain
> Covered with jungle; on one slope, a chateau
> With garden, courtyard, a rococo fountain,
> And, faces down, hands tied, six bodies in a row.
>   (Barth, 1)

However Barth will come to see his Vietnam experience and its agonies of east-west confrontation, in chiseled quatrains he lets us know that his war will be counterpoised against the earlier heroic trials of the Homeric myth.

More than a half dozen of the poems in this chapbook are cast in letter form; "Last Letter" is dedicated to "J. H. who threw himself on a grenade to save the lives of six men with him." Beginning with an episode on patrol, the poem ends:

This afternoon, we found twelve carcasses
Around bomb craters. Though I choked on the smell
Of maggot-breeding flesh at first, I bless

Those bodies now, for they are flaunting hell;
Bless them, for they are shattered and awry;
Bless them, for I have heard the words they tell:

"Come, friend; it is not difficult to die."
    (Barth, 16)

Like Hector whirling in the grip of Achilles or the maggot-crawling flesh of these corpses or, as with the stilled bodies of Barth's "Prologue," death itself creates its own unhearing, its own unfeeling; but for the man of duty, facing death is the one duty that the soldier must know not to push aside. The issue is still the definition of manhood as the definition of courage. Other poems using rhyme and meter in ways not foreign to them, speak directly to literary predecessors like Owen, Blunden, and Sassoon. Barth's literary epigraphs are plentiful. For this poet, tradition is not only active, but interactive and deeply shadowing. Like W. D. Ehrhart and Keith Douglas before him, he writes the war poem we have come to recognize, about the man sighting his weapon, in "Longinus in Vietnam":

They command; and I obey,
collecting my combat pay.
Peasant, soldier— it's all one
on this hill where, like passion
seeking an object, I wait
and, watching, I concentrate.
It's truth of a kind, this sense
of sighting down the long lens
at men who scurry to loss,
hung on my spiderweb cross.
    (Barth, 4)

Truth comes down the barrel of a gun, in an ironic revision of Longinus's sublime where, in the production of pagan awe and terror, the wartime goal of the killer comes to displace any idea of Christian self-sacrifice. Wilfred Owen,

Randall Jarrell, and Keith Douglas—each blends the victimization of the one who wounds with the one who is wounded, both wounded and wounder falling to the common mutilations of war. Barth's detachment is chillier. His poem centers on the moment when all the crucifying takes place on the martyred enemy body, at least for now. The only modern touch seems his speaker's acceptance of command hierarchy; for this Longinus, there is no Homeric duel fought between equals, but peasant or soldier is equally minion of the faceless, disembodied military will.

Doug Anderson recasts his free-verse vision of *The Iliad*, in a sharper, more antagonistic dialogue with Homer. In "Spoken by the Sentry at Achilles' Tent," and in "Homer Does Not Mention Him," Anderson amplifies key passages and fills in narrative gaps, looking at the status and visibility of foot soldier and captive woman. Choosing the reworkings born of his time, and with the egalitarian insights of Vietnam behind him, Anderson adds the grunt to Homer's forces, enlarges the subject of a woman's entrapment in war, denies glory, and moves to the antiheroic and the nontraditional form.

R.L. Barth's closeness to Homer does not lie in his burnishing of the particulars of consciousness. Making poems with the human believability of Homer's people is not his concern. Jonathan Shay, citing "Priam's nightmare vision of his own fate in the conquered city" (Shay, 132), shows the round weight of Homer's consciousness, in which the characters' bleak fates spell out fully and inexorably. Barth's ironic detachment from people is closer in style to Muir; like Muir, his poetry is traditional, conventional, but not necessarily Homeric.

Doug Anderson, however distant his literary technique from the hexameters of Greek epic, nonetheless accepts the reality of Homer's people and the words they move in: as if the text were a fluid stream, a kind of liquid mirror that the poet enters, his writerly reading a twist of the mirror substance. It is hardly new, of course, to rewrite Homer. The Homeric text itself is the product of reworking its own generative series of poems and stories. Much as Ovid's *Heroides* does, Anderson embroiders on Briseis, Achilles' famous chattel, taken from him by Agamemnon, and for whom Achilles withdraws from the Greek side in pique. Long after she has left the scene in the quarrel of book 1, Briseis bursts into book 9 after Patroclus's death. It is the moment when she breaks from her previous muteness and near invisibility, opening her mouth to mourn Patroclus and, in the process, voice her own history of grief, that floors every attentive reader.

Since her importance consists solely of what is done to her on the decisive command of others, it might not have mattered, ever, that she had nothing to

say for herself, if Homer in one of those anticipatorily Shakespearian moments, had not stepped in suddenly to give her this remarkable scene:

> And so Briseis returned, like golden Aphrodite,
> but when she saw Patroclus lying torn by the bronze
> she flung herself on his body, gave a piercing cry
> and with both hands clawing deep at her breasts,
> her soft throat and lovely face, she sobbed,
> a woman like a goddess in her grief, "Patroclus—
> dearest joy of my heart, my harrowed, broken heart!
> I left you alive that day I left these shelters,
> now I come back to find you fallen, captain of armies!

Her grief is a big surprise. We had not expected it of her: so far, she has been
a parcel of goods passed back and forth between the contending warriors with
about as much voice as a lamb chop. She has served silently, a name to spark
the quarrel between the Greek leaders. Now she continues:

> So grief gives way to grief, my life one endless sorrow!
> The husband to whom my father and noble mother gave me,
> I saw him torn by the sharp bronze before our city,
> and my three brothers—a single mother bore us:
> my brothers, how I loved you!—
> you all went down to death on the same day . . .
> But you, Patroclus, you would not let me weep,
> not when the swift Achilles cut my husband down,
> not when he plundered the lordly Mynes' city—
> not even weep! No, again and again you vowed
> you'd make me godlike Achilles' lawful wedded wife,
> you would sail me west in your warships, home to Phthia
> and there with the Myrmidons hold my marriage feast.
> So now I mourn your death—I will never stop—
> you were always kind."
>   (*Iliad* 19.332–55)

Briseis's great moment begins as a male wish fulfillment; initially, she is
brought on as a representative of "Sincere Mourning," someone whose
craven loveliness merely enhances the power and glory of the fallen warrior

who once in kindness pitied her. But how the lines run away with Homer; in one of those stunning, flash appearances, Briseis steps out as breathing flesh, born complete from Homer's brow, a recognizable woman with an aching history all of her own.[5]

Each packed detail shows that Briseis was never her own to give away. A father and a noble mother gave her to her husband; there was at least a kind of early nuclear family because she and her three brothers were all born to that noble mother. But this family bond crumbled—typically, only the fate of the men being mentioned—but they all went down to death, brothers and husband, presumably the father as well, while the husband was cut down by the man who would claim her next. The kicker here is that Patroclus, "kind" Patroclus, forbade her tears for any of this: the one solid hope he could think to offer her was that at least the wrapping on her present slave package could be regal. Achilles would marry her; from vulnerable captive, she could make it not to a precarious concubinage, but to the greater security of queenship.

Sorrow is constant and unremitting in Briseis's brief biography. Feelings seem an irrelevant indulgence, given how little she can minister to them; even grief in these savage circumstances is a fragile, detachable ribbon that flutters through the incidental kindness of strangers: once fastened, huge tears are let to fall, standing in for all the unshed tears of a lifetime. In the wartime existence of a female chattel, tears are the rare luxury, flooding in on the pretext of weeping for others, in this case, for a downed man.

Ovid, struck by what Homer has rendered, gives us a monologue where Briseis writes to Achilles, after the unsuccessful Greek embassy. In Harold Isbell's commentary on this poem of Ovid's, he writes: "It is the fear of desertion that colors and shapes her life and provides the context within which this letter is written" (Ovid, 19–27). Briseis in Isbell's translation moves from tears of pathos to taunts to admonition and pleading to threats of suicide then back again to pleading. It is an expressive but also commonplace trajectory. That love is opportunistic, and springs frankly from what the lover needs, is not in question. In order to survive in a world of war and conquest, Ovid's Briseis demands Achilles' protection, and her request for his "love" is this barely concealed need. If a history of feeling could ever be written, we might say that this view represents the relation between the sexes as a blunt power relation, solely a matter of patronage given or patronage denied.

Doug Anderson changes nothing essential in his reading of Homer's particulars; it is what he adds that is of interest. Like Homer, he understands the reticent helplessness of Briseis. In his poem, titled "Spoken by The Sentry at

Achilles' Tent," once again Briseis comes into view obliquely. Anderson begins with the questions many of my Vassar students have when they encounter Briseis in book 9:

> Why did the girl Briseis weep for Patroclus?
> Taken from her father by Achilles, raped,
> then seized by Agamemnon, raped again.
> Then Agamemnon gave her back to bribe Achilles
> to return so the sea would not froth red
> with our cut throats. But upon returning to Achilles' tent
> she saw Patroclus, dead, his stiffening beauty
> stretched out on a cot, the demi-god insane with grief.
> I watched her throw herself across the corpse and sob.
> They say even Achilles' horses wept for Patroclus
> but why this girl, sixteen, who could not wish
> any of us well? Perhaps because she saw
> her own spoiled body lying there, her ruined life.
>
> > (Anderson, 41)

Speculation about her future occupies the poem's middle section, a future teetering between various forms of bondage, with consolations either as light or heavy dressing. The speaker continues:

> Patroclus was seventeen,
> the boy who speaks to you the same.
> Brought here because I can put an arrow
> through a halter ring at a hundred meters,
> tell a hummock from a creeping man on a moonless night
> but most important because I can keep my mouth shut,
> my feelings hid, even what I feel now.

He identifies with her; each is inhabited by the exigencies of rank and gender. Feelings as we understand them are a luxury for both of them, which grows as anything daily trodden underfoot can, yielding to the crush of circumstance. And he concludes:

> I Spiros, son of a sandalmaker, entrust to you this secret:
> I would take her home and love her as she is,

lay my hand on her heart and leave it there
until she remembers that she has one.

        (Anderson, 41)

It does not matter that Homer caught Briseis crying, and in a briefly confessional mode. The twentieth-century soldier who hears knows that sons of sandal-
makers rarely talk in Homer, even less than captive women do. And he is determined to add them to the record. In "Homer Does Not Mention Him," Petros
the stone cutter comes home limping, his shoulder ruined from swinging a short
sword, "Lungs rotten from the choking / yellow dust, sleeping cold nights / on
the plain under a spear-propped shield, heart hard as his heels from killing."
Homer, says Jonathan Shay, "entirely omitted the soldier's experience of short-
age and privation" (Shay, *Achilles*, 121). At home, Petros's wife sees him:

> not as Penelope knew Odysseus disguised
> but as a woman who sees a husband, only older,
> something unnameable gone out of him.

Elsewhere,

> The markets of Argos filling with the crutched
> and nubbled with their olive bitter mouths;
> a blind hoplite lifting his robe to show
> his testicles gone, people throwing money in his hat;
>
>   (Anderson, 38)

Working within his own grim realism, the twentieth-century poet cannot
bring us to see the consequences of war as soaring tragedy. Instead, beside the
Homeric recognition of war's broken families, he leaves us with a more pervasive sense of war's damaged and damaging masculinity. For Anderson, in a
denial of heroic power, Odysseus proves a lying butcher; Achilles in Hades is
"at last no larger and no smaller / than you are, and no shame in that" (Anderson, 42).

When Anderson gets around to "Erebus," though, there is a conflation of
the huge past with the demanding present. Along with the lurching rhythms
and diminutions of war's aftermath, there is still the example of Homer to follow in the return to the dead, performed by so many Vietnam War poets. Anderson's speaker is caught again by Vietnam:

You have the dream again: monsoon season, jungle,
a muddy village road; you are naked,
stumbling along a paddy dike across an open field
where C. W. killed all the pigs
but once into the trees
there is only thickening jungle,
canopy hung with smoldering flares.
You stumble into an open field,
cupping your balls,
and from the next treeline
you hear music, Motown, Aretha,
who used to throb from the mortar pits
where the brothers slung round after round down the tubes,
a little respect
and when you enter the village, ashamed,
you see men you tagged dead
and choppered out like sides of beef,
grinning at you from around a fire,
and the old women, the children
who didn't move quick enough, all the Cong,
they are there too,
and the ones from the day so many died
you tore up your own clothes for bandages;
all there and singing, lit amber by the fire.

Many others enter, snatches of experience recapitulated. In the ending of the
sequence, a buddy who survived, only to die at home, "killed in a drug deal,"
speaks:

All of us are here, he says, *sit down,*
we'll get you some clothes,
you're home now, easy,
remember what you used to say?
You're going to be fine, my man,
you're going home,
just don't fade out on me,
hey, what's your mother's maiden name?
        (Anderson, 44–45)

Is it that home for the soldier is only in hell? Or that only memory of the dead, and long, restless, helpless concourse with them, and with those who wrote solidly about them, can truly heal?

Both R. L. Barth and Doug Anderson, even in their different engagements with Homer, show the endlessly recursive nature of literary movement, in which one source is always the ground of an individual life, and the other source is always other literature. New and memorable form teases the older artist for the human constant; each living voice of the present has to back talk, adding fresh texture, fresh detail to the volatile mix of what war has been or is going to be. Some generations are inevitably more contentious than others and train their pictures of the worlds that should come closer to us than others. While the next war poets may not be able to show more than what was acutely and freshly terrible, at least they prop up a continued resistance to violent means, a resistance that, with a feeble stubbornness, is still amassed at no slower rate than our capacity to invent new kinds of killing.

Notes

1. Introduction: The Dignities of Danger

1. See instructive charts and tables in Dan Smith, *The State of War and Peace Atlas* (Oslo: Penguin Books/The International Peace Research Institute, 1997), 24–25.
2. This poem of Sassoon's, cited by its opening line, is published with earlier deletions bracketed, as well as final emendations, in Jon Silkin, ed., *The Penguin Book of First World War Poetry* (London: Penguin, 1981), 124. Silkin notes that the manuscript he reproduces for his anthology was given to him in Sassoon's home in 1965 (127).
3. Ian Hamilton, ed. *The Poetry of War, 1939–45* (London: Alan Ross, 1965), includes Norman Cameron's "Black Takes White" without comment.

5. Randall Jarrell's War

1. Jarrell has in mind here several aphorisms of William Blake's, including "To generalize is to be an idiot." Or, in the *Annotations to Sir Joshua Reynolds*, "Singular & Particular Detail is the Foundation of the Sublime." See Blake, 637.
2. "During World War II 25 percent of military personnel never left the United States and only about one in eight actually saw combat. In World War II only 34.1 percent of army personnel was engaged in purely military occupations. Thus, the increasingly 'civilian' nature of many military duties, more than 10 percent of which were administrative and clerical, made possible the employment of women in the defense establishment." Susan M. Hartmann, *The Home Front and Beyond: American Women in the 1940s* (Boston: Twayne, 1982), 34.
3. "Thus, the direct inflicting of misery and harm on the enemy population was one of the three main tools in the hands of the mediaeval commander, along with battle and siege. . . . for nothing in the late mediaeval conception of chivalry forbade direct attacks on the "civilian" population, just as nothing prevented the bombing of Dresden and Nagasaki in the twentieth century: the population at large was seen as the mast of the enemy's ship of state, and so a legitimate target of attack, for it was only by the support of the commons that a king could wage war" (Clifford J.

Rogers, "The Age of the Hundred Years' War," in *Mediaeval Warfare: A History*, ed. Maurice Keen [Oxford: Oxford University Press, 1999], 153). It is the same rationale, of course, in what has come to be styled postmodern war, in which civilians are designated as terrorist support,and are equally and remorselessly targeted.

4. Jarrell noted at the Pfeiffer College reading (see note 6, below) that the aria is drawn from Giacomo Meyerbeer's opera *Vasco da Gama*, celebrating the vision of the New World. That the denizens of the New World paradise were returning to bomb the Old World seems an irony Jarrell is tapping us to notice.

5. Donald W. Hastings, David G. Wright, and Bernard C. Glueck comment that combat fatigue for airmen was strictly correlated with numbers of missions flown, not to any previous record of emotional distress. In the European Theater of Operations, 25 missions were at first standard, which was then upped to 30, and the worst tension occurred in anticipation of the final mission. See the restricted report by Hastings, Wright, and Glueck, *Psychiatric Experiences of the Eighth Air Force*, (New York: Josiah Macy, Jr. Foundation, 1944), issued to Air Force flight surgeons in August 1944. Other reports possibly familiar to Jarrell include a piece by Brendan Gill, interviewing a pilot in *The New Yorker* of 12 August 1944. Hallock, the pilot, is quoted saying: "It was getting close to the end and my luck was bound to be running out faster and faster. . . . The twenty-ninth mission was to Thionville, in France, and all I thought about on that run was 'One more, one more, one more.'"

6. *Randall Jarrell Reads and Discusses His Poems Against War*, recorded 30 April 1961, Caedmon SWC1363, 1972, audiotape.

7. Jarrell was no doubt acutely aware of the high risk life that World War II pilots led. John Keegan gives these numbers in *Fields of Battle*: "The Army Air Forces lost 52,173 aircrew in combat in the Second World War, four-fifths of them in Europe and the majority of these from the Eighth Air Force bomber crews who flew from Britain. . . . There was roughly, an even chance of surviving the course; put the other way about, there was an even chance of not." See Keegan, *Fields of Battle*, 331.

8. James Dickey's work in midcareer and earlier provides an interesting comparison with Jarrell's treatment of boyhood. Dickey, who according to his biographer, Henry Hart, inflated the number, danger, and impact of the actual combat missions in the Pacific that he flew, internalizes war guilt in "The Firebombing." This poem, written in the free verse forms of the 1960s, but dealing with World War II, points toward the anguish of guilt expressed in Vietnam-war-veteran poetry. Poems like "The Sheepchild" and "Cherrylog Road," in which the adolescent speaker is "wild to be wreckage forever" also deal with an untamed sexuality and exultant adolescent destructiveness that is never part of Jarrell's take on boy pilots.

6. "Cry for us all, for learning our lessons well": American Poets of the Vietnam War

1. These medals were a potent means of symbolic protest, of course, as well as of proud credentialing. On 23 April 1971, some of these same medals no doubt found their way into the shower of medals thrown over the six-foot fence erected at the bottom

of the steps of the Capitol in Washington, D.C. The fence, designed to keep the Vietnam Veterans Against the War from getting any closer to official chambers, stood against approximately eight hundred veterans who participated in this protest action, named Dewey Canyon III after illicit army operations into Laos, in a ritual return of their medals. Each return—in one notable case by a Gold Star mother, Louise Ransom, representing her dead son, was accompanied by short, often quite passionate speeches against the continuation of the war. In Gloria Emerson's account:

> Sometimes, after a man had hurled a bit of ribbon or a Bronze Star or a Purple Heart over a high wire fence the police put in front of the steps of the Capitol, he would break down and be hugged by other men. They were free at last to do it. No one was ashamed of crying or holding on to each other. Some threw in fury, others in sorrow, but nearly all made faces as they did it.

See Gloria Emerson, *Winners and Losers: Battles, Retreats, Gains, Losses, and Ruins from the Vietnam War*, (New York: W. W. Norton, 1976; reprint, 1992), 331.

The ceremony, called by its organizers "A short incursion into the country of Congress," was the culmination of a week of protests and demands. See details in Richard Stacewicz, *Winter Soldiers: An Oral History of the Vietnam Veterans Against the War*, (New York: Twayne, 1997), 233–51; also Gerald Nicosia, *Home to War: A History of the Vietnam Veterans' Movement* (New York: Crown Publishers, 2001), chapter 3. That other writers like Guenter Lewy, (in *America in Vietnam* [New York: Oxford, 1978], 316–17, 319), indicate that a few of the veterans misrepresented their service records or may have retrieved their medals after the ceremony does not destroy the force of the majority action.

2. This theme, or "the moment when," is treated at considerable length, and with some slight gain of effectiveness, in Tim O'Brien's account of the death of Curt Lemon in "How to Tell a True War Story," in *The Things They Carried* (Boston: Houghton Mifflin, 1990), 75–91.

3. "Independent surveys indicate that the total number of American women, both military and civilian, working in Vietnam during the war years is somewhat between 33,000 and 55,000. No one seems to have an accurate count. This apparent lack of data on the part of the Department of Defense and the State Department both serves as a reminder of government mishandling of information during the Vietnam War and points to the more general belief that war is men's business." Kathryn Marshall, *In the Combat Zone: An Oral History of American Women in Vietnam, 1966–1975* (Boston: Little, Brown, 1987), 4.

4. In her foreword to Lady Borton's *After Sorrow: An American Among The Vietnamese*, Grace Paley points out that Borton was the woman who led the first reporters to My Lai (*After Sorrow*, xv).

5. Malcolm Willcock speculates about the consistency of her character. In the lines cited, "It appears for the first time that she has been married . . . This is in conflict with the description of her as "daughter of Briseis" in l.392 and 9.132, for that suggests an unmarried girl. Strangely, too, her fate has been closely similar to that of Andromache, who lost father and brothers in the same expedition in which Briseis lost husband and brother (see Willcock, 1.184 n).

Works Cited

Alighieri, Dante. *The Inferno*. Trans. Robert Pinsky. New York: Farrar, Straus & Giroux, 1994.

Anderson, Doug. *The Moon Reflected Fire*. Cambridge, Mass.: Alice James Books, 1994.

Appy, Christian G. *Working Class War: American Combat Soldiers and Vietnam*. Chapel Hill: University of North Carolina Press, 1993.

Archilochos. *Carmina Archilochi: The Fragments of Archilochos*. Trans. Guy Davenport. Berkeley: University of California Press, 1964.

Auden, W. H. Correspondence. Letters to James and Tania Stern. Berg Collection, New York Public Library.

——. *The Dyer's Hand And Other Essays*. New York: Vintage, 1968.

——. *The English Auden: Poems, Essays, and Dramatic Writings, 1927–1939*. Ed. Edward Mendelson. New York: Random House, 1977.

——. Manuscripts. Manuscripts Room, Add 61838, British Library.

——. *The Prolific and the Devourer*. New York: Ecco Press, 1976. Reprint, 1981.

——. *Spain*. London: Faber and Faber, 1937.

Auden, W. H., and Christopher Isherwood. *Journey to A War*. New York: Paragon House, 1939. Reprint, 1990.

Auden, W. H., and Louis MacNeice. *Letters from Iceland*. London: Faber and Faber, 1937.

Balaban, John. *Ca Dao Vietnam: Vietnamese Folk Poetry*. Greensboro, N.C.: Unicorn Press, 1980.

——. *Remembering Heaven's Face*. Athens: The University of Georgia Press, 2002.

Barbusse, Henri. *Under Fire: The Story of a Squad*. Trans. Fitzwater Wray. New York: E. P. Dutton and Company, 1917. Reprint, 1937.

Barth, R. L. *Forced Marching to the Styx*. Van Nuys, Calif.: Perivale Press, 1983.

Bates, Scott. *Poems of War Resistance*. New York: Grossman, 1969.

Bayley, John. "Slaughter and the Real Right Thing." Review of *Wilfred Owen: A Biography*, by Jon Stallworthy. *Times Literary Supplement* 3793 (15 November 1974): 1273–74.

Bishop, Elizabeth. *The Complete Poems, 1927–1979*. New York: Farrar, Straus and Giroux, 1983.

——. Correspondence. Houghton Library, Harvard University.

———. *One Art: Letters*. Ed. Robert Giroux. New York: Farrar, Straus & Giroux, 1994.

Blake, William. *The Poetry and prose of William Blake*. Ed. David V. Erdman. New York: Doubleday, 1965.

Blunden, Edmund. *The Poems, 1914–1930*. London: Cobden Sanderson, 1930.

———. *Selected Poems*. Ed. Robyn Marsack. London: Carcanet Press, 1982.

———. *Undertones of War*. London: Cobden Sanderson, 1935.

———. *War Poets, 1914–1918*. London: The British Council and The National Book League, Longmans, Green and Company, 1958.

Blythe, Ronald, ed. *Components of the Scene*. Harmondsworth, U.K.: Penguin Books, 1966.

Booth, Allyson. *Postcards from the Trenches*. New York: Oxford University Press, 1966.

Borton, Lady. *After Sorrow: An American Among the Vietnamese*. Foreword by Grace Paley. New York: Viking, 1995.

———. *Sensing the Enemy: An American Woman Among the Boat People of Vietnam*. Garden City, N.Y.: Dial Press, 1984.

Brooks, Gwendolyn. *Blacks*. Chicago: Third World Press, 1987. Reprint, 1994.

Brown, D. F. *Returning Fire*. San Francisco: San Francisco State University Press, 1984.

Brownmiller, Susan. *Against our Will: Men, Women, and Rape*. New York: Simon and Schuster, 1975.

Bucknell, Katherine, and Nicholas Jenkins, eds. *The Map of All My Youth*. Vol. 1 of *Auden Studies*. Oxford: Clarendon Press, 1993.

Burlingham, Dorothy, and Anna Freud. *War and Children*. New York: Medical War Books, 1943.

Campbell, James. "Combat Gnosticism." *New Literary History* 30, no. 1 (winter 1999): 203–15.

Cameron, Norman. "Black Takes White." In *The Poetry of War, 1939–45*, ed. Ian Hamilton, p. 53. London: Alan Ross Ltd., 1965.

Carrington, Charles. *Soldier from the Wars Returning*. New York: David McKay, 1965.

Carruth, Hayden. "Melancholy Monument." *The Nation*, 7 July 1969. Reprinted in *Working Papers: Selected Essays and Reviews*. Athens: The University of Georgia Press, 1982, 156–160.

Connolly, David. *Lost in America*. Woodbridge, Conn.: Vietnam Generation, Inc., and Burning Cities Press, 1994.

Cowdrey, Albert E. *Fighting for Life: American Military Medicine in World War II*. New York: The Free Press, 1994.

Crane, Conrad C. *Bombs, Cities, and Civilians: American Airpower Strategy in World War II*. Lawrence, Kans.: University Press of Kansas, 1993.

Cummings, E. E. *Poems, 1923–1954*. New York: Harcourt, Brace & Co., 1954.

Currey, R. N. "Poets of the 1939–1945 War." London: The British Council and The National Book League, publication by Longmans, Green & Company, 1960.

Davenport-Hines, Richard. *Auden*. New York: Vintage Books, 1999.

Davidson, Mildred. *The Poetry Is in the Pity*. London: Chatto & Windus, 1972.

Dickey, James. "Randall Jarrell." In *Randall Jarrell, 1914–1965*. Ed. Robert Lowell, Peter Taylor, and Robert Penn Warren, 35–48. New York: Farrar, Straus & Giroux, 1967.

Donne, John. *The Complete Poetry of John Dunne*. Ed. John T. Shawcross. New York: Doubleday Anchor, 1967.

Douglas, Keith. *Alamein to Zem Zem*. Ed. Desmond Graham. London: Faber & Faber, 1992.

——. *The Complete Poems*. Ed. Desmond Graham. Introduction by Ted Hughes. Oxford: Oxford University Press, 1998.

——. Douglas Papers. Correspondence, drafts, miscellaneous prose. Manuscripts Room, British Library.

——. *A Prose Miscellany*. Ed. Desmond Graham. Manchester: Carcanet Press, 1985.

Ecksteins, Modris. *Rites of Spring: The Great War and the Birth of the Modern Age*. New York: Doubleday, 1989.

Ehrenreich, Barbara. *Blood Rites*. New York: Henry Holt, 1997.

Ehrhart, W. D. *Beautiful Wreckage: New and Selected Poems*. Easthampton, Mass.: Adastra Press, 1999.

——. *Busted: A Vietnam Veteran in Nixon's America*. Amherst: University of Massachusetts Press, 1995.

——, ed. *Carrying the Darkness: The Poetry of the Vietnam War*. Lubbock, Tex.: Texas Tech University Press, 1985. Reprint, 1989.

——. *The Distance We Travel*. Easthampton, Mass.: Adastra Press, 1993.

——. *In the Shadow of Vietnam: Essays, 1977–1991*. Jefferson, N.C.: McFarland, 1991.

——, ed. *Unaccustomed Mercy: Soldier-Poets of The Vietnam War*. Lubbock, Tex.: Texas Tech University Press, 1989

——. *Vietnam–Perkasie: A Combat Marine Memoir*. London. MacFarlane, 1983.

——. "War, Poetry, and Ethics: A Symposium." *War, Literature, and The Arts: An International Journal of the Humanities* 10, no. 2 (1998):5–41.

Eliot, T. S. *The Complete Poems and Plays, 1909–1950*. New York: Harcourt Brace, 1952.

Ellis, John. "Reflections on the 'Sharp End' of War." in *Time to Kill: The Soldier's Experience of War in the West, 1939–45*, ed. Paul Addison and Angus Calder, 12–18. London: Pimlico, 1997.

——. *The Sharp End: The Fighting Man in World War II*. London: Pimlico, 1993.

Emerson, Gloria. *Winners and Losers: Battles, Retreats, Gains, Losses, and Ruins from the Vietnam War*. New York: W. W. Norton, 1976. Reprint, 1985.

Featherstone, Simon. *War Poetry: An Introductory Reader*. New York: Routledge, 1995.

Fein, Richard. "Randall Jarrell's World of War." In *Critical Issues in Randall Jarrell*, ed. Suzanne Ferguson, 149–62. Boston: G. K. Hall, 1983.

Felman, Shoshana. "Education and Crisis, or the Vicissitudes of Teaching." In *Trauma: Explorations in Memory*, ed. Cathy Caruth, 13–60. Baltimore: Johns Hopkins, 1995.

Fenton, James. *The Strength of Poetry: Oxford Lectures*. New York: Farrar, Straus & Giroux, 2001.

Flint, R. W. "On Randall Jarrell." In *Randall Jarrell, 1914–1965*, ed. Robert Lowell, Peter Taylor, and Robert Penn Warren, 76–85. New York: Farrar, Straus, & Giroux, 1967.

Flynn, Richard. *Randall Jarrell and the Lost World of Childhood*. Athens: The University of Georgia Press, 1990.

Fuller, Roy. *Collected Poems, 1936–1961*. Philadelphia: Dufour Editions, 1962.

Fussell, Paul. *Doing Battle: The Making of a Skeptic*. Boston: Little, Brown and Company, 1996.

——. *The Great War and Modern Memory*. Oxford: Oxford University Press, 1977.

——. *Thank God for the Atom Bomb and Other Essays*. New York: Simon & Schuster, 1988.

——. *Wartime: Understanding and Behavior in the Second World War*. New York: Oxford University Press, 1989.

Gascoigne, George. "The fruites of Warre." In *The Posies*. Vol. 1 of *The Complete Works of George Gascoigne*, ed. John W. Cunliffe, 139–84. Cambridge: Cambridge University Press, 1907.

Gilbert Sandra M., and Susan Gubar. *Sexchanges*. Vol. 2 of *No Man's Land: The Place of The Woman Writer in the Twentieth Century*. New Haven: Yale University Press, 1989.

Gill, Brendan. "Young Man Behind Plexiglass." *The New Yorker*. 12 August 1944, 26–37.

Glasser, Ronald J. *365 Days*. New York: George Braziller, 1971.

Graham, Desmond. *Keith Douglas, 1920–1944*. London: Oxford University Press, 1974.

Graves, Robert. *Good-Bye to All That*. 1929. Reprint, New York: Anchor Books, Doubleday, 1998.

——. "The Poets of World War II." In *The Common Asphodel: Collected Essays on Poetry, 1922–1949*, 307–12. London; Hamish Hamilton, 1949.

Gurney, Ivor. *Severn and Somme and War's Embers*. Ed. R. K. R. Thornton. London: Carcanet Press, 1987. Reprint, Ashington, U.K.: The Mid Northumberland Arts Group and Carcanet Press, 1997.

Hamilton, Ian, ed. *The Poetry of War, 1939–45*. London: Alan Ross, 1965.

Hardy, Thomas. *The Complete Poetical Works of Thomas Hardy*. Ed. Samuel Hynes. 3 vols. Oxford: The Clarendon Press, 1982.

Hartmann, Susan M. *The Home Front and Beyond: American Women in the 1940s*. Boston: Twayne, 1982.

Hasford, Gustav. *The Short-Timers*. New York: Harper & Row, 1979. Reprint, Bantam, 1983.

Hastings, Donald W., David G. Wright, and Bernard C. Glueck. *Psychiatric Experiences of the Eighth Air Force*. New York: Josiah Macy, Jr. Foundation, 1944.

Hemingway, Ernest. *Collected Poems*. Only information available: "Pirated Edition. San Francisco: 1960." Acquired: City Lights Bookstore, San Francisco, ca. 1960.

——. *A Farewell to Arms*. New York: Scribner, 1969.

Henderson, Hamish. *Elegies: For the Dead in Cyrenaica*. Edinburgh: EUSPB, n.d. Possible prior publication: John Lehmann, 1948.

Hibbert, Christopher. *Wellington: A Personal History*. Reading, Mass.: Addison Wesley, 1997.

Hill, Geoffrey, "'I in Another Place': Homage to Keith Douglas." *Stand* 6, no. 4 (1964–1965): 6–13.

Hinojosa, Rolando. *Korean Love Songs*. Berkeley: Justa, 1978.

Housman, A. E. *The Collected Poems of A. E. Housman*. New York: Holt, Rinehart & Wilson, 1965.

Howard, Michael. "Military Experience in European Literature." In *The Lessons of History*, 177–87. New Haven: Yale University Press, 1991.

Huddle, David. *Stopping by Home*. Salt Lake City: Peregrine Books, 1988.

Hudgins, Andrew. *After the Lost War*. Boston: Houghton Mifflin Books, 1988.

Hughes, Ted. *The Hawk in the Rain*. London: Faber and Faber, 1957.

———. Introduction to *Complete Poems*, by Keith Douglas. Ed. Desmond Graham. Oxford: Oxford University Press, 1998.

———. *Wolfwatching*. New York: Farrar, Straus & Giroux, 1989.

Hulme, T. E. *Further Speculations*. Ed. Samuel Hynes. Lincoln, Nebr.: University of Nebraska Press, 1962.

Huston, Nancy. "The Matrix of War: Mothers and Heroes." In *The Female Body in Western Culture*, ed. Susan Robin Suleiman, 119–36. Cambridge: Harvard University Press, 1986.

Hynes, Samuel. *The Auden Generation: Literature and Politics in the 1930s*. New York: The Viking Press, 1972. Reprint, 1976.

———. *The Soldiers' Tale: Bearing Witness to Modern War*. New York: Penguin, 1997.

———. *A War Imagined*. New York: Atheneum, 1991.

Isherwood, Christopher. *Lions and Shadows*. London: Hogarth Press, 1938.

———. "Some Notes on the Early Poetry." In *W. H. Auden: A Tribute*, ed. Stephen Spender, 74–78. New York: MacMillan, 1975.

Jaeger, Lowell. *War on War*. Logan: Utah State University Press, 1988.

Jarrell, Randall. *Blood for a Stranger*. New York: Harcourt Brace, 1942.

———. *The Complete Poems*. New York: Farrar, Straus and Giroux, 1969.

———. "Go, Man, Go!" *Mademoiselle* 45 (May 1957): 98–99. Reprint, in Jarrell, *Kipling, Auden, and Co.*, 287–84. New York: Farrar, Straus & Giroux, 1980.

———. Jarrell Papers. Correspondence, drafts, unpublished papers. Berg Collection, New York Public Library.

———. "Levels and Opposites: Structure in Poetry." *The Georgia Review* 50, no. 4 (winter 1996): 697–713.

———. *Little Friend, Little Friend*. New York: Dial Press, 1945.

———. *Losses*. New York: Harcourt Brace, 1948.

———. "Poetry in War and Peace." *Partisan Review* (winter 1945). Reprint, in Jarrell, *Kipling, Auden, and Co.: Essays and Reviews, 1935–1964*, 127–34. New York: Farrar, Straus & Giroux, 1980.

———. *Randall Jarrell Reads and Discusses His Poems Against War*. Recorded 30 April 1961. Caedmon SWC1363, 1972. Audiocassette.

———. *Randall Jarrell's Letters*. Ed. Mary Jarrell. Boston: Houghton Mifflin, 1985.

Keegan, John. *The Face of Battle*. New York: Viking, 1976.

———. *Fields of Battle*. New York: Alfred A. Knopf, 1996.

Kendrick, William. *The Wound Within: America in the Vietnam Years, 1945–1974*. Boston: Little, Brown, 1974.

Kerr, Douglas. "The Discipline of the Wars: Army Training and the Language of Wilfred Owen." *The Modern Language Review* (1992): 287–99.

Keyes, Sidney. *Collected Poems of Sidney Keyes*. Ed. Michael Meyer. London: Routledge, 1945.

Kinzie, Mary. "The Man Who Painted Bulls." *The Southern Review* n.s. 16 (1980): 829–52.

———. "A New Sweetness: Randall Jarrell and Elizabeth Bishop." In *The Cure of Poetry in an Age of Prose*, 65–100. Chicago: The University of Chicago Press, 1993.

Knox, Bernard, ed. *The Norton Book of Classical Literature*. New York: W. W. Norton, 1993.

Komunyakaa, Yusef. *Blue Notes: Essays, Interviews, and Commentaries*. Ed. Radiclani Clytus. Ann Arbor: University of Michigan Press, 2000.

———. *Dien Cai Dau*. Hanover, N.H.: Wesleyan University Press, 1988.

———. *Neon Vernacular: New and Selected Poems*. Hanover, N.H.: Wesleyan University Press, 1993.

Kunitz, Stanley. "Michael Casey." In *A Kind of Order, A Kind of Folly: Essays and Conversations*, 276–81. Boston: Little Brown, 1975.

Larkin, Philip. *Collected Poems*. Ed. Anthony Thwaite. London and New York: Farrar, Straus & Giroux, The Marvell Press, 1989.

———. *Required Writing: Miscellaneous Pieces, 1955–1982*. Ann Arbor: University of Michigan Press, 1999.

———. *Selected Letters of Philip Larkin, 1940–1985*. Ed. Anthony Thwaite. New York: Farrar, Straus & Giroux, 1992.

Lewis, Alun. *Selected Poetry and Prose*. Introduced by Ian Hamilton. London: Allen and Unwin, 1966.

Lewis, C. Day. *Collected Poems of C. Day Lewis*. London: Jonathan Cape and Hogarth Press, 1954.

Lewy, Guenter. *America in Vietnam*. New York: Oxford, 1978.

Lin, Maya. "Making the Memorial." *New York Review of Books* 47, no. 17 (2 November, 2001): 33–35.

Lowell, Robert. Correspondence. Special Collections. Vassar College.

———. *Life Studies* and *For the Union Dead*. New York: Farrar, Straus & Giroux, 1964.

———. "Randall Jarrell." In *Randall Jarrell, 1914–1965*, ed. Robert Lowell, Peter Taylor, and Robert Penn Warren, 101–17. New York: Farrar, Straus & Giroux, 1967.

MacDiarmid, Hugh. *Selected Poems*. Ed. David Craig and John Manson. London: Penguin Books, 1970.

MacNeice, Louis. *Modern Poetry: A Personal Essay*. Oxford: Oxford University Press, 1938.

Mahony, Phillip, ed. *From Both Sides Now: The Poetry of the Vietnam War and Its Aftermath*. New York: Scribner, 1998.

Marshall, Kathryn. *In the Combat Zone: An Oral History of American Women in Vietnam, 1966–1975*. Boston: Little, Brown, 1987.

McCarthy, Gerald. *War Story: Vietnam War Poems*. Trumansburg, N.Y.: The Crossing Press, 1977.

McGrath, Thomas. "Ode for the American Dead in Asia." Reprint, in *Retrieving the Bones: Stories and Poems of the Korean War*. Ed. W. D. Ehrhart and Philip K. Jason. New Brunswick, N.J.: Rutgers University Press, 1999. Published earlier as "Ode for the American Dead in Korea." In McGrath, *Selected Poems, 1938–1988*. Port Townsend, Wash.: Copper Canyon, 1988.

Mithers, Carol Lynn. "Missing in Action: Women Warriors in Vietnam." In *The Vietnam War and American Culture*, ed. John Carlos Rowe and Rick Berg, 75–91. New York: Columbia University Press, 1991.

Moore, Marianne. *The Complete Poems of Marianne Moore*. New York: MacMillan, 1981.

Motion, Andrew. *A Writer's Life: Philip Larkin*. New York: Farrar, Straus and Giroux, 1993.

Muir, Edwin. *Collected Poems, 1921–1958*. London: Faber and Faber, 1960.

Mydans, Seth. "A Fallen Saigon Rises Again in the West." *New York Times* Friday, 5 April 2002.

Nemerov, Howard. *The Collected Poems of Howard Nemerov*. Chicago: University of Chicago Press, 1977.

Nicosia, Gerald. *Home to War: A History of the Vietnam Veterans' Movement*. New York: Crown Publishers, 2001.

Nye, Jim. *Aftershock: Poems and Prose from the Vietnam War*. El Paso, Tex.: Cinco Puntos Press, 1991.

O'Brien, Tim. "How to Tell a True War Story." In *The Things They Carried*, 75–91. Boston: Houghton Mifflin, 1990.

Orwell, George. "Inside the Whale." 1940. Reprint, in *The Complete Works of George Orwell*, ed. Peter Davison. Vol. 12, 86–115. London: Secker and Warburg, 1998.

——. "Political Reflections on the Crisis." 1938. Reprint, in *The Complete Works of George Orwell*, ed. Peter Davison. Vol. 11, 242–46. London: Secker and Warburg, 1998.

Ovid. "Briseis to Achilles." In *Heroides*. Translated and annotated by Harold Isbell, 19–27. London: Penguin, 1990.

Owen, Wilfred. *Collected Letters*. Ed. Harold Owen and John Bell. Oxford: Oxford University Press, 1967.

——. *The Collected Poems of Wilfred Owen*. Ed. C. Day Lewis. New York: New Directions, 1965.

——. *The Complete Poems and Fragments*. 2 vols. Ed. Jon Stallworthy. New York: W. W. Norton, 1983.

——. Correspondence, drafts, miscellaneous prose. British Library.

——. Correspondence. Harry Ransom Research Center, Austin, Texas.

Paret, Peter. *Imagined Battles: Reflections of War in European Art*. Chapel Hill, N.C.: The University of North Carolina Press, 1997.

Pope, Jessie. "The Call." In *Scars Upon My Heart: Women's Poetry and Verse of the First World War*, ed. Catherine Reilly, 88. London: Virago Press, 1981.

Pound, Ezra. *Gaudier-Brzeska*. New York: New Directions, 1970.

Pritchard, William. *Randall Jarrell: A Literary Life*. New York: Farrar, Straus & Giroux, 1990.

Ramazani, Jahan. *Poetry of Mourning: The Modern Elegy from Hardy to Heaney*. Chicago: University of Chicago Press, 1994.

Regan, Geoffrey. *Back Fire: The Tragic Story of Friendly Fire in Warfare from Ancient Times to The Gulf War*. London: Robson Books, 1995.

Ritterbusch, Dale. *Lessons Learned: Poetry of The Vietnam War and Its Aftermath*. Woodbridge, Conn.: Viet Nam Generation, Inc. and Burning Cities Press, 1995.

Rogers, Clifford J. "The Age of the Hundred Years' War." In *Mediaeval Warfare: A History*, ed. Maurice Keen. Oxford: Oxford University Press, 1999.

Rosenberg, Isaac. *The Collected Works of Isaac Rosenberg*. Ed. Ian Parsons. New York: Oxford University Press, 1979.

Roszak, Betty, and Theodore Roszak, eds. *Masculine/Feminine*. New York: Harper and Row, 1969.

Rottmann, Larry, Jan Berry, and Basil T. Paquet, eds. *Winning Hearts and Minds*. New York: McGraw-Hill, 1972.

Sandburg, Carl. *Complete Poems*. New York: Harcourt, Brace and Co.: 1950.

Sassoon, Siegfried. *Collected Poems, 1908–1956*. London: Faber and Faber, 1947. Reprint, 1984.

———. *The Complete Memoirs of George Sherston*. London: Faber and Faber, 1972.

———. "The rank stench of those bodies haunts me still." In draft form in *The Penguin Book of First World War Poetry*. Ed. John Silkin, 124–27. London: Penguin, 1981.

———. *Siegfried's Journey, 1916–1920*. London: Faber and Faber, 1945.

———. *Siegfried Sassoon's Diaries, 1915–1918*. Ed. Rupert Hart Davis. London: Faber and Faber, 1983.

———. *The War Poems*. London: Faber and Faber, 1983.

Scammell, William. *Keith Douglas: A Study*. London: Faber and Faber, 1988.

Scannell, Vernon. *Collected Poems, 1950–1993*. London: Robson Books, 1993.

———. *Not Without Glory: Poets of the Second World War*. London: Woburn Press, 1976.

Schwartz, Delmore. "On *Little Friend, Little Friend*." In *Randall Jarrell, 1914–1965*, ed. Robert Lowell, Peter Taylor, and Robert Penn Warren, 184–87. New York: Farrar, Straus & Giroux, 1967.

Seymour-Smith, Martin. *Robert Graves: His Life and Work*. New York: Holt, Rinehart & Winston, 1982.

Shakespeare, William. *King Henry V*. Ed. Andrew Gurr. Cambridge: Cambridge University Press, 1992.

Shapiro, Karl. "The Death of Randall Jarrell." In *Randall Jarrell, 1914–1965*, ed. Robert Lowell, Peter Taylor, and Robert Penn Warren, 195–229. New York: Farrar, Straus & Giroux, 1967.

Shay, Jonathan. *Achilles in Vietnam: Combat Trauma and the Undoing of Character*. New York: Simon and Schuster, 1995.

———. *Odysseus in America*. New York: Scribner, 2003.

Shephard, Ben. *A War of Nerves: Soldiers and Psychiatrists in the Twentieth Century*. Cambridge: Harvard University Press, 2001.

Sherry, Michael C. *The Rise of American Airpower: The Creation of Armageddon*. New Haven: Yale University Press, 1987.

Shields, Bill. *drinking gasoline in hell*. Wichita, Kans.: Mumbles, 1989.

Silkin, John, ed. *The Penguin Book of First World War Poetry*. London: Penguin, 1981.

Simpson, Louis. *Collected Poems*. New York: Paragon House, 1990.

Sisson, C. H. *An Assessment: English Poetry, 1900–1950*. New York: Methuen, 1981.

Sleigh, Tom. "At the End of Our Good Day." *Partisan Review* 59 (1992): 147–55.

Smith, Dan. *The State of War and Peace Atlas*. Oslo: Penguin Books, The International Peace Research Institute, 1997.

Spender, Stephen. *Collected Poems, 1928–1985*. New York: Random House, 1986.

Stacewicz, Richard. *Winter Soldiers: An Oral History of the Vietnam Veterans Against the War*. New York: Twayne, 1997.

Steiner, George. *The Death of Tragedy*. New York: Hill & Wang, 1963.

Stevens, Wallace. "Adagia." In *Opus Posthumous: Poems, Plays, Prose*. Ed. Samuel French Morse. New York: Knopf, 1957.

St. John, David. *Study for the World's Body*. New York: Harper Collins, 1994.

Strachan, Hew. "The Soldier's Experience in Two World War: Some Historiographical Comparisons." In *Time To Kill*, ed. Paul Addison and Angus Calder, 315–32. London: Pimlico, 1997.

Swift, Jonathan. *Gulliver's Travels*. Dublin: George Faulkner, 1735. Reprint, New York: Collier, 1962.

Swinden, Patrick. "Larkin and the Exemplary Owen." *Essays in Criticism*, 1994: 315–32.

Symons, Julian. *An Anthology of War Poetry*. Harmondsworth, U.K.: Penguin, 1942.

Tate, James. *The Lost Pilot*. New Haven: Yale University Press, 1967.

Taylor, Sandra C. *Vietnamese Women at War: Fighting for Ho Chi Minh and the Revolution*. Lawrence, Kans.: University Press of Kansas, 1999.

Tennyson, Alfred, Lord. *Poetical Works*. London: Oxford University Press, 1963.

Thomas, Dylan. *The Collected Poems of Dylan Thomas*. New York: New Direction, 1953.

Toynbee, Philip. *Friends Apart*. London: MacGibbon & Kee, 1954.

Tritle, Lawrence A. *From Melos to My Lai: War and Survival*. New York: Routledge, 2000.

Tuchman, Barbara W. *A Distant Mirror: The Calamitous Fourteenth Century*. New York: Ballantine Books, 1979.

Van Devanter, Lynda, and Joan A. Furey, ed. *Visions of War, Dreams of Peace: Writings of Women in the Vietnam War*. New York: Warner Books, 1991.

Van Devanter, Lynda, and Christopher Morgan. *Home Before Morning: The Story of an Army Nurse in Vietnam*. New York and Toronto: Beaufort Books, 1983.

Vassiltchikov, Marie. *Berlin Diaries, 1940–1945*. New York: Alfred A. Knopf, 1987.

Vietnam Veterans Against the War. *The Winter Soldier Investigation: An Inquiry into American War Crimes*. Boston: Beacon Press, 1972.

Voigt, Ellen Bryant. "Lost and Found." *The Southern Review* 38, no. 2 (spring 2000): 377–98.

Wagner, Erica. *Ariel's Gift*. New York: W. W. Norton and Company, 2000.

Webb, Barry. *Edmund Blunden: A Biography*. New Haven: Yale University Press, 1990.

Weigl, Bruce. *The Circle of Hanh: A Memoir*. Grove Press, New York: 2000

———. *Song of Napalm*. New York: The Atlantic Monthly Press, 1988.

———. *What Saves Us*. Evanston, Ill.: Triquarterly Books, Northwestern University Press, 1992.

Weigl, Bruce, and Thanh T. Nguyen. *Poems from Captured Documents*. Amherst, Mass.: The University of Massachusetts Press, 1994.

Welland, D. S. R. *Wilfred Owen: A Critical Study*. London: Chatto and Windus, 1968.

Willcock, Malcolm M. *A Companion to the* Iliad. Chicago: The University of Chicago Press, 1976.

Wilson, Keith. *Graves Registry and Other Poems*. Livingston, Mont.: Clark City Press, 1992.

Winter, Denis. *Death's Men: Soldiers of the Great War*. New York: Penguin, 1979.

Woods, Gregory. *Articulate Flesh: Male Homo-Eroticism and Modern Poetry*. New Haven: Yale University Press, 1987.

Wright, Stuart. *Randall Jarrell: A Descriptive Bibliography, 1929–1983*. Charlottesville: University Press of Virginia, 1986.

Yeats, William Butler. *Letters on Poetry from W. B. Yeats to Dorothy Wellesley*. Oxford: Oxford University Press, 1940.

——, ed. *The Oxford Book of Modern Verse, 1892–1935*. Oxford: Clarendon Press, 1952.

——. *The Poems of W. B. Yeats*. Ed. Richard C. Finneran, New York: Macmillan, 1983.

Index

Dickey, James, 205, 232; "The Firebombing," 342n.8
Dickinson, Emily, 178
division between combatants and noncombatants, xii; World War I, 12–16, 20, 28–29, 67, 103; World War II, 7, 103, 201
domestic war, 104–5
Donne, John, 194
Douglas, Keith, 6–7, 11, 21, 36, 98, 102, 251; absurdity in, 149–50; antiheroic poetry, 132–34, 156–57; artwork, 119, 121, 151, 159; Auden's influence on, 7, 83; black humor, 131–32, 157, 159; bodies in poems of, 121, 126–30, 140–44, 149, 158; comparison to Jarrell, 174–75; connections between sense and feeling in, 150–51; death in works of, 125–31, 137–40; death of, 119, 172–73; detachment, 125, 146, 160; detail in, 149; eagerness to serve, 145–46; early works, 126–27; England, view of, 164–65, 170; fatalism, 119, 122–23, 137, 139, 163–65, 240; figure of Jew and, 169–72; horsemanship, 134–35; injury, 125, 157–59; language of, 150, 161–62; literary reference in, 147, 150; mental preparation for death, 164–65; metaphysical context in, 160–61; militarist propensity, 119–20, 123, 170; military analysis in, 151–52, 155–56; naturalistic metaphor, 147–48; regimental life, 134–36; revisions, 137–38; schooling, 122–23; self-discovery, 165–67; war poetry, view of, 84–85, 98, 102, 161–62; women, view of, 121–22, 145, 164; on writing in the field, 21–22; Works: "Actors Waiting in the Wings of Europe," 168–69; *Alamein to Zem Zem*, 17, 144–59, 172, 200; "Aristocrats" ("Sportsmen"), 133, 153; "Bête Noire," 165–67; "Cairo Jag," 124–25; *Complete Poems*, 143; "A Dead Gunner," 140; "Dead Men," 19, 125–26, 141; "Desert

Flowers," 131; "Gallantry," 132–33; "A God Is Buried," 127; "The Hand," 169; "How to Kill," 11, 17, 19, 128, 130–31, 137–39, 141, 152, 159, 239, 273; "Landscape with Figures," 143–44; "Landscape with Figures 3," 167; "The Last Laugh," 131–32; "The Marvel," 160; "On a Return from Egypt," 173; "Poets in This War," 84; "The Prisoner," 126; *Prose Miscellany*, 84–85; "Russians," 127; "Saturday Evening in Jerusalem," 169; "Simplify Me When I'm Dead," 127–28; "Snakeskin and Stone," 137–38; "Sniper," 137; "Tel Aviv," 168; "This is the Dream," 168; "Vergissmeinnicht," 19, 124, 140–42, 160
Douglas, Marie, 122
draft resisters, 269
drama, 1–2
dreams, 19, 53, 204–5, 208
Duncan, Don, M/Sgt., 244, 245

Eberhart, Richard, 83
egalitarian themes, 23
Ehrhart, W. D., 261, 267–68, 277, 312–13, 326; *Beautiful Wreckage*, 287–89; *Busted*, 240, 267; *Carrying the Darkness: The Poetry of the Vietnam War* (ed. Ehrhart), 236, 260–70, 295; "Guerrilla War," 245–46; "How It All Comes Back," 270; "Hunting," 239–40
Eisler, Elizabeth, 219
Eksteins, Modris, 67
elegy, 2–3, 34–35, 115, 130, 143, 160, 162, 187
Eliot, T. S., 22, 102; "East Coker," 104; "Little Gidding," 97
Elizabeth I, 15
Ellis, John, 112, 203
empire, 11–13
enemy, 10–11, 18–20, 53, 218–19, 273; as double, 128, 137, 139–40, 273; erotic portrayal of, 293–95

Isherwood, Christopher, 31, 91–92, 157; *The Ascent of F6* (with Auden), 94–95; on Auden, 94–95; *Journey to a War* (with Auden), 91–92, 105

James, William, 269
jargon, 253–54
Jarrell, Randall, 6–7, 21, 22–23, 28, 147, 160, 293; ambivalence, 190–91; Bishop and, 228–32; childhood in poems of, 200, 204, 207–8; children, poems about, 214–18; comic sense, 178; commodification, view of, 183–86; criticism of, 232–33; dreamwork in poems of, 204–5, 208; as enlisted man, 179; flatness of language, 176–77, 199; impersonal style, 185–86, 211; language of, 176–77, 184–85, 199, 210–11, 233; letters to Mackie Langham, 184, 185, 192, 212–14; machine imagery, 188–89; Marxist views of, 184, 185–86; masculinity and, 190–91, 212–22; on military destructiveness, 179–80; mother figure in poems of, 187–90, 213–14, 216; passion for planes and flying, 204–7; pity in works of, 191–94; Pulitzer Prize and, 228–29; state, view of, 180, 182–83, 190–91, 199–200, 211, 214; tenderness, 187, 213–14, 222, 239, 294; Works: "2nd Air Force," 186, 187–90, 192, 199; 182,"Pilots, Man Your Planes," 206; "1914," 185; "1945: The Death of the Gods," 210–11; "Absent with Official Leave," 207; "The Angels at Hamburg," 215; "The Black Swan," 207; *Blood for a Stranger*, 219; "Burning the Letters," 176, 187, 213; "A Camp in the Prussian Forest," 216–18; "Come to the Stone . . . ", 215; *The Complete Poems*, 174, 214, 225; "The Dead Wingman," 182; "The Death of the Ball Turret Gunner," 186, 190, 196, 214, 234; "The Difficult Resolution," 204–5; "The Dream of Waking," 191, 192, 194–96, 199, 208; "Eighth Air Force," 190, 213, 222, 223–25, 239; "The Eland," 207; "The Emancipators," 182, 184; "Levels and Opposites: Structure in Poetry," 197–98; "The Lines," 207; *Little Friend, Little Friend*, 181–87, 191, 210, 218, 219; "Losses," 190, 191, 192–94, 199, 206, 210, 234, 239; *The Lost World*, 174, 192, 220; "A Lullaby," 199–200; "Mail Call," 207, 209–10; "Next Day," 187; "An Officers' Prison Camp Seen from a Troop Train," 218–19; "One Pound Wonder Tablet," 208–9; "A Pilot from the Carrier," 181, 186, 206, 233; "Poetry in War and Peace," 225–27; "Prisoners," 218–19; "Protocols," 102, 214, 215, 218; *Selected Poems*, 176, 186, 214; "The Sick Nought," 182, 185, 186, 207, 214; "Siegfried," 176, 206; "Soldier [T. P.]," 209; "The Soldier," 182–84, 185, 186; "Title Pending," 209; "The Truth," 102, 219–22; "The Wide Prospect," 184; "The Woman at the Washington Zoo," 187, 213, 234
Jones, Bill, "The Body Burning Detail," 259
Jones, David, *In Parenthesis*, 1–2
justice, 224

Keats, John, 162
Keegan, John, 20, 275; *Fields of Battle*, 207
Kendrick, William, 283
Kerr, Douglas, 55, 59, 80
Kettlewell, Penny, "The Coffee Room Soldier," 320
Keyes, Sidney, 22; *Eight Oxford Poets*, 113; "War Poet," 110–11
Kinzie, Mary, 204–5, 214
Kirstein, Lincoln, 96
Knox, Bernard, 4

meditation, poetry of, 97–98

Meirsons, Olga, 170

memoir, 28

memorials: Menin Gate, 239, 277–78, 325; Vietnam War, 273–74, 325–26. *See also* commemoration

mercenaries, 12

military: American *vs.* European views of, 201; noncombatant personnel, 202–3, 341n.2; as predatory mechanism, 200–201

military hierarchy, 128, 178; Vietnam War, 278–79; World War I, 18, 20–21

Miller, Henry, 93

mines, 158–59

Mithers, Carol Lynn, 305, 312, 319–20

Moncrieff, C. K. Scott, 60

Moore, Marianne, 201; "In Distrust of Merits," 180, 225–27, 230, 234

moral justification of war, 37–40

Morgan, Christopher, 321

mother figure, 24, 44–48, 57–58, 187–90, 213–14, 216, 304

Motion, Andrew, 114; *A Writer's Life*, 33

mourning, 2; censorship and World War I, 14–16; Vietnam War poetry, 246–47; in World War II poetry, 246

Muir, Edwin, 334; "Ballad of Hector in Hades," 331–32

munition maker, 7, 27

murder, killing in war as, 12, 89–92, 223–25, 325

mutability, 125

Mydans, Seth, 241

My Lai massacre, 317, 343n.4

mystery, 249

myth, 37

narrative, 251–52

Nation, The, 227

national borders, 27

nationalism, 99; Vietnamese style, 290–91

naturalistic war fiction, 29

Nemerov, Howard, "Redeployment," 105

"New Guy" (McDonald), 301–3

New Republic, The, 227

New Statesman, 93

noncombatants, military personnel, 202–3, 341n.2

noncombatants, poetry by, 11–12, 180, 202, 331–32. *See also* civilian poetry; Douglas, Keith; Jarrell, Randall; women writers

North Africa, 139–40

nostalgia, 34–36, 46, 189–90

nurses, 312–13, 315, 319–24

Nye, Jim, 261, 316; *After Shock*, 281; "Aftershock 1," 281; "Career Choice," 286; "Chimaera," 286; "Dead Weight," 274; "It Don't Mean Nuthin'," 272; "It's Too Late," 265–66; "Water Detail," 298, 300–301

observer-combatant, 140–42, 144

observers, World War II poetry, 242–43

officer-poets, 20

original sin, 118

Orwell, George, 88–90, 93–94, 107; *Adelphi*, 88; "Inside the Whale," 93

otherness, 17–18

Ovid, *Heroides*, 334, 336

Owen, Susan, 55, 57

Owen, Wilfred, 5–6, 14, 18–25, 31, 41, 133, 178, 225; biblical references in, 65–66; black humor in, 131–32; as caretaker, 55, 57; civilians, view of, 29, 48, 61–62; combat experience, 53–54, 64–65; death of, 18, 50; erotic emphasis, 54–55, 59–60; fatalism, 62–63; fraternity of battlefield in works of, 48, 50–55; homosexuality of, 50, 55, 116; homosexual themes, 107–8; injury, 64–65; letters home, 55–57; masculinity in, 18–25; mother figure in works of, 45–48; mythic elements in poetry of, 62–63, 65–66; pity in works of, 71–74, 251; Sassoon and, 53–54, 58–59, 65; style, 72, 76–79; tenderness, 6, 50–51, 55, 222–23; victimhood in, 6, 18, 25, 29, 75–76, 334; view of leadership, 18;

Sandburg, Carl, "Grass," 258
Sassoon, Siegfried, 14, 16, 18, 20, 29, 48–50, 136, 258; meets Owen, 53–54, 65; statement against war, 178–79; Works: "Counter-Attack," 128–29; "Glory of Women," 44, 47–48; "How to Die," 128, 131; "On Passing the New Menin Gate," 239, 277–78, 325; *War Poems*, 14
Saving Private Ryan, 10
Scammell, William, 123, 160
Scannell, Vernon, 33, 83–84, 98, 112; "The Great War," 33; *Not Without Glory*, 83–84
Schwartz, Delmore, 199
Sebastian, Saint, 26
self-consciousness, 248–49, 251, 252
senses, 150–51
sentimentality, 46, 48, 116–17, 134
September 11th terrorist attacks, 37
sexuality: bonds of death, 43–44; fear and, 60–61; Vietnam War poetry, 29–30, 300–305, 307, 309–10
Shakespeare, William: *Henry V*, 1, 18–19, 43–44, 136; *King Lear*, 173
shame, 8, 23, 92
Shapiro, Karl, 23, 83, 177–78, 180, 232
Shay, Jonathan, 253, 334
Shelley, Percy Bysshe, 90; "The Revolt of Islam," 81
Shephard, Ben, 166–68
Sherry, Michael C., 267
Sherwood Rangers, 135
Shields, Bill, "Coming Home," 324–25
Simpson, Louis, 250–51; "The Battle," 249–50; "Memories of A Lost War," 250
Sino-Japanese war, 157
Sisson, C. H., 71–72
Sitwell, Edith, 98
Sitwell, Osbert, 80
Sleigh, Tom, 187–88, 196–97
soldier-civilian relations, 6 7, 23, 25–28

soldier-poets, xi, 324; as agent-victim, 8, 20, 178, 237–38; literacy, 11, 16, 70, 203, 235; recognition of responsibility, 237–39. *See also* Vietnam War poetry; World War I poetry; World War II poetry
soldiers: boy-pilots, 181, 188, 190, 192–93, 342n.8; boy status of, 223–24; feminized, 305–6
Spanish Civil War, 86–89, 143
Sparta, 4
Spender, Stephen, 98, 202; "Ultima Ratio Regum," 143
sporting code, 20, 134
Stalin, Joseph, 94
Stallworthy, Jon, 54, 62, 65, 77, 116
Starbuck, George, 230
state, 180, 190–91, 199–200, 211, 214; death ascribed to, 182–83
Steiner, George, 175
Stern, James, 96
Stevens, Wallace, "Adagia," 252
Stewart, Frank, "Black Winter," 269–70
stoic endurance, 6, 201, 251, 325
Strachan, Hew, 117
Sutton, J. B., 114
Swift, Jonathan, 37–38, 134, 183
Swinden, Patrick, 76–77
Symons, Julian, 102

Tate, Allen, 206, 211–12; "Ode to Our Young Pro-Consuls of the Air," 186
Tate, James, "The Lost Pilot," 35
Taylor, Sandra C., 297
technology of war, 17, 23, 38–39, 253–54
television, 283
Tennyson, Alfred: "The Charge of the Light Brigade," 11; *The Holy Grail and Other Poems*, 63
Thanh T. Nguyen, 330
Thomas, Dylan, 266; "Refusal to Mourn the Death, by Fire, of a Child in London," 102, 246
totalitarianism, 200

violence: moral justification of, xii, 37–40; Victorian acceptance of, 118–19

visionary-ecstatic mode, 206–7

Visions of War, Dreams of Peace (ed. Van Devanter and Furey), 236, 312–15

visual imagery, 16–17, 29, 330–31

Voigt, Ellen Bryant, 213, 222

Wagner, Erica, 32

war: attraction of, 31–36; changing conditions of, 22–23, 38–39, 103, 235; domestic, 104–5; ethics of, 180, 251, 268; moral justification of, 37–40; as pathology, 5, 38; rationale for, 36–41; as test of masculinity, 8–11, 31, 89, 98, 146, 308, 333. *See also* industrial warfare

War and Children (Burlingham), 220

war poetry: cultural functions of, 16–17; definitions, 102, 112–13, 177–78; "Democratic principle," 97–98, 108, 238; eroticism in, 54–55, 59 60, 116, 132–33, 142, 293–95, 303; personal experience as precondition for, 89, 121, 175, 226, 248–49. *See also* Vietnam War poetry; World War I poetry; World War II poetry

warrior, label of, 89

Wars of the Roses, 1

waste, death as, 182, 183, 226

weapons displays, xiii-xiv

Weigl, Bruce, 20, 29, 263, 329; "Burning Shit at An Khe," 260; *The Circle of Hanh*, 271; "The Kiss," 257–58; "The Last Lie," 265; *Poems from Captured Documents* (with Thanh), 330; "Short," 302–3; *Song of Napalm*, 260, 330; "What Saves Us," 303–5

Welland, Denis, 81

Wellington, Duke of, 20, 201–2

West, Rebecca, 21

Whitman, Walt, 27, 242

Wiesel, Elie, 75

Williams, William Carlos, 198

Wilson, Keith, *Graves Registry and Other Poems*, 330

Winning Hearts and Minds: War Poems by Vietnam Veterans (ed. Rottmann, Barry, and Paquet), 236–38, 247–49, 255, 295

Winter, Denis, 26, 46

Winter Soldier Investigation, The: An Inquiry into American War Crimes, 236, 238, 244, 255–56

witness to war, 7, 38, 75, 98, 119, 163, 238; to cruelty, 262–63; self-consciousness, 248–49, 251, 294; visual display, 124–25

women: in armed forces, 38–39, 323–24, 343n.3; blood imagery and, 44–46; as bystanders, 225–27; as captives, 334–38; as caretakers, 313, 325; childbirth, 44–46; defense work, 201; deflection of power relations, 308–10; experience of war, 23–25, 229; in labor force, 30; mother figure, 44–48, 187–90, 213–14, 216, 304; as not-men, 305; nurses, 312–13, 315, 319–24; rape of, 30, 308 9, 311; sexuality, and Vietnam War poems, 29–30, 300–305, 307, 309–10; support of war, 25, 47–48, 51–52, 225, 231–32; veterans as nonpersons, 323 24; Vietnamese soldiers, 297–99; in Vietnam War poetry, 297–311, 334. *See also* women writers

women writers, 8 9, 203, 312, 314; on Vietnam War, 261, 312–30. *See also* Bishop, Elizabeth; Moore, Marianne; Pope, Jessie

Woods, Gregory, 16–17

Woolf, Virginia, 110, 229

Wordsworth, William, "The Happy Warrior," 77

World War I, xiii-xiv; air war, 74–75; casualties, 14, 84; censorship, 14–16, 67; division between combatants and noncombatants, 7, 14, 103; trench warfare, 15, 47–48, 61, 64, 282–83; victimhood, 103–4, 180, 239

World War I poetry, 6, 7, 21; eroticism in, 42–44, 54–55, 59–60, 116; homosexual themes, 24, 107–8, 116; by noncombatants, 331–32; victimhood, 6, 18, 25, 29, 70, 75, 103, 180, 239

World War II: casualties, 27, 36, 84, 183, 201–3, 267; division between combatants and noncombatants, 7, 103, 201; fraternity of battlefield, 136–37, 154, 155, 194–95; gender roles, 201; mobility of warfare, 22, 85; rear echelons, 112, 202–3

World War II poetry, 6, 21; belatedness of, 22, 84–85, 98, 102, 251; despair, 21, 108–10; effect of World War I on, 31–35, 84, 108–10, 117, 160, 251; traditional form, 84, 107–8, 117, 163, 251; women and family issues, 24–25

Wright, Stuart, 219

writing workshops, 329

Yeats, W. B., 76, 331; "An Irish Airman Foresees his Death," 74–75, 77; view of Owen, 71–74, 331

Further Acknowledgments

DOUG ANDERSON, "Infantry Assault," "Xin Loi," "Purification," "Two Boys," "Spoken by the Sentry at Achilles Tent," "Homer Does Not Mention Him," and "Erebus," from *The Moon Reflected Fire* (Alice James Books, 1994) Used by permission of the author.

PHILIP APPLEMAN, "Peace with Honor," from *Carrying the Darkness: The Poetry of the Vietnam War*, ed. W. D. Ehrhart (Texas Tech University Press 1989). Used by permission of the author.

W. H. AUDEN, "September 1, 1939," "In Time of War," "But in the evening . . . ," and "The Unknown Citizen," from *Selected Poems*, ed. Edward Mendelson (Vintage Books, 1979).

R. L. BARTH, "Prologue, Reading the Iliad," "Last Letter," and "Longinus in Vietnam," from *Forced Marching to the Styx* (Perivale Press, 1983; reprint, University of New Mexico Press, 2003). Used by permission of the author.

EDMUND BLUNDEN, "Concert Party: Busseboom," from *Selected Poems* (Carcanet, 1982).

D. F. BROWN, "When I Am Nineteen I Am a Medic," "Dead Weight," "Still Later There Are War Stories," and "Proofs," from *Returning Fire* (San Francisco University Press, 1984). Used by permission of the author.

MICHAEL CASEY, "Bummer," from *Obscenities* (Yale University Press, 1972; reprint, Carnegie Mellon, 2001). Used by permission of the author.

BAO-LONG CHU, "This Is the House I Pass Daily," from *From Both Sides Now: The Poetry of the Vietnam War and Its Aftermath*, ed. Phillip Mahony (Scribner, 1998).

HORACE COLEMAN, "OK Corral East," "Brothers in the Nam," and "A Black Soldier Remembers," from *In the Grass* (Vietnam Generation, Inc., and Burning Cities Press, 1995). Used by permission of the author.

DAVID CONNOLLY, "It Don't Mean Nothin," "A Goodbye," "The Little Man," "Tet, Plus Twenty Four," and "Our Fourth LT," from *Lost in America* (Vietnam Generation, Inc. and Burning Cities Press, 1994). Used by permission of the author.

GUY DAVENPORT, trans., "Some Saian Mountaineer" and "Kindly pass the cup," from *Carmina Archilochi: The Fragments of Archilochus* (University of California Press, 1964).

GWENDOLYN BROOKS, "Negro Hero," from *Blacks* (Third World Press, 1987). Used by consent of Brooks Permissions.

KEITH DOUGLAS, "Cairo Jag," "Dead Men," "The Prisoner," "Russians," "Simplify Me When I'm Dead," "How to Kill," "Gallantry," "Aristocrats," "Vergissmeinnicht," "Landscape with Figures," "Words," "Bête Noire," "Landscape with Figures 3," "Tel Aviv," "This Is the Dream," "Actors Waiting in the Wings of Europe," "Saturday Evening in Jerusalem," and "On A Return from Egypt," from *The Complete Poems*, ed. Desmond Graham (Oxford University Press, 1998).

W. D. EHRHART, "Hunting," "Guerilla War," "How It All Comes Back," and "Beautiful Wreckage," from *Beautiful Wreckage: New and Selected Poems* (Adastra Press, 1999). Used by permission of the author.

T. S. ELIOT, "East Coker," from *The Complete Poems and Plays: 1909-1950* (Harcourt Brace, 1958). Used by permission of Harcourt Brace.

ROBERT FAGLES, trans., 9:73-75 and 19:332-55 from *The Iliad*, Homer (Penguin, 1990).

BRIAN ALEC FLOYD, "Sergeant Brandon Just. U.S.M.C.," from *The Long War Dead* (Avon Books, 1976).

ROY FULLER, "What Is Terrible," "Follower's Song," "War Poet," and "During A Bombardment by V-Weapons," from *Collected Poems, 1936-1961* (Dufour Editions, 1962).

JON FORREST GLADE, "Shitbirds" and "Blood Trail," from *From Both Sides Now*, ed. Phillip Mahony (Scribner, 1998).

IVOR GURNEY, "To His Love," from *War's Embers* (Carcanet, 1997).

SUE HALPERN, "I Am A Veteran of Vietnam," from *Winning Hearts and Minds*, ed. Jan Barry, Larry Rottmann, and Basil Paquet (McGraw Hill, 1972).

GUSTAV HASFORD, "Bedtime Story," from *Carrying the Darkness*, ed. W. D. Ehrhart (Texas Tech University Press, 1989).

DAVID HUDDLE, "Work" and "Vermont," from *Stopping By Home* (Peregrine Smith, 1988). Used by permission of the author.

TED HUGHES, "Six Young Men" and "For the Duration," from *The Hawk in the Rain* (Faber & Faber, 1957) and *Wolfwatching* (Farrar, Straus & Giroux, 1991).

LOWELL JAEGER, "The Trial," from *From Both Sides Now*, ed. Phillip Mahony (Scribner, 1998).

BILL JONES, from *From Both Sides Now*, ed. Mahony (Scribner, 1998).

PENNY KETTLEWELL, "The Coffee Room Soldier," from *Visions of War, Dreams of Peace*, ed. Lynda Van Devanter and Joan Furey (Warner Books, 1991).

SIDNEY KEYES, "War Poet," from *Collected Poems of Sidney Keyes*, ed. Michael Meyer (Routledge, 1945).

YUSEF KOMUNYAKAA, "The Dead at Quang Tri," "You and I Are Disappearing," "Fragging," "Ambush," "Jungle Surrender," "Hanoi Hannah," "Tu Do Street," "Sappers," "We Never Know," "Starlight Scope Myopia," "Tunnels," and "Dui Boi, Dust of Life," taken from *Dien Cai Dao* (Wesleyan University Press, 1988).

GREG KUZMA, "Peace, So That," from *Poetry* 120, no. 6 (1972), "Poetry Against the War" special issue. Used by permission of the author.

PHILIP LARKIN, "Conscript" and "MCMXIV," from *Collected Poems*, ed. Anthony Thwaite (Farrar, Straus & Giroux, 1989).

MCAVOY LAYNE, "On the Yellow Footprints," from *How Audie Murphy Died in Vietnam* (Doubleday, 1973).

ALUN LEWIS, "The Peasants" and "The Soldier," from *Selected Poetry and Prose*, ed. Ian Hamilton (Allen & Unwin, 1966).

C. DAY LEWIS, "Where are the War Poets," "Will It Be So Again?" and "The Nabara," taken from *Collected Poems of C. Day Lewis* (Jonathan Cape/Hogarth Press, 1954).

HUGH MACDIARMID, "Another Epitaph on an Army of Mercenaries," from *Selected Poems* (Penguin, 1970). Used by permission of New Directions Publishing Corporation.

GERALD MCCARTHY, "Untitled" and "War Story," from *War Story: Vietnam War Poems* (The Crossing Press, 1977). Used by permission of the author.

WALTER MCDONALD, "Hauling Over Wolf Creek Pass in Winter" and "Rocket Attack," from *Carrying the Darkness*, ed. W. D. Ehrhart (Texas Tech University Press, 1989). Used by permission of the author.

MARIANNE MOORE, "In Distrust of Merits," from *The Complete Poems of Marianne Moore* (Macmillan, 1981). Used by permission of Marianne Craig Moore.

HOWARD NEMEROV, "Redeployment," from *The Collected Poems of Howard Nemerov* (University of Chicago Press, 1977). Used by permission of Margaret Nemerov.

JIM NYE, "It's Too Late," "Chimaera," "It Don't Mean Nuthin," "Aftershock," and "Water Detail," from *Aftershock* (Cinco Puntos Press, 1991). Used by permission of the author.

WILFRED OWEN, "Greater Love," "Dulce et Decorum Est," "The Next War," "Disabled," "Who Is the God of Canongate," "Hospital Barge," "The Parable of the Old Man and the Young," "Insensibility," "Sonnet on Seeing a Piece of Our Heavy Artillery Brought into Action, " and "Strange Meeting," from *The Complete Poems and Fragments of Wilfred Owen*, ed. Jon Stallworthy (W. W. Norton, 1983), vols. 1 and 2.

BASIL PAQUET, "Mourning the Death, By Hemorrhage, of A Child from Honai" and "Basket Case," from *Carrying the Darkness*, ed. W. D. Ehrhart (Texas Tech University Press, 1989).

JESSIE POPE, "The Call," from *Scars Upon My Heart: Women's Poetry and Verse of the First World War*, ed. Catherine Reilly (Virago Press, 1981).

HENRY REED, "The Naming of Parts," from *A Map of Verona* (Jonathan Cape/Random House, 1946).

ELLIOTT RICHMAN, "The Woman He Killed," from *From Both Sides Now*, ed. Phillip Mahony (Scribner, 1998).

DALE RITTERBUSCH, "What There Is," from *Lessons Learned: Poetry of the Vietnam War and Its Aftermath* (Vietnam Generation, Inc./Burning Cities Press, 1995). Used by permission of the author.

ISAAC ROSENBERG, "Dead Man's Dump," from *The Collected Works of Isaac Rosenberg* (Oxford University Press, 1979).

SIEGFRIED SASSOON, "On Passing the New Menin Gate," "Glory of Women," "Counter-Attack," and "—the rank stench of those bodies haunts me still," from *The War Poems* (Faber & Faber, 1983).

VERNON SCANNELL, "The Great War," from *Collected Poems* (Robson Books, 1993).

BILL SHIELDS, "Coming Home," from *From Both Sides Now*, ed. Phillip Mahony (Scribner, 1998).

LOUIS SIMPSON, "The Battle" and "Memories of A Lost War," from *Collected Poems* (Paragon House, 1990).

STEPHEN SPENDER, "Ultima Ratio Regum," from *Collected Poems, 1928-1985* (Random House, 1986).

FRANK STEWART, "Black Winter," from *Carrying the Darkness*, ed. W. D. Ehrhart (Texas Tech University Press, 1989). Used by permission of the author.

DAVID ST. JOHN, "Six/Nine/Forty-four," from *Study for the World's Body* (Harper, 1994). Used by permission of the author.

JAMES TATE, "The Lost Pilot," from *The Lost Pilot* (Yale University Press, 1967).

DYLAN THOMAS, "A Refusal to Mourn the Death By Fire of a Child in London," from *The Collected Poems of Dylan Thomas* (New Directions Press, 1953).

BARBARA TRAN, "The Women Next Door," from *From Both Sides Now*, ed. Phillip Mahony (Scribner, 1998).

BRUCE WEIGL, "The Kiss," "Burning Shit at An Khe," "Song of Napalm," "The Last Lie," and "What Saves Us," from *Song of Napalm* (The Atlantic Monthly Press, 1988) and *What Saves Us* (Triquarterly Books, 1992). Used by permission of the author.

Every effort has been made to secure permissions for the quotations in this book. Rights holders of any selection not credited should contact Lorrie Goldensohn in care of Columbia University Press, 61 West 62nd Street, New York, NY 10023.